THE GREAT SEAL OF THE STATE OF NEW YORK

EXCELSIOR

D1456132

Standard 3 Social Studies: Geography

Students will: use a variety of intellectual skills to demonstrate their understanding of the geography of the interdependent world in which we live—local, national, and global—including the distribution of people, places, and environments over the Earth's surface.

3.1   Geography can be divided into six essential elements which can be used to analyze important historic, geographic, economic, and environmental questions and issues. These six elements include: the world in spatial terms, places and regions, physical settings (including natural resources), human systems, environment and society, and the use of geography. (Adapted from The National Geography Standards, 1994: Geography for Life)

3.2   Geography requires the development and application of the skills of asking and answering geographic questions; analyzing theories of geography; and acquiring, organizing, and analyzing geographic information. (Adapted from: The National Geography Standards, 1994: Geography for Life)

Standard 4 Social Studies: Economics

Students will: use a variety of intellectual skills to demonstrate their understanding of how the United States and other societies develop economic systems and associated institutions to allocate scarce resources, how major decision-making units function in the U.S. and other national economies, and how an economy solves the scarcity problem through market and nonmarket mechanisms.

4.1   The study of economics requires an understanding of major economic concepts and systems, the principles of economic decision making, and the interdependence of economies and economic systems throughout the world.

4.2   Economics requires the development and application of the skills needed to make informed and well-reasoned economic decisions in daily and national life.

Standard 5 Social Studies: Civics, Citizenship, and Government

Students will: use a variety of intellectual skills to demonstrate their understanding of the necessity for establishing governments; the governmental system of the U.S. and other nations; the U.S. Constitution; the basic civic values of American constitutional democracy; and the roles, rights, and responsibilities of citizenship, including avenues of participation.

5.1   The study of civics, citizenship, and government involves learning about political systems; the purposes of government and civic life; and the differing assumptions held by people across time and place regarding power, authority, governance, and law. (Adapted from The National Standards for Civics and Government, 1994)

5.2   The state and federal governments established by the Constitutions of the United States and the State of New York embody basic civic values (such as justice, honesty, self-discipline, due process, equality, majority rule with respect for minority rights, and respect for self, others, and property), principles, and practices and establish a system of shared and limited government. (Adapted from The National Standards for Civics and Government, 1994)

5.3   Central to civics and citizenship is an understanding of the roles of the citizen within American constitutional democracy and the scope of a citizen's rights and responsibilities.

5.4   The study of civics and citizenship requires the ability to probe ideas and assumptions, ask and answer analytical questions, take a skeptical attitude toward questionable arguments, evaluate evidence, formulate rational conclusions, and develop and refine participatory skills.

New York Academic Content Standards

Standard 1 Social Studies: History of the United States and New York

Students will: use a variety of intellectual skills to demostrate their understanding of major ideas, eras, themes, developments, and turning points in the history of the United States and New York.

1.1 The study of New York State and United States history requires an analysis of the development of American culture, its diversity and multicultural context, and the ways people are unified by many values, practices, and traditions.

1.2 Important ideas, social and cultural values, beliefs, and traditions from New York State and United States history illustrate the connections and interactions of people and events across time and from a variety of perspectives.

1.3 Study about the major social, political, economic, cultural, and religious developments in New York State and United States history involves learning about the important roles and contributions of individuals and groups.

1.4 The skills of historical analysis include the ability to: explain the significance of historical evidence; weigh the importance, relilability, and validity of evidence; understand the concept of multiple causation; understand the importance of changing and competing intrepretations of different historical developments.

Standard 2 Social Studies: World History

Students will: use a variety of intellectual skills to demostrate their understanding of major ideas, eras, themes, developments, and turning points in world history and examine the broad sweep of history from a variety of perspectives.

2.1 The study of world history requires an understanding of world cultures and civilizations, including an analysis of important ideas, social and cultural values, beliefs, and traditions. This study also examines the human condition and the connections and interactions of people across time and space and the ways different people view the same event or issue from a variety of perspectives.

2.2 Establishing timeframes, exploring different periodizations, examining themes across time and within cultures, and focusing on important turning points in world history help organize the study of world cultures and civilizations.

2.3 Study of the major social, political, cultural, and religious developments in world history involves learning about the important roles and contributions of individuals and groups.

2.4 The skills of historical analysis include the ability to investigate differing and competing interpretations of the theories of history, hypothesize about why interpretations change over time, explain the importance of historical evidence, and understand the concepts of change and continuity over time.

NEW YORK

PROGRAM AUTHORS

James A. Banks, Ph.D.
Kevin P. Colleary, Ed.D.
Walter C. Parker, Ph.D.

STATE CONSULTANTS

Karen Ward Mahar, Ph.D.
Dr. Thomas A. Rumney
Rose Ann Terrance-Mohawk
Jason Young, Ph.D.

Mc Graw Hill **Macmillan McGraw-Hill**

Acknowledgments

PROGRAM AUTHORS

James A. Banks, Ph.D.
Russell F. Stark University
  Professor and Director, Center for
  Multicultural Education
University of Washington
Seattle, Washington

Kevin P. Colleary, Ed.D.
Curriculum and Teaching Department
Graduate School of Education
Fordham University
New York, New York

Walter C. Parker, Ph.D.
Professor of Education and Chair
  of Social Studies Education
University of Washington
Seattle, Washington

HISTORIANS/SCHOLARS

Karen Ward Mahar, Ph.D.
Associate Professor of History
Siena College
Loudonville, New York

Dr. Thomas A. Rumney
Professor of Geography
Plattsburgh State University
Plattsburgh, New York

Rose Ann Terrance - Mohawk
Grades 3–4 Teacher
Monica B. Leary Elementary School
Rush, New York

Jason Young, Ph.D.
Assistant Professor
SUNY Buffalo
Buffalo, New York

PRIMARY SOURCES RESEARCH

Library of Congress
Pubishing Office
Washington, D.C.

GRADE LEVEL CONSULTANTS

Marilyn Barr
Assistant Superintendent for Instruction
Clyde-Savannah Central School
Clyde, New York

Deborah Giannuzzi
Assistant Principal
P.S. 180 Homewood School
Brooklyn, New York

Patti Staebell
Fifth Grade Teacher
Elba Central School
Elba, New York

Jennifer Tomm, NBCT
Social Studies Lead Teacher
Rochester City School District
Rochester, New York

Students with print disabilities may be eligible to obtain an accessible, audio version of the pupil edition of this textbook. Please call Recording for the Blind & Dyslexic at 1-800-221-4792 for complete information.

About the Cover: Front: Niagara Falls (bottom) and the Manhattan skyline (top) are world famous sights. The Empire State Building is on the right. Back: The New York State Capitol was completed in 1899. It is the third Capitol Building in Albany.

ACKNOWLEDGMENTS

Grateful acknowledgment is given to the following authors, composers, and publishers. Every effort has been made to trace the ownership of all copyrighted material and to secure the necessary permissions to reprint these selections. In the case of some selections for which acknowledgment is not given, extensive research has failed to locate the copyright holders.

Listening to the Land: Conversations About Nature, Culture and Eros, by Derrick Jensen. Copyright © 2004 by Chelsea Green Publishing Company. All Rights Reserved. Used by Permission

Dark Rivers Run Deep: An interview with Robert Kennedy, Jr., and John Cronin, by Sally Richards, San Francisco, 1998. From <http://www.SallyRichards.com> Copyright © by Sally Richards. All Rights Reserved. Used by Permission.

(continued on page R37)

A

The McGraw·Hill Companies

**Macmillan
McGraw-Hill**

Published by Macmillan/McGraw-Hill, of McGraw-Hill Education, a division of The McGraw-Hill Companies, Inc., Two Penn Plaza, New York, New York 10121.

Copyright © 2007 by Macmillan/McGraw-Hill. All rights reserved. No part of this publication may be reproduced or distributed in any form or by any means, or stored in a database or retrieval system, without the prior written consent of The McGraw-Hill Companies, Inc., including, but not limited to, network storage or transmission, or broadcast for distance learning.

Printed in the United States of America

ISBN 0-02-151269-8

1 2 3 4 5 6 7 8   027/10 09 08 07 06

Contents

Unit 1 New York and Its First People 2

v

Reference Section

Skills and Features

Charts, Graphs, and Diagrams

City of Rochester Expenses, 2003–2005

Expenses (in Millions of Dollars)

310
300
290
280
270
260

2003–2004   2004–2005   2005–2006
Year

Source: *City of Rochester*

Maps

ABOUT THE BIG IDEA

The Big Ideas in this textbook are important ideas in social studies. They will help you understand each unit and its New York Standards.

The Big Idea question for each unit appears on its opening pages. As you review each lesson, look for the Write About the Big Idea question in the Lesson Review. The question helps you answer the Big Idea question for the unit. When you finish each unit, complete the Big Idea activities. They will help you review what you have learned. Finally, you will find a list of three books that will help you learn more about the Big Idea.

Each unit starts with a Big Idea question.

A graphic organizer helps you organize information for the Big Idea question.

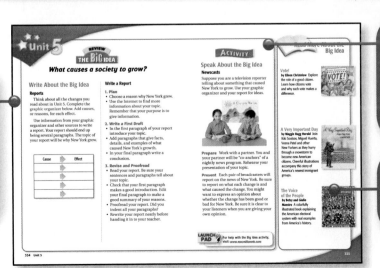

Each unit ends with a Write About the Big Idea to review what you have learned.

The Big Idea Activity lets you work with classmates on a project based on the Big Idea.

These books can help you learn more about the Big Idea.

Reading Your Textbook

This book is organized to help you understand and apply social studies content and skills as you read.

- **Unit Opener** and **People Who Make a Difference** pages introduce you to the people and places in the unit.

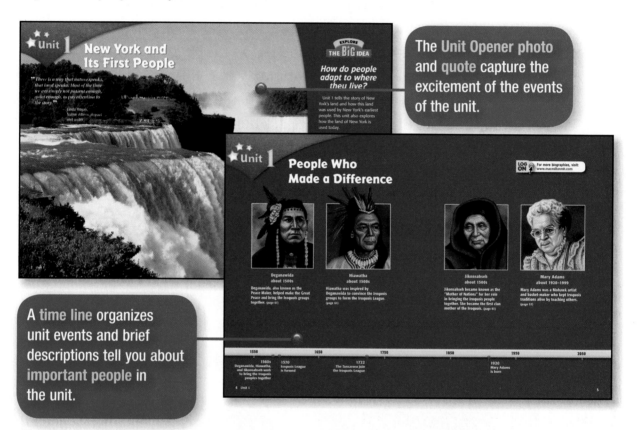

The **Unit Opener** photo and **quote** capture the excitement of the events of the unit.

A **time line** organizes unit events and brief descriptions tell you about important people in the unit.

- **Chapter Opener** pages introduce you to the time and place of events you will read about.

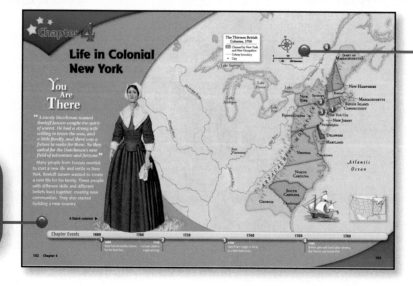

A **map** helps you see the locations of places from the chapter.

A **time line** organizes important chapter events.

Lesson Opener pages prepare you before you read.

Focus questions set a purpose for reading.

Graphic organizers help you organize information as you read.

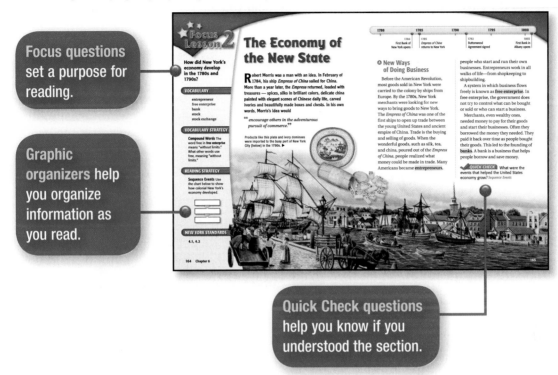

Quick Check questions help you know if you understood the section.

Lesson Review pages test your understanding of the lesson.

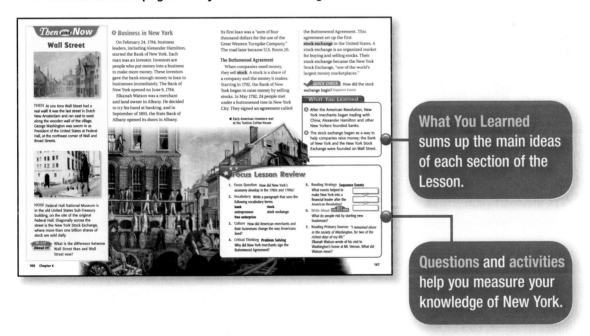

What You Learned sums up the main ideas of each section of the Lesson.

Questions and activities help you measure your knowledge of New York.

Reading Social Studies pages teach reading skills that help you understand social studies content.

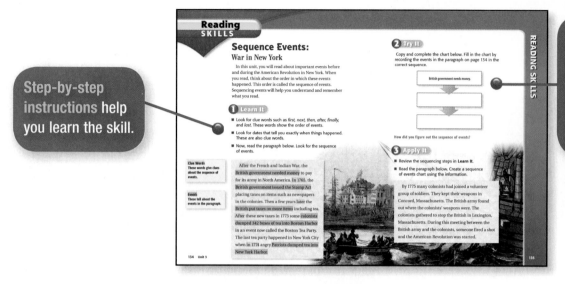

Step-by-step instructions help you learn the skill.

Graphic organizers help you apply the skill to the content.

Biographies and **Primary Sources** bring the past alive.

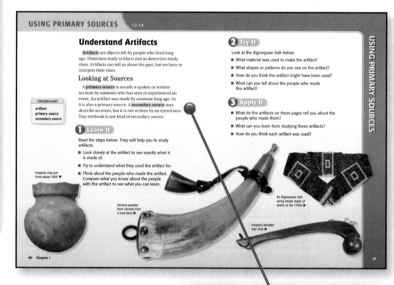

Biographies help you learn about the lives of people who have made a difference in New York and the United States.

Primary Sources let you see and study words and possessions of people from New York's past.

Citizenship pages show real-life participation in democracy.

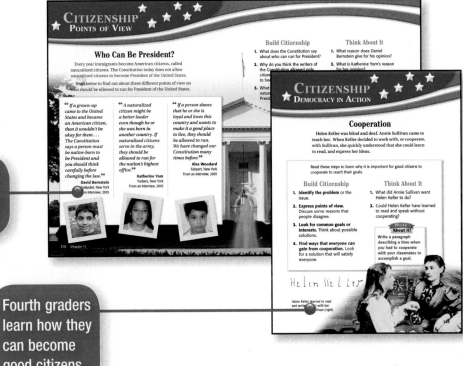

People explain their views on events and issues in New York.

Fourth graders learn how they can become good citizens

Readers' Theater and **Literature** bring New York history alive.

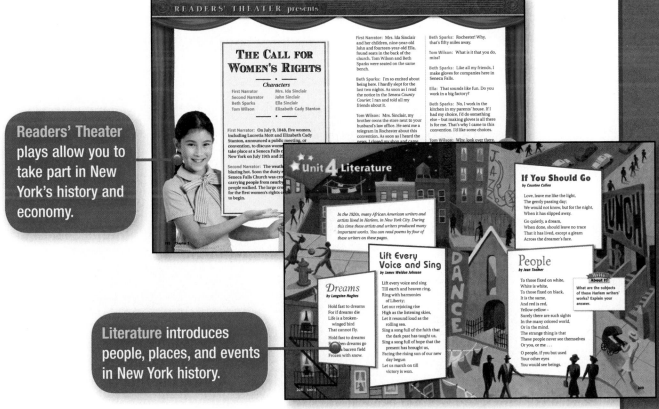

Readers' Theater plays allow you to take part in New York's history and economy.

Literature introduces people, places, and events in New York history.

GEOGRAPHY HANDBOOK

GEOGRAPHY AND YOU

Geography is the study of our Earth and the people who live here. Most people think of geography as learning about cities, states, and countries, but geography is more than that. Geography includes learning about bodies of water, such as oceans, lakes, and rivers. Geography helps us learn about land, such as plains and mountains. Geography also helps us learn how to use land and water wisely.

Did you know that people are part of geography, too? Geography includes the study of how people adapt to live in a new place. How people move around, how they move goods, and how ideas travel from place to place are also parts of geography.

In fact, geography includes so many things that geographers have divided this information into six elements, or ideas, so you can better understand them.

SIX ESSENTIAL ELEMENTS

The World in Spatial Terms: Where is a place located, and what land or water features does this place have?

Places and Regions: What is special about a place, and what makes it different from other places?

Physical Systems: What has shaped the land and climate of a place, and how does this affect the plants, animals, and people there?

Human Systems: How do people, ideas, and goods move from place to place?

Environment and Society: How have people changed the land and water of a place, and how have the land and water affected people of a place?

Uses of Geography: How does geography influence events in the past, present, and the future?

FIVE THEMES OF GEOGRAPHY

You have read about the six elements of geography. The five themes of geography are another way of dividing the ideas of geography. The themes, or topics, are **location**, **place**, **region**, **movement**, and **human interaction**. Using these five themes is another way to understand events you read about in this book.

1. LOCATION

Sagamore Hill, Theodore Roosevelt's home on Long Island

In geography, location means an exact spot on the planet. A location is usually a street name and number. You write a location when you address a letter.

2. PLACE

Niagara Falls from the U.S. side

A place is described by its physical features, such as rivers, mountains, or valleys. You would also include the human features, such as cities, language, and traditions, in the description of a place.

3. REGION

Hyde Park, New York

A region is a larger area than a place or a location. The people in a region are affected by landforms. Their region has typical jobs and customs. For example, many people in the Finger Lakes Region make a living from farming or tourism at the beautiful lakes.

4. MOVEMENT

Adirondacks North Creek, New York

Throughout history, people have moved to find better land or a better life. Geographers study why these movements occurred. They also study how people's movements have changed a region.

5. HUMAN INTERACTION

Erie Canal at Little Falls, New York

Geographers are interested in how people adapt to their environments. Geographers also study how people change their environments. This interaction between people and their environments determines how land is used for cities, farms, or parks.

DICTIONARY OF GEOGRAPHIC TERMS

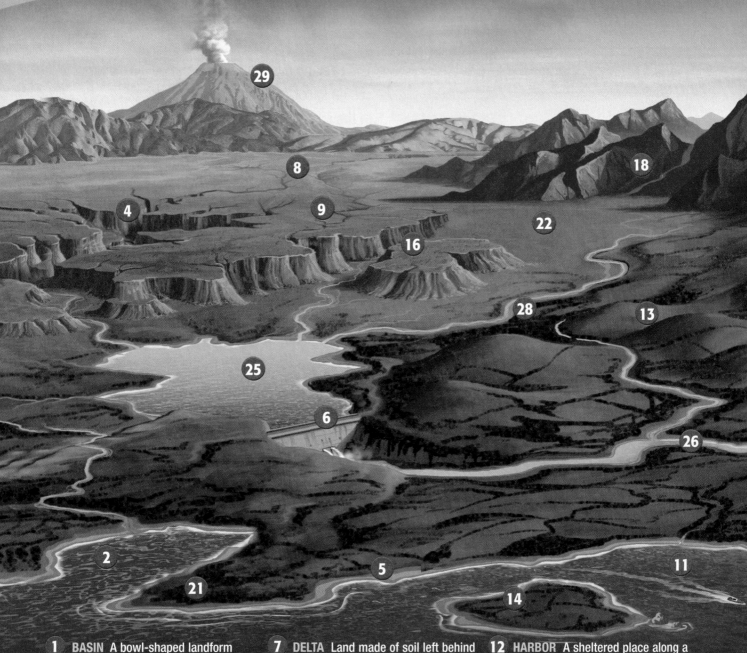

1 BASIN A bowl-shaped landform surrounded by higher land

2 BAY Part of an ocean or lake that extends deeply into the land

3 CANAL A channel built to carry water for irrigation or transportation

4 CANYON A deep, narrow valley with steep sides

5 COAST The land along an ocean

6 DAM A wall built across a river, creating a lake that stores water

7 DELTA Land made of soil left behind as a river drains into a larger body of water

8 DESERT A dry environment with few plants and animals

9 FAULT The border between two of the plates that make up Earth's crust

10 GLACIER A huge sheet of ice that moves slowly across the land

11 GULF Part of an ocean that extends into the land; larger than a bay

12 HARBOR A sheltered place along a coast where boats dock safely

13 HILL A rounded, raised landform; not as high as a mountain

14 ISLAND A body of land completely surrounded by water

15 LAKE A body of water completely surrounded by land

16 MESA A hill with a flat top; smaller than a plateau

17 MOUNTAIN A high landform with steep sides; higher than a hill

18 MOUNTAIN PASS A narrow gap through a mountain range

19 MOUTH The place where a river empties into a larger body of water

20 OCEAN A large body of salt water; oceans cover much of Earth's surface

21 PENINSULA A body of land nearly surrounded by water

22 PLAIN A large area of nearly flat land

23 PLATEAU A high, flat area that rises steeply above the surrounding land

24 PORT A place where ships load and unload their goods

25 RESERVOIR A natural or artificial lake used to store water

26 RIVER A stream of water that flows across the land and empties into another body of water

27 SOURCE The starting point of a river

28 VALLEY An area of low land between hills or mountains

29 VOLCANO An opening in Earth's surface through which hot rock and ash are forced out

30 WATERFALL A flow of water falling vertically

Looking at Earth

Earth and the Globe

From outer space, Earth looks like a big blue ball with brown spots. In order to see a complete view of Earth, we use a globe. A globe is a special map that is shaped like a sphere, or ball. The globe is a model of Earth. It shows what the land and water look like on Earth.

The large areas of land on Earth are called continents. There are seven continents on Earth. Their names are Africa, Antarctica, Asia, Australia, Europe, North America, and South America.

The big bodies of water are called oceans. The names of the four oceans are the Arctic, Atlantic, Indian, and Pacific oceans.

Hemispheres

The equator is an imaginary line on Earth. It divides the sphere of Earth in half. A word for half a sphere is hemisphere. The prefix "hemi" means half. Geographers divide Earth into four hemispheres.

All the land and oceans north of the equator are in the Northern Hemisphere. All the land and oceans south of the equator are in the Southern Hemisphere.

There is another imaginary line on Earth that runs from the North Pole to the South Pole. It is called the prime meridian. It divides Earth into the Eastern Hemisphere and the Western Hemisphere.

🌎 What continents are located on the equator?

🌎 In which two hemispheres is North America?

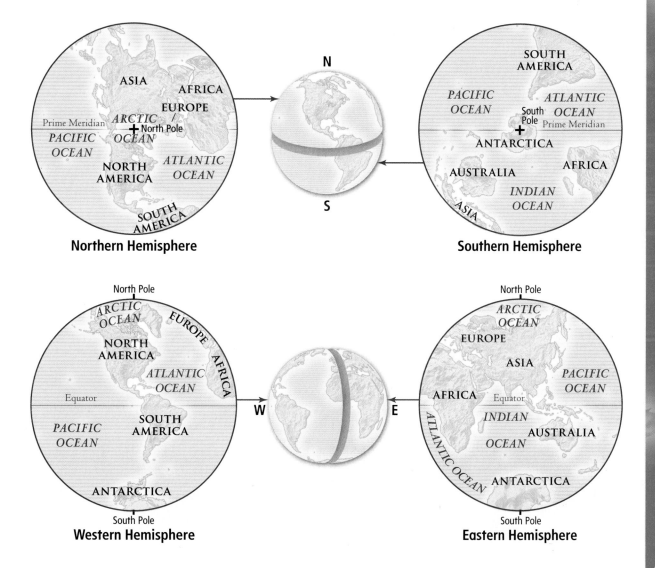

Reading a Map

Maps are drawings of places on Earth. Most maps have standard features to help you read the map. One piece of information on a map is direction. The main directions are north, south, east, and west. These are called cardinal directions.

Map Title Map titles tell you what information is on the map.

Regions of the United States: Political

RUSSIA

CANADA

AK

Juneau★

0   200   400 miles
0   200   400 kilometers

CANADA

WA
★Olympia

★Helena
MT

ND
★Bismarck

MN

MI

★Salem
OR

ID
★Boise

SD
★Pierre

St. Paul
★

WI

Madison
★

WY

Cheyenne
★

IA
Des Moines
★

IL

Carson
City
★

Salt Lake
City★

NE
Lincoln★

Springfield★

Sacramento
★

NV

UT

Denver
★
CO

Topeka
★
KS

Jefferson
City★
MO

CA

AZ
Phoenix
★

Santa Fe
★
NM

Oklahoma
City
★
OK

AR
Little
Rock★

MS

PACIFIC
OCEAN

TX

Austin
★

Jackson★
LA

Baton Rouge★

Gulf of Mexico

Honolulu★
HI

0   100   200 miles
0   100   200 kilometers

MEXICO

Map Key

Midwest
Mountain
Northeast
Southeast
Southwest
West
National boundary
State boundary
⊛ National capital
★ State capital

Map Key This is the map key or legend. It helps you understand the colors or special symbols on a map.

Inset Map An inset map is a small map that shows an area that is too large, too small, or too far away to be on the main map.

Locator A locator map is a small map set into the main map. It shows the location on Earth of the main map.

The areas between the cardinal directions are called intermediate directions. These are northeast, southeast, southwest, and northwest. You use directions to describe one place in relation to another. For example, Albany, New York, is northeast of Harrisburg, Pennsylvania.

🌐 **About how far is it from Albany, New York to Richmond, Virginia?**

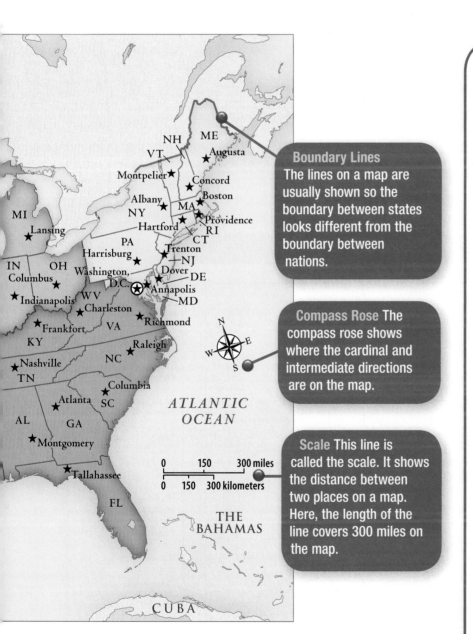

Boundary Lines The lines on a map are usually shown so the boundary between states looks different from the boundary between nations.

Compass Rose The compass rose shows where the cardinal and intermediate directions are on the map.

Scale This line is called the scale. It shows the distance between two places on a map. Here, the length of the line covers 300 miles on the map.

State Abbreviations

On this map, the name of each state is shortened, or abbreviated. The abbreviations were invented by the United States Postal Service. Maps often use these abbreviations when there is not enough room to write the whole state name.

AK	ALASKA	MT	MONTANA
AL	ALABAMA	NC	NORTH CAROLINA
AR	ARKANSAS	ND	NORTH DAKOTA
AZ	ARIZONA	NE	NEBRASKA
CA	CALIFORNIA	NH	NEW HAMPSHIRE
CO	COLORADO	NJ	NEW JERSEY
CT	CONNECTICUT	NM	NEW MEXICO
DE	DELAWARE	NV	NEVADA
FL	FLORIDA	NY	NEW YORK
GA	GEORGIA	OH	OHIO
HI	HAWAII	OK	OKLAHOMA
IA	IOWA	OR	OREGON
ID	IDAHO	PA	PENNSYLVANIA
IL	ILLINOIS	RI	RHODE ISLAND
IN	INDIANA	SC	SOUTH CAROLINA
KS	KANSAS	SD	SOUTH DAKOTA
KY	KENTUCKY	TN	TENNESSEE
LA	LOUISIANA	TX	TEXAS
MA	MASSACHUSETTS	UT	UTAH
MD	MARYLAND	VA	VIRGINIA
ME	MAINE	VT	VERMONT
MI	MICHIGAN	WA	WASHINGTON
MN	MINNESOTA	WI	WISCONSIN
MO	MISSOURI	WV	WEST VIRGINIA
MS	MISSISSIPPI	WY	WYOMING

Special Purpose Maps

Grid Maps

This map has a special grid. Each box on a grid can be named by a number and a letter. For example, you might want to find Ticonderoga in B-3. Put one finger on the letter B along the side of the map. Put another finger on the number 3 at the top. Move your fingers down and across the map until they meet. You have found B-3 on the grid. Now look for Ticonderoga inside Box B-3.

You can use an index to locate places on a map more quickly. Entries in an index are listed in alphabetical order. Find the name of the place in the index, and then use the grid number and letter to locate it on the map.

🌐 Find Saranac Lakes on the map. What grid box is it in?

🌐 What are the grid number and letter for Elizabethtown?

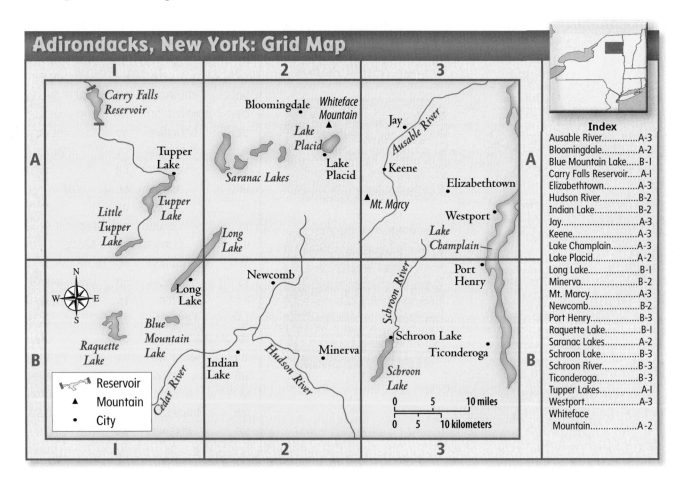

Adirondacks, New York: Grid Map

Reservoir
▲ Mountain
• City

| 0 | 5 | 10 miles |
| 0 | 5 | 10 kilometers |

Index

Ausable River	A-3
Bloomingdale	A-2
Blue Mountain Lake	B-1
Carry Falls Reservoir	A-1
Elizabethtown	A-3
Hudson River	B-2
Indian Lake	B-2
Jay	A-3
Keene	A-3
Lake Champlain	A-3
Lake Placid	A-2
Long Lake	B-1
Minerva	B-2
Mt. Marcy	A-3
Newcomb	B-2
Port Henry	B-3
Raquette Lake	B-1
Saranac Lakes	A-2
Schroon Lake	B-3
Schroon River	B-3
Ticonderoga	B-3
Tupper Lakes	A-1
Westport	A-3
Whiteface Mountain	A-2

Historical Maps

Some maps show an area as it appeared at a certain time. This kind of special purpose map is a historical map. You will learn more about historical maps in Using Primary Sources on pages 120-121. Historical maps are maps that show information about the past and how things appeared at that time. Sometimes they show events and where they occured. Other times they just show where people lived. You need to use a key to read a historical map.

🌐 In what colonies are the three settlements located?

🌐 What colonies are part of the New England colonies?

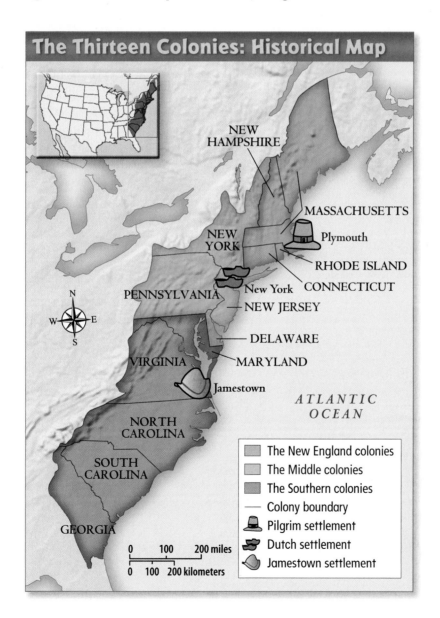

The Thirteen Colonies: Historical Map

NEW HAMPSHIRE

MASSACHUSETTS

Plymouth

NEW YORK

RHODE ISLAND

CONNECTICUT

New York

PENNSYLVANIA

NEW JERSEY

N
W — E
S

DELAWARE

VIRGINIA

MARYLAND

Jamestown

ATLANTIC OCEAN

NORTH CAROLINA

SOUTH CAROLINA

GEORGIA

- ⬛ The New England colonies
- ⬛ The Middle colonies
- ⬛ The Southern colonies
- — Colony boundary
- 🎩 Pilgrim settlement
- Dutch settlement
- Jamestown settlement

0   100   200 miles
0   100   200 kilometers

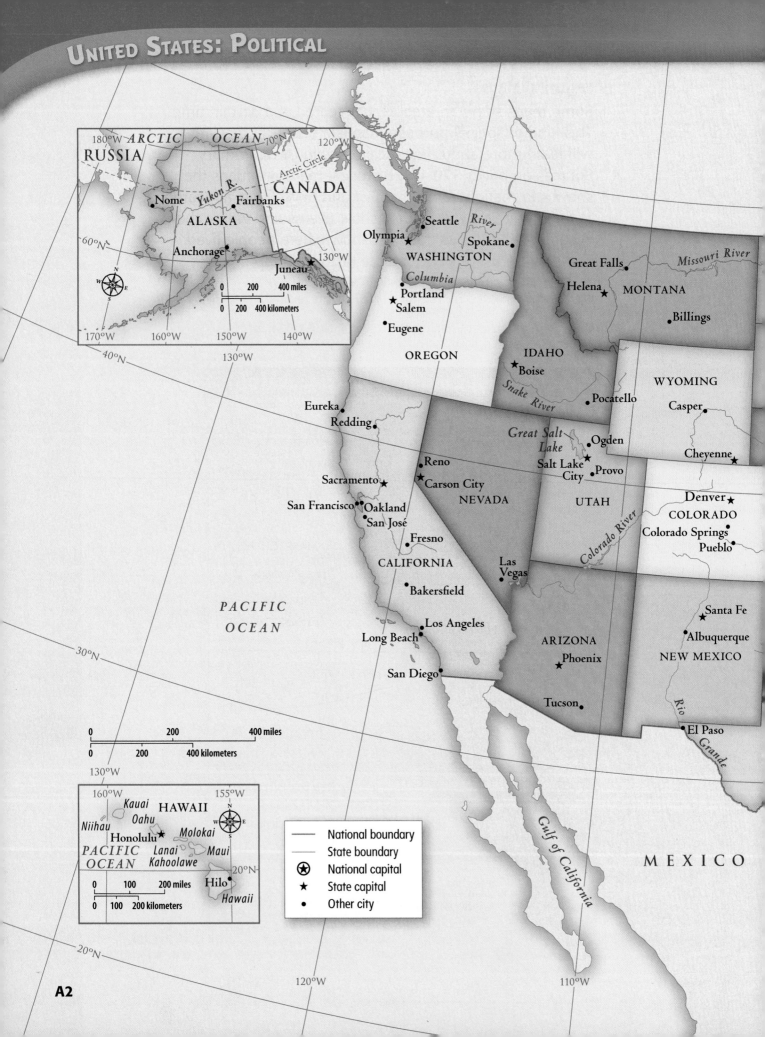

ARCTIC OCEAN
180°W · 70°N · 120°W

RUSSIA
CANADA
Arctic Circle
Nome · Yukon R. · Fairbanks
ALASKA
60°N
Anchorage · 130°W
Juneau
0 200 400 miles
0 200 400 kilometers
170°W · 160°W · 150°W · 140°W
40°N · 130°W

Seattle
Olympia
WASHINGTON · Spokane
Columbia
Portland
Salem
Eugene
OREGON

River
Great Falls
Helena · MONTANA
Billings
Missouri River

IDAHO
Boise
Snake River
Pocatello
WYOMING
Casper
Cheyenne

Eureka
Redding

Great Salt Lake
Ogden
Reno · Salt Lake City · Provo
Sacramento · Carson City
San Francisco · Oakland
San José
NEVADA
UTAH
Fresno
CALIFORNIA
Las Vegas
Bakersfield

Denver
COLORADO
Colorado Springs
Pueblo
Colorado River

PACIFIC OCEAN

30°N

Los Angeles
Long Beach
San Diego

ARIZONA
Phoenix
Tucson

Santa Fe
Albuquerque
NEW MEXICO

El Paso
Rio Grande

0 200 400 miles
0 200 400 kilometers
130°W

160°W · HAWAII · 155°W
Kauai
Niihau · Oahu
Honolulu · Molokai
PACIFIC · Lanai · Maui
OCEAN · Kahoolawe
20°N
Hilo
0 100 200 miles
0 100 200 kilometers
Hawaii

Gulf of California

MEXICO

——	National boundary
——	State boundary
⊛	National capital
★	State capital
•	Other city

20°N
120°W · 110°W

A2

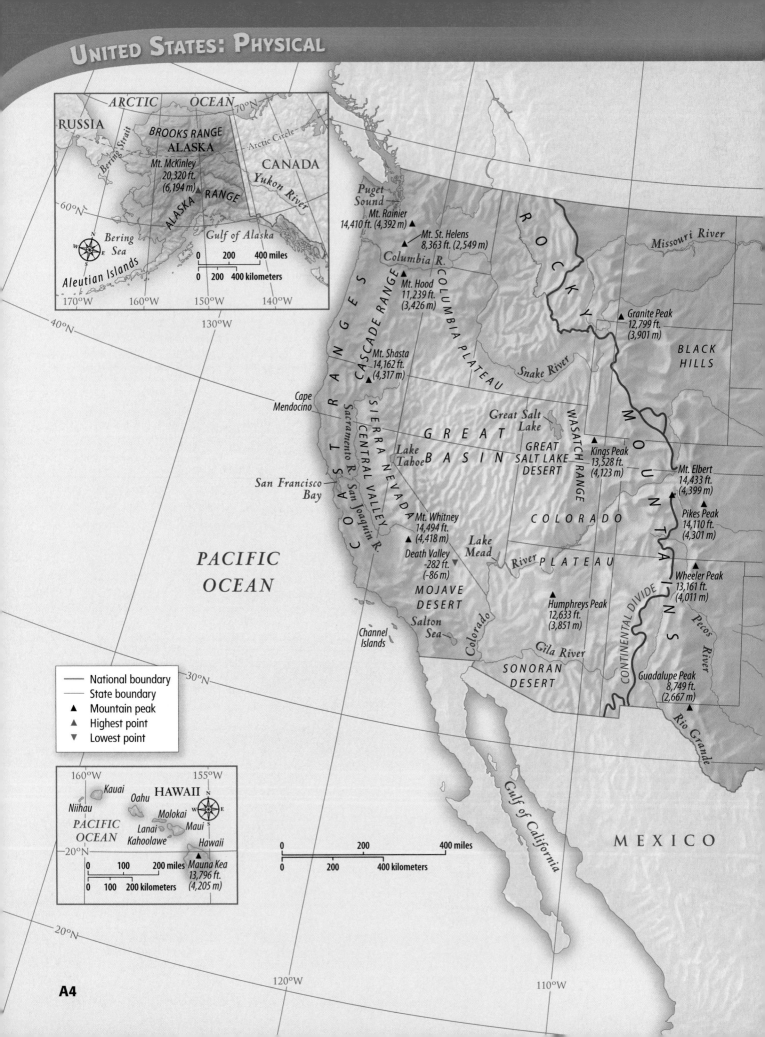

ARCTIC OCEAN
70°N

RUSSIA

BROOKS RANGE
ALASKA

Arctic Circle

CANADA

Mt. McKinley
20,320 ft.
(6,194 m)

Yukon River

ALASKA RANGE

60°N

Bering Sea

Gulf of Alaska

N
W   E
S

Aleutian Islands

0   200   400 miles
0   200   400 kilometers

170°W   160°W   150°W   140°W

40°N   130°W

Puget Sound

Mt. Rainier
14,410 ft. (4,392 m)

Mt. St. Helens
8,363 ft. (2,549 m)

Columbia R.

CASCADE RANGE

Mt. Hood
11,239 ft.
(3,426 m)

COLUMBIA PLATEAU

ROCKY

Missouri River

Granite Peak
12,799 ft.
(3,901 m)

BLACK HILLS

Mt. Shasta
14,162 ft.
(4,317 m)

Snake River

Cape Mendocino

Sacramento R.

SIERRA NEVADA

CENTRAL VALLEY

Great Salt Lake

GREAT BASIN

WASATCH RANGE

MOUNTAINS

Lake Tahoe

GREAT SALT LAKE DESERT

Kings Peak
13,528 ft.
(4,123 m)

Mt. Elbert
14,433 ft.
(4,399 m)

San Francisco Bay

San Joaquin R.

COLORADO

Pikes Peak
14,110 ft.
(4,301 m)

Mt. Whitney
14,494 ft.
(4,418 m)

Lake Mead

PACIFIC OCEAN

Death Valley
-282 ft.
(-86 m)

Colorado River

PLATEAU

Wheeler Peak
13,161 ft.
(4,011 m)

MOJAVE DESERT

Humphreys Peak
12,633 ft.
(3,851 m)

CONTINENTAL DIVIDE

Pecos River

Salton Sea

Channel Islands

Colorado

Gila River

SONORAN DESERT

Guadalupe Peak
8,749 ft.
(2,667 m)

Rio Grande

30°N

National boundary
State boundary
▲ Mountain peak
▲ Highest point
▼ Lowest point

160°W   155°W

Kauai

Oahu   HAWAII

Niihau

Molokai

PACIFIC OCEAN

Lanai   Maui
Kahoolawe

N
W   E
S

Hawaii

20°N

0   100   200 miles
0   100   200 kilometers

Mauna Kea
13,796 ft.
(4,205 m)

0   200   400 miles
0   200   400 kilometers

Gulf of California

MEXICO

20°N

120°W   110°W

CANADA

Lake of the Woods

MESABI RANGE

Lake Superior

GREAT LAKES

GREAT PLAINS

Lake Michigan

Lake Huron

St. Lawrence River

WHITE MOUNTAINS

Mt. Washington
6,288 ft.
(1,917 m)

GREEN MOUNTAINS

ADIRONDACK MOUNTAINS

Lake Ontario

Cape Cod

Mississippi River

Lake Erie

ALLEGHENY PLATEAU

Hudson River

Long Island

40°N

CENTRAL PLAINS

Susquehanna River

ALLEGHENY MOUNTAINS

Missouri River

Platte River

Wabash River

River

Ohio River

APPALACHIAN MOUNTAINS

Potomac River

Delaware Bay

Chesapeake Bay

PIEDMONT

Arkansas River

INTERIOR PLAINS

OZARK PLATEAU

Tennessee River

Mt. Mitchell
6,684 ft.
(2,037 m)

Cape Hatteras

ATLANTIC OCEAN

OUACHITA MOUNTAINS

Mississippi River

Savannah River

Red River

ATLANTIC COASTAL PLAIN

Brazos River

Alabama River

Chattahoochee River

30°N

Colorado River

EDWARDS PLATEAU

GULF COASTAL PLAIN

Mobile Bay

Galveston Bay

Mississippi River Delta

Lake Okeechobee

THE BAHAMAS

Gulf of Mexico

N
W   E
S

Florida Keys

Straits of Florida

CUBA

20°N

100°W

90°W

80°W

A5

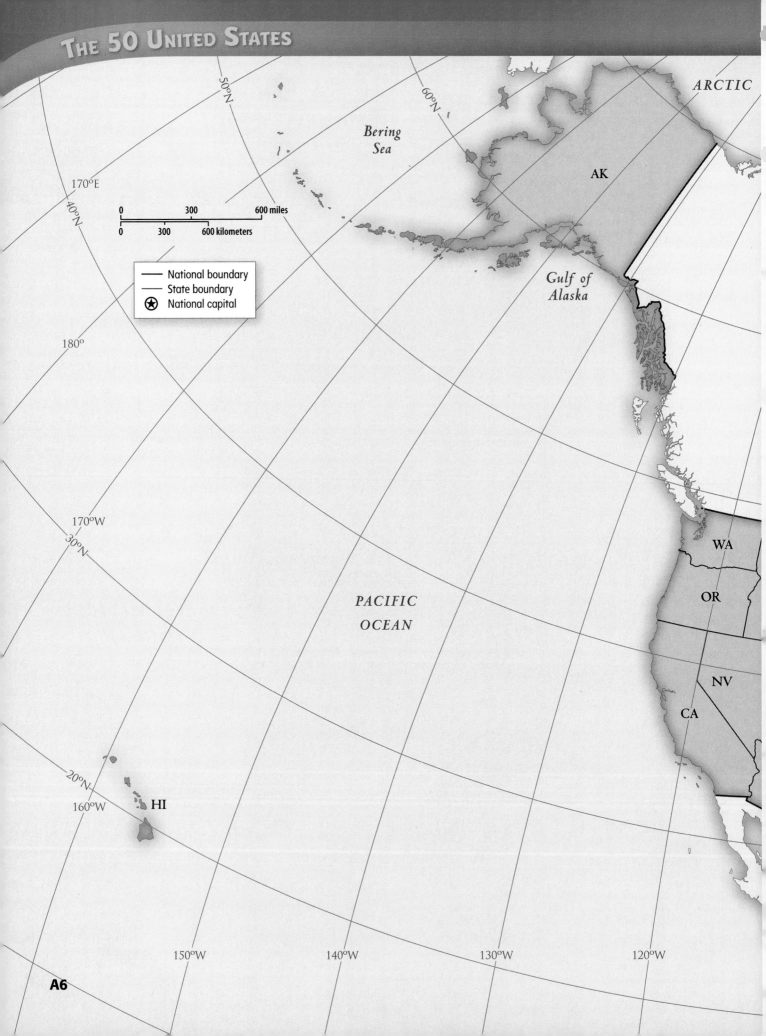

ARCTIC

Bering
Sea

AK

Gulf of
Alaska

170°E

50°N

60°N

40°N

0   300   600 miles
0   300   600 kilometers

—— National boundary
—— State boundary
⊛ National capital

180°

170°W

30°N

PACIFIC
OCEAN

WA

OR

NV

CA

20°N

160°W HI

150°W   140°W   130°W   120°W

OCEAN

GREENLAND
(Denmark)

20°W

60°N

30°W

40°W

Labrador
Sea

50°N

CANADA

Hudson
Bay

50°W

Lake
Superior

ME

MT

ND

MN

VT NH

Lake
Huron

Lake
Ontario

NY

MA
CT

40°N

ID

SD

WI

MI

RI

WY

Lake
Michigan

Lake
Erie

PA

NJ
DE
MD

60°W

UT

NE

IA

IN

OH

ATLANTIC
OCEAN

Washington, D.C.

CO

KS

MO

WV

VA

KY

AZ

NM

OK

AR

TN

NC

SC

MS

AL

GA

30°N

TX

LA

FL

THE
BAHAMAS

MEXICO

N
W   E
S

Gulf of
Mexico

80°W

CUBA

70°W

20°N

110°W

100°W

90°W

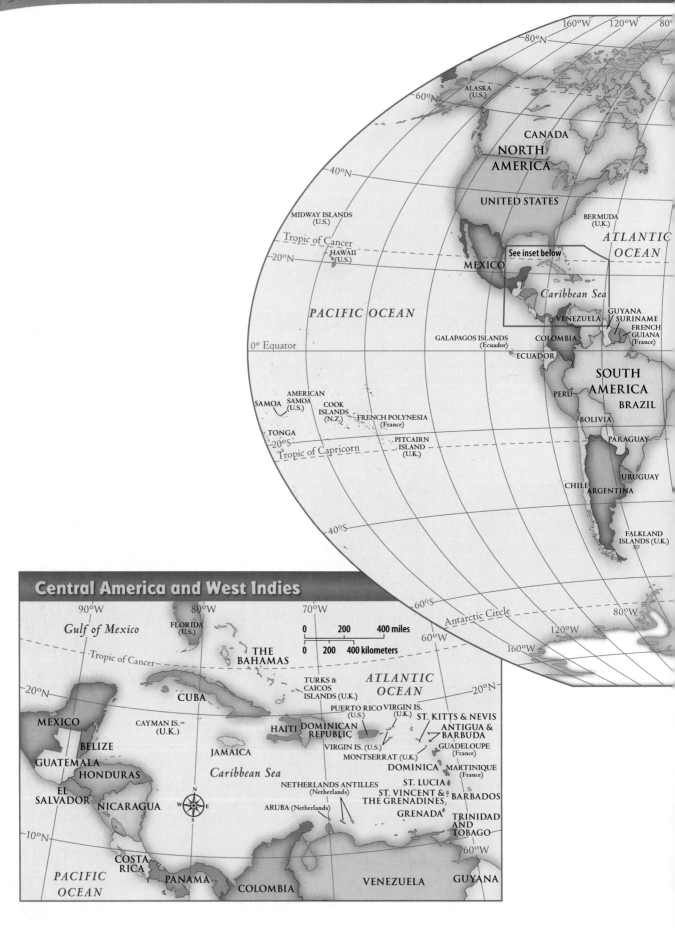

160°W   120°W   80

80°N

60°N

ALASKA
(U.S.)

CANADA

NORTH
AMERICA

40°N

UNITED STATES

BERMUDA
(U.K.)

ATLANTIC
OCEAN

MIDWAY ISLANDS
(U.S.)

Tropic of Cancer

See inset below

20°N

HAWAII
(U.S.)

MEXICO

Caribbean Sea

GUYANA
SURINAME
FRENCH
GUIANA
(France)

VENEZUELA

PACIFIC OCEAN

GALAPAGOS ISLANDS
(Ecuador)

COLOMBIA

0° Equator

ECUADOR

SOUTH
AMERICA

PERU

BRAZIL

AMERICAN
SAMOA
(U.S.)

COOK
ISLANDS
(N.Z.)

BOLIVIA

SAMOA

FRENCH POLYNESIA
(France)

TONGA

PARAGUAY

20°S

Tropic of Capricorn

PITCAIRN
ISLAND
(U.K.)

CHILE

URUGUAY

ARGENTINA

40°S

FALKLAND
ISLANDS (U.K.)

60°S

Antarctic Circle

80°W

Central America and West Indies

90°W   80°W   70°W

Gulf of Mexico

FLORIDA
(U.S.)

0   200   400 miles

0   200   400 kilometers

Tropic of Cancer

THE
BAHAMAS

ATLANTIC
OCEAN

20°N

TURKS &
CAICOS
ISLANDS (U.K.)

20°N

CUBA

PUERTO RICO
(U.S.)

VIRGIN IS.
(U.K.)

ST. KITTS & NEVIS

MEXICO

CAYMAN IS.
(U.K.)

HAITI

DOMINICAN
REPUBLIC

VIRGIN IS. (U.S.)

ANTIGUA &
BARBUDA

GUADELOUPE
(France)

BELIZE

JAMAICA

MONTSERRAT (U.K.)

GUATEMALA

Caribbean Sea

DOMINICA

MARTINIQUE
(France)

HONDURAS

NETHERLANDS ANTILLES
(Netherlands)

ST. LUCIA

EL
SALVADOR

NICARAGUA

ST. VINCENT &
THE GRENADINES

BARBADOS

ARUBA (Netherlands)

GRENADA

TRINIDAD
AND
TOBAGO

10°N

60°W

COSTA
RICA

PACIFIC
OCEAN

PANAMA

COLOMBIA

VENEZUELA

GUYANA

120°W

60°W

160°W

60°S

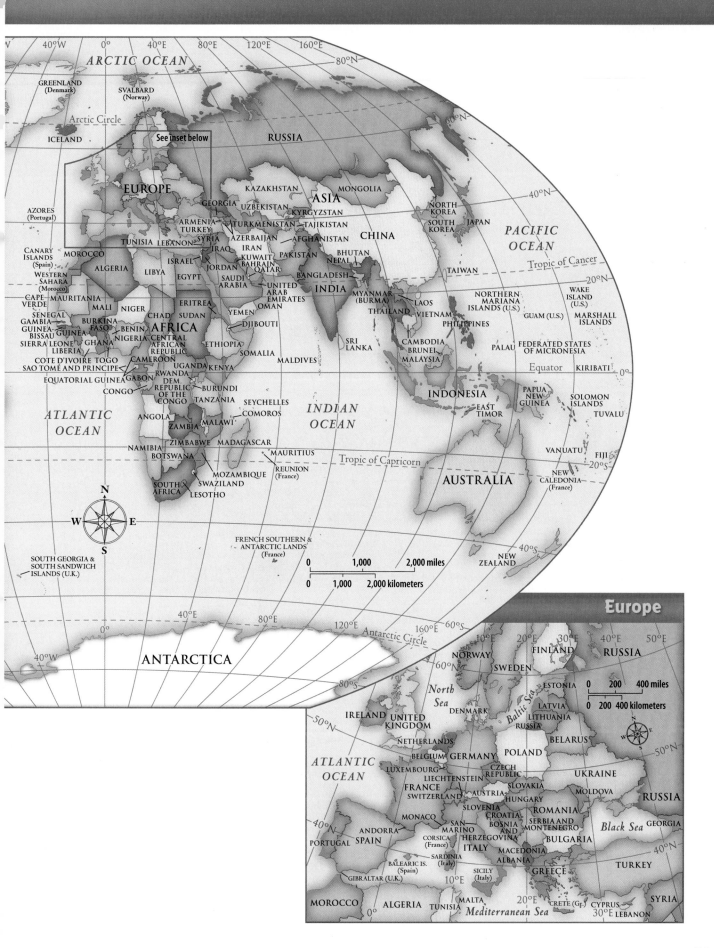

ARCTIC OCEAN

80°N

40°W   0°   40°E   80°E   120°E   160°E

GREENLAND
(Denmark)

SVALBARD
(Norway)

RUSSIA

Arctic Circle

60°N

ICELAND

See inset below

EUROPE

KAZAKHSTAN   MONGOLIA

40°N

AZORES
(Portugal)

GEORGIA   UZBEKISTAN   ASIA

ARMENIA   KYRGYZSTAN
TURKEY   TAJIKISTAN

NORTH
KOREA

SOUTH   JAPAN
KOREA

PACIFIC
OCEAN

CANARY
ISLANDS
(Spain)

TUNISIA LEBANON   SYRIA   AZERBAIJAN   AFGHANISTAN   CHINA

IRAQ   IRAN

MOROCCO   ISRAEL   KUWAIT PAKISTAN   NEPAL   BHUTAN

Tropic of Cancer

WESTERN
SAHARA
(Morocco)

ALGERIA   LIBYA   JORDAN BAHRAIN QATAR   BANGLADESH   TAIWAN   20°N

EGYPT   SAUDI   UNITED
ARABIA   ARAB   INDIA   MYANMAR   LAOS
EMIRATES   (BURMA)

NORTHERN
MARIANA
ISLANDS (U.S.)

WAKE
ISLAND
(U.S.)

CAPE MAURITANIA   ERITREA   OMAN   THAILAND VIETNAM   GUAM (U.S.)   MARSHALL
VERDE   ISLANDS

MALI   NIGER   CHAD   SUDAN   YEMEN   PHILIPPINES

SENEGAL   DJIBOUTI   SRI
GAMBIA   BURKINA   BENIN   AFRICA   CENTRAL   ETHIOPIA   LANKA   CAMBODIA   PALAU   FEDERATED STATES
GUINEA-   FASO   NIGERIA AFRICAN   BRUNEI   OF MICRONESIA
BISSAU GUINEA   REPUBLIC   SOMALIA   MALDIVES   MALAYSIA
SIERRA LEONE GHANA   Equator   KIRIBATI   0°
LIBERIA   CAMEROON   UGANDA KENYA
COTE D'IVOIRE TOGO
SAO TOME AND PRINCIPE   GABON   RWANDA   INDONESIA   PAPUA
EQUATORIAL GUINEA   DEM.   BURUNDI   NEW   SOLOMON
CONGO   REPUBLIC   INDIAN   EAST   GUINEA ISLANDS
OF THE   TANZANIA   OCEAN   TIMOR
CONGO   SEYCHELLES   TUVALU

ATLANTIC
OCEAN   ANGOLA   ZAMBIA MALAWI COMOROS

ZIMBABWE MADAGASCAR   VANUATU   FIJI

NAMIBIA   MAURITIUS   AUSTRALIA   20°S
BOTSWANA   REUNION   Tropic of Capricorn   NEW
(France)   CALEDONIA
MOZAMBIQUE   (France)
SOUTH SWAZILAND
AFRICA LESOTHO

N
W   E
S

FRENCH SOUTHERN &
ANTARCTIC LANDS
(France)   0   1,000   2,000 miles   NEW   40°S
ZEALAND
SOUTH GEORGIA &
SOUTH SANDWICH   0   1,000   2,000 kilometers
ISLANDS (U.K.)

40°E   80°E   120°E   60°S

0°   Antarctic Circle

40°W   ANTARCTICA   80°S

Europe

10°E   20°E   30°E   40°E   50°E

FINLAND   RUSSIA
NORWAY
60°N   SWEDEN

North   ESTONIA   0   200   400 miles
Sea   LATVIA   0   200   400 kilometers
IRELAND UNITED   DENMARK   LITHUANIA
KINGDOM   RUSSIA   BELARUS
NETHERLANDS   POLAND   N
W   E
ATLANTIC   BELGIUM GERMANY   CZECH   UKRAINE   S
OCEAN   LUXEMBOURG   REPUBLIC
LIECHTENSTEIN   SLOVAKIA   MOLDOVA   50°N
FRANCE   AUSTRIA   HUNGARY   RUSSIA
SWITZERLAND   SLOVENIA   ROMANIA
MONACO   CROATIA   SERBIA AND   Black Sea GEORGIA
ANDORRA   SAN   BOSNIA MONTENEGRO
MARINO   AND
PORTUGAL SPAIN CORSICA HERZEGOVINA BULGARIA
(France)   ITALY   MACEDONIA   40°N
BALEARIC IS.   SARDINIA   ALBANIA   TURKEY
(Spain)   (Italy)   GREECE
GIBRALTAR (U.K.)   SICILY
10°E   (Italy)   CRETE (Gr.) CYPRUS
MOROCCO ALGERIA TUNISIA MALTA   SYRIA
20°E   Mediterranean Sea 30°E LEBANON

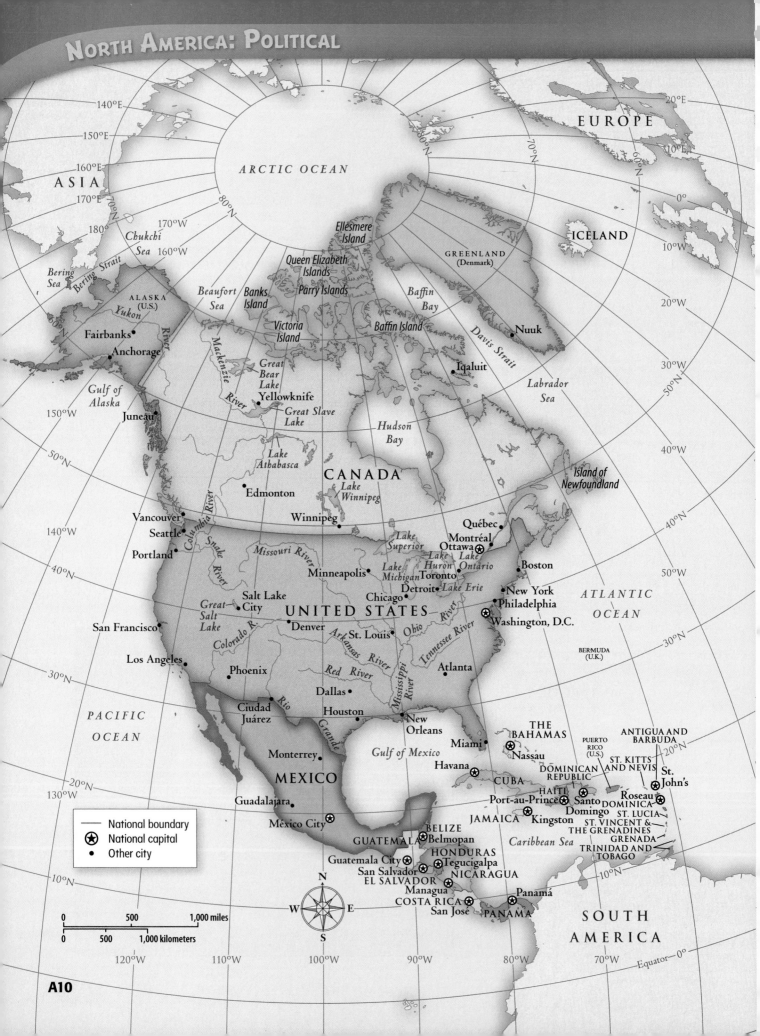

NORTH AMERICA: POLITICAL

ASIA

ARCTIC OCEAN

EUROPE

Chukchi Sea

Bering Sea

Bering Strait

ICELAND

Ellesmere Island

Queen Elizabeth Islands

GREENLAND (Denmark)

Parry Islands

Banks Island

Beaufort Sea

Baffin Bay

ALASKA (U.S.)

Yukon River

Fairbanks •

Anchorage •

Victoria Island

Baffin Island

Nuuk •

Mackenzie River

Davis Strait

Gulf of Alaska

Great Bear Lake

Yellowknife •

Iqaluit •

Labrador Sea

Juneau •

Great Slave Lake

Hudson Bay

Lake Athabasca

CANADA

Island of Newfoundland

Edmonton •

Lake Winnipeg

Vancouver •

Winnipeg •

Québec •

Seattle •

Lake Superior

Montréal •

Portland •

Columbia River

Ottawa ⊛

Boston •

Snake River

Missouri River

Lake Michigan

Lake Huron

Lake Ontario

Minneapolis •

Toronto •

Lake Erie

New York •

Salt Lake City •

Detroit •

Philadelphia •

Chicago •

Washington, D.C. ⊛

San Francisco •

Great Salt Lake

Denver •

St. Louis •

Ohio River

Tennessee River

ATLANTIC OCEAN

UNITED STATES

Colorado R.

Arkansas River

Los Angeles •

Phoenix •

Red River

Mississippi River

Atlanta •

BERMUDA (U.K.)

PACIFIC OCEAN

Dallas •

Ciudad Juárez •

Rio Grande

Houston •

New Orleans •

Miami •

THE BAHAMAS

PUERTO RICO (U.S.)

ANTIGUA AND BARBUDA

Monterrey •

Gulf of Mexico

Nassau •

MEXICO

Havana •

DOMINICAN REPUBLIC

ST. KITTS AND NEVIS

St. John's ⊛

CUBA

HAITI

Santo Domingo ⊛

Roseau ⊛

Guadalajara •

Port-au-Prince ⊛

DOMINICA

ST. LUCIA

México City ⊛

JAMAICA

Kingston ⊛

ST. VINCENT & THE GRENADINES

BELIZE

Caribbean Sea

GRENADA

GUATEMALA

Belmopan •

HONDURAS

TRINIDAD AND TOBAGO

Guatemala City ⊛

Tegucigalpa ⊛

San Salvador ⊛

NICARAGUA

EL SALVADOR

Managua ⊛

Panamá ⊛

COSTA RICA

PANAMA

SOUTH AMERICA

San José ⊛

N
W   E
S

— National boundary
⊛ National capital
• Other city

0   500   1,000 miles

0   500   1,000 kilometers

140°E 150°E 160°E 170°E 180° 170°W 160°W 150°W 130°W 120°W 110°W 100°W 90°W 80°W 70°W

20°E 10°E 0° 10°W 20°W 30°W 40°W 50°W

80°N 70°N 60°N 50°N 40°N 30°N 20°N 10°N

60°N 50°N 40°N 30°N 20°N 10°N Equator—0°

CENTRAL AMERICA

Caribbean Sea

15°N — 75°W — 15°N

Barranquilla
Maracaibo
Valencia · Caracas
Lake Maracaibo
Orinoco River
VENEZUELA
Georgetown
Paramaribo
GUYANA
Cayenne
SURINAME
FRENCH GUIANA (France)

ATLANTIC OCEAN

Medellín
Gulf of Panama
Bogotá
Cali
Magdalena River
COLOMBIA

Quito
Equator — 0°
ECUADOR
GALAPAGOS ISLANDS (Ecuador)
Guayaquil
Iquitos
Negro River
Manaus
River
Belém
Amazon River
Equator — 0°

Trujillo
PERU
Callao · Lima
Cuzco
Arequipa
Lake Titicaca
La Paz
BOLIVIA
Sucre
Madeira River
Tapajós River
Xingu River
BRAZIL
São Francisco River
Recife
Salvador (Bahía)
Brasília
Belo Horizonte
River
Paraguay River
Paraná
15°S — 15°S

PARAGUAY
Rio de Janeiro
São Paulo
Tropic of Capricorn
Antofagasta
Asunción
Porto Alegre
Tucumán
CHILE
Paraná River
Uruguay River
Córdoba
Rosario
URUGUAY
Valparaíso
Santiago
ARGENTINA
Buenos Aires
Montevideo
Rio de la Plata
Concepción
Colorado River
30°S — 30°S

PACIFIC OCEAN

ATLANTIC OCEAN

National boundary
National capital
Other city

45°S — 45°S

0   400   800 miles
0   400   800 kilometers

FALKLAND ISLANDS (ISLAS MALVINAS) (U.K.)

Strait of Magellan
Punta Arenas

SOUTH GEORGIA (U.K.)

105°W   90°W   75°W   60°W   45°W   30°W

New York: Political

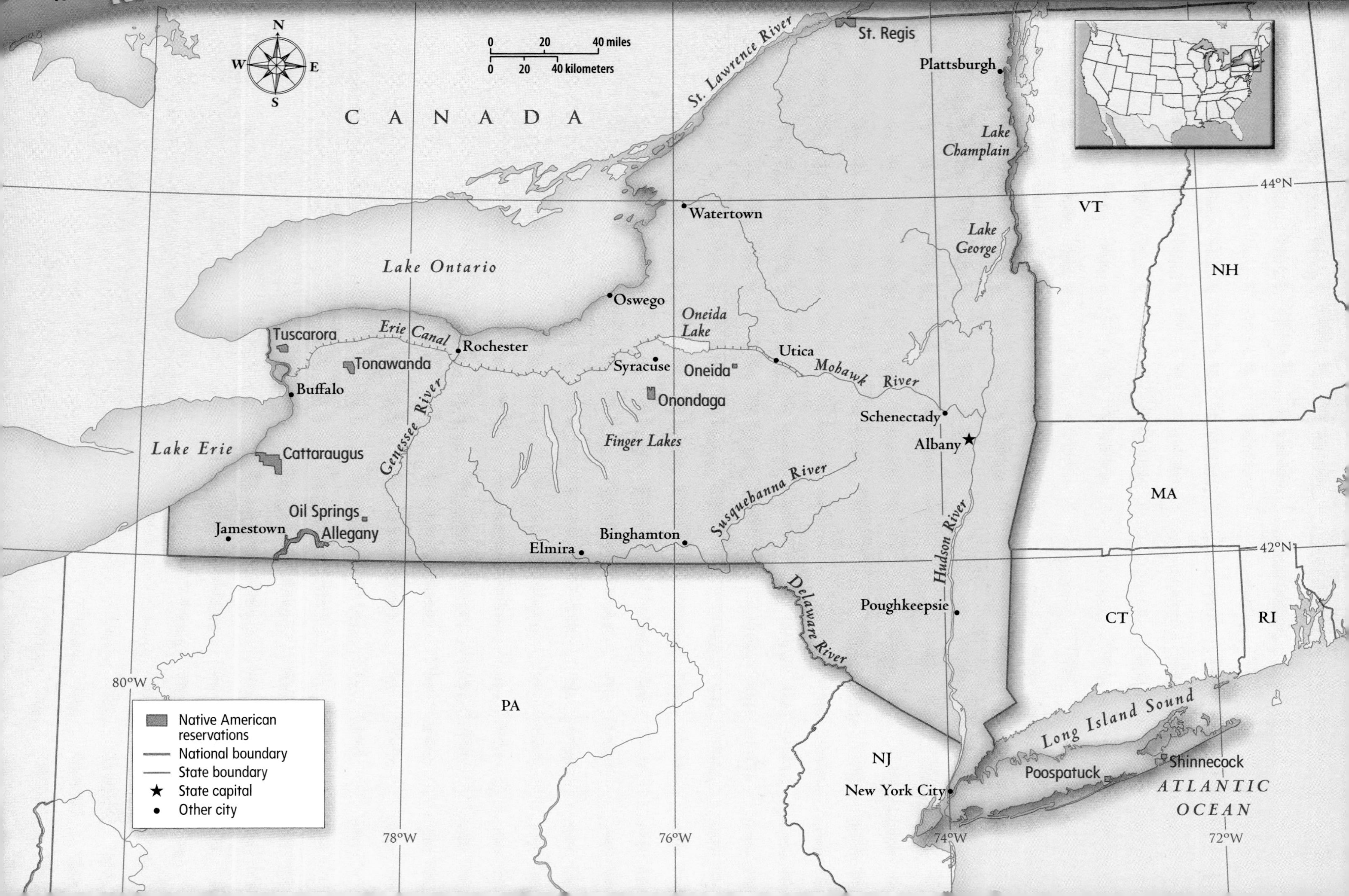

CANADA

St. Lawrence River

St. Regis

Plattsburgh •

Lake Champlain

Lake George

Watertown •

Oswego •

Lake Ontario

Oneida Lake

Utica •

Mohawk River

Schenectady •

★ Albany

Hudson River

Poughkeepsie •

Oneida

Syracuse •
Onondaga

Finger Lakes

Rochester •

Erie Canal

Genesee River

Tonawanda

Tuscarora

Buffalo •

Cattaraugus

Oil Springs
Allegany

Jamestown •

Lake Erie

Binghamton •

Susquehanna River

Elmira •

Delaware River

New York City •

NJ

PA

Long Island Sound

Shinnecock

Poospatuck

ATLANTIC OCEAN

VT

NH

MA

CT

RI

N
W E
S

40 miles
40 kilometers
0 20 40
0 20 40

44°N
42°N
80°W
78°W
76°W
74°W
72°W

Native American reservations
National boundary
State boundary
★ State capital
• Other city

A12

NEW YORK: PHYSICAL

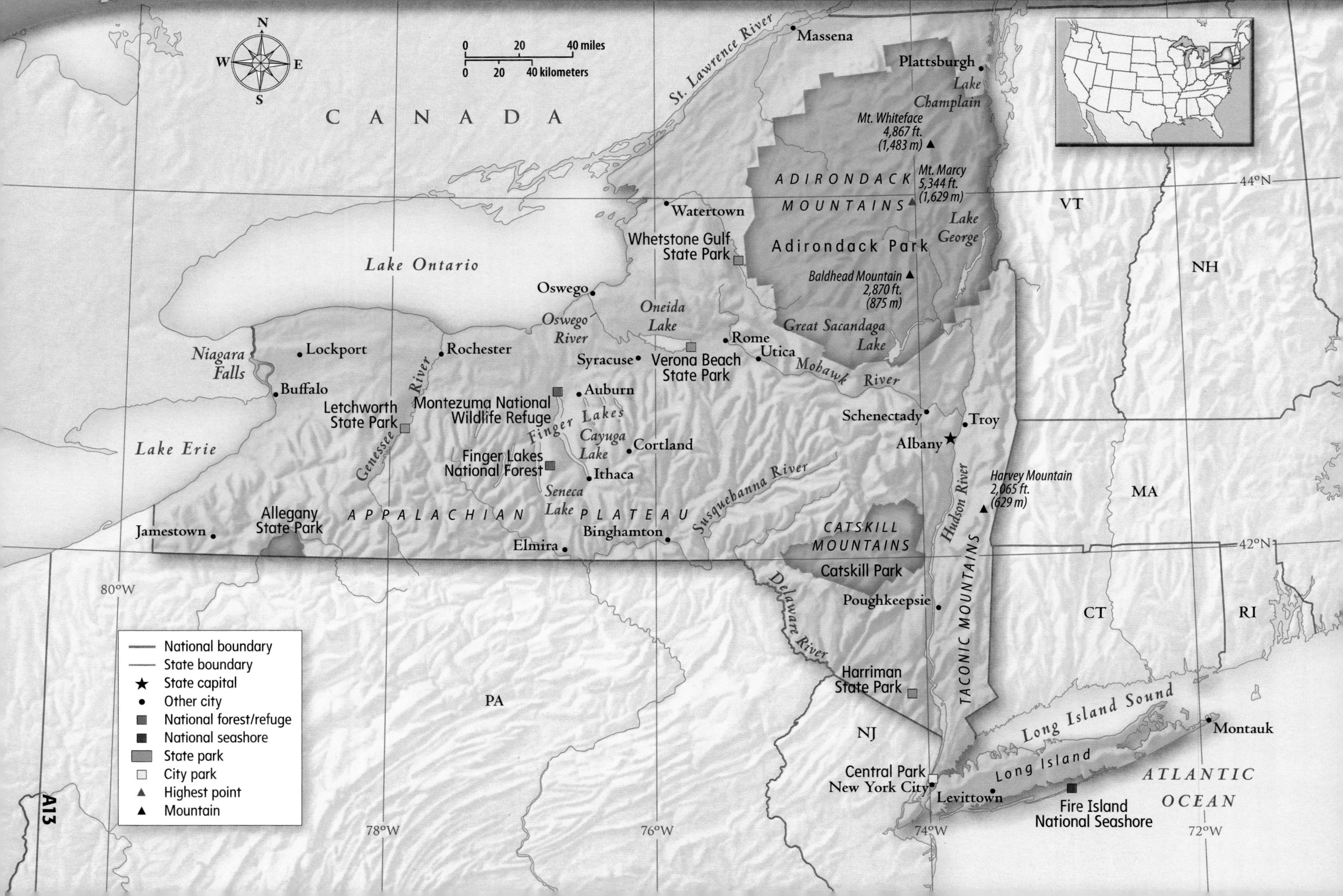

CANADA

St. Lawrence River

Massena

Plattsburgh

Lake Champlain

ADIRONDACK

Mt. Whiteface
4,867 ft.
(1,483 m) ▲

Mt. Marcy
5,344 ft.
(1,629 m) ▲

Lake George

MOUNTAINS

Adirondack Park

Baldhead Mountain
2,870 ft.
(875 m) ▲

Great Sacandaga Lake

Watertown

Whetstone Gulf
State Park

Rome

Utica

Mohawk River

Schenectady

Troy

★ Albany

Hudson River

Harvey Mountain
2,065 ft.
(629 m) ▲

TACONIC MOUNTAINS

Oswego

Oswego River

Oneida Lake

Verona Beach
State Park

Syracuse

Auburn

Cortland

Ithaca

Finger Lakes

Cayuga Lake

Seneca

Susquehanna River

CATSKILL
MOUNTAINS

Catskill Park

Poughkeepsie

Delaware River

Harriman
State Park

NJ

Central Park
New York City

Levittown

Fire Island
National Seashore

Long Island

Long Island Sound

Montauk

ATLANTIC
OCEAN

RI

MA

CT

VT

NH

Rochester

Genesee River

Montezuma National
Wildlife Refuge

Finger Lakes
National Forest

Elmira

Binghamton

Lake PLATEAU

APPALACHIAN

Letchworth
State Park

Lockport

Buffalo

Niagara
Falls

Lake Ontario

Lake Erie

Jamestown

Allegany
State Park

PA

Scale

| 40 miles |
| 40 kilometers |

0   20   40 miles
0   20   40 kilometers

N E S W

Legend

———	National boundary
|	State boundary
★	State capital
●	Other city
■	National forest/refuge
■	National seashore
▬	State park
□	City park
▲	Highest point
▲	Mountain

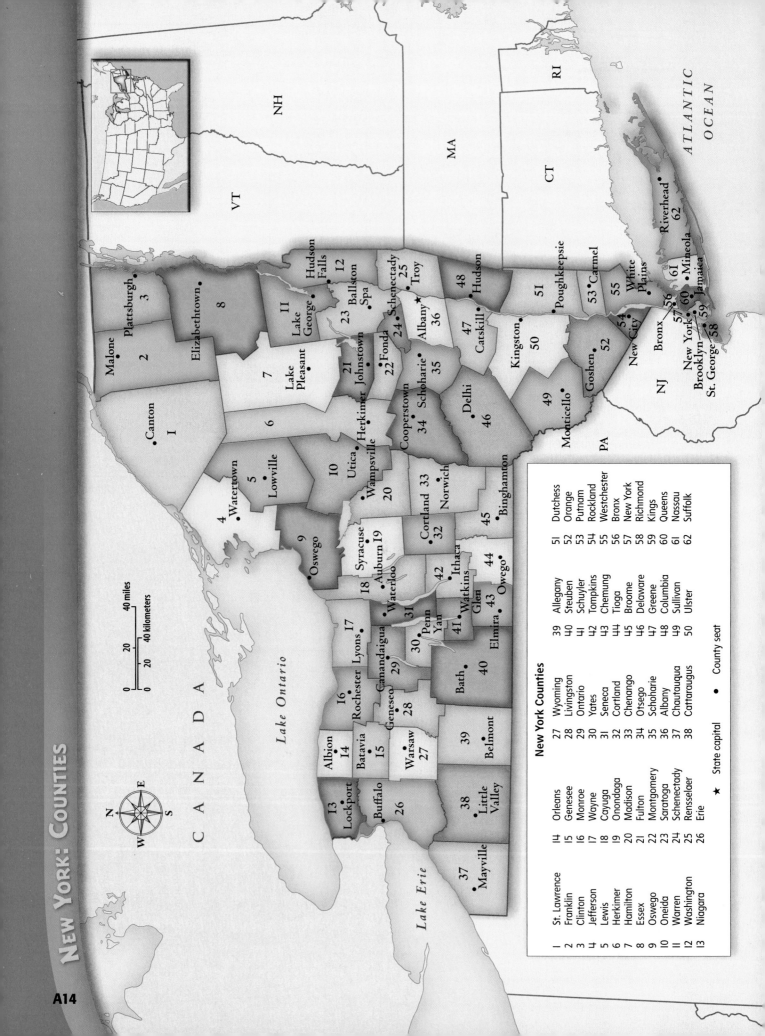

NEW YORK: COUNTIES

A14

ATLANTIC OCEAN

RI

NH

MA

CT

VT

CANADA

Lake Ontario

Lake Erie

N **E** **S** **W**

40 miles
20
40 kilometers
0   20   40
0

Malone 2
Plattsburgh 3
Canton I
Elizabethtown 8
Lake George II
Hudson Falls I2
Ballston Spa 23
Schenectady 25
Troy
Albany ★ 36
Schoharie 35
Hudson 48
Catskill 47
Kingston 50
Poughkeepsie 5I
Carmel 53
White Plains 55
Riverhead 62
Mineola 6I
Jamaica 60
New York 57
Brooklyn 59
St. George 58
Bronx 56
New City 54
Goshen 52
Monticello 49
Delhi 46
Cooperstown 34
Fonda 22
Johnstown 2I
Herkimer 7
Lake Pleasant 6
Watertown 4
Lowville 5
Utica I0
Wampsville 20
Syracuse
Auburn I9
Waterloo I8
Oswego 9
Cortland 33
Norwich 32
Binghamton 45
Ithaca 42
Watkins Glen 4I
Owego 44
Elmira 43
Penn Yan 30
Canandaigua 29
Lyons I7
Rochester I6
Geneseo 28
Bath 40
Warsaw 27
Belmont 39
Little Valley 38
Mayville 37
Buffalo 26
Batavia I5
Albion I4
Lockport I3

NJ

PA

New York Counties

I	St. Lawrence	I4	Orleans	27	Wyoming	39	Allegany	5I	Dutchess
2	Franklin	I5	Genesee	28	Livingston	40	Steuben	52	Orange
3	Clinton	I6	Monroe	29	Ontario	4I	Schuyler	53	Putnam
4	Jefferson	I7	Wayne	30	Yates	42	Tompkins	54	Rockland
5	Lewis	I8	Cayuga	3I	Seneca	43	Chemung	55	Westchester
6	Herkimer	I9	Onondaga	32	Cortland	44	Tioga	56	Bronx
7	Hamilton	20	Madison	33	Chenango	45	Broome	57	New York
8	Essex	2I	Fulton	34	Otsego	46	Delaware	58	Richmond
9	Oswego	22	Montgomery	35	Schoharie	47	Greene	59	Kings
I0	Oneida	23	Saratoga	36	Albany	48	Columbia	60	Queens
II	Warren	24	Schenectady	37	Chautauqua	49	Sullivan	6I	Nassau
I2	Washington	25	Rensselaer	38	Cattaraugus	50	Ulster	62	Suffolk
I3	Niagara	26	Erie						

★ State capital
● County seat

New York Counties

County Name	County Seat	County Name	County Seat	County Name	County Seat	County Name	County Seat
Albany (36)	Albany	Franklin (2)	Malone	Oneida (10)	Utica	Schuyler (41)	Watkins Glen
Allegany (39)	Belmont	Fulton (21)	Johnstown	Onondaga (19)	Syracuse	Seneca (31)	Waterloo
Bronx (56)	Bronx	Genesee (15)	Batavia	Ontario (29)	Canandaigua	Steuben (40)	Bath
Broome (45)	Binghamton	Greene (47)	Catskill	Orange (52)	Goshen	Suffolk (62)	Riverhead
Cattaraugus (38)	Little Valley	Hamilton (7)	Lake Pleasant	Orleans (14)	Albion	Sullivan (49)	Monticello
Cayuga (18)	Auburn	Herkimer (6)	Herkimer	Oswego (9)	Oswego	Tioga (44)	Owego
Chautauqua (37)	Mayville	Jefferson (4)	Watertown	Otsego (34)	Cooperstown	Tompkins (42)	Ithaca
Chenango (33)	Norwich	Kings (59)	Brooklyn	Putnam (53)	Carmel	Ulster (50)	Kingston
Chemung (43)	Elmira	Lewis (5)	Lowville	Queens (60)	Jamaica	Warren (11)	Lake George
Clinton (3)	Plattsburgh	Livingston (28)	Geneseo	Rensselaer (25)	Troy	Washington (12)	Hudson Falls
Columbia (48)	Hudson	Madison (20)	Wampsville	Richmond (58)	Saint George	Wayne (17)	Lyons
Cortland (32)	Cortland	Monroe (16)	Rochester	Rockland (54)	New City	Westchester (55)	White Plains
Delaware (46)	Delhi	Montgomery (22)	Fonda	St. Lawrence (1)	Canton	Wyoming (27)	Warsaw
Dutchess (51)	Poughkeepsie	Nassau (61)	Mineola	Saratoga (23)	Ballston Spa	Yates (30)	Penn Yan
Erie (26)	Buffalo	New York (57)	Manhattan	Schenectady (24)	Schenectady		
Essex (8)	Elizabethtown	Niagara (13)	Lockport	Schoharie (35)	Schoharie		

Unit 1
New York and Its First People

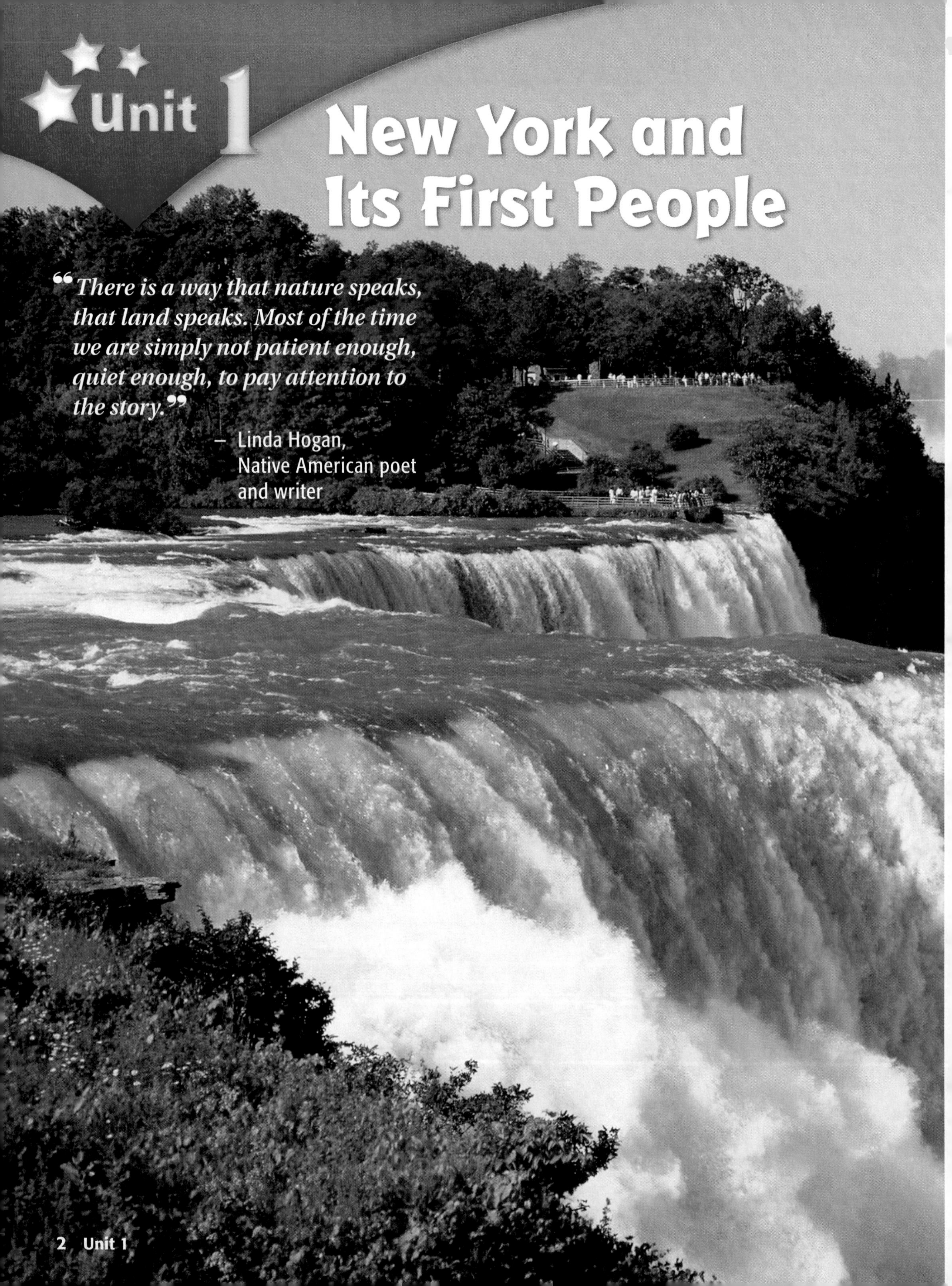

"There is a way that nature speaks, that land speaks. Most of the time we are simply not patient enough, quiet enough, to pay attention to the story."

– Linda Hogan,
Native American poet
and writer

◀ Niagara Falls

How do people adapt to where they live?

Unit 1 tells the story of New York's land and how this land was used by New York's earliest people. This unit also explores how the land of New York is used today.

As you read the chapters in this unit, think about how the land of New York has influenced and shaped the people who have lived here.

Copy and fill in the graphic organizer below with details from the Unit. List some of the ways people have adapted. The first one has been started for you.

Region	Natural Resources	Climate	How People Adapt
1. Northern New York	1. Adirondack Mountains	1.	1.
2.	2.	2.	2.
3.	3.	3.	3.
4.	4.	4.	4.

People Who Made a Difference

Deganawida
about 1500s

Deganawida, also known as the Peace Maker, helped make the Great Peace and bring the Iroquois groups together. (page 61)

Hiawatha
about 1500s

Hiawatha was inspired by Deganawida to convince the Iroquois groups to form the Iroquois League. (page 61)

1550   1650   1750

1560s
Deganawida, Hiawatha, and Jikonsahseh work to bring the Iroquois peoples together

1570
Iroquois League is formed

1722
The Tuscarora join the Iroquois League

LOG ON For more biographies, visit: www.macmillanmh.com

Jikonsahseh
about 1500s

Jikonsahseh became known as the "Mother of Nations" for her role in bringing the Iroquois people together. She became the first clan mother of the Iroquois. (page 61)

Mary Adams
about 1920–1999

Mary Adams was a Mohawk artist and basket-maker who kept Iroquois traditions alive by teaching others. (page 57)

1850   1950   2050

1920
Mary Adams
is born

Turtle's Race with Bear

A Seneca Story

It was an early winter, cold enough so that the ice had frozen on all the ponds, and Bear...came to the edge of a great pond and saw Turtle....

"Hah," shouted Bear..."What are you looking at, Slow One?"

Turtle looked at Bear. "Why do you call me slow?"

Bear snorted. "You are the slowest of the animals. If I were to race you, I would leave you far behind."

"My friend," Turtle said, "let us have a race to see who is the swiftest...You will run along the banks of the pond...I will make holes in the ice...and stick my head out when I reach it."

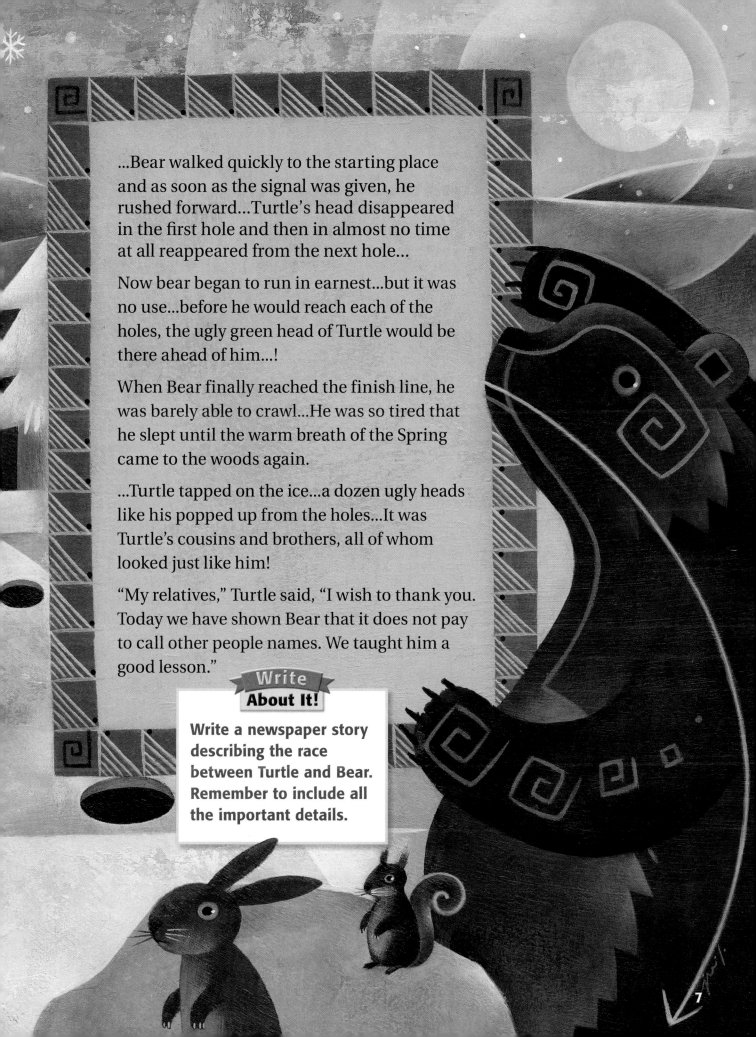

...Bear walked quickly to the starting place and as soon as the signal was given, he rushed forward...Turtle's head disappeared in the first hole and then in almost no time at all reappeared from the next hole...

Now bear began to run in earnest...but it was no use...before he would reach each of the holes, the ugly green head of Turtle would be there ahead of him...!

When Bear finally reached the finish line, he was barely able to crawl...He was so tired that he slept until the warm breath of the Spring came to the woods again.

...Turtle tapped on the ice...a dozen ugly heads like his popped up from the holes...It was Turtle's cousins and brothers, all of whom looked just like him!

"My relatives," Turtle said, "I wish to thank you. Today we have shown Bear that it does not pay to call other people names. We taught him a good lesson."

Write About It!

Write a newspaper story describing the race between Turtle and Bear. Remember to include all the important details.

Identify Main Idea and Details:
New York's Resources

Looking for main ideas and details when you read will help you better understand the subject that you are reading. The main idea is what a passage is all about. Often the main idea is stated in the first sentence in a paragraph. The details tell more about the main idea. Keeping track of main ideas and details will help you to organize and remember information.

 Learn It

- Identify the information in the paragraph.

- Decide if the first sentence states the main idea.

- Look for details. Think about what these details describe.

- Now read the paragraph below. Look for the main idea and details.

Main Idea
The first sentence often states the main idea.

Details
These sentences give details about Watkins Glen.

One of New York's most beautiful and famous physical features is the gorge, or narrow canyon, at Watkins Glen. It is over $1\frac{1}{2}$ miles long. Watkins Glen also has 19 waterfalls and trails that run alongside the gorge.

Try It

Copy and complete the chart below. Fill in the chart by listing the main idea and details from the paragraph on page 8.

MAIN IDEA AND DETAILS CHART

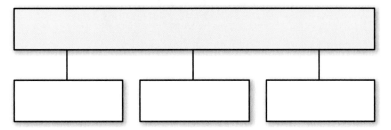

How did you find the main idea and supporting details?

Apply It

- Review the steps for finding the main idea and details in **Learn It**.

- Read the paragraph below. Create a main idea and details chart using the information.

Watkins Glen has a gorge trail with views of all the waterfalls. Starting at the west end, the first waterfall you will see is Cavern Cascade, a free-falling waterfall. Another major waterfall is Central Cascade, which is the highest in the park. The last waterfalls on the trail are a series of cascades known as Pluto Falls. Watkins Glen is a wonderful place to visit.

Chapter 1

The Land of New York

You Are There

"... to find the air and the water [exciting]; to be refreshed by a morning walk or an evening [stroll]; to be thrilled by the stars at night; to be [happy] over a bird's nest or a wildflower in spring — these are some of the rewards of the simple life."

Naturalist John Burroughs wrote these words in 1908. He lived in the Catskill Mountains.

In this chapter, you will learn about New York's land and its uses. You will also find out how New York's land is being used today.

◀ John Burroughs

4 •Buffalo

Lake Erie

Jamestown• **1**

1 Allegany State Park

2 Hudson River

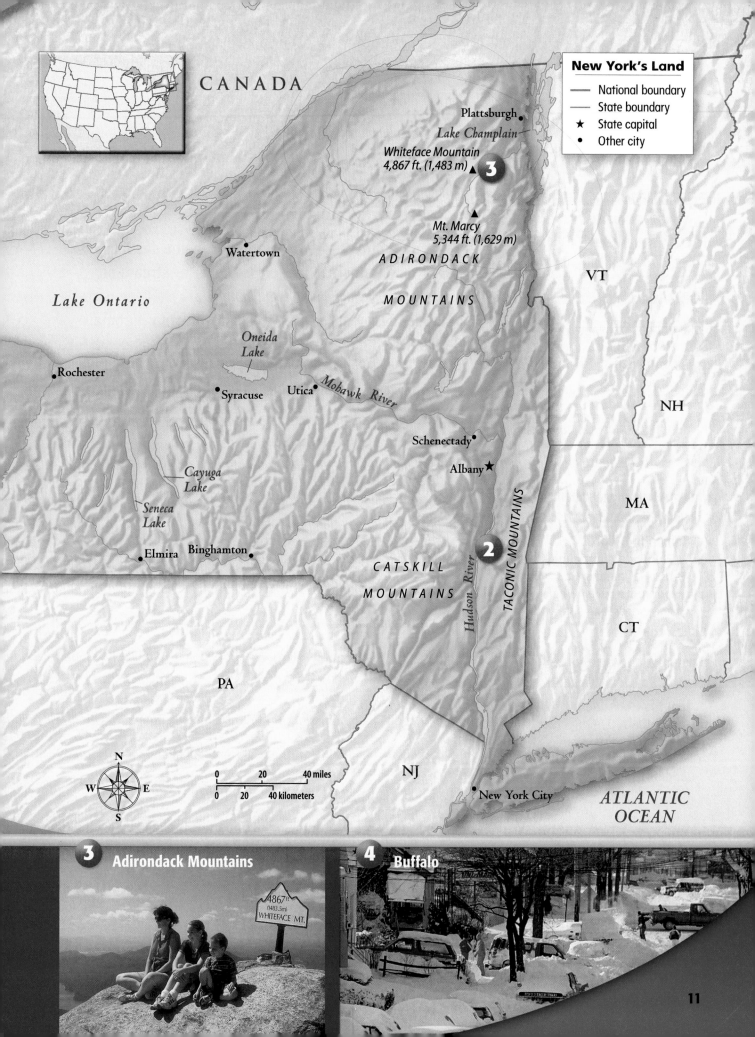

CANADA

Plattsburgh

Lake Champlain

Whiteface Mountain
4,867 ft. (1,483 m) ▲ **3**

▲
Mt. Marcy
5,344 ft. (1,629 m)

A D I R O N D A C K

M O U N T A I N S

• Watertown

VT

Lake Ontario

Oneida Lake

• Rochester

• Syracuse

Utica • *Mohawk River*

NH

Cayuga Lake

Schenectady •

Albany ★

Seneca Lake

MA

• Elmira • Binghamton

C A T S K I L L

M O U N T A I N S

Hudson River

TACONIC MOUNTAINS **2**

CT

PA

N
W E
S

| 0 | 20 | 40 miles |
| 0 | 20 | 40 kilometers |

NJ

• New York City

ATLANTIC OCEAN

New York's Land
— National boundary
— State boundary
★ State capital
• Other city

3 Adirondack Mountains

4867 ft
(1483.5m)
WHITEFACE MT.

4 Buffalo

New York's Regions

What types of land and water are found in New York?

VOCABULARY

geography
continent
landform
valley
plateau
glacier
region
natural resource

VOCABULARY STRATEGY

Compound Words
Landform is a compound word. That means it has two or more parts. What do the words **land** and **form** mean?

READING STRATEGY

Identify Main Idea and Details Use the chart below to list the main idea and details about landforms found in New York.

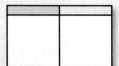

NEW YORK STANDARDS

3.1, 3.2

Look out your classroom window. Can you see hills or mountains? Do you cross a river or stream on your way to school? Is there a lake nearby? These parts of the land may not appear to change in your lifetime. However in the lifetime of Earth, they have changed a lot. Thousands of years ago, most of New York was covered with huge sheets of ice. As the ice melted, it left hills and lakes. You might have visited one of these lakes, or climbed one of these hills.

Ⓐ Where is New York?

Geography is the study of Earth and of the ways people, plants, and animals use it. Describing a place by its location on Earth is also part of geography.

New York state has a "global address," or an address on Earth. Part of New York's global address is the United States. The United States has a global address, too. It is a part of North America, which is a **continent**, one of Earth's seven great bodies of land.

New York's Land

Landforms are a part of geography too. A landform is a natural feature on Earth's surface. The Hudson River Valley is a landform in New York. A **valley** is the low land between hills or mountains, often with a river. The Finger Lakes are another New York landform. They spread out like fingers on a hand. Can you find the Finger Lakes on the map?

Another type of landform in New York are mountains. The Taconic and Catskill mountains are part of the Appalachian Mountain Range that runs through the state. The Appalachian **Plateau** is in Central New York. A plateau is a large area that rises steeply above the surrounding land. The third mountain range, the largest in New York, is the Adirondack Mountains.

QUICK CHECK What are some of the landforms in New York?
Main Idea and Details

New York is located in North America. ▼

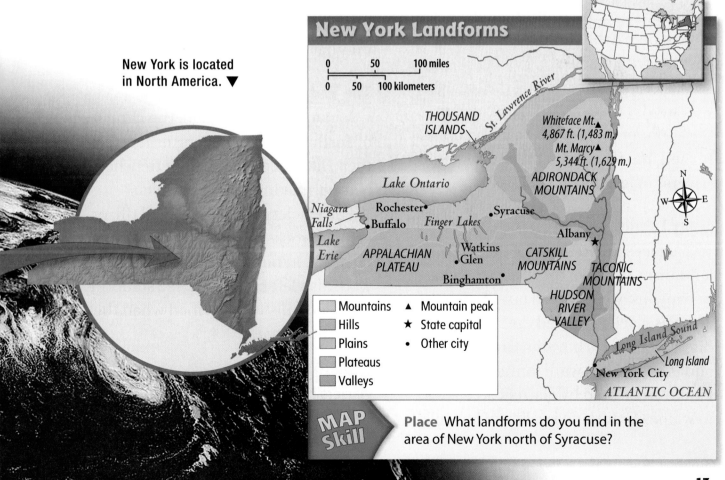

New York Landforms

0   50   100 miles
0   50   100 kilometers

St. Lawrence River

THOUSAND ISLANDS

Whiteface Mt.▲ 4,867 ft. (1,483 m.)
Mt. Marcy▲ 5,344 ft. (1,629 m.)

ADIRONDACK MOUNTAINS

Lake Ontario

Niagara Falls
Rochester•
•Buffalo   Finger Lakes   •Syracuse

Lake Erie

APPALACHIAN PLATEAU

Watkins Glen•

Albany ★

CATSKILL MOUNTAINS

TACONIC MOUNTAINS

Binghamton•

HUDSON RIVER VALLEY

Long Island Sound

Long Island

•New York City

ATLANTIC OCEAN

N W E S

- Mountains
- Hills
- Plains
- Plateaus
- Valleys

▲ Mountain peak
★ State capital
• Other city

MAP Skill

Place What landforms do you find in the area of New York north of Syracuse?

13

Glaciers like this once covered New York State. ▲

❸ The Ice Age

About 20,000 years ago, most of the northern United States was covered by giant sheets of ice, called **glaciers**. These glaciers moved slowly across much of the land. This time in history is called the Ice Age. During the Ice Age almost all of what is now New York was covered with glaciers.

The temperature during the Ice Age was so cold that snow did not melt in the summer. As snow kept piling up, it turned into ice, which then turned into "rivers" of ice, or glaciers.

Many Landforms

Glaciers shaped many of the landforms of New York. Deep trenches, or canyons, were carved out in some areas as glaciers moved the rocks and dirt away. This is how the Great Lakes and Finger Lakes were formed. Another landform created by glaciers is called a moraine. A moraine is a line of low hills formed by rocks pushed at the front of a glacier.

Glaciers did not cover the entire southwestern part of New York, so part of this region has a different landscape from the rest of the state. Allegany State Park, in this area, has gentle rounded hills. This is how much of New York State may have looked before the Ice Age.

The End of the Ice Age

About 10,000 years ago, the climate of Earth changed. Glaciers melted, and their water filled some of the trenches left behind, making lakes and rivers.

The glaciers also left behind till, or soil and rocks. This rich soil is good for farming. Landforms called drumlins were also left behind. These smoothly rounded hills were formed when the glaciers melted.

QUICK CHECK What landforms did glaciers help form in New York?
Main Idea and Details

ⓒ Six Areas of New York

New York can be divided into six geographical **regions**. A region is an area with common features such as landforms, rivers, or **natural resources**. A natural resource is something found in nature that people can use. Different resources create different kinds of jobs. For example, a region with good soil would have jobs in farming. On the other hand, people in Northern New York might work at jobs on the many lakes or in the forests found there.

The Identity of a Region

Regions have identities, or a combination of characteristics, that make them different. For example, Western New York is mostly flat. Many people work in transportation because of the region's location near Lake Erie. These different landforms and jobs are part of Western New York's identity.

The Finger Lakes region has rich farmland and many beautiful lakes. Northern New York is a popular vacation spot because of the Adirondack Mountains.

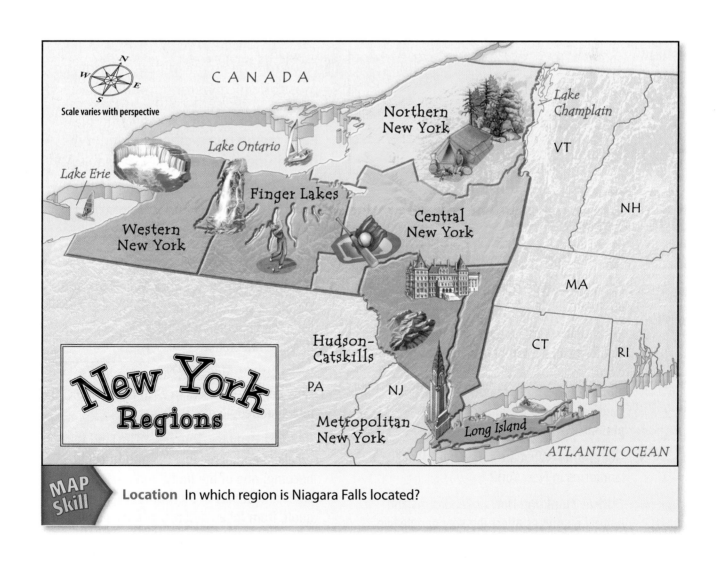

MAP Skill **Location** In which region is Niagara Falls located?

The Six Regions of New York

Region	Major Cities	Landforms
Western New York	Buffalo Dunkirk	Genesee River Niagara Falls
Finger Lakes	Ithaca Syracuse	Finger Lakes Appalachian Plateau
Northern New York	Potsdam Ticonderoga	Mt. Marcy St. Lawrence River
Central New York	Albany Utica	Mohawk and Hudson Rivers
Hudson-Catskill Region	Poughkeepsie Kingston	Hudson River Catskill Mountains
Metropolitan New York City	New York City Yonkers	Long Island

CHART Skill What landforms are in Western New York?

Other New York Regions

The Hudson-Catskill region inspired artists in the 1800s. In Unit 2, you will read "Rip Van Winkle," which takes place in the Catskill Mountains.

The Metropolitan New York region includes Long Island. This area is known for its cities, and beaches.

QUICK CHECK How are the regions of New York alike and different? *Compare and Contrast*

What You Learned

A New York has a "global address." It is in the United States.

B New York has many different landforms, most of which were formed by glaciers.

C New York is divided into six regions. Each region has a different identity based upon the resources available.

Focus Lesson Review

1. **Focus Question** What types of land and water are found in New York?

2. **Vocabulary** Write a paragraph describing the landforms of New York using these vocabulary words.
   glacier   region
   landform   valley
   plateau

3. **Geography** What are some important landforms in New York?

4. **Critical Thinking** How do landforms and natural resources affect the way people live in your region?

5. **Reading Strategy Identify Main Idea and Details** Use the chart to list details about landforms in New York State.

6. **Write About THE BIG IDEA** How do the resources in each region affect the jobs that people do?

7. **Reading Primary Sources** "The land is excellent and agreeable . . . and [it could become] one of the finest and most fruitful lands in that part of the world." What does this quote from Johan de Laet, a Dutch geographer, tell you about the region?

Express Your Opinion

As governor of New York, Theodore Roosevelt worked to protect New York's natural areas.

> **"** *I recognize the right . . . of this generation [people today] to develop and use the natural resources of our land; but I do not recognize the right to waste them . . .* **"**

Theodore Roosevelt expressed, or stated, his opinion about the importance of nature. Read these steps to learn how to express your opinion.

Build Citizenship

1. **Identify the problem** or the issue you are concerned about.

2. **Get information** from newspapers, magazines, television, reference books, and the Internet.

3. **Look for solutions.** Share ideas. Ask others what they think.

4. **Express your opinion** in a letter or an article.

Think About It

1. What was Theodore Roosevelt expressing his opinion about?

2. In Roosevelt's opinion, what should Americans do?

3. How might people express their opinions today?

Write About It!

Pick a problem or an issue that is important to your school or community. Write a letter to the school newspaper expressing your opinion about this issue.

17

Understand Latitude and Longitude

VOCABULARY

latitude
longitude
global grid
degree
parallel
meridian

Geographers use maps with grids. Grids are lines that cross each other on a map. The grid system is based on a set of lines called **latitude** and **longitude**. Lines of longitude and latitude cross to form a pattern on a map called a **global grid**.

Lines of latitude and longitude measure distance in **degrees**. The symbol for degrees is °.

1 Learn It

- Lines of latitude are called **parallels**. Parallels north of the equator are labeled N. Parallels south of the equator are labeled S.

- Lines of longitude are called **meridians**. The prime meridian is the starting place for measuring distance from east to west. Meridians east of the prime meridian are labeled E. Meridians west of the prime meridian are labeled W.

- Look at Map A on page 19. This map is a global grid. It can be used to locate any place on Earth.

- When you locate a place on a map, give the latitude first and longitude second.

2 Try It

- Locate Rome, on Map A. Is Rome east or west of the prime meridian?

- Use Map B to locate the cities near the "addresses" below. Name each city.

    44°N, 74°W

    42°N, 76°W

Lines of Latitude

Lines of Longitude

Map A
Global Grid

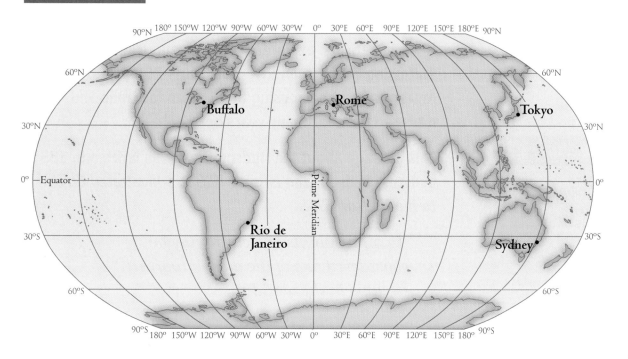

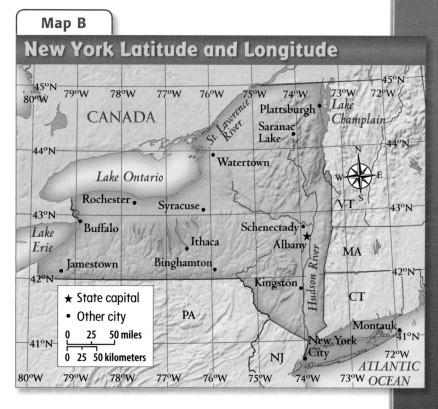

③ Apply It

- Look at Map A. Give the latitude and longitude of the city on the map that is in New York State.

- Now look at Map B. Find the latitude and longitude that is closest to Watertown. Can you also find the latitude and longitude that is closest to where you live?

Map B
New York Latitude and Longitude

★ State capital
• Other city

0 25 50 miles
0 25 50 kilometers

Rivers and Lakes

How do New Yorkers use their waterways?

VOCABULARY

goods
source
tributary
mouth
border
boundary
harbor
coast

VOCABULARY STRATEGY

Root Words The word **tributary** comes from tribute, meaning "a payment or gift." A tributary flows into a larger river. What does **contribute** mean?

READING STRATEGY

Identify Cause and Effect Use the chart below to list waterways and how they affect life in New York.

NEW YORK STANDARDS

3.1, 3.2

By the 1800s, explorers, settlers, and traders had been using the Hudson River for nearly 200 years. Native Americans had been using the Hudson for trade and transportation for many years before that.

This passage about the Hudson River was written in 1851 by Henry Wilson, and is from *Wilson's Illustrated Guide to the Hudson River*.

>" *In many points of view, it may be considered one of the most important streams in the world . . .* "

● New York Waterways

Water is a precious natural resource. You read about natural resources in Lesson 1. The people of New York have used water in many ways. Early peoples used waterways, such as rivers and streams, to move from place to place. Waterways were also used to move **goods**, or products to different locations.

Mid-Hudson Bridge at Poughkeepsie ▼

New York Rivers

The place where a river begins is called its **source**. As a river flows from its source, smaller rivers may flow into it. These smaller rivers are called **tributaries** [TRIB yoo tair eez]. The end of a river is where it empties into an ocean, lake, or larger river. This place is called the **mouth** of the river.

The source of the Hudson River is Lake Tear-in-the-Clouds in the Adirondack Mountains. The Hudson flows more than 300 miles to its mouth at New York Harbor. The river was named for Henry Hudson. You will learn more about Henry Hudson later in this book.

The Mohawk River is a tributary of the Hudson. It was also a "Highway to the West" as European settlers moved into western New York State.

The St. Lawrence River separates New York from Canada. The Thousand Islands (actually 1,700!) are found at the beginning of this river.

The Niagara River begins at Lake Erie and empties into Lake Ontario in western New York. Niagara Falls, which is about halfway down the river, is one of the most famous waterfalls in the United States.

QUICK CHECK Why was the Mohawk River important to settlers? *Cause and Effect*

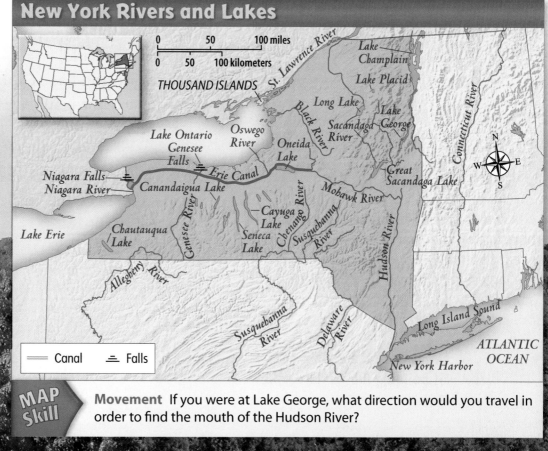

New York Rivers and Lakes

THOUSAND ISLANDS

St. Lawrence River

Lake Champlain

Lake Placid

Long Lake

Lake George

Sacandaga River

Black River

Connecticut River

Lake Ontario
Genesee Falls

Oswego River

Oneida Lake

Niagara Falls
Niagara River

Erie Canal

Canandaigua Lake

Great Sacandaga Lake

Mohawk River

Lake Erie

Chautauqua Lake

Genesee River

Cayuga Lake

Seneca Lake

Chenango River

Susquehanna River

Hudson River

Allegheny River

Susquehanna River

Delaware River

Long Island Sound

New York Harbor

ATLANTIC OCEAN

0   50   100 miles
0   50   100 kilometers

— Canal   ≛ Falls

N W E S

MAP Skill **Movement** If you were at Lake George, what direction would you travel in order to find the mouth of the Hudson River?

21

Then and Now

Great Sacandaga Lake

THEN Until 1930 the Sacandaga River would regularly flood. This photo shows Albany flooded by the Sacandaga River before the dam was built.

NOW After the Conklingville Dam was built to stop the river from flooding, the Great Sacandaga Lake was created. It is the largest lake formed by a dam in the state. Today people use it for fishing, boating, and waterskiing.

Write About It! What were the good results of building the Conklingville Dam?

B New York Lakes

New York has many kinds of lakes—large lakes, small lakes, even lakes shaped like fingers. Some lakes are the sources of important rivers. Others are important transportation routes. Still others help to form **borders** between states and countries. A border is a line that people agree on that divides one place from another. Another word for border is **boundary**. Lake Champlain in northern New York forms part of the border between New York and Vermont.

The Great Lakes

The Great Lakes are five large lakes in the northern part of the United States. From west to east, they are called Lake Superior, Lake Huron, Lake Michigan, Lake Erie, and Lake Ontario. They form the largest body of fresh water in the world.

Lake Erie and Lake Ontario are on the western border of New York. Lake Ontario is the smallest of the Great Lakes. It is connected to many of New York's waterways. Lake Erie carries goods to many cities in New York, such as Buffalo.

QUICK CHECK Why are lakes important to New York? *Summarize*

C New York and the Ocean

The mouth of the Hudson River opens into New York **Harbor**. A harbor is a sheltered body of water along a coast where boats can dock. New York Harbor is in the southeast corner of New York state. This is where New York borders the Atlantic Ocean. New York Harbor is one of the finest natural harbors in the world. It has been an important harbor for shipping since the 1600s.

Montauk Point Lighthouse on Long Island ▶

New York's Long Island extends 118 miles east to west. The south **coast** of Long Island is bordered by the Atlantic Ocean. A coast is the land along an ocean. Long Island Sound lies between the north side of the island and the coast of New York and Connecticut.

✓ **QUICK CHECK** Why are waterways important for New York? *Summarize*

What You Learned

A New York's waterways are an important natural resource. Many cities are built on these waterways.

B New York has many lakes and is located on the Great Lakes.

C New York's waterways have helped it become an important center for trade.

★ Focus Lesson Review

1. **Focus Question** How do New Yorkers use their waterways?

2. **Vocabulary** Write a paragraph about waterways in New York using the vocabulary words listed below.
   source   harbor
   tributary   mouth

3. **Geography** Which bodies of water form borders of New York?

4. **Critical Thinking Make Decisions** Why did New Yorkers build the Conklingville Dam?

5. **Reading Strategy Identify Cause and Effect** What effect does each waterway have on New Yorkers?

6. **Write About THE BIG IDEA** In what ways have people used the waterways in New York State?

7. **Reading Primary Sources** "I was told that the river was unfit to swim in. My grandfather was a fisherman . . . my father learned how to swim in the river . . . What happened to my family's river?" What change is the speaker talking about?

How do climate and weather affect the people of New York?

VOCABULARY

weather
climate
temperature
sea level
elevation
precipitation

VOCABULARY STRATEGY

Suffixes The words **elevation** and **precipitation** end in the suffix **-tion**. This suffix turns a verb, such as elevate, into a noun. What are some other nouns ending in **-tion**.

READING STRATEGY

Identify Main Idea and Details Use the chart below to list details about this main idea: Weather and Climate in New York.

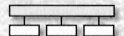

NEW YORK STANDARDS

3.1, 3.2

New York's Seasons

This is how John Burroughs described a snowstorm in New York's Catskill Mountains. How would you describe your favorite New York weather?

> "*Look up at the miracle of the falling snow, the air a dizzy maze [puzzle] of whirling . . . flakes, noiselessly transforming the world . . .*"

Ⓐ Wind, Rain, and Snow in New York

Weather is the condition of the air at a certain time and in a certain place. Wind, rain, and snow are all parts of weather. The pattern of weather in a certain place over many years is called **climate**. Weather and climate may vary in different areas of the same state.

Landforms and Climate

Landforms affect the weather of an area. If the land is high, the air is usually cooler. Water can also make an area cooler. Wind blowing over the water carries cooler air. In the winter the winds off the Great Lakes can bring snow. This is why Buffalo and other regions of upstate of New York are said to be in the "snow belt."

Temperature measures how hot or cold the air is. The temperature of an area changes from season to season. What do you know about temperature changes during the year?

Southeastern New York lies on the Atlantic Ocean, at **sea level**. Sea level is the height of land where it meets the sea.

The height of land above sea level is called **elevation**. Sea level has an elevation of zero feet. Higher elevations are cooler than lower elevations. So the mountainous regions of New York are usually cooler year round than the areas that are at a lower elevation. Look at the map on this page to see the average January temperatures throughout New York.

QUICK CHECK What is the difference between weather and climate? *Main Idea and Details*

In winter, trees in the Catskill Mountains are covered with snow or ice. ▼

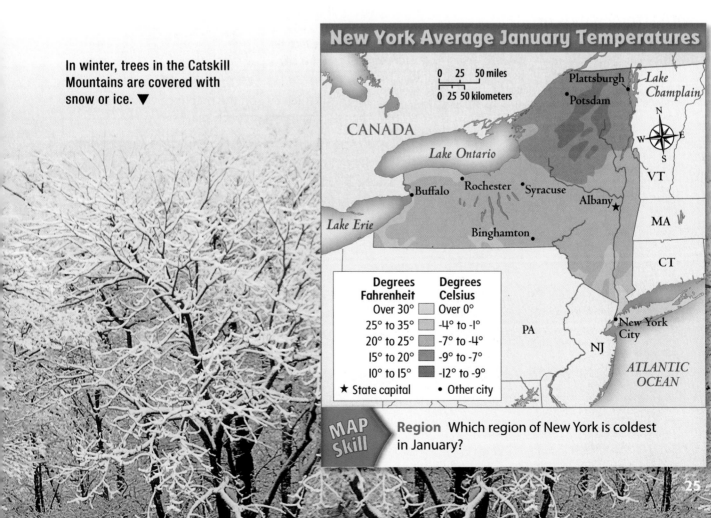

New York Average January Temperatures

Degrees Fahrenheit	Degrees Celsius
Over 30°	Over 0°
25° to 35°	-4° to -1°
20° to 25°	-7° to -4°
15° to 20°	-9° to -7°
10° to 15°	-12° to -9°

★ State capital   • Other city

MAP Skill **Region** Which region of New York is coldest in January?

B Rain and Snow

Precipitation is another part of the weather and climate of an area. Precipitation is the amount of moisture that falls as rain, snow, sleet, or hail.

Location can affect how much precipitation an area will get. You have already read how the areas around Lake Erie and Lake Ontario get a lot of snow in the winter because precipitation comes in over the lakes. Look at the map. How much precipitation is there in the area where you live?

Extreme Weather

Sometimes the weather in New York can be pleasant, but it can also be extreme, with strong winds or heavy precipitation.

Blizzards are one example of extreme weather in New York. A blizzard is a snowstorm with very strong winds. During a blizzard, schools and businesses might have to close. It may be dangerous for drivers and sometimes airports are closed down.

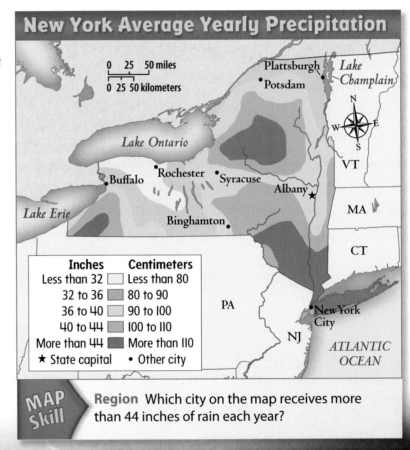

New York Average Yearly Precipitation

Inches	Centimeters
Less than 32	Less than 80
32 to 36	80 to 90
36 to 40	90 to 100
40 to 44	100 to 110
More than 44	More than 110
★ State capital	• Other city

MAP Skill

Region Which city on the map receives more than 44 inches of rain each year?

A lightning storm near Centerport on Long Island ▲

▲ Heavy rains flood New York City streets.

Learning About Your Weather

It is important to know about the weather, because it affects the things that you do every day. You can find information about the weather in your area by reading a newspaper, watching television weather reports, or using the Internet.

QUICK CHECK What are some ways weather can affect our lives? *Draw Conclusions*

What You Learned

A Weather is determined by the temperature and precipitation of an area. The climate is the long-term pattern of weather in a certain area over time.

B New York can experience extreme weather, such as blizzards.

Focus Lesson Review

1. **Focus Question** How do climate and weather affect the people of New York?

2. **Vocabulary** Write a description of the weather in your area using the vocabulary terms below.
   - elevation
   - temperature
   - precipitation
   - weather
   - sea level

3. **Geography** How can landforms affect weather?

4. **Critical Thinking Problem Solving** How do people adapt when they live in an area with a lot of precipitation?

5. **Reading Strategy Identify Main Idea and Details** What are some things that affect climate in New York?

6. **Write About THE BIG IDEA** Think about the weather in your area. How do you adapt to the changing weather?

7. **Reading Primary Sources** "The men must have gotten out through the second story door, around the huge snow drifts, somehow, and to the barn for shovels, and then dug their way back to the house." How did these people adapt to extreme weather?

Problem Solving

Problem solving is finding answers, or **solutions**, to problems. You can use the following problem-solving steps to solve big or small problems.

VOCABULARY

solution
consequence

1 Learn It

- Identify a problem. You need to know what the problem is before you can solve it.

- Gather information. Find out as much as you can about the problem.

- Identify your choices. Looking at different choices can help you to choose a solution.

- Think about the **consequences**. Every choice has a consequence, or result. Some consequences are better than others.

- Choose a solution. The best solutions have the best results.

- Think about the results of your choice. Was it the best solution? Would another solution have produced a better result?

◄ New Yorkers work to clean up the banks of one of New York's rivers.

② Try It

- In Lesson 2, you learned about New York's waterways.

- Identify a water problem found in New York. Organize your information in the graphic organizer below to help you.

Identify Problem

⬇

Identify choices and consequences

⬇

Make choices

- Gather information about this problem.

- Identify the choices for solving this problem.

- Think about the consequences of these choices.

- Choose the best solution.

③ Apply It

- Identify a problem in your school or community.

- Use the steps in Learn It to suggest a solution.

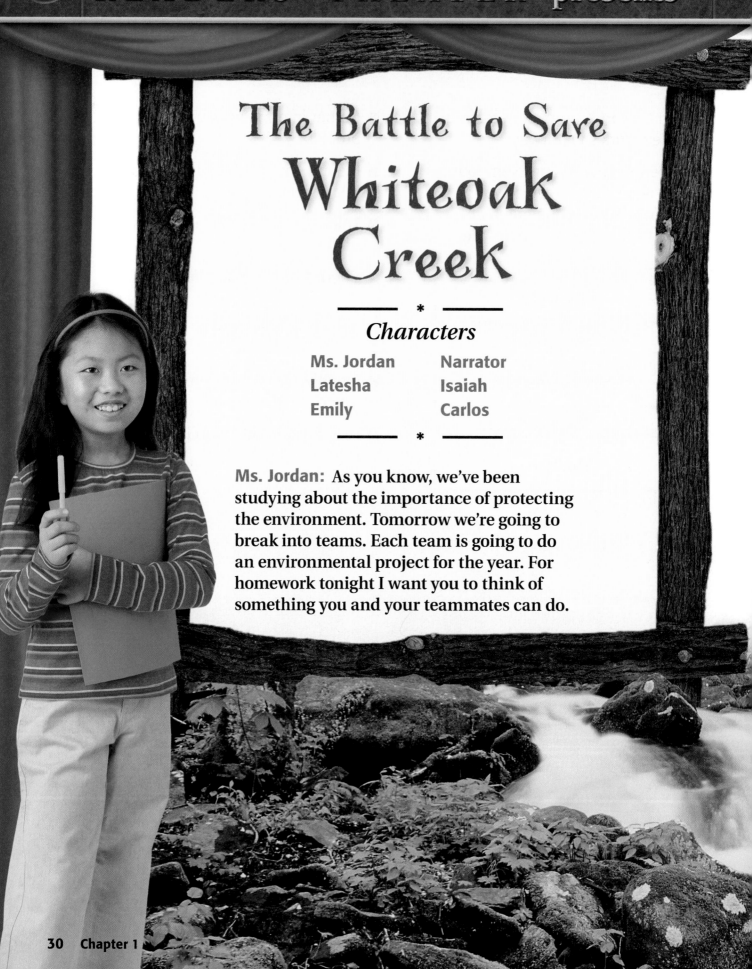

The Battle to Save Whiteoak Creek

* * *

Characters

Ms. Jordan	Narrator
Latesha	Isaiah
Emily	Carlos

* * *

Ms. Jordan: As you know, we've been studying about the importance of protecting the environment. Tomorrow we're going to break into teams. Each team is going to do an environmental project for the year. For homework tonight I want you to think of something you and your teammates can do.

Latesha: And I thought we weren't going to have any homework tonight!

Emily: How are we supposed to save the planet? We're just kids.

Narrator: Later that afternoon Carlos and Isaiah walk home along Whiteoak Creek after soccer practice.

Isaiah: Are those old tires over there?

Carlos: Yeah, and check out that mattress and table over there.

Isaiah: How did this stuff get here?

Carlos: People just dump stuff here, and they bring more all the time. My mom says it didn't used to be like this. When my uncle was our age he used to fish here. He'd catch trout and my mom's family would eat them for dinner.

Isaiah: If there are any fish in that creek now I wouldn't want to eat them.

Narrator: The boys soon arrive in front of Carlos's house.

Isaiah: Will you be on my team in Ms. Jordan's class?

Carlos: Sure. If you can think of a great project.

Isaiah: I was counting on you to do that. See you tomorrow.

Help save Whiteoak Creek

Narrator: The next day, Ms. Jordan divides the class up into teams. Isaiah, Carlos, Latesha, and Emily are on the same team.

Latesha: Okay, anybody have any brilliant ideas to save the planet?

Carlos: Actually, yes. I think we should clean up Whiteoak Creek. It's near where Isaiah and I live.

Isaiah: That's a big project.

Latesha and Emily: We better see this Whiteoak Creek.

Narrator: After school Carlos, Isaiah, Emily, and Latesha head to the creek. Carlos hands everyone a big garbage bag. The kids start putting bottles, cans, candy wrappers, and other trash into the garbage bags. Soon their bags are almost full.

Latesha: We'll never be able to clean this place up.

Emily: I've got an idea. Why don't we ask if we can make this an entire class project?

Isaiah: That's the best idea I've heard all day!

Narrator: The next day the team tells Ms. Jordan and the rest of the class about Whiteoak Creek and Carlos's idea to clean it up.

Ms. Jordan: What do you think class? All in favor raise your hand.

Narrator: Everyone's hand went up. Soon the entire class was spending time at the creek cleaning up. Parents pitched in on weekends to help. Still, the students would find new garbage on the creek banks. Back in class, the group talked about what to do.

Latesha: This is a creek, not a dump! The people who put their garbage here should be punished!

Emily: We should put up a sign telling people not to dump stuff here.

Ms. Jordan: Both of those ideas are good. Let's write to the city council and ask them to help us.

Narrator: Soon a sign was posted on the road above the creek. It said, "NO DUMPING. MINIMUM FINE $200." But that wasn't the only sign needed to protect the creek.

Ms. Jordan: Class, you've done a great job. But we still need to do something about the garbage in the creek that we can't pick up.

Isaiah: What kind of garbage is that?

Ms. Jordan: When people wash their car or change the oil in their car out in front of their house, sometimes the dirty water or oil goes down the drain in the street. The rain then carries it into Whiteoak Creek.

Emily: Okay, so we have to keep people from dumping stuff in the drains. But how do we do that?

Latesha: Where my grandmother lives, they have signs on the drains to remind people whatever goes down them will end up in a river.

Narrator: The class painted signs on storm drains that led to the creek. "Dump No Waste. Drains to Stream."

Ms. Jordan: Class, we only have a few minutes before the bell rings, but I have an announcement to make. You did an amazing job on this project. You should be very proud.

Write About It!

Write your own Readers' Theater play about an environmental project.

Resources of New York

What resources are important to New York State?

VOCABULARY

environment
renewable resource
nonrenewable resource
conservation
raw materials
economy

VOCABULARY STRATEGY

Prefix The word **nonrenewable** has the prefix **non-**. **Non-** means "not." What other words start with this prefix?

READING STRATEGY

Compare and Contrast
Use the Venn diagram below to compare and contrast the resources of two regions in New York.

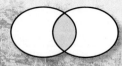

NEW YORK STANDARDS

3.1, 3.2, 4.1, 4.2, 5.1

The sound and power of Niagara Falls fill visitors with wonder. Others prefer the warm, sandy beaches of Long Island. Some like to hike the Adirondack Mountains. The Finger Lakes offer swimming and boating. New York offers a wide variety of natural beauties to its citizens and their visitors.

Ⓐ Many Natural Resources

Natural resources come from the **environment**, or the surroundings in which people, plants, and animals live.

As you learned earlier, forests are a natural resource. Other resources include minerals, such as iron and copper, fuels such as oil and coal, and rich farming soil.

Natural resources, such as wood, are used to make goods such as chairs. ▶

Using Resources

Some resources, called **renewable resources**, can be replaced. Trees are one renewable resource. People can plant new trees to replace the ones that are cut down.

Resources called **nonrenewable resources** cannot be replaced. Some nonrenewable resources in New York are minerals, such as iron, and fossil fuels, such as oil and natural gas.

When resources are nonrenewable, people need to practice **conservation**. Conservation is the careful use of natural resources. Recycling, or reusing, materials is one way to conserve resources. If cans and bottles are recycled, fewer new cans or bottles need to be made.

Another part of conservation is making sure that resources, such as water, stay clean. Read why Robert Kennedy, Jr., thinks it is important to protect New York's water.

> **QUICK CHECK** How are renewable and nonrenewable resources alike and different? *Compare and Contrast*

PRIMARY SOURCES

Dark Rivers Run Deep
by Sally Richard quoting
Robert Kennedy, Jr. • 1998

" *We look forward to the day when there's a Baykeeper or Riverkeeper on every <u>significant</u> body of water in America. . . we're protecting it because it enriches us. It's really about protecting our own backyard, our community— our quality of life.* "

<u>significant</u> large

Write About It!

What does Robert Kennedy, Jr., hope to see one day?

◄ **Forests around Lake George may supply wood for woodcarvers.**

Using New York's Resources

Each region of New York has natural resources. These resources affect the kinds of jobs people do. The map below shows some of New York's natural resources. Use the map and graph below to answer the questions.

New York's Natural Resources

Corn
Grapes
Fish
Stone
Fruit
Sand and Gravel
Oil and Natural Gas
Salt
Forest
Vegetables

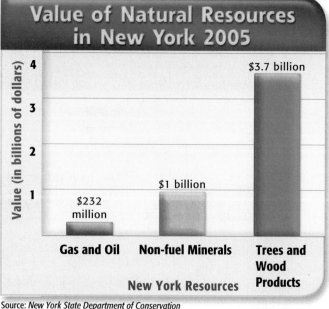

Value of Natural Resources in New York 2005

Value (in billions of dollars)

- Gas and Oil — $232 million
- Non-fuel Minerals — $1 billion
- Trees and Wood Products — $3.7 billion

New York Resources

Source: *New York State Department of Conservation*

Think About Resources

1. In what parts of the state are oil and natural gas found?

2. What natural resource contributed the most to New York's economy in 2005?

3. What information does the map give you that you can't find on the graph?

ⓑ People and Resources

New York has another resource, its people. People make **raw materials** into useful products. Raw materials are resources that can be changed into something usable. Iron, for example, can be made into steel for buildings or automobiles. The way a place uses or produces natural resources, goods, and services is its **economy**.

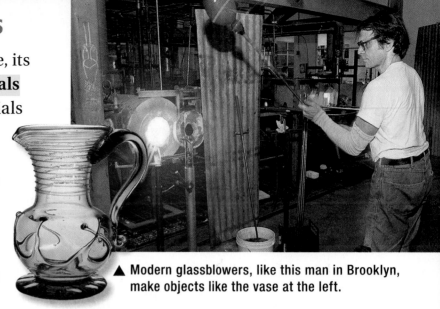

▲ Modern glassblowers, like this man in Brooklyn, make objects like the vase at the left.

Jobs and the Economy

The jobs available in a region depend on its resources. In the past, cities grew up near natural resources. For example, Schuyler County has two fields for salt mining. What kinds of jobs are important where you live?

QUICK CHECK How do resources affect jobs and the economy?

Cause and Effect

What You Learned

ⓐ New York has both renewable and nonrenewable resources. It is necessary to conserve resources so that we have them in the future.

ⓑ Resources, including people, are important to the economy of an area. Resources affect the types of jobs that are available.

⭐ Focus Lesson Review

1. **Focus Question** What resources are important to New York State?

2. **Vocabulary** Write about resources in New York using the vocabulary terms listed below.
   economy   raw material
   environment   renewable resource
   nonrenewable resource

3. **Geography** Trace a map of New York. Place cities and resources on your map.

4. **Critical Thinking** **Make Decisions** In what ways are people the most important resource in New York?

5. **Reading Strategy** **Compare and Contrast** How are resources such as water and fuels alike? How are they different?

6. **Write About** THE **BIG** IDEA Write about some ways that you can conserve the natural resources that you use every day.

7. **Reading Primary Sources** "A house well-constructed of oak bark . . . contained a great quantity of maize [corn], and beans of the last year's growth . . ."

   Name some of the resources Henry Hudson mentions in this quotation.

Read Time Lines

VOCABULARY

time line

A **time line** is a diagram that shows when events took place. You can see the date an event happened. A time line also shows whether one event happened before or after another event. You can also use the time line to find out how much time passed between events.

John Burroughs was a naturalist and writer who lived in New York for most of his life. He wrote about the Catskill Mountains.

1 Learn It

■ Read the title of the time line. The title is "The Life of John Burroughs." The title summarizes the main topic of the time line.

■ Find out how many years each part on the time line shows. Time lines are divided into equal parts. Each part covers a certain number of years. On this time line, each part is 20 years.

■ Read the events from left to right. The earliest event on a time line is on the left side. Each event to the right happens later. The last event on the right side of the time line shows the most recent event.

■ On this time line, you can see the date of John Burroughs' birth on the left. The date of his death is on the right.

The Life of John Burroughs

| 1830 | 1850 | 1870 | 1890 | 1910 | 1930 |

1837
Born in Roxbury, New York

1864
Moved to Washington, D.C.

1867
Wrote his first book

1873
Returns to New York

1908
Completes his 20th book

1921
Dies while traveling

2 Try It

Look at the time line on page 38 to answer the questions below.

- Did Burroughs return to New York before or after he wrote his first book?

- In what year did Burroughs complete his 20th book?

- How many years passed between Burroughs' return to New York and his death?

3 Apply It

Use the time line on this page to answer the questions below.

- When was the Catskill Forest Preserve established?

- How many years were there between the creation of Fire Island National Seashore and Gateway National Recreation Area?

- Was the Adirondack Park or Appalachian National Scenic Trail created first?

Parks in New York State

1885	1905	1925	1945	1965	1985

1885 Catskill Forest Preserve established

1892 Adirondack Park created

1937 Appalachian National Scenic Trail is opened

1964 Fire Island National Seashore created

1974 Gateway National Recreation Area established in New York City

John Burroughs (bearded) traveled with his friends, (from left to right) Thomas Edison, Henry Ford, and Harvey Firestone. ▶

Understand Artifacts

Artifacts are objects left by people who lived long ago. Historians study artifacts just as detectives study clues. Artifacts can tell us about the past, but we have to interpret their clues.

Looking at Sources

A **primary source** is usually a spoken or written account by someone who has seen or experienced an event. An artifact was made by someone long ago. So it is also a primary source. A **secondary source** may describe an event, but it is not written by an eyewitness. Your textbook is one kind of secondary source.

VOCABULARY

artifact
primary source
secondary source

1 Learn It

Read the steps below. They will help you to study artifacts.

- Look closely at the artifact to see exactly what it is made of.

- Try to understand what they used the artifact for.

- Think about the people who made the artifact. Compare what you know about the people with the artifact to see what you can learn.

Iroquois clay pot from about 1500 ▼

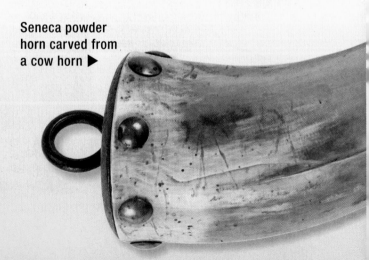

Seneca powder horn carved from a cow horn ▶

 **Try It**

Look at the Algonquian belt below.

■ What material was used to make the artifact?

■ What shapes or patterns do you see on the artifact?

■ How do you think the artifact might have been used?

■ What can you tell about the people who made this artifact?

3 Apply It

■ What do the artifacts on these pages tell you about the people who made them?

■ What can you learn from studying these artifacts?

■ How do you think each artifact was used?

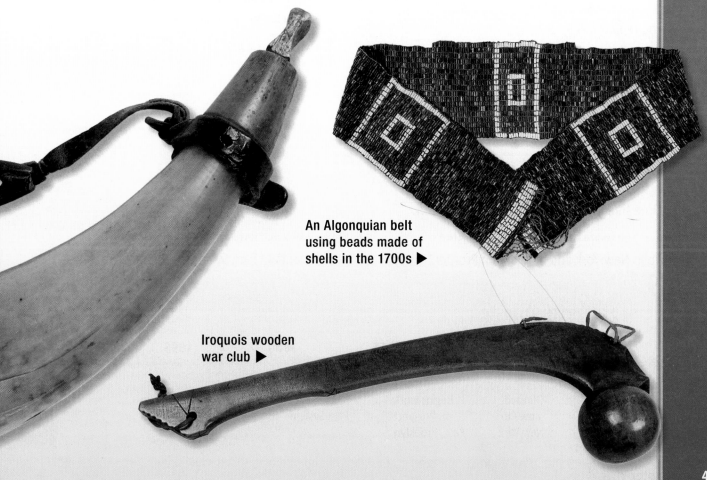

An Algonquian belt using beads made of shells in the 1700s ▶

Iroquois wooden war club ▶

Chapter 1 Review

FOCUS Vocabulary Review

Copy the sentences below on a separate sheet of paper. Use the list of vocabulary words to fill in the blanks.

landform **tributary**
climate **economy**

1. A ________ is a stream that joins a river.
2. The ways that people make, sell, and use goods is called ________.
3. A __landform__ is a natural feature on Earth.
4. ________ is the pattern of weather in a place over a long time.
5. Test Preparation A natural material that can be replaced is a ________.
   (A) **landform** (C) **renewable resource**
   (B) **mouth** (D) **nonrenewable resource**

FOCUS Comprehension Check

6. How did glaciers create landforms in New York?
7. What makes the identity of a region?
8. What is the mouth of a river? Where is the mouth of the Hudson River?
9. How do landforms affect the climate of a region?
10. What is the difference between renewable and nonrenewable resources?
11. Critical Thinking How does climate affect the lives of people in New York?
12. Critical Thinking In what ways do people change the environment?

FOCUS Use the Time Line

Use the time line below to answer each question.

13. How many years passed between Olmsted's move to New York and his work on Prospect Park?
14. How old was Olmsted when he began to work on the Buffalo Park System?

The Life of Frederick Olmsted

1820 1835 1850 1865 1880 1895 1910

1822 Frederick Law Olmsted is born in Connecticut

1840 Olmsted moves to New York

1865 Begins work on Prospect Park, Brooklyn

1868 Started Buffalo Park System

1903 Dies in Massachusetts

Understand Latitude and Longitude

Write a complete sentence to answer each question.

15. What do lines of latitude measure?

16. Why is it useful to know about lines of latitude or longitude?

17. **Test Preparation** Look at the map of New York on this page. Which city is closest to 43°N, 76°W?

18. **Test Preparation** The pattern of lines of latitude and longitude crossing over Earth is called the _____.

    (A) meridian   **(C) degrees**
    (B) global grid   **(D) equator**

Hudson River Valley

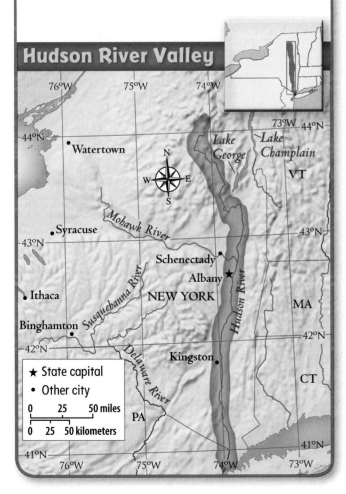

★ State capital
• Other city

0   25   50 miles
0   25   50 kilometers

Constructed Response Questions

Read the passage and write a complete sentence to answer each question.

> ❝ *New York's annual Arbor Day observance is an important way to recognize the critical [important] role trees play in our local communities and in our daily lives. Trees help clean the air we breathe, beautify our neighborhoods, conserve energy, and provide . . . habitat for wildlife.* ❞

19. What is the purpose of Arbor Day?

20. Name three important ways that trees play a part in our lives.

21. **Make a Poster** Work in groups to create a chart of renewable and nonrenewable resources.

22. **Persuasive** Write a letter telling how to protect natural resources in your region.

LOG ON For help with the process of writing, visit: www.macmillanmh.com

Chapter 2

New York State's Early People

You Are There

> **In making any law, our chiefs must always consider three things: the effect of their decision on peace; the effect on the natural world; and the effect on seven generations in the future. We believe that all lawmakers should be required to think this way, that all constitutions should contain these rules.**

These words are from Carol Jacobs, a Native American leader, in a speech to the United Nations in 1995. Who were some of New York's early peoples? In this chapter, you will learn about the first settlers of New York.

Lake Erie

◀ Modern Cayuga Woman

Chapter Events	1500	1550

1500
Algonquians and Iroquois are important Native American groups in New York

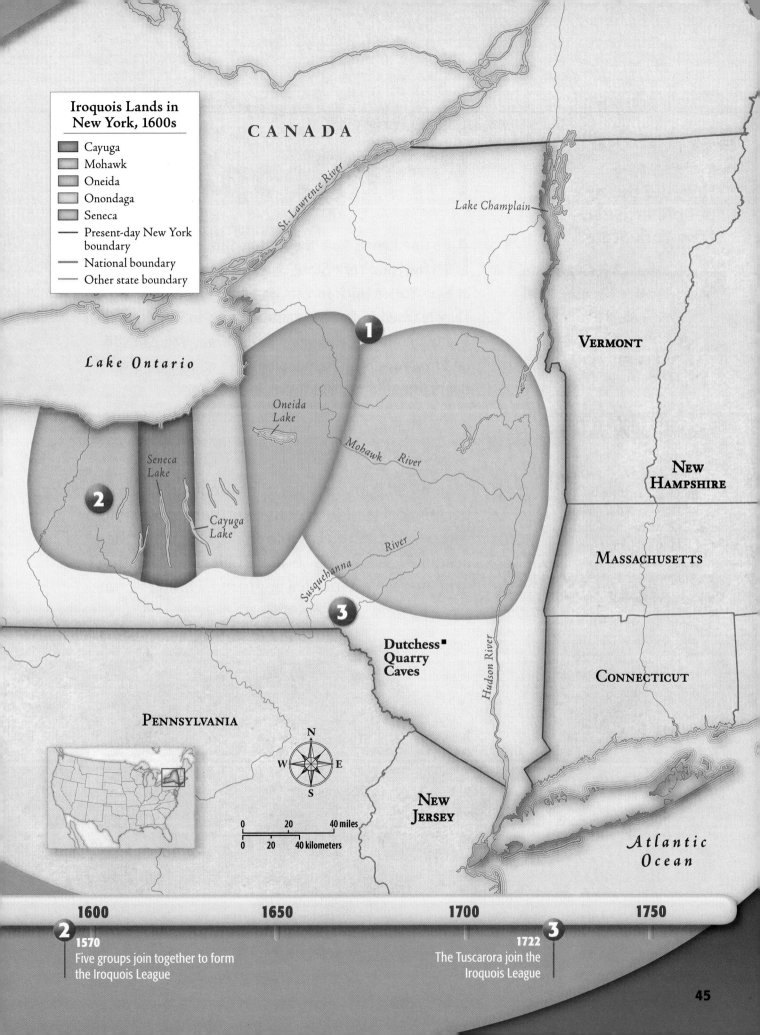

Iroquois Lands in New York, 1600s

- Cayuga
- Mohawk
- Oneida
- Onondaga
- Seneca
- —— Present-day New York boundary
- —— National boundary
- —— Other state boundary

CANADA

St. Lawrence River

Lake Champlain

Lake Ontario

1

VERMONT

Oneida Lake

Seneca Lake

2

Mohawk River

Cayuga Lake

NEW HAMPSHIRE

River

MASSACHUSETTS

Susquehanna

3

Dutchess Quarry Caves

Hudson River

CONNECTICUT

PENNSYLVANIA

N
W E
S

NEW JERSEY

| 0 | 20 | 40 miles |
| 0 | 20 | 40 kilometers |

Atlantic Ocean

| 1600 | 1650 | 1700 | 1750 |

2
1570
Five groups join together to form the Iroquois League

3
1722
The Tuscarora join the Iroquois League

VOCABULARY

archaeologist
prehistory
hunter-gatherer
agriculture

VOCABULARY STRATEGY

Prefixes The prefix **pre-** means "before." **Prehistory** means "the time before written records." What other words start with this prefix?

READING STRATEGY

Identify Main Idea and Details Use the chart below to list the main idea and supporting details of this lesson.

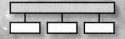

NEW YORK STANDARDS

1.1, 1.2, 1.3, 1.4

New York's First People

No one knows how the first people came to what is now New York State. We know that they settled in New York's thick forests and along its many rivers. They learned to live by planting crops in the rich soil and by hunting the animals in the area. You can still find evidence of these people in the names we give rivers, mountains, and towns in New York.

Ⓐ Coming to North America

About 40,000 years ago, the climate of Earth became colder. Much of the Northern Hemisphere was covered in thick rivers of ice. This made the ocean levels lower. A "bridge" of land connecting Asia and North America appeared. Hunters from

about 40,000 years ago
Ice Age begins

about 12,000 years ago
People settle
in New York

about 11,000
years ago
Ice Age ends

Asia followed animals across the land bridge to what is today Alaska. People may also have come across a land bridge from Europe, or traveled to the Americas by boat. For thousands of years people continued to move across North and South America. Around 12,000 years ago, people began to settle in what is today called New York State.

Learning About the Past

Have you ever found an old arrowhead? An arrowhead is an artifact, an object made by people who lived in the past. As you read on pages 40–41, artifacts can teach us about the tools people made, the foods they might have eaten, and the kinds of shelters they lived in.

The first people in New York may have lived in caves like these. ▼

An **archaeologist** (AHR kee AWL uh jist) is a scientist who studies artifacts. Archaeologists found many artifacts in the Dutchess Quarry Caves in Orange County. They found arrowheads made of stone and animal bones from animals such as caribou (KAR ih boo). The artifacts were about 12,000 years old. They came from **prehistory**, or the time before written records.

QUICK CHECK What are artifacts and what can we can learn from them?
Main Idea and Details

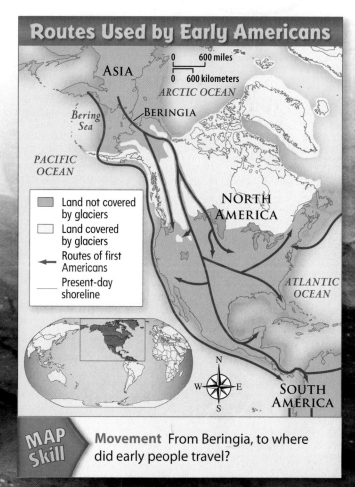

Routes Used by Early Americans

ASIA

0   600 miles
0   600 kilometers

ARCTIC OCEAN

Bering
Sea

BERINGIA

PACIFIC
OCEAN

Land not covered
by glaciers

Land covered
by glaciers

Routes of first
Americans

Present-day
shoreline

NORTH
AMERICA

ATLANTIC
OCEAN

SOUTH
AMERICA

MAP Skill

Movement From Beringia, to where did early people travel?

B Prehistoric New York

The first people who lived in New York were hunters who followed herds of animals such as caribou and mastodons. Mastodons no longer exist. They looked like elephants, but they had thick furry coats so they could survive in the Ice Age cold. The hunters used the animals they hunted for food. They probably also made clothes from the animal skins and fur.

Hunters made tools from the animal bones and from stone. They made arrows and spear points for hunting. They also made tools for cutting up animals and for sewing their clothes.

Hunting

In addition to hunting, early people in New York also gathered food. They found roots, nuts, and berries and other food from plants. **Hunter-gatherers** are people who find food both by hunting animals and by gathering plants.

The life of hunter-gatherers centered on the family. Four to ten families would travel together, camping near lakes or rivers for water. They could also catch fish for food in the lakes. Travelers sometimes traded with other groups for goods they needed.

▼ Mastodons lived in the New York area during the Ice Age.

Early Farmers

About 11,000 years ago, Earth began to get warmer. Some ice and snow melted. The cold season was shorter and there was less snowfall. Plants had longer seasons to grow.

As the ice melted, the water filled lakes, ponds, and wetlands where new plants and animals could live. These new sources of food helped the human population to grow and settle in new areas.

▲ Some types of squash

Agriculture began more than 1,000 years ago. Agriculture is growing crops and raising animals. The first farmers planted corn, beans, and squash. People now had a steady source of food.

People still hunted, but now they built villages near their fields. They dried food to store for the winter or in case crops failed. Farmers could also trade the extra food they raised for other goods.

QUICK CHECK List the events that led up to people living in villages. *Sequence Events*

What You Learned

Ⓐ People came to North America during the Ice Age. They followed animals across a land bridge.

Ⓑ People in what is now New York hunted and gathered food. Later they learned to farm and to live in villages.

★★★ Focus Lesson Review

1. **Focus Question** How did the first people arrive in New York State?

2. **Vocabulary** Write a summary of this lesson using the vocabulary terms below.
   **archaeologist   hunter-gatherer
   prehistory**

3. **Technology** How did tools change the way early people lived?

4. **Critical Thinking** **Problem Solving** What problem did the discovery of agriculture solve?

5. **Reading Strategy** **Identify Main Idea and Details** How did climate affect the lives of prehistoric people?

6. **Write About** THE **BiG** IDEA Describe how people lived as hunter-gatherers.

7. **Reading Primary Sources** "An intact [unbroken] clay pot is a rare find for archaeologists." Why might an intact artifact be rare?

Use Elevation Maps

VOCABULARY

elevation map

New York has two major mountain ranges—the Adirondack Mountains and the Catskill Mountains. How can you tell which mountains are the highest? For this kind of information, you need an **elevation** (el uh VAY shun) **map**. Elevation is the height of the land above sea level. The elevation at sea level is zero feet.

1 Learn It

To read elevation maps, follow these steps using the map on page 51.

- Read the map title. The title of the map is "New York: Elevation."

- Elevation maps use colors to show the height, or elevation, of land. Different colors mean different heights.

- The map key tells you what each color on the map means. For example, all the yellow areas are between 1,600 and 3,300 feet (500 and 1,000 meters) above sea level.

2 Try It

Use the map on page 51 to answer these questions.

- Which mountain range covers the largest area?

- What is the elevation of the city of Elmira?

- Where is the highest point in New York?

Heart Lake in the Adirondack Mountains ▼

3 Apply It

- How can an elevation map, like the one below, help you learn about geography?

- What else can an elevation map tell you about plants, resources, and people of an area?

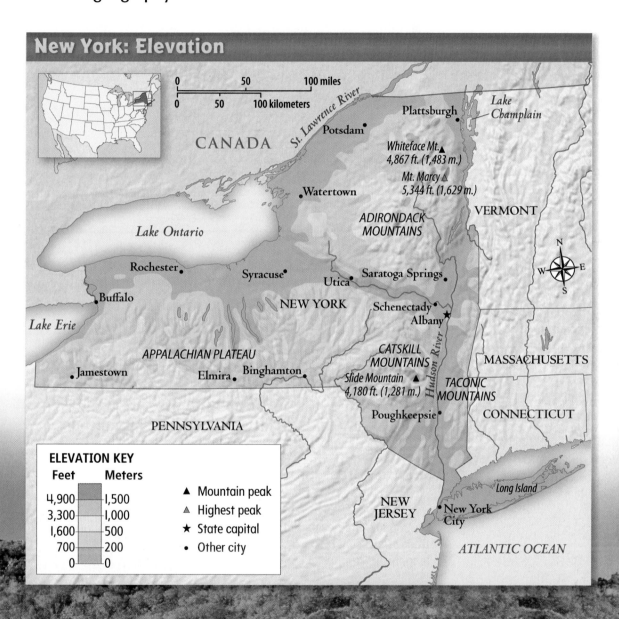

New York: Elevation

0   50   100 miles
0   50   100 kilometers

CANADA
St. Lawrence River
Potsdam
Plattsburgh
Lake Champlain
Whiteface Mt. ▲ 4,867 ft. (1,483 m.)
Mt. Marcy △ 5,344 ft. (1,629 m.)
Watertown
ADIRONDACK MOUNTAINS
VERMONT
Lake Ontario
Rochester
Syracuse
Utica
Saratoga Springs
Buffalo
NEW YORK
Schenectady
Albany
Lake Erie
APPALACHIAN PLATEAU
CATSKILL MOUNTAINS
Hudson River
MASSACHUSETTS
Jamestown
Elmira
Binghamton
Slide Mountain ▲ 4,180 ft. (1,281 m.)
TACONIC MOUNTAINS
CONNECTICUT
PENNSYLVANIA
Poughkeepsie
Long Island
NEW JERSEY
New York City
ATLANTIC OCEAN

ELEVATION KEY

Feet	Meters
4,900	1,500
3,300	1,000
1,600	500
700	200
0	0

▲ Mountain peak
△ Highest peak
★ State capital
• Other city

51

Focus Lesson 2

How did people live in the Eastern Woodlands?

VOCABULARY

heritage
longhouse
wigwam
ancestor
reservation

VOCABULARY STRATEGY

Word Origins Wigwam comes from the Algonquian word *wik* or *wig*, which means "to live in." A wigwam is the name of an Algonquian tent or home.

READING STRATEGY

Compare and Contrast
Use a Venn diagram to compare and contrast two Native American groups.

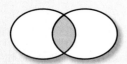

NEW YORK STANDARDS

1.1, 1.2, 1.3
1.4, 2.2, 2.4

Native Americans of New York

Telling stories has been an important way for Native Americans to share their values and culture. Native American historian Suzanne Guerra described the tradition this way:

> " . . . *Storytelling isn't just entertainment . . . Stories teach you how to be a human being.* "

A People of the Eastern Woodlands

In the 1300s, Native Americans hunted, gathered berries and nuts, and farmed in the Eastern woodlands. The Eastern woodlands were an area of large forests that stretched from the Mississippi River to the Atlantic Ocean.

We know about Native American life from the stories they told. These stories tell us about their **heritage**. Heritage is the history, traditions, beliefs, and customs shared by a group of people.

An Iroquois man in front of a reconstructed longhouse. ▶

1200	1300	1400	1500	1600	1700

about 1200
Native American groups settle in the Eastern Woodlands

1500
Iroquois and Algonquian are the two main groups of Native Americans in New York

1609
Europeans meet Native Americans of the Eastern Woodlands

Two Native American Groups

By the 1500s, there were two large Native American groups in what is now New York State. They were grouped by the language they spoke. The Algonquian (al GON kee an) group included the Mahican (ma HEE kahn), Shinnecock (SHIH nuh kahk), and Lenni Lenape (LEH nee LEN nah pee). They lived on Long Island and in the Hudson River Valley.

The Iroquois (IR uh koy) included the Mohawk, Seneca, Oneida (oh NI duh), Onondaga (ahn un DAH guh), and Cayuga (kah YOO guh) in Central and Western New York.

The name Iroquois may have come from an Algonquian word meaning "red snakes." The name was not meant to be friendly. Algonquian and Iroquois groups often fought.

The Iroquois called themselves the Hodenosaunee (ho den oh SAH nee), meaning "people of the **longhouse**." A longhouse is a long wooden building housing more than one family.

QUICK CHECK What made the Iroquois and Algonquian different? *Compare and Contrast*

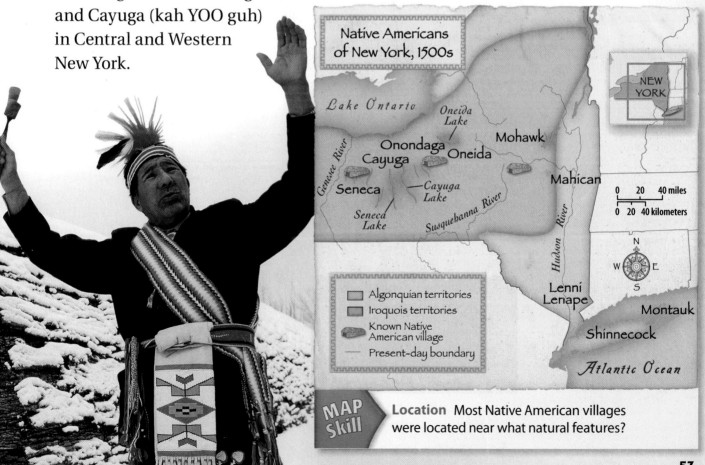

Native Americans of New York, 1500s

NEW YORK

Lake Ontario

Oneida Lake

Genesee River

Onondaga   Mohawk

Cayuga   Oneida

Seneca   Cayuga Lake

Susquehanna River

Mahican

Seneca Lake

Hudson River

Lenni Lenape

Montauk

Shinnecock

Atlantic Ocean

0   20   40 miles
0   20   40 kilometers

N W E S

- Algonquian territories
- Iroquois territories
- Known Native American village
- Present-day boundary

MAP Skill

Location Most Native American villages were located near what natural features?

53

ⓑ Life in the Eastern Woodlands

Most of the Iroquois people lived in longhouses. Archaeologists have found remains of longhouses as long as a football field.

The diagram below shows a typical longhouse. The longhouse was divided into separate rooms opening onto a long hallway. Most of the people in each longhouse were related. There was one room for each family. Imagine living in one house with all your cousins, uncles, and aunts!

The longhouse probably smelled of woodsmoke and foods drying for the winter. You would hear babies crying and people talking in other rooms. The longhouse was warm and safe. What would you have liked about life in a longhouse?

Another kind of shelter was a **wigwam**. This smaller house was made from arched poles covered with bark. Some Algonquian groups lived in wigwams, although others also lived in longhouses like the Iroquois.

An Iroquois Longhouse

elm tree bark

smoke hole

storage platform

sleeping platform

preparing animal skins

Building Villages

The Iroquois and Algonquian had similar ways of life. They usually built villages near fields and grew corn, beans, and squash. These crops, called the Three Sisters, were often grown together.

Everyday Living

Tasks were divided between men and women. Men fished, hunted, and traded with other groups. They also built houses and the walls around the village. They defended the village from attack.

Women planted and harvested crops. They dried foods for the winter months. They cooked meals, and they cared for the children. Families would work together to catch fish in the spring.

Children learned the skills they would need as adults. Boys learned how to hunt and to build shelters. Girls were taught how to cook and make pottery and clothing.

QUICK CHECK What jobs were done by men and which were done by women? *Summarize*

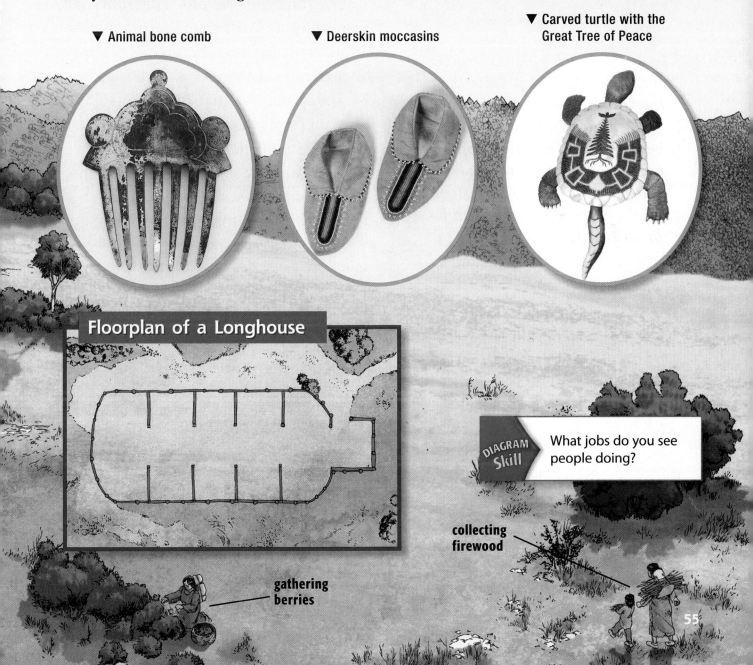

▼ Animal bone comb

▼ Deerskin moccasins

▼ Carved turtle with the Great Tree of Peace

Floorplan of a Longhouse

DIAGRAM Skill > What jobs do you see people doing?

collecting firewood

gathering berries

A section from
Sky Spirit
an Iroquois story

"Long, long ago, one of the Spirits of the Sky World came down and looked at Earth. As he travelled over it, he found it beautiful, and so he created people to live on it. Before returning to the sky, . . . he gave them names, called the people all together, and spoke his parting words:

'To the Mohawks, I give corn. To the patient Oneidas, I give the nuts and the fruit of many trees. To the industrious Senecas, I give beans. To the friendly Cayugas, I give the roots of plants to be eaten. To the wise and eloquent Onondagas, I give grapes and squashes to eat and tobacco to smoke at the camp fires.'"

Write About It! Why do you think the Sky Spirit gave each group a different gift? What might he have wanted the Iroquois peoples to do?

● Stories Tell History

Native Americans use stories to tell their history and to teach important lessons about life. Often a storyteller talks about **ancestors**. An ancestor is a person in a family who lived in the past. Look at the Primary Source on this page. It tells an Iroquois story about how their groups began.

A Living Tradition

Native Americans continue to keep their traditions alive through stories and celebrations. The Iroquois communities still meet for ceremonies and festivals, to celebrate their Native American heritage.

Today, many Native Americans live on **reservations**, or land set aside by the United States government for Native Americans to use. Reservations have their own stores, schools, libraries, museums, and health centers.

▼ Onondaga people at a cultural festival near Syracuse.

Native Americans Today

Native Americans are important members of the New York community today. Did you know that Native Americans helped build many of the skyscrapers in our cities? Members of the Mohawk group are especially famous for this skill. They are called ironworkers.

Perry Ground is a famous Iroquois storyteller. Mary Adams, a Mohawk, is famous for making traditional baskets. Ted Williams of the Tuscarora group is a medicine man who has written books about his people. Have you ever watched people play lacrosse? This popular sport was invented by Native Americans living along the St. Lawrence River in New York and Ontario.

QUICK CHECK How do Native Americans celebrate their culture today?
Summarize

▼ Lacrosse is a popular team sport today.

What You Learned

A Two Native American groups, the Iroquois and Algonquian, live in New York.

B In the past, both groups lived in similar ways, and used the resources of the local forests and rivers.

C Stories are an important part of Native American life and help children to learn traditions and proper behavior.

Focus Lesson Review

1. **Focus Question** How did people live in the Eastern Woodlands?

2. **Vocabulary** Write a paragraph using each vocabulary word.
   ancestor   longhouse
   heritage   reservation

3. **History** How do we learn about Native American history and traditions?

4. **Critical Thinking** **Problem Solving** How did Native Americans organize villages to get food and shelter?

5. **Reading Strategy** **Compare and Contrast** Compare and contrast how Native Americans live today with how they lived in the past.

6. **Write About** 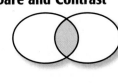 How did Native Americans use natural resources?

7. **Reading Primary Sources** "In the autumn small parties would leave the villages for the annual hunt . . . spring was the fishing season." Why might these events have taken place at particular times of the year?

Young Native Americans Long Ago

Native American children of long ago helped their parents in many important ways. Boys learned to hunt and fish with their fathers and elder brothers. Girls learned to gather plants with their mothers. Girls also learned to weave baskets and make meals. Just like you, Native American children played games and looked after their younger brothers and sisters.

This lacrosse stick has a shorter handle for a child to use. ▶

◀ Boy in traditional dress

George Catlin painted this Iroquois mother and her child in a carrying cradle in 1835. ▶

◀ These moccasins from the 1800s show traditional Iroquois bead work.

▲ A child's canoe

Write About It!

Write about how the lives of Native American children might have been similar to your own.

This Iroquois doll is made from corn husks and dressed in traditional clothing. ▶

Girl in traditional dress ▶

LOG ON For more about young people in history, visit: www.macmillanmh.com

The Iroquois League

Why did the Iroquois form the Iroquois League?

VOCABULARY

league
clan
clan mother
council
sachem
wampum

VOCABULARY STRATEGY

Word Origins The word "**league**" comes from a Latin word *legare*, which means "to tie together." What other kinds of leagues can you name?

READING STRATEGY

Sequence Events Use the chart below to show how the Iroquois League was formed.

NEW YORK STANDARDS

1.1, 1.2, 1.3
1.4, 5.1

In this lesson you will learn how the Iroquois people learned to help each other and to work together. Deganawida, an Iroquois leader, told his people to live together in peace.

> 66 *We bind ourselves together by taking hold of each other's hands so firmly and forming a circle so strong that if a tree should fall upon it, it could not shake nor break it, so that our people and grandchildren shall remain in the circle in security, peace, and happiness.* 99

▼ Hiawatha and Deganawida share their plan with Jikonsahseh.

1500	1600	1700	1800

1570
The Iroquois
League is formed

1722
The Tuscarora join the
Iroquois League

Ⓐ The Great Peace

For many years, Iroquois groups fought among themselves over farmlands and hunting areas. Many people were killed and the Iroquois were unhappy.

Around 1570, five Iroquois groups agreed to stop fighting. The Iroquois call this agreement the Great Peace.

The Iroquois League

According to Iroquois legend, Deganawida (day gahn uh WEE dah) brought the Iroquois together. He told the Iroquois that they should stop fighting and work together in peace. A woman named Jikonsahseh (jih KON sah say) agreed with Deganawida.

She helped convince the Seneca to join the Great Peace. Deganawida is called the Peace Maker, and Jikonsahseh is called the Mother of Nations. An Onondaga leader, Hiawatha, traveled from village to village with Deganawida. Hiawatha was a good speaker and convinced many Iroquois to join the peace.

The Mohawk, the Seneca, the Cayuga, the Oneida, and the Onondaga came together to form the Iroquois **League**. A league is a group of people who join together for a common goal. In 1722 the Tuscarora joined the Iroquois League. The League is also called the Six Nations.

✓ **QUICK CHECK** What events led up to the Great Peace? *Sequence Events*

61

Ⓑ How the League Worked

Deganawida wanted the Iroquois to stop fighting and to make decisions for the good of all. He said that the league

> *will take the form of a longhouse, in which there are many fires, one for each family, yet all live as one household . . . They shall have one mind and live under one law. Thinking shall replace killing.*

The Great Laws

Deganawida met with leaders around a tall pine tree called the Tree of the Great Peace. The tree was a symbol of the strength of the Iroquois League.

There were laws to protect the rights of Iroquois people. Each person had the right to speak freely. Everyone had a

▲ Wampum belts had great value to Native Americans.

right to food, clothing, and shelter. Each Iroquois nation also had the right to practice its own religion. Iroquois lands were open to all members of the league.

Choosing League Leaders

The Iroquois were divided into many **clans**. A clan is group of people who share the same ancestors. The clans were named for animals such as the wolf, turtle, and bear.

The head of each clan was the **clan mother**. The clan mother and the other women of the clan chose men

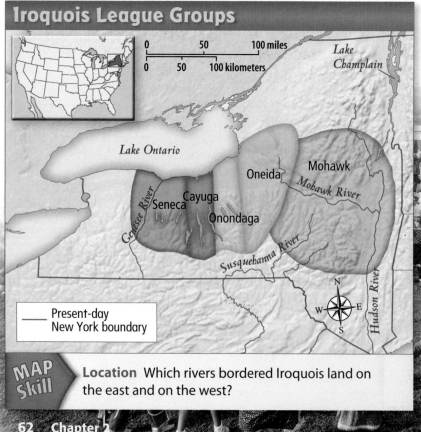

Iroquois League Groups

0   50   100 miles
0   50   100 kilometers

Lake Champlain

Lake Ontario

Oneida

Mohawk

Mohawk River

Seneca   Cayuga

Genesee River

Onondaga

Susquehanna River

Hudson River

N
W   E
S

___ Present-day New York boundary

MAP Skill   **Location** Which rivers bordered Iroquois land on the east and on the west?

Onondaga Iroquois cultural dance on the reservation at Nedrow, New York ▼

to serve in the village council. Women also chose the members of the Grand Council and replaced a leader who was not doing his job.

The Grand Council

The Iroquois leaders made laws for the group. Fifty chiefs from all the nations came together to make decisions. This was called the Grand Council. A **council** is a group of people who meet to talk and make decisions. The council had the power to keep peace and to protect the people of the league.

Onondaga Oren Lyons at work on his "Tree of Peace."

Iroquois Village Council

Council Leaders
made plans and decisions

Respected Older People
gave advice

Clan Mothers
appointed council leaders

Village Members
attended councils and had a right to speak

CHART Skill   Who appointed council leaders?

Every year the Grand Council met in the Onondaga lands, in the central area of what is now New York. The 50 members of the Grand Council were called **sachems** (SAY chumz).

The Grand Council settled differences between the nations of the Iroquois League. The sachems also made decisions about how to deal with people outside of the league.

It is said that when a sachem spoke to the council, he held **wampum**, a string of polished beads made from shells. Some historians believe the Iroquois ideas of government influenced the men who organized the American government.

✓ **QUICK CHECK** What was the role of women in Iroquois life? *Main Idea and Details*

C The League Today

The Iroquois League still exists today. In the year 2000 there were more than 70,000 people in North America who were either Iroquois or had Iroquois ancestors. Many of them live in New York. Some of them live on reservations, and others live in cities and towns.

Modern Iroquois leader speaks to a public meeting. ▼

The Iroquois no longer live in longhouses and rarely dress like their ancestors. However traditions, special days, art, music, and storytelling still keep their heritage alive. The Grand Council continues to meet in Onondaga. The sachems listen to readings of the Great Law, just as they did more than 400 years ago.

QUICK CHECK How did the Iroquois League solve problems? *Problem Solving*

What You Learned

A Around 1570, five groups joined together in the Iroquois League. The Tuscarora joined in 1722.

B The Iroquois League set up laws that protected the rights of individuals and of the groups.

C The Iroquois League continues to meet today.

★ Focus Lesson Review

1. **Focus Question** Why did the Iroquois form the Iroquois League?

2. **Vocabulary** Write a description of the Iroquois League using each of the following vocabulary terms.

   clan   league
   clan mother   sachem
   council   wampum

3. **Government** How was the Iroquois Grand Council like a modern government?

4. **Critical Thinking Recognize Point of View** Why did the Grand Council include sachems from all Iroquois groups?

5. **Reading Strategy Sequence Events** Explain how the Grand Council reached a decision.

6. **Write About THE BIG IDEA** Why do you think the Iroquois League decided to share resources?

7. **Reading Primary Sources** "We must have but one voice. Many voices makes confusion." Explain how this statement by Hiawatha supports the idea of working together in the Iroquois League.

Hiawatha 1500s

Hiawatha was probably a member of the Onondaga group. What we know about him comes from stories told by the Iroquois. Some of these stories are legends, but we do know that he helped bring the Iroquois together.

According to some stories, a man named Atotarho killed Hiawatha's wife and family. Hiawatha came to believe that the killing must end. Hiawatha decided to forgive Atotarho. Hiawatha said,

> **"Our strength is not in the war club and arrows alone, but in wise counsels [advice]."**

Hiawatha convinced the Iroquois nations to join a league. The league would make laws based on fairness and justice. Hiawatha's actions showed the Iroquois the power of justice and peace.

 Write About It! Why did Hiawatha forgive Atotarho?

 LOG ON For more biographies, visit: www.macmillanmh.com

The Life of Hiawatha

1500	1540	1580

about 1500
Hiawatha is born in the early 1500s

about 1565
Hiawatha speaks to the Iroquois groups about forming a league

1570
The Iroquois League is formed

Chapter 2 Review

FOCUS Vocabulary Review

Copy the sentences below on a separate sheet of paper. Use the list of vocabulary words to fill in the blanks.

ancestor	agriculture
sachem	wampum

1. _____ is growing crops and raising animals.

2. An _____ is a member of a family who lived in the past.

3. A _____ was a council member of the Iroquois League.

4. _____ was polished beads used by Native Americans.

5. **Test Preparation** A _____ is land set aside for Native Americans by the U.S. government.

   (A) heritage   (C) longhouse
   (B) reservation   (D) sachem

FOCUS Comprehension Check

6. How do some historians think early people arrived in North America?

7. When did New York's Native Americans begin to farm and build villages?

8. Which area of New York State was settled by the Algonquians?

9. **Critical Thinking** Why are stories from the past important to modern Native Americans?

10. **Critical Thinking** Why might other Native American groups have wanted to join the Iroquois League?

FOCUS Use the Time Line

Use the time line below to answer each question.

11. How many years does this time line show?

12. Did people begin farming before or after the Iroquois League formed?

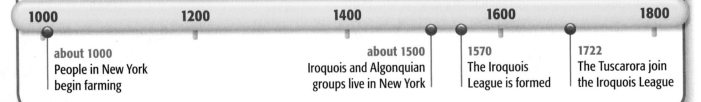

1000	1200	1400	1600	1800

about 1000
People in New York begin farming

about 1500
Iroquois and Algonquian groups live in New York

1570
The Iroquois League is formed

1722
The Tuscarora join the Iroquois League

Reading Elevation Maps

Write a complete sentence to answer each question.

13. What do the colors on an elevation map key mean?

14. How might an elevation map help people decide where to live?

15. **Test Preparation** The elevation of Mount Marcy is about _____.

(A) **5000 meters** (C) **600 meters**

(B) **5000 feet** (D) **600 feet**

16. **Test Preparation** The highest mountain on the map is _____.

(A) **Mt. Marcy** (C) **Mt. Katahdin**

(B) **Mt. Washington** (D) **Whiteface Mountain**

New England Elevation

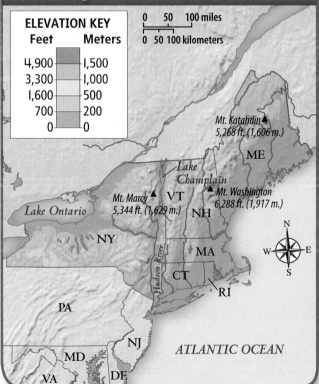

ELEVATION KEY

Feet	Meters
4,900	1,500
3,300	1,000
1,600	500
700	200
0	0

0   50   100 miles
0 50 100 kilometers

Mt. Katahdin
5,268 ft. (1,606 m.)

ME

Lake Champlain

Mt. Marcy
5,344 ft. (1,629 m.)

VT

Mt. Washington
6,288 ft. (1,917 m.)

NH

Lake Ontario

NY

Hudson River

MA

CT

RI

PA

N
W   E
S

NJ

MD

ATLANTIC OCEAN

VA   DE

Constructed Response Questions

Read this selection from the Iroquois Constitution. Answer the questions below.

" All Lords of the Five Nations . . . must be honest in all things. They must not *idle* or gossip, but be men [having] honorable qualities . . ."

idle: be lazy

17. What kinds of people did the leaders of the League need to be?

18. Why do you think this was a part of the Iroquois Constitution?

19. **Write a Skit** In small groups, write and perform a short skit showing what the Iroquois leaders might have talked about as they set up the Iroquois League.

20. **Expository** Write a paragraph that describes the Iroquois League.

LOG ON For help with the process of writing, visit: www.macmillanmh.com

Unit 1 Review and Test Prep

Comprehension and Critical Thinking Check

1. What makes a place part of a **region**?

2. What are three types of landforms that could be created by **glaciers**?

3. How does **elevation** change the temperature of an area?

4. How do **archaeologists** study history?

5. What is the difference between a **renewable resource** and a **nonrenewable resource**?

6. What is one example of **conservation**?

7. What foods would a **hunter-gatherer** eat?

8. What would the inside of a **longhouse** look like?

9. **Critical Thinking** What effect would a lack of resources have on an area's **economy**?

10. **Critical Thinking** Who do you think had more power in the Iroquois government, a **clan mother** or a **sachem**? Explain your answer.

Reading Skills Check

Identify Main Idea and Details

Copy this graphic organizer. Reread "Landforms and Climate" on page 25. Use the graphic organizer to identify the main idea and details of this reading selection. Answer the questions.

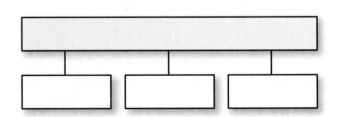

11. What is the main idea from the selection?

12. What is one supporting detail for the main idea?

13. How did you identify the details in the selection?

Base your answers to questions 14 and 15 on the information in the box below.

- The Iroquois lived in upstate New York between Niagara Falls and the Adirondack Mountains.

- There were about 20,000 Iroquois in the five groups in the Iroquois League in 1680.

- The Iroquois League expanded by defeating other Native Americans and then by "adopting" the defeated people.

- The Mohawk were the largest group in the Iroquois League.

14. These statements show that the Iroquois people had

(A) a strong government.

(B) a weak government.

(C) many enemies.

(D) wise leaders.

15. Within the Iroquois League, the Mohawk were

(A) the strongest soldiers.

(B) a defeated group.

(C) in charge of government.

(D) the largest group.

Write About History

16. Persuasive Write a letter to leaders of New York State about some of the natural resources in your area. Explain what you think should be done with these resources.

17. Descriptive Write a description of life inside an Iroquois longhouse or Algonquian wigwam.

18. Expository Think about how Iroquois groups made decisions. Write a one-paragraph summary of the Iroquois system.

LOG ON For help with the process of writing, visit: www.macmillanmh.com

REVIEW

THE BIG IDEA

How do people adapt to where they live?

Write About the Big Idea

Expository Essay

Think about what you learned about New York's geography, climate, and natural resources as you read Unit 1. Complete the chart below by filling in details from the chapters.

Use your chart to help you write an essay about one of the six regions in New York. Your essay should answer the Big Idea question "How do people adapt to where they live?"

You might describe the geography, people, climate, and resources of the area you choose. Be sure to begin with an introduction. Include one paragraph for each main reason. End with a concluding paragraph.

Region	Natural Resources	Climate	How People Adapt
1. Northern New York 2. 3. 4.	1. Adirondack Mountains 2. 3. 4.	1. 2. 3. 4.	1. 2. 3. 4.

Write an Expository Essay

1. Plan
- To begin, you will need to decide what your essay topic is.
- Develop a plan. This plan should include researching your topic. Organize your information by writing an outline or filling a graphic organizer.

2. Write a First Draft
- Use the information from your outline or organizer to write each paragraph.
- Focus on getting your thoughts on paper.

3. Revise and Proofread
- Read your essay.
- Make sure that you stated the main idea in the introduction.
- Be sure you included details.
- Be sure you restated the main idea in the last paragraph.
- Proofread your essay, fixing any errors and checking spelling, capitalization, and punctuation.
- Rewrite your essay neatly.

ACTIVITY

Speak About the Big Idea

Travel Advertisement

Create a television advertisement for a region of New York. You will want to use exciting words and descriptions that would make people want to come there. You might make a colorful brochure or poster that you can show during the ad to promote the region.

Prepare Work in small groups. Each group should choose a region to promote. Consider including information about your region's climate, natural resources, tourist attractions, cities, or national parks. Use information from Unit 1 and your notes. You may want to gather additional information by using the Internet, your school library, or your local library.

Present Each member of the group should present some information about the area.

 LAUNCH PAD For help with the Big Idea activity, visit: www.macmillanmh.com

Read More About the Big Idea

The Discovery of The Americas
by Betsy and Giulio Maestro
Learn how people walked and sailed to North America and how they adapted to the geography of the land they settled.

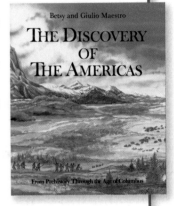

Hudson, The Story of a River
by Robert Baron and Thomas Locker
This beautifully illustrated book describes the history and natural beauties of the river.

The Iroquois Indians
by Bill Lund
Learn about the culture of the Iroquois. Look at modern photographs showing the lives of the Iroquois today.

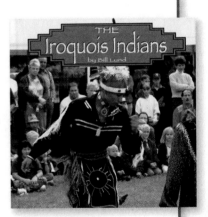

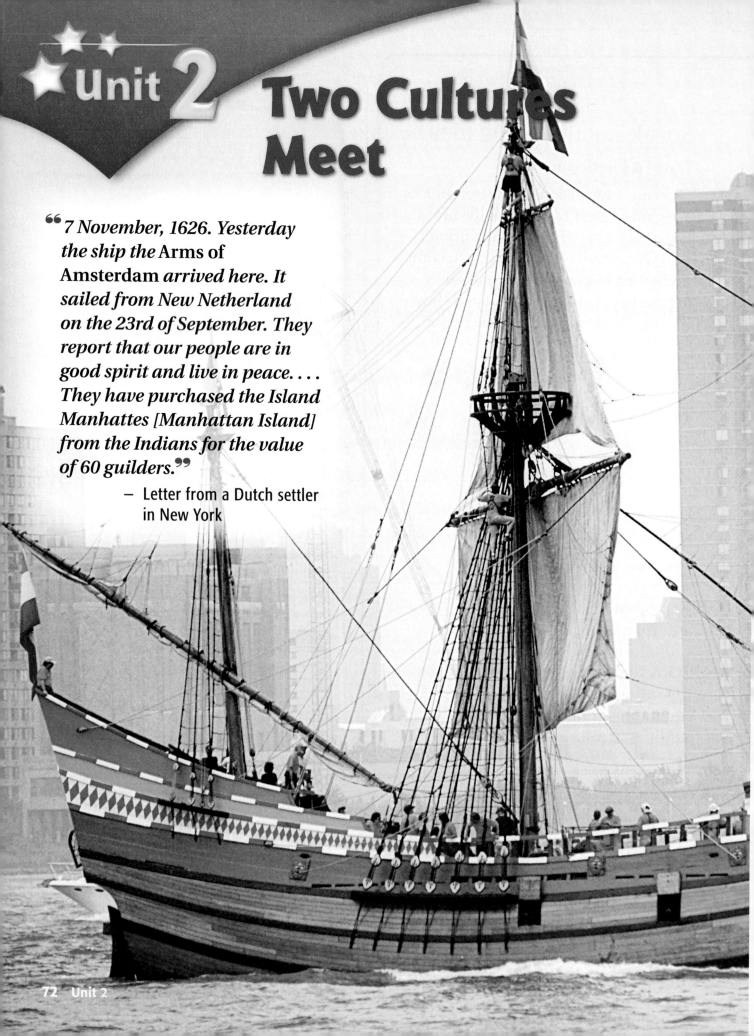

Unit 2

Two Cultures Meet

"*7 November, 1626. Yesterday the ship the* Arms of Amsterdam *arrived here. It sailed from New Netherland on the 23rd of September. They report that our people are in good spirit and live in peace. . . . They have purchased the Island Manhattes [Manhattan Island] from the Indians for the value of 60 guilders.*"

— Letter from a Dutch settler in New York

What happens when different peoples first meet?

In Unit 1 you read about Native Americans in New York. In Unit 2 you will learn how the lives of these first settlers changed when Europeans arrived. As you read the unit, look for changes caused by their meeting.

Copy the graphic organizer below. As your read the chapters in this unit, look for changes caused by the arrival of Europeans.

Fill in the graphic organizer with details telling how different groups affected Native Americans living in New York.

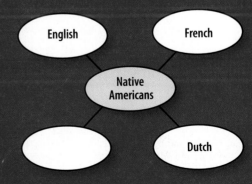

English   French

Native Americans

Dutch

◄ A modern reconstruction of the "Half Moon," Henry Hudson's ship, sails past modern buildings.

73

People Who Made a Difference

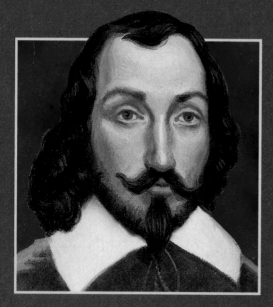

Samuel de Champlain
1567–1635

Samuel de Champlain founded Quebec, in what is today Canada, in 1608. He also explored the land of northern New York. (page 84)

Anne Hutchinson
1591–1643

Anne Hutchinson had to leave the New England colonies because of her religious beliefs. The Dutch let her settle north of New Amsterdam. (page 90)

1600   1615   1630

1609
Samuel de Champlain explores northern New York

1626
Tammany allows Dutch to settle on Manhattan Island

LOG ON For more biographies, visit:
www.macmillanmh.com

Tammany
1600s

According to one legend, Tammany, a Lenni Lenape leader, sold Dutch colonists the right to settle on Manhattan Island in 1626. (page 89)

Peter Stuyvesant
1592–1672

Peter Stuyvesant was the last Dutch governor of New Netherland. While he was unpopular with some colonists, Stuyvesant was a good leader. He was forced to surrender his colony to the British. (page 90)

1645   **1660**   **1675**

1642
Anne Hutchinson moves to New Netherland

1664
Peter Stuyvesant is last Dutch governor of New Netherland

RIP VAN WINKLE

by Washington Irving
retold by Catherine Storr

Washington Irving (1783–1859) was one of the first writers of the United States. He retold many legends of Colonial New York. One of his most famous stories concerns Rip Van Winkle, a Dutch settler in the Hudson River Valley.

More than one hundred years ago, there was a man called Rip Van Winkle. He and his family lived in a village in the Catskill Mountains near the great Hudson River. Rip was a kind man. He liked talking with his friends at the village inn, and he often played with the children of the village.

He would help his neighbors with any kind of work they had. But Rip hated to do any kind of work on his own farm. His fences were always broken. His cows were always wandering off. And weeds seemed to grow faster than his crops. . .

One day Rip . . . took his gun and his dog Wolf, and he went off towards the mountains. After some time, he sat down on a grassy hill to enjoy the lovely fall day.

Down one side of the mountain, Rip could see the Hudson River and mile after mile of rich forest. On the other side, the mountain was dark and wild and filled with rocks. When the long blue evening shadows moved across the valley, Rip knew it was time to start back. Just as he was about to leave, he heard a voice.

"Rip Van Winkle! Rip Van Winkle!"

Rip looked around, but he didn't see anyone. Then the voice called again. Wolf growled, and Rip felt afraid. Then Rip saw a strange figure coming toward him. It was an old man dressed in old-fashioned clothes. He was carrying a barrel, and, as he came near, he made signs to Rip to help him. They took turns carrying the barrel up a steep path. From time to time, Rip heard a rumbling noise that sounded like thunder.

Soon they reached an opening, and Rip saw a grassy meadow. A group of old men were playing ninepins. The men did not speak, and their faces were very serious. Then Rip realized that the sound that he thought was thunder was really the rumbling of huge balls rolling over the ground.

Write About It!

What do you think will happen next? Write an ending to the story.

Summarize:
The First Europeans in New York

Summarizing, or stating the important ideas in a reading selection, will help you understand social studies better. A summary states the main ideas but leaves out minor, or smaller, details. Summarizing will help you understand and remember what you read.

▲ Giovanni da Verrazano

1 Learn It

- Read the selection and find the main ideas. Restate these ideas briefly in your summary.

- Find important details and combine them in your summary.

- Now read the selection below and think about how you would summarize the information.

Main Idea
The first European explorer reached what is now New York in 1524.

Detail
He was an Italian, but he was sent by the king of France.

Main Idea
This explorer was different from Christopher Columbus.

Detail
He knew that he had not reached Asia.

Giovanni da Verrazano was the first European explorer to reach what is now New York in 1524. He was from Italy, a country in Europe, but he was sent to explore by the king of France. This meant that any land he visited would be claimed by France. He sailed all the way up the Atlantic coast of North America.

Giovanni da Verrazano was different from Christopher Columbus. He knew that he had not reached Asia. During Verrazano's explorations, he and a few of his sailors met some Native Americans.

2 Try It

Copy and complete the summary chart below. Fill in the chart by summarizing the paragraphs on page 78.

SUMMARY CHART

Paragraph 1	Paragraph 2

How did you decide which information would help you summarize the paragraphs?

3 Apply It

- Review the steps for summarizing in **Learn It**.

- Read the selection below. Create a summary chart to summarize the paragraphs.

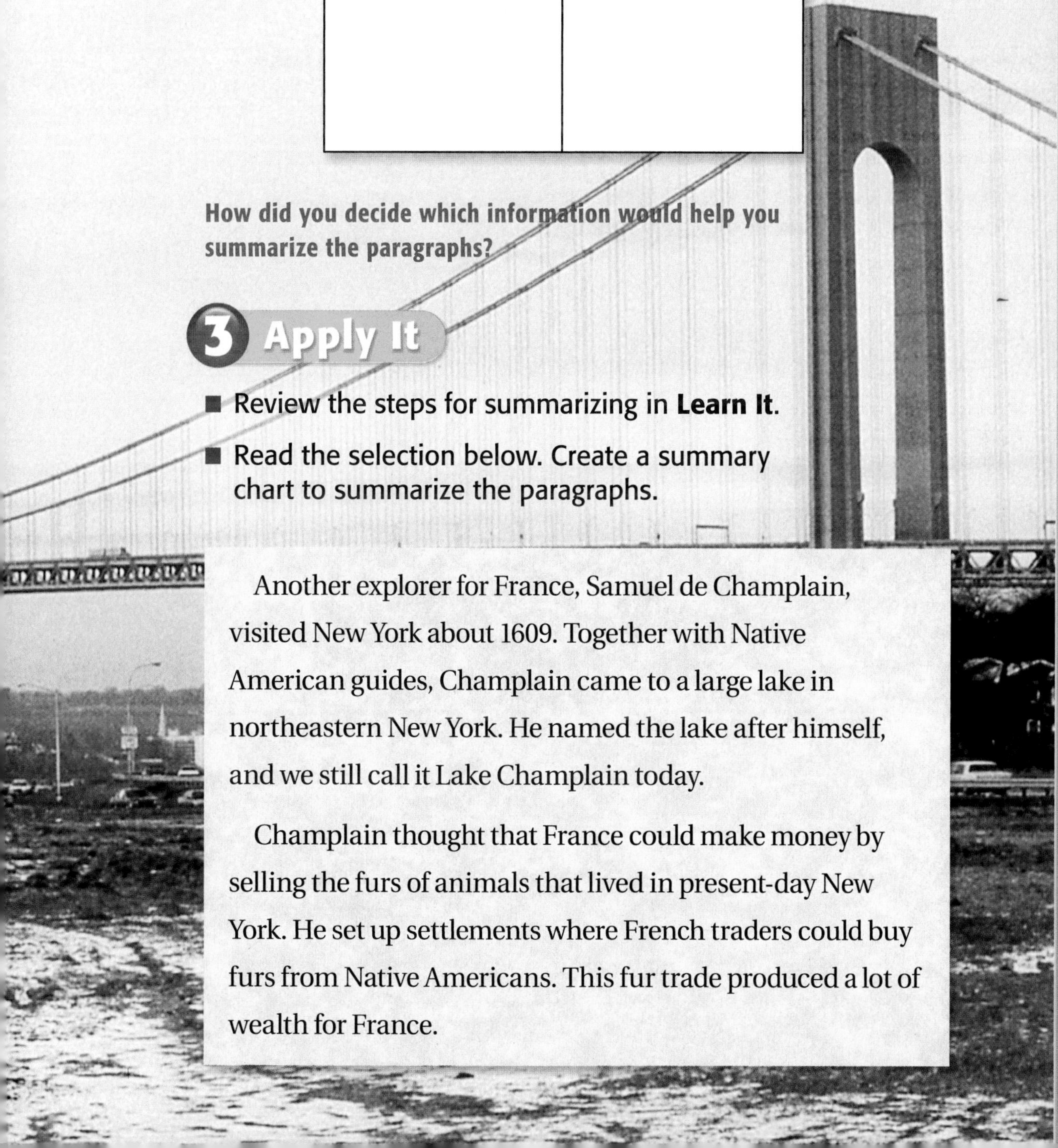

Another explorer for France, Samuel de Champlain, visited New York about 1609. Together with Native American guides, Champlain came to a large lake in northeastern New York. He named the lake after himself, and we still call it Lake Champlain today.

Champlain thought that France could make money by selling the furs of animals that lived in present-day New York. He set up settlements where French traders could buy furs from Native Americans. This fur trade produced a lot of wealth for France.

Chapter 3

Europeans Explore New York

You Are There

"*The country is good and pleasant, the climate is healthy, notwithstanding the sudden changes of cold and heat. The sun is very warm, the winter is fierce and severe and continues fully as long as in our country. . . . The ground is fertile enough to reward labor, but they must clear it well, and till it, just as our lands require.*"

Suppose that you arrived in New York in the early 1600s, as Jonas Michel did. In this chapter, you will learn about European settlers who came to New York.

Lake Erie

◄ Dutch settler
Jonas Michel

Chapter Events   1520   1550   1580

1
1524
Giovanni da Verrazano sails
into New York Harbor

Dutch Settlement in New York

Legend:
- New Netherland, 1609–1664
- Present-day New York boundary
- National boundary
- Other state boundary
- • City/settlement
- ( ) Present-day cities

N W E S (compass rose)

CANADA

St. Lawrence River

Lake Champlain

Lake Ontario

VT

Oneida Lake

Mohawk River

Fort Orange• (Albany)

NH

Cayuga Lake

Seneca Lake

Susquehanna River

MA

Connecticut River

Hudson River

CT

PA

Delaware River

Long Island Sound

Long Island

New Amsterdam (New York)

1 **2**
3 **4**

NJ

Atlantic Ocean

0   20   40 miles
0   20   40 kilometers

1610   **1640**   **1670**

2 1624
The Dutch settle in New Netherland

3 1647
Peter Stuyvesant becomes governor of New Netherland

4 1664
The English capture New Netherland

VOCABULARY

explorer
Northwest Passage
trading post
colony

VOCABULARY STRATEGY

Word Origins A **colony** is a group of people who settle in a new land. The word comes from the Latin word *colonia*, which means "settler." What other words use this Latin root?

READING STRATEGY

Summarize Use the chart below to summarize why explorers came to New York.

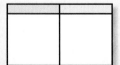

NEW YORK STANDARDS

1.1, 1.2, 1.3, 2.1, 2.2, 3.1, 4.1

Looking for New Routes

It is the year 1524. You are a French sailor who has spent weeks in a small wooden boat crossing the Atlantic Ocean. You have no idea what lies ahead. No European has ever sailed to this place before. You hope that the people of the region will be friendly. Later your captain writes:

"*So we took the small boat up the river to a land which we found densely [thickly] populated. The people . . . came toward us joyfully, uttering loud cries of wonderment. . . .*"

Henry Hudson met Native Americans as he explored the Hudson River (below) on his ship, *Half Moon* (left), or *Naive Maen* in Dutch. ▼

1490	1520	1550	1580	1610

1492
Christopher Columbus
lands in the Americas

1524
Giovanni da Verrazano sails
into New York Harbor

1609
Samuel de Champlain explores
New York; Henry Hudson
explores the Hudson River

Ⓐ Europeans Reach the Americas

In the late 1400s, Europeans began to look for a water route to the rich spice markets found in Asia. An **explorer** travels to unfamiliar places to find out about them. One explorer, Christopher Columbus, thought he could reach Asia by sailing westward across the Atlantic Ocean. In 1492, instead of Asia, Columbus sailed to the Bahama Islands in the Caribbean Sea. Columbus did not realize that he had reached a world Europeans knew nothing about.

The First Europeans in New York

By the 1500s, many more explorers came to North America and the land of New York. These Europeans believed that there must be a **Northwest Passage**, a water route across North America to reach Asia. The country that found this water route would grow rich from trade with Asia.

Giovanni da Verrazano

You read the words of Giovanni da Verrazano (joh VAHN nee duh vair uh ZAHN oh) at the beginning of this lesson. Although an Italian sea captain, he sailed for the king of France in 1524. He did not find the Northwest Passage, but he was probably the first European to see what is now New York. Verrazano realized he was not in Asia, but he hoped this new land might have riches and products for Europeans to buy. Today a part of New York Harbor north of Staten Island is called Verrazano Narrows in this explorer's honor.

QUICK CHECK What were Columbus and other explorers looking for when they sailed west across the Atlantic Ocean? *Summarize*

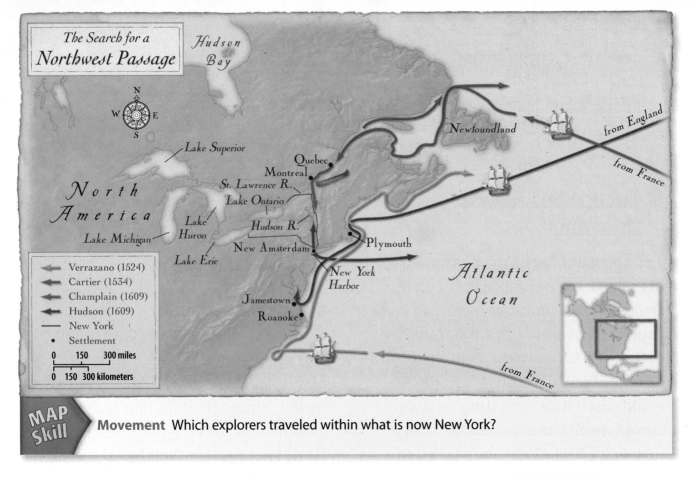

The Search for a
Northwest Passage

North America

- Verrazano (1524)
- Cartier (1534)
- Champlain (1609)
- Hudson (1609)
- New York
- Settlement

0   150   300 miles
0 150 300 kilometers

Hudson Bay

Newfoundland

from England

from France

Quebec
Montreal
St. Lawrence R.
Lake Ontario
Hudson R.
New Amsterdam
New York Harbor
Plymouth

Lake Superior
Lake Michigan
Lake Huron
Lake Erie

Jamestown
Roanoke

Atlantic Ocean

from France

MAP Skill **Movement** Which explorers traveled within what is now New York?

B Other Europeans Explore

European kings wanted to find a water route to the riches of Asia. They also hoped that there were riches in the lands of the Americas.

Verrazano was not the only explorer sent to North America by a French king. In 1534 King Francis I of France sent Jacques Cartier (ZHAHK kahr TYAY) to explore North America. Cartier sailed up the St. Lawrence River. This river flows from the Great Lakes to the Atlantic Ocean. Cartier hoped that this river might be the famous Northwest Passage. He claimed the valley of the river for France.

The French in New York

Samuel de Champlain (duh sham PLAYN) was another French explorer.

In 1608 he set up a **trading post**—a place to trade products with others. Quebec, the name of Champlain's trading post, became a French **colony**. A colony is a place ruled by another country. In 1609 Champlain explored what is now northern New York with some Algonquian guides. He saw and named Lake Champlain.

The French Make an Enemy

During this journey, Champlain's group met some Iroquois, who were enemies of the Algonquian. The French had guns, which the Iroquois had never seen before. They helped the Algonquian defeat the Iroquois. This defeat made the Iroquois into enemies of the French for years to come.

Henry Hudson

The Dutch, people from the Netherlands, hired an English sea captain named Henry Hudson. In September 1609, Hudson sailed up the Hudson River. He hoped he had found a Northwest Passage to Asia. However, what Hudson explored was a large river. The river was later named for Hudson.

▲ Henry Hudson

Hudson met and traded with Native Americans called the Lenni Lenape. The Lenape called Hudson's ship a "very large house," which is probably how his brightly-painted ship looked.

Hudson wrote:

❝ *The land was pleasant with grass and flowers . . . We found very loving people . . .* ❞

Although Henry Hudson did not find a Northwest Passage, his reports of rich soil and friendly people encouraged the Dutch to start a very important colony.

✓ **QUICK CHECK** What did European explorers find in North America? *Main Ideas and Details*

What You Learned

A Christopher Columbus and other Europeans reached the Americas while searching for a sea route from the Atlantic to the Pacific Ocean.

B Other European explorers explored north on the Hudson River and south from Canada into what is now New York.

★ Focus Lesson Review

1. **Focus Question** Why were Europeans exploring land in New York?

2. **Vocabulary** Describe French voyages using these vocabulary terms.
   - colony
   - explorer
   - Northwest Passage
   - trading post

3. **Geography** What geographic features in New York are named for explorers?

4. **Critical Thinking Make Decisions** Think about the explorers' descriptions of land in New York. Why do you think people settled in New York?

5. **Reading Strategy Summarize** How did Native Americans and Champlain work together?

6. **Write About** THE BIG IDEA Write a paragraph describing what you think European explorers and Native Americans might have learned about each other at their first meetings.

7. **Reading Primary Sources** What have you learned about the Native Americans' reactions to the European explorers?

Make Decisions

In Lesson 1, you read about the early explorers who came to New York. These explorers made a **decision**, or choice, to explore new lands.

Decision making is a skill you will use every day. Decisions may be simple, like deciding what clothes to wear, or more difficult, like deciding to learn a new sport. The steps below will help you make the right decisions.

VOCABULARY

decision
goal
option

1 Learn It

- To make a decision, know your **goal**. Your goal is what you want to get.

- Identify each **option**, or possible choice. For any decision, you will have at least two choices.

- Predict the results of each option.

- Choose the option that seems most likely to help you reach your goal.

2 Try It

Read the paragraphs on page 87. Think about the decision Lee has to make. Answer the questions.

- What is Lee's goal?

- What are Lee's options to reach his goal?

- What might be the result if Lee chooses his first option?

- Which option would best help Lee reach his goal?

Lee's goal
I want to find out more about this flower.

One option
I'll dig it up, and study it at home.

Another option
Maybe I could take a photograph of the flower and show it to my science teacher.

Lee's family was hiking in the Adirondack Mountains. At the side of the trail, Lee saw a beautiful wildflower. "I wonder what this flower is," Lee said. "I want to find out more about this flower. I'll dig it up, and study it at home."

Then Lee remembered reading about wildflowers in his science class. Wildflowers are an important part of the environment. "I think I should leave the wildflower here," Lee thought. "Maybe I could take a photograph of the flower and show it to my science teacher."

3 Apply It

- Think of a decision you have made recently.
- Follow the steps in **Learn It** to tell about your options.
- Tell how your decision helped you reach your goal.

The Dutch Settle New York

How did the colony of New Netherland begin to grow?

VOCABULARY

culture
investor
profit
patroon
tenant farmer
tolerance
slavery

VOCABULARY STRATEGY

Suffixes When the suffix **-or** is added to a verb, it describes what a person does. The verb *invest* means "use money to make a profit." What do you think an **investor** does?

READING STRATEGY

Compare and Contrast Use the chart below to compare and contrast life for Native Americans and Dutch colonists.

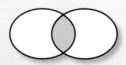

NEW YORK STANDARDS

1.1, 1.2, 1.3, 1.4, 2.1, 2.2, 2.3, 2.4, 3.1, 4.1, 4.2, 5.1

From its very earliest days, the Dutch colony attracted people from many countries and cultures. It must have been an exciting time for the early settlers as they moved into a strange new place.

In the 1640s, the settlement of New Amsterdam was a center of activity. Isaac Jogues, a Frenchman, described the young settlement:

66 *There were persons there of eighteen different languages; they are scattered here and there on the river, above and below as the beauty and convenience of the spot invited each to settle.* 99

ⓐ New Netherland

The Dutch came to North America to make money from animal furs. Many Europeans wanted fur coats to wear during the cold winters. The Dutch hoped

1620	1630	1640	1650

1621
Dutch West
India Company
is formed

1624
Dutch settle in
New Netherland

1647
Peter Stuyvesant becomes
governor of New Netherland

to make money by buying furs from Native Americans and selling them in Europe.

In 1621 Dutch businessmen created the Dutch West India Company. The Dutch government gave the company the right to trade in North and South America. The company quickly made plans to set up a trading colony on the Hudson River in 1624.

The First Dutch Settlements

The Dutch called their colony New Netherland in honor of their home country. At first most colonists settled around Fort Orange, near present-day Albany.

In 1626, Peter Minuit, the first Dutch governor, "bought" Manhattan Island from the Native Americans living

there. According to legend, he bought the land from the Lenni Lenape chief, Tammany. Minuit traded blankets and other valuable trade goods in exchange for the land.

The Native Americans believed that they were selling Minuit only the right to use the land. In their **culture**, people did not "own" land. A culture is a way of life a group of people share. As time passed, Europeans and Native Americans would continue to fight over New York's land.

QUICK CHECK How did the Native Americans view trade differently from the Dutch? *Compare and Contrast*

The harbor (inset) at New Amsterdam quickly became a busy port with ships from many nations. ▼

Ⓑ A Trading Colony

The money for the Dutch West India Company came from **investors**, people who give money to a business. When a business sells its products, it charges more than the products cost to make. This price difference is called a **profit**. A profit is the money a business earns after it pays for tools, salaries, and other costs. Investors get a share of the profit.

To encourage settlement in New Netherland, the company gave large areas of land to **patroons**. A patroon was a landowner who brought 50 settlers to the colony to live on his land.

Many people who moved to New Netherland became **tenant farmers**. These people farmed land owned by a patroon and paid rent in cash or crops. Few tenant farmers were able to save money to buy their own land.

The largest city in New Netherland was New Amsterdam. Most leaders in New Amsterdam followed the Dutch tradition, or custom, of **tolerance**. Tolerance is being accepting of differences. You can read about the Company's tolerance in the Primary Source. The Dutch treated most people fairly even if they had different beliefs. Anne Hutchinson, for example, came to New Netherland when her religious beliefs forced her to leave New England.

However, not all people in New Amsterdam were treated fairly. Some people were brought from Africa to work on the land. These Africans were forced into **slavery**. Slavery is making a person work for no money and without the freedom to leave. Some enslaved people were able to earn their freedom. However, many did not. The colony of New Netherland, which later became New York, was a colony with many enslaved workers.

New Netherland Gets a New Governor

Peter Stuyvesant (STY vuh suhnt) became the governor, or leader, of the New Netherland colony in 1647. He was a forceful leader who tried to strengthen New Netherland.

PRIMARY SOURCES

A section of a letter from the

Dutch West India Company

to the governor of New Netherland, 1663

❝ *Allow everyone to have his own belief, as long as he behaves quietly and legally, gives no* _offense_ *to his neighbors and does not* _oppose_ *the government.* ❞

_____

offense a cause of anger
oppose be against

Write About It! Why do you think the Dutch West India Company was in favor of tolerance?

Stuyvesant did improve the colony. He made fire safety laws and created a police force called "Rattle Watch." His biggest problems came from the English colonies located north and south of New Netherland. Settlers from these colonies were taking land that Stuyvesant believed belonged to his colony. Soon, New Netherland was drawn into war over this land.

QUICK CHECK Why did many different people choose to settle in New Amsterdam? *Main Idea and Details*

Governor Peter Stuyvesant and a soldier beside the wall of the Dutch fort at New Amsterdam ▼

What You Learned

A Wealthy Dutch investors formed the Dutch West India Company and established the colony of New Netherland.

B Dutch and people from other countries were encouraged to settle in New Netherland.

★ ★ ★ Focus Lesson Review

1. **Focus Question** How did the colony of New Netherland begin to grow?

2. **Vocabulary** Write about life in New Netherland using the following vocabulary terms.

   investor   tenant farmer
   patroon   tolerance
   slavery

3. **Economics** Why did the Dutch West India Company establish New Netherland?

4. **Critical Thinking Problem Solving** How did the Dutch West India Company hope to get settlers for its colony?

5. **Reading Strategy Compare and Contrast** Use the graphic organizer to compare and contrast patroons and tenant farmers in New Netherland.

6. **Write About THE BIG IDEA** Write a paragraph describing what the colonies and the Native Americans thought they were getting when Peter Minuit purchased Manhattan Island.

7. **Reading Primary Sources** "Whatever we desire . . . is here to be found. If you will come here with your family you will not regret it. " Do you think the writer of this letter liked New Netherland? Why do you think so?

Read Circle and Line Graphs

VOCABULARY

graph
circle graph
line graph

A **graph** is a diagram that shows information. A **circle graph** shows a whole amount and its parts. Because the pieces of the circle graph look like slices of a pie, circle graphs are sometimes called *pie graphs*.

A **line graph** shows only whole amounts, but it shows how those amounts change over time. Each point on a line graph is labeled to tell you how many years or how much of something is shown.

Circle graphs and line graphs are only two of many types of graphs.

1 Learn It

- Circle graphs are used to show the parts of a whole. Each "slice" on a circle graph has a label that tells you what that part represents. Graph A on page 93 is a circle graph.

- The title of the circle graph is "Population of New Amsterdam in the 1660s." What was the largest group of colonists at that time?

- Line graphs are used to show how something changes over time. Graph B on page 93 is a line graph.

- The numbers and labels on the left side of the line graph represent the population of New York colony. The labels at the bottom show the years that the graph covers.

- The red line in the graph shows population changes of New York colony over 30 years. Each dot on the line stands for the population during a particular year.

② Try It

Look at the graphs on this page. Answer the questions.

- Which graph would you use to find the population of New York in 1665?

- What percentage of the colonists were not Dutch in the 1660s?

- Between which years did the population of the colony increase most quickly?

③ Apply It

Make a circle graph of your own. Your circle graph should show how you spend your time during one weekday.

- The whole graph should equal 24 hours, or one day.

- Use slices to show how many hours you are in school, how many hours you sleep, how many hours you do homework, and so on.

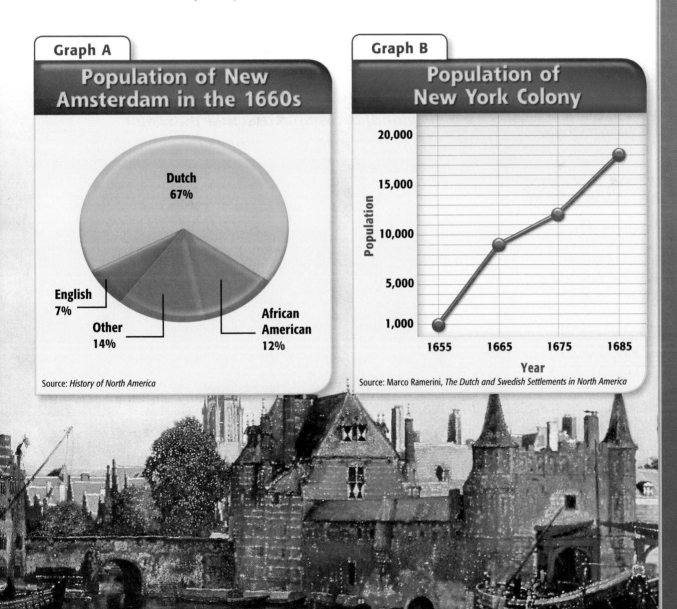

Graph A

Population of New Amsterdam in the 1660s

Dutch 67%

English 7%

Other 14%

African American 12%

Source: *History of North America*

Graph B

Population of New York Colony

Source: Marco Ramerini, *The Dutch and Swedish Settlements in North America*

Focus Lesson 3

New York Becomes an English Colony

What Dutch traditions continued after New Netherland became an English colony?

VOCABULARY

proprietor
free trade

VOCABULARY STRATEGY

Compound Words
Free trade is an open compound. Put the meanings of **free** and **trade** together. What other open compounds can you name?

READING STRATEGY

Identify Main Idea and Details Use the chart below to list the main idea and supporting details of this lesson.

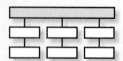

NEW YORK STANDARDS

1.1, 1.2, 1.3, 1.4
2.1, 2.2, 3.1, 4.1
5.1, 5.3

Samuel Drisius was a leader of the Dutch Church in New Amsterdam. In the summer of 1664, he recorded an important event:

"*On the 26th of August there arrived in the Bay of the North River, near Staten Island, four great men-of-war [warships] . . . well manned with sailors and soldiers. They were provided with a patent [order] . . . from the King [of England] to demand and take possession of this province, in the name of His Majesty.*"

The English victory changed New Amsterdam to New York City. ▼

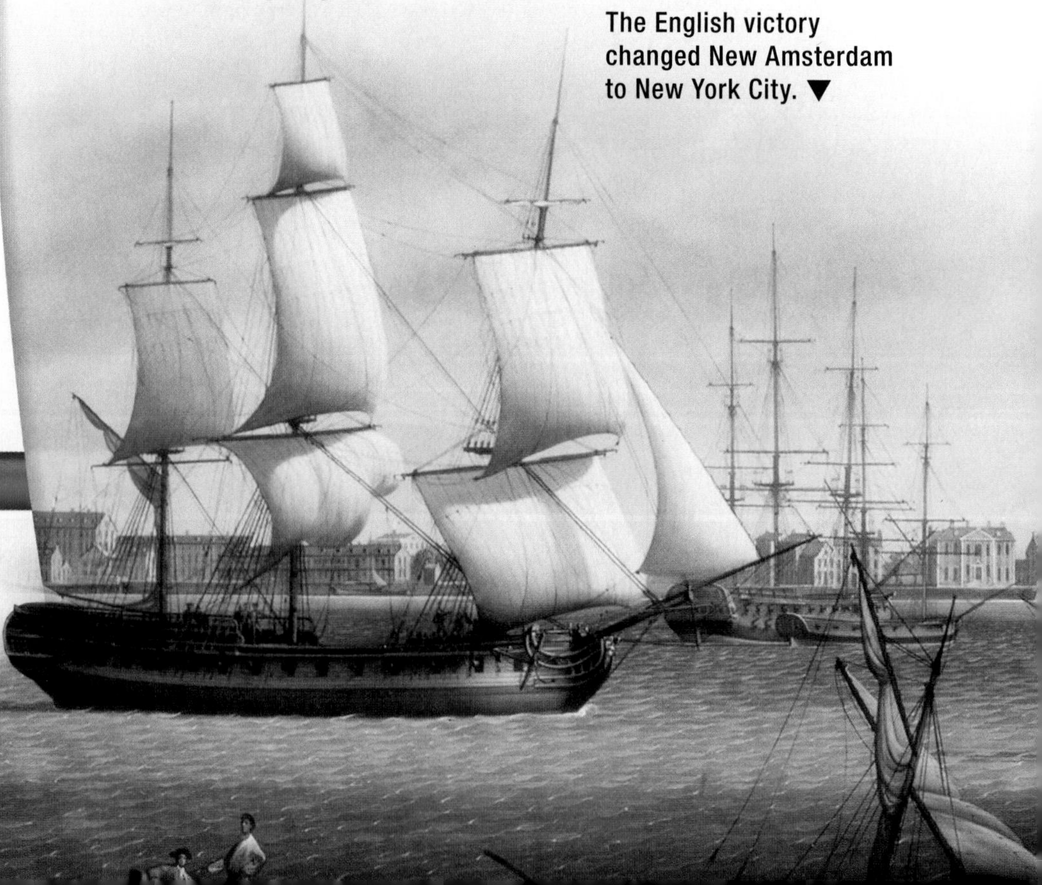

1630	1640	1650	1660	1670

1638
Colony of New
Sweden established

1655
Stuyvesant captures
Swedish settlements

1664
English capture
New Netherland

Ⓐ New Sweden

In March 1638 Sweden, another European country, established the colony of New Sweden in North America. This colony was located south of New Netherland in what is now Delaware. The settlers of New Sweden built the first log cabins in North America.

Governor Stuyvesant of New Netherland thought the Swedes were living on land that belonged to his colony. In 1655 Stuyvesant captured the Swedish settlements.

The End of Dutch Rule

For much of the 1600s, England and the Netherlands were at war. In 1664, English warships appeared in the harbor of New Amsterdam.

Governor Stuyvesant wanted to fight the English, but most of the city's settlers did not. Their fort was falling down, and the city's walls needed repairs.

The sight of the powerful English warships convinced the people of New Amsterdam to surrender. The city gave up without a single shot being fired.

QUICK CHECK Why did the people of New Amsterdam surrender their colony to the English? *Main Idea and Details*

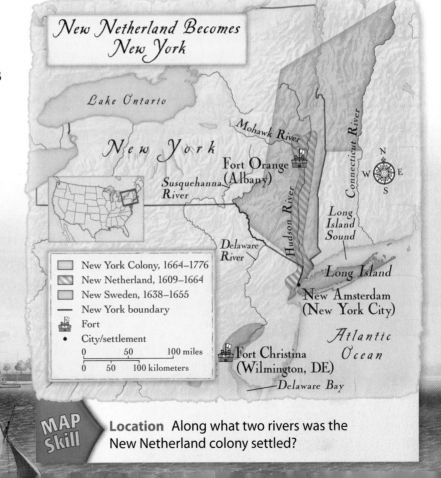

New Netherland Becomes New York

Lake Ontario

New York

Mohawk River

Fort Orange (Albany)

Susquehanna River

Hudson River

Connecticut River

Long Island Sound

Delaware River

Long Island

New Amsterdam (New York City)

Atlantic Ocean

Fort Christina (Wilmington, DE)

Delaware Bay

☐ New York Colony, 1664–1776
▨ New Netherland, 1609–1664
☐ New Sweden, 1638–1655
— New York boundary
🏰 Fort
• City/settlement

0   50   100 miles
0   50   100 kilometers

MAP Skill

Location Along what two rivers was the New Netherland colony settled?

DATAGRAPHIC

Wealth in the Colonies

The English colonies produced valuable crops and products. Some people made fortunes trading these goods. However, wealth was not equally distributed. Some colonists had more money than others. These two graphs show you how wealth changed in the 1700s and who owned most of that wealth.

Wealth in the Colonies, 1700s

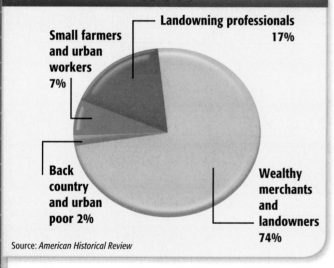

Landowning professionals 17%

Small farmers and urban workers 7%

Back country and urban poor 2%

Wealthy merchants and landowners 74%

Source: *American Historical Review*

Value of Exports from the Colonies

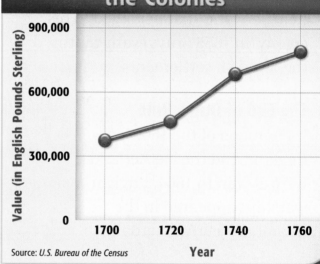

Source: *U.S. Bureau of the Census*

Think About the Colonies

1. Who owned most of the wealth in the 13 colonies?

2. In general, was trade increasing or decreasing during this period?

3. Do you think the wealth of landowners and merchants was increasing or decreasing?

❸ The Colony Becomes New York

The new **proprietor**, or owner of the colony, was James, the Duke of York. He renamed his new colony New York. The city of New Amsterdam was renamed New York City.

The Duke of York gave part of his new colony to two friends, Lord Berkeley and George Carteret. Together they formed another colony called New Jersey. New Jersey was named for the island of Jersey in England.

With the capture of New Netherland in 1664, England now controlled most of the land along the Atlantic Coast.

The New York Colony

Much of life stayed the same for the colonists of New York after the English took control. The Dutch practice of tolerance continued and the economy continued to grow.

The Duke of York wisely allowed some Dutch traditions to continue, such as freedom of religion and **free trade**, or trade without restrictions or charges. One hundred years later, many of the original Dutch ideas became important parts of a new American government.

QUICK CHECK Why did the Duke of York allow the citizens in New Netherland to continue their lives unchanged? *Make Inferences*

What You Learned

Ⓐ Sweden established a colony called New Sweden south of New Netherland. New Netherland became an English colony.

Ⓑ The Dutch traditions of religious tolerance and other freedoms continued in the English colony.

⭐ Focus Lesson Review

1. **Focus Question** What Dutch traditions continued after New Netherland became an English colony?

2. **Vocabulary** Write about the economy of New York colony using these terms.
   proprietor   free trade

3. **Government** How did Dutch traditions shape New York colony?

4. **Critical Thinking** **Make Decisions** What made the Dutch colonists surrender to the English warships?

5. **Reading Strategy** **Main Idea and Details** Use the graphic organizer to find the main idea and details about the New York colony.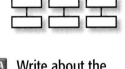

6. **Write About** THE BIG IDEA Write about the struggles between different European colonies in North America.

7. **Reading Primary Sources** The Duke of York ordered his soldiers to treat the people of New Amsterdam "with all humility and gentleness." What did he mean by these words?

Could Settlers Have Lived Peacefully with Native Americans?

As you have learned, settlers in New York and Native Americans often disagreed. Was there some way the two groups could have lived together? Read below to find out about three different points of view.

❝*The purpose of the British [English] colonies was to move people from England to America. The Iroquois did not have the power . . . to withstand a growing European population . . . taking their land.*❞

Hiram L. Smith
Onondaga College
Syracuse, New York
From an interview, 2005

❝*The Dutch understood [the Iroquois] way of owning and sharing land. They understood that people who shared the land were allies . . . The English should have tried to understand the ways of native peoples.*❞

Sheree Bonaparte
St. Regis Mohawk Tribe
Akwesasne, New York
From an interview, 2005

❝*Most British colonists . . . stayed within English society. They had much less day to day contact . . . with Native peoples . . . so they were less likely to treat [them] as equals.*❞

Erik Seeman
State University of New York (SUNY)-Buffalo
Buffalo, New York
From an interview, 2005

Build Citizenship

1. What was the purpose of English colonies in North America?

2. How were Native Americans treated differently by the Dutch?

3. Why were the English less likely to treat Native Americans as equals?

Think About It

1. What reasons does Sheree Bonaparte give for her opinion?

2. Why does Hiram Smith think that events had to turn out as they did?

3. On what idea do all three speakers agree?

Write About It!

Do you think fighting over land in New York could have been avoided? Why or why not? Write a paragraph that expresses your opinion. Give reasons for your answer.

Chapter 3 Review

Vocabulary Review

FOCUS

Copy the sentences below on a separate sheet of paper. Use the list of vocabulary terms to fill in the blanks.

colony	patroon
Northwest Passage	tolerance

1. _____ is the fair treatment of people regardless of religion, custom, and beliefs.

2. A _____ is a place ruled by another country.

3. The _____ is a water route believed to run across North America.

4. A _____ is a Dutch citizen given large areas of land to settle in New Netherland.

5. **Test Preparation** The practice of making one person work for another without pay or a chance to be free.

   (A) **explorer**   (C) **tenant farmer**
   (B) **slavery**   (D) **fleet**

Comprehension Check

FOCUS

6. Why did Dutch investors form New Netherland?

7. Who was the first European to explore what is now New York Harbor?

8. Why did the Dutch surrender New Amsterdam to the English?

9. What important contribution did the settlers of New Sweden make?

10. Which European explorer was first to explore the Hudson River and trade with the Lenni Lenape?

11. **Critical Thinking** How did the capture of New Netherland improve England's position in North America?

12. **Critical Thinking** Why do you think many non-Dutch people moved to New Netherland?

Use the Time Line

FOCUS

Use the time line below to answer each question.

13. How long was New Netherland a Dutch colony?

14. How many years after the Dutch formed New Netherland did Peter Minuit buy land on the island of Manhattan?

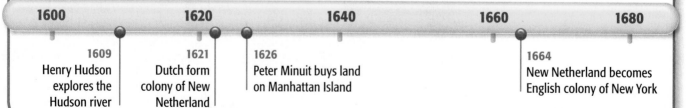

1600	1620	1640	1660	1680

1609
Henry Hudson explores the Hudson river

1621
Dutch form colony of New Netherland

1626
Peter Minuit buys land on Manhattan Island

1664
New Netherland becomes English colony of New York

Read Circle and Line Graphs

Write a complete sentence to answer each question.

15. What are circle graphs used to show?

16. In the line graph below, between which years did the population of New York colony increase the least?

17. **Test Preparation** What does each dot represent on the graph below?

18. **Test Preparation** What information does this graph show?

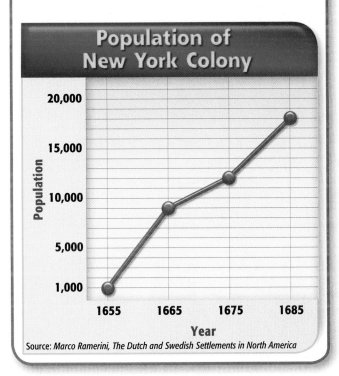

Population of New York Colony

Source: *Marco Ramerini, The Dutch and Swedish Settlements in North America*

Using Primary Sources

CRQ

Constructed Response Questions

Read the quotation and answer the questions that follow.

> *"So when any ship shall return from a voyage, the general or commanders of the fleets (groups of ships), shall be obliged [required] to come and report to us the success of the voyage of such ship or ships, within ten days after their arrival, and shall deliver and leave us with a report in writing . . ."*

19. What two things were required of ship captains?

20. How long were ship captains given to do these tasks?

Hands-on Activity

21. **Prepare and Perform a Skit** Work in groups to write a skit about the purchase of Manhattan Island. One group should be the European settlers and the other group the Native Americans. Try to make as fair a trade as possible. Remember that the Native Americans did not think that land could actually be owned.

Write About History

22. **Narrative** Suppose you are a colonist who just arrived in New Netherland. Write a letter to a family member in Europe describing your life in the new colony.

LOG ON For help with the process of writing, visit: www.macmillanmh.com

Life in Colonial New York

You Are There

"*A sturdy Dutchman named Roeloff Jansen caught the spirit of unrest. He had a strong wife willing to brave the seas, and a little family, and there was a future to make for them. So they sailed for the Dutchman's new field of adventure and fortune.*"

Many people from Europe wanted to start a new life and settle in New York. Roeloff Jansen wanted to create a new life for his family. These people with different skills and different beliefs lived together, creating new communities. They also started building a new country.

A Dutch colonist ▶

Mississippi River

Missouri River

Chapter Events	1680	1700	1720

1
1683
New York Assembly chosen
for the first time

2
1710
German settlers
begin arriving

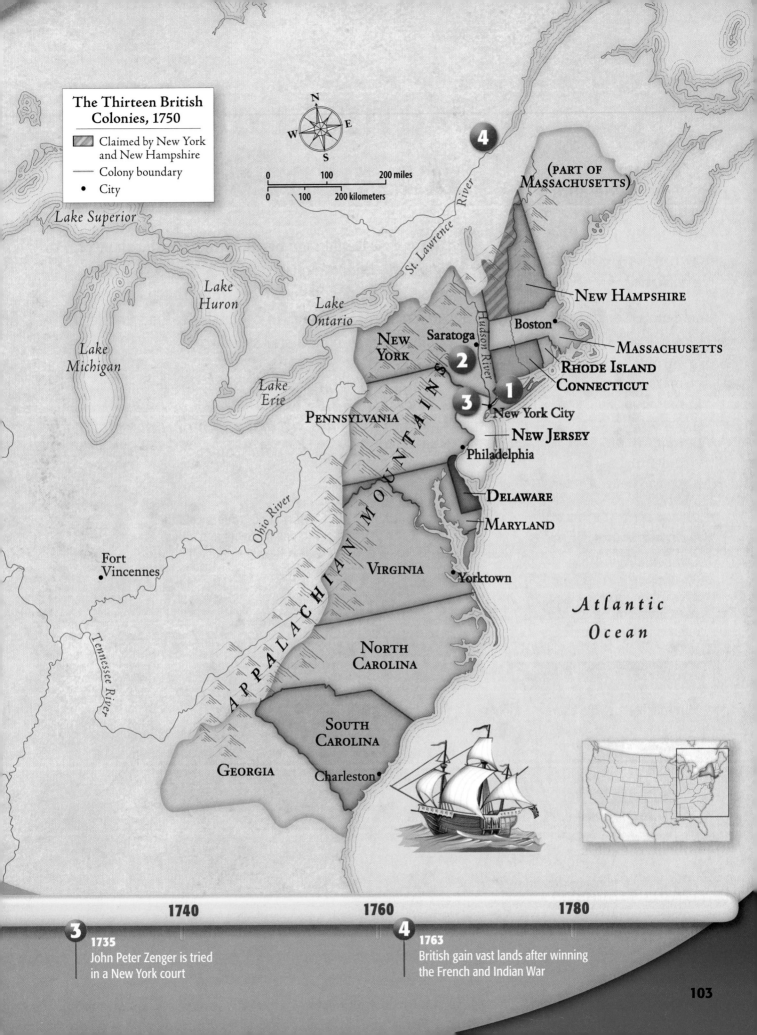

The Thirteen British Colonies, 1750

Claimed by New York and New Hampshire
Colony boundary
• City

N W E S

0   100   200 miles
0   100   200 kilometers

Lake Superior

Lake Huron

Lake Michigan

Lake Ontario

Lake Erie

St. Lawrence River

Hudson River

4

(PART OF MASSACHUSETTS)

NEW HAMPSHIRE

Boston

NEW YORK

Saratoga

2

3

1

MASSACHUSETTS

RHODE ISLAND
CONNECTICUT

New York City

NEW JERSEY

PENNSYLVANIA

Philadelphia

DELAWARE

MARYLAND

Fort Vincennes

Ohio River

A P P A L A C H I A N   M O U N T A I N S

VIRGINIA

Yorktown

Atlantic Ocean

Tennessee River

NORTH CAROLINA

SOUTH CAROLINA

GEORGIA

Charleston

1740   **1760**   **1780**

3
1735
John Peter Zenger is tried in a New York court

4
1763
British gain vast lands after winning the French and Indian War

How did trade and agriculture help build a strong economy in colonial New York?

VOCABULARY

surplus
manor
merchant
export
import
indentured servant
packet boat

VOCABULARY STRATEGY

Compound Words
A **packet boat** carried packets, or packages. What are some other open compound words?

READING STRATEGY

Summarize Use the chart to summarize why New York was a good place for Europeans to settle.

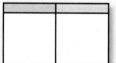

NEW YORK STANDARDS

1.1, 1.2, 1.3, 3.1
4.1

Farmers and Townspeople

In 1664 New Netherland became the English colony of New York. Under English rule, New York increased its trade and its population. The former Dutch colony became one of the leaders of colonial life. King Charles II of England wrote to his sister in France:

> ❝*You will have heard of our taking of New Amsterdam, which lies just by New England. Tis a place of great importance to trade, and a very good town.*❞

New York farmers sold their crops in towns and cities like New York City. ▼

1660	1670	1680	1690

1664
English ships capture
New Amsterdam

1673
Dutch briefly
recapture
New York

1685
The Duke of York
becomes England's
King James II

Ⓐ Colonial Farmers

During the 1600s countries in Europe had many wars about religion and politics. Many people decided to come to New York to escape from these wars. The Dutch spirit of tolerance continued in English New York. European settlers were treated fairly here even if they had different beliefs. Immigrants from France, Germany, and other countries in Europe used their skills to begin a new life in New York.

Settlers Become Farmers

The New York area had rich farmland. Farmers were able to produce a **surplus**, more than they needed. The extra crops were then sold to markets in other North American colonies and to colonies in the area around the Caribbean Sea.

Farming was hard work and many children helped on the farms. Boys fed pigs, watered horses, and herded cows. Girls spun linen, did laundry, made butter, and milked cows.

Most early farms were in the Hudson and Mohawk river valleys. People used the rivers to transport their wheat and corn to market. The Iroquois, whom you have read about, controlled much of upstate New York, so there were not many settlers there.

Some farms were on **manors**, large pieces of land divided up into several farms and rented by landowners to farmers.

QUICK CHECK Why did many Europeans move to New York to live?
Summarize

Notice the Dutch "half doors" on this Dutch farmhouse in Kinderhook, New York. ▼

▲ Ports in early New York may have looked much like this historic site today.

ⓑ New York Builds Trade

Under the Dutch, New Amsterdam had been an important port. Renamed New York City, it continued to be the most important city in the colony. **Merchants**, or people who buy and sell goods, traded many products in New York. Wheat, furs, meat, lumber, fish, and vegetables were **exported**. An export is something sold or traded to another country.

However, the colony was not able to make all the manufactured items it needed. Glassware, china, and luxury fabrics were **imported** from England. An import is something brought into a country for sale. In addition, New York imported sugar and molasses from the islands in the Caribbean Sea. In time this trade would lead to trade with Africa, which brought a great deal of money to New York. It also made New York a center for the Atlantic slave trade.

Ships from the Caribbean and from Africa brought enslaved Africans to New York. Here the enslaved Africans were sold and transported to other colonies. Ships from Europe also brought **indentured servants**. An employer paid for the servant to come to the colonies. The servant then had to work a certain number of years to pay for his or her ticket. Indentured servants worked until they were free, but enslaved people were almost never given their freedom.

The waterfront of New York City was crowded and busy. Sailors loaded and unloaded **packet boats**, boats that carried letters and other goods from England. The waterfront smelled of imported coffee, spices, and sugar.

Streetsellers called out to buyers, and merchants discussed deals. It was exciting and probably a bit confusing to the newcomers.

New York Grows

New York's population and economy grew. Farmers came to towns to sell their goods and buy goods from Europe. Craftworkers set up small shops to make and sell items such as iron tools and saddles.

During the colonial period, New York attracted many new settlers. New York became a major center of export for the colonies. By the late 1700s, New York City was one of the largest cities in North America.

QUICK CHECK How did New York become one of the largest cities in the colonies? *Cause and Effect*

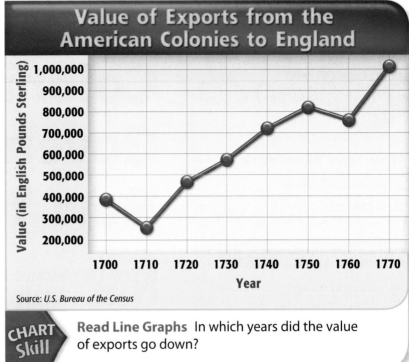

Value of Exports from the American Colonies to England

Source: *U.S. Bureau of the Census*

CHART Skill **Read Line Graphs** In which years did the value of exports go down?

What You Learned

A European farmers who settled in New York colony built a strong agricultural economy.

B Skilled merchants helped make New York an important trading center.

Focus Lesson Review

1. **Focus Question** How did trade and agriculture help build a strong economy in colonial New York?

2. **Vocabulary** Write a paragraph about colonial New York using the following terms.
   indentured servant   **packet boat**
   manor   **surplus**

3. **Economics** Why did New York become a leading trade center in the 1700s?

4. **Critical Thinking Problem Solving** How did New York farmers get their crops to markets?

5. **Reading Strategy Summarize** How did trade affect life in New York in the 1700s?

6. **Write About** 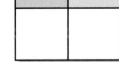 How were the experiences of European settlers, indentured servants, and enslaved people both similar and different?

7. **Reading Primary Sources** Reread the words of Charles II on page 104. Why was he glad to have captured New York City?

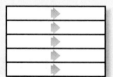
How was New York organized as a British colony?

VOCABULARY

royal colony
sheriff
government
legislature
assembly
tax

VOCABULARY STRATEGY

Word Origins The word **sheriff** comes from an old English word that means the royal law officer of a shire, or county. What other terms do we use for law officers today?

READING STRATEGY

Identify Cause and Effect Use the chart below to show how Great Britain's government affected New York.

	▶
	▶
	▶
	▶
	▶

NEW YORK STANDARDS

1.1, 1.2, 1.3, 2.1, 5.1, 5.2, 5.3

Colonial Government in New York

New York became a bustling colony under the English. Visitors did not expect to see a city of this size on the edge of North America. One British naval officer wrote:

> ❝ *I had no idea of finding a place in America, consisting of near 2,000 houses, elegantly built of brick, raised on an eminence [high place] and the streets paved and spacious.* ❞

Ⓐ A British Colony

As you have read, the Dutch colony of New Netherland became the English colony of New York. In 1707 England and Scotland joined to form the kingdom of Great Britain. English colonies, including New York, now became British colonies.

1683
Assembly is chosen for the first time

1710
British lawmakers set up a colonial postal service based in New York

1735
John Peter Zenger is tried in a New York court

1754
Many battles of the French and Indian War fought in New York

A Royal Colony

In 1685 the Duke of York became King James II of England. New York then became a **royal colony**. This meant that New York belonged to the king or queen. The first royal governor, Richard Nicolls, was chosen to carry out the king's wishes in the colony.

Other officials helped the governor run the colony. **Sheriffs** were county officials who made sure that laws were obeyed.

The citizens of New York were just like citizens of Great Britain. However, there was one big difference. Citizens of New York could not vote in elections for Parliament, the elected group who made laws for Britain and its colonies. New Yorkers resented having to obey people they had not chosen. Many of these laws affected trade in the colonies and with foreign countries. These laws would later cause trouble in the colonies.

QUICK CHECK Why were New Yorkers angry about British trade laws? *Cause and Effect*

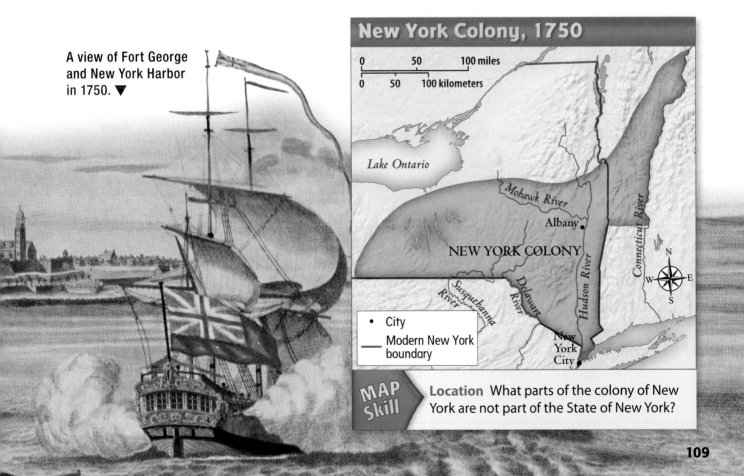

A view of Fort George and New York Harbor in 1750. ▼

New York Colony, 1750

0 50 100 miles
0 50 100 kilometers

Lake Ontario

Mohawk River

Albany

NEW YORK COLONY

Connecticut River

Hudson River

Susquehanna River

Delaware River

New York City

N W E S

• City
— Modern New York boundary

MAP Skill **Location** What parts of the colony of New York are not part of the State of New York?

109

B The Colonial Government

A **government** is the system which runs a country, state, or city. Colonial New Yorkers demanded a **legislature**, or a group of elected citizens to make laws. In 1683 they were allowed to elect members to a legislature, called an **assembly**. However only wealthy white men could vote in these elections. The Assembly members voted on issues such as **taxes**, money collected to pay the costs of government. New York had an elected legislature, but it was still

This royal badge has the letters GR for "George Rex," or King George. ▶

under the control of the king and the governor. This led to problems in the 1700s.

Colonial New York also had judges. One famous trial was an important step in giving Americans freedom of the press. This is the right to print or tell the news without fear of punishment. You will read about this trial in the Biography on the next page.

✓ **QUICK CHECK** Why was freedom of the press important? *Summarize*

What You Learned

A New York became a royal colony under the rule of Great Britain.

B Colonial New York had an assembly that voted on issues such as taxes; however, the British king still had control over the colony.

★ Focus Lesson Review

1. **Focus Question** How was New York organized as a British colony?

2. **Vocabulary** Write a paragraph about government in colonial New York using the following vocabulary terms.
   assembly royal colony
   government tax
   legislature

3. **Government** What government group made laws for Great Britain and its colonies?

4. **Critical Thinking** **Problem Solving** How did the citizens of New York try to get more power?

5. **Reading Strategy** **Identify Cause and Effect** Use the chart to show how the Assembly affected government in New York.

6. **Write About**  When Great Britain took over New Netherland, in what way did the colonists not become full British citizens?

7. **Reading Primary Sources** Reread the naval officer's words on page 108. Draw a picture of New York City in the 1700s using his description.

John Peter Zenger 1697–1746

John Peter Zenger was born in Germany. In 1710, when he was 13 years old, he sailed to New York with his family. In New York, Zenger was indentured to a printer for eight years. Zenger opened his own printing business in 1726.

Zenger created a newspaper called the *New York Weekly Journal* in 1733. He printed articles criticizing Governor William Cosby. Cosby had Zenger arrested for libel. Libel is printing false statements that hurt someone's reputation.

Andrew Hamilton was Zenger's lawyer. He argued that the information in the articles was true, so Zenger was not guilty of libel.

"No nation . . . ever lost the liberty of freely speaking, writing, or publishing [without losing] their liberty in general."

The jury agreed, and Zenger was set free. His case helped create freedom of the press in America. Americans have the right to report news without fear of punishment.

Write About It! How did Zenger's case help printers and publishers?

LOG ON For more biographies, visit: www.macmillanmh.com

The Life of John Peter Zenger

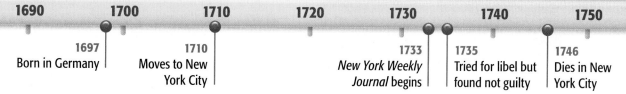

1690	1700	1710	1720	1730	1740	1750
1697 Born in Germany		**1710** Moves to New York City		**1733** *New York Weekly Journal* begins	**1735** Tried for libel but found not guilty	**1746** Dies in New York City

Philipsburg Manor

Philipsburg Manor, in the Hudson River Valley, was owned by Frederick Philipse, the richest man in the New York colony in the 1700s. Today, you can visit and experience life on a working manor in the early days of New York.

Philipsburg Manor

① Festivals ▼

Pinkster Day is an annual festival. Originally, African workers celebrated spring on this day.

ACTIVITY

Use the map to write directions for a walk through Philipsburg Manor. Be sure to include each of the four sites shown on these pages.

2 The Grist Mill ▲

The mill at the manor was powered by water turning the mill-wheel.

3 The Manor House ▼

The bridge across the mill stream leads to the barns, workshops, and the stone manor house.

4 The Herb Garden ▼

Today volunteers do the daily tasks of life on the Philipsburg Manor. This woman weeds the herb garden.

LOG ON For virtual field trips, visit: www.macmillanmh.com

113

Life in New York Colony

How did people live in colonial New York?

VOCABULARY

ally
Triangle Trade
market economy

VOCABULARY STRATEGY

Word Origins An **ally** is a friend. The word comes from a word that means "friend" or "helper." What do you think an **alliance** is?

READING STRATEGY

Compare and Contrast
Use the diagram below to compare farm and city life in colonial New York.

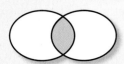

NEW YORK STANDARDS

1.1, 1.2, 1.3
3.1, 4.1

Not everyone who started a new life in the North American colonies found happiness. For most immigrants, life in the New York colony was very hard work. Many were disappointed with what they found. Gottlieb Mittelberger, a school teacher from Germany, was disappointed with his new life:

> " *Work and labor in this new and wild land are very hard. . . . Work mostly consists in cutting wood, felling oak-tree, rooting out, or as they say there, clearing large tracts of forest.* "

1680	1700	1720	1740	1760

1677
French settlers arrive in New York

1710
Germans settle along the Hudson River

1712
Uprising ends in defeat for enslaved Africans

1741
Enslaved Africans blamed for New York City fire

1763
Britain wins the French and Indian War

Ⓐ A Royal Colony

When the British took over New York colony, they wanted colonists to follow their laws. However, the British government still kept many of the original Dutch traditions.

A steady stream of settlers came from Europe to New York. Many came looking for a place to practice their religious beliefs in peace. They came to New York because of its tradition of tolerance. In 1677 a group of French settlers arrived and set up communities, such as New Paltz, in the Hudson River Valley. Around 1710 many Germans began coming to New York and they also settled along the Hudson River Valley.

▼ A colonial farmer used oxen to pull a wooden plow before planting crops.

The British ruler, Queen Anne, sent many of these new settlers to the colonies. She sympathized with their religious beliefs, and she hoped they would set up industries to help the British navy. The navy plan failed, but the settlers stayed and started farms and villages.

Looking for Land

One problem the new settlers faced was trying to find available land. The patroon system tied up large areas of the Hudson River Valley. New settlers could not settle on land in western New York because it belonged to the Iroquois League. The Iroquois were **allies**, or friends, of the British. The British had signed a treaty with the Iroquois protecting their lands from European settlement.

Some settlers moved to Pennsylvania or New Jersey, where land was easier to buy. In spite of this, the population of New York continued to increase during the 1700s.

✓ **QUICK CHECK** How did life change for Europeans who settled in New York?
Compare and Contrast

115

B Going to Work

New York City and Albany were busy port cities. Most colonists lived in these two cities. However, smaller towns and villages grew up all along the river. Farmers sold their crops in the larger towns where they also bought goods they needed for their farms.

Enslaved Workers

Life did not improve for one group of colonists, enslaved Africans. Some New York merchants grew wealthy through the slave trade. The slave trade ran from Africa to the islands in the Caribbean Sea and then to the American colonies. This created a triangle. This trade is sometimes called the **Triangle Trade**.

Most of these enslaved workers lived in Albany and New York City. New York had one of the largest enslaved populations in the colonies.

New York slaveholders worried that enslaved Africans might fight for their freedom. In 1712 a group of Africans did fight. They burned houses and attacked white colonists in New York City. Soldiers put down the revolt and the leaders were executed.

In 1741 a mysterious fire destroyed several official buildings in Manhattan. Enslaved Africans had nothing to do with the fire. They were blamed anyway, and many were executed.

European Settlement in New York Colony, 1775

CANADA

St. Lawrence River

Lake Ontario

Lake Erie

Mohawk River

Glen Falls • Salem
German Flats • Cambridge
Canajoharie • Albany

Kingston • Germantown
New Paltz
Newburgh CT
Minisink

Hudson River

Long Island Sound

PA

New York City

Southampton
Long Island

ATLANTIC OCEAN

N E W S

0   50   100 miles
0   50   100 kilometers

■ European settlements
— New York Colony boundary
— Present-day boundary

MAP Skill **Movement** Along which New York rivers were most settlements built?

This reenactor works in a New York museum shop as an enslaved African would have done in the 1700s. ▼

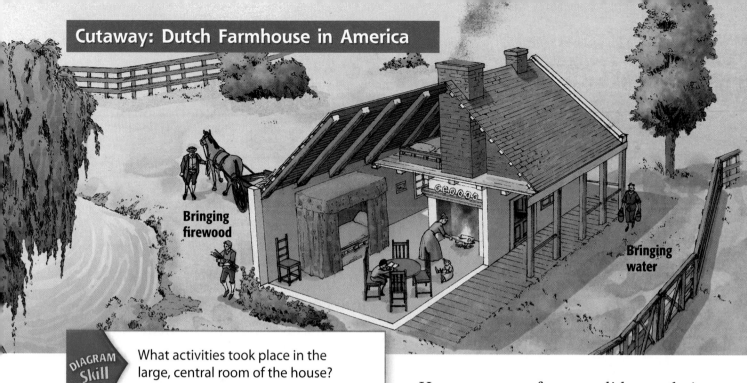

Cutaway: Dutch Farmhouse in America

Bringing firewood

Bringing water

DIAGRAM Skill What activities took place in the large, central room of the house?

Family Work

Everyone worked in colonial New York, even children. Many products that we buy in stores today had to be made by hand in the home during the colonial period. Colonists even had to make their own candles and soap.

Some families owned small shops, such as printing shops, bake shops, or woodworking shops. Sundays were the only time when colonists did not work. On Sundays most colonists went to church. Afterward they would spend time together as families.

Farm Life

Many families did not own shops, or even their own land. They were tenant farmers, who worked on land owned by someone else. New York's patroon system employed many tenant families. These families were often very poor.

However, some farmers did own their land. They had to clear the land before they could farm it. Other colonists bought land close to colonial settlements from Native American peoples.

City Life

Towns grew as more crops and more goods were produced. Look at the map on page 116 to see where people lived. People went to the towns to sell their crops and to buy what they needed. This is called a **market economy**, an economy in which people decide for themselves what to sell or buy.

In the 1700s the British government introduced laws that took away many rights that women, the enslaved, and children had had under the Dutch. For example women were no longer allowed to own property.

QUICK CHECK Why did many settlers become tenant farmers?
Make Inferences

117

Then and Now

New Paltz

THEN New Paltz, New York, was founded in 1677. Some of the stone houses built by the original settlers are still in use in the town today. You can see how the first settlers in this Hudson River town lived.

NOW Today New Paltz includes a National Historic District. The town of New Paltz is a busy center of shops and offices. There is also a state university at New Paltz.

Write About It! How is New Paltz today the same as the original settlement? How is it different?

● Trouble with France

France and Great Britain fought four wars in North America during the 1700s. French armies from eastern Canada and their Native American allies had invaded New York several times and burned farms and villages.

New France had fewer colonists than the British colonies, but it did have a strong French army. The French moved into northern New York and built a fort on Lake Champlain, near present-day Ticonderoga. This powerful fort was a threat because it could cut off communication by land between the New England colonies and the British colonies to the south.

The French and Indian War

The final war in this British-French contest was called the French and Indian War, which began in 1754. At first the war went well for France. British general Edward Braddock was defeated and killed near what is now Pittsburgh, Pennsylvania, in 1755. In 1756 the French captured Fort William Henry near Lake George, New York.

However, in 1759 Quebec was captured. The French lost their colony in Canada forever. The French were no longer able to threaten the British colonies in North America. Colonial soldiers had fought well and gained skills in the war. The world of the 13 colonies had changed by the time the peace treaty was signed in 1763.

This war had been expensive. The British government badly needed money. It decided to raise taxes in the colonies. They had fought the war to protect the colonies, so the colonists should pay part of the costs. This decision would be a main cause of the American Revolution.

QUICK CHECK How did the war affect feelings between the colonies and Great Britain? *Cause and Effect*

The flag of Great Britain combined the flags of England and Scotland. ▼

What You Learned

A The royal colony of New York continued to attract settlers from many European countries.

B Merchants, enslaved people, and farmers from many countries helped to create a strong economy in New York.

C The French and British fought four wars in North America, ending with the French defeat in the French and Indian War.

Focus Lesson Review

1. **Focus Question** How did people live in colonial New York?

2. **Vocabulary** Write a paragraph about colonial life in New York using the following terms.
   ally
   market economy
   Triangle Trade

3. **Geography** Why were major settlements in New York first formed near major rivers?

4. **Critical Thinking Problem Solving** Why did the British allow New Netherland colonists to keep many of their laws?

5. **Reading Strategy Compare and Contrast** Compare and contrast your life with that of a child in colonial New York.

6. **Write About THE BIG IDEA** Suppose you are a new settler in New York in 1750. Write a paragraph about your first day in the new colony.

7. **Reading Primary Sources** An Albany citizen in the 1760s described her town, " . . . *at evening the herd returned altogether . . . along the wide and grassy street.*" How have New York towns changed since the late 1600s? Write a paragraph describing the change.

The LIBRARY *of* CONGRESS

VOCABULARY

map

Understand Historical Maps

A **map** is a kind of picture of Earth. A map can be a primary source. By studying historical maps, you can learn what people in the past knew about their world. For example, a European map of the world before 1492 would not have shown the Americas because Europeans did not know the two continents existed.

Looking at Historical Maps

Historians study maps and charts to learn about people in the past. The map on page 121 has clues to help you learn more about Dutch New York.

1 Learn It

Read the steps below. They will help you to find information on maps.

■ Read the title of the map. What does the title tell you about the information on the map?

■ Study the map for clues. What information looks familiar, or like a modern map?

■ Try to understand what the map designers wanted to tell their readers about their world.

2 Try It

■ Look at the map on page 121. Read the title. *Novi Belgii* means "New Netherland."

■ Look at the map of North America on page A10. What landforms do you recognize?

■ Is New Netherland larger or smaller than the state of New York today?

■ What do the pictures on the map tell you?

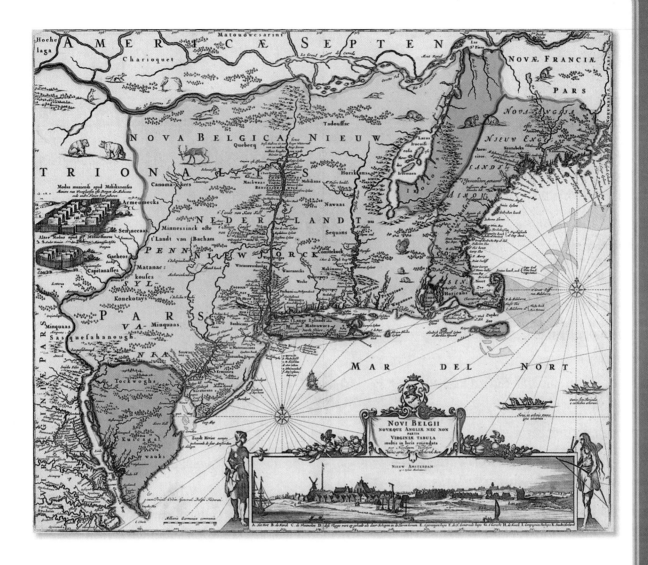

3 Apply It

- Draw or trace the outline of New York State on a sheet of paper.

- Draw and label landforms.

- Label the Iroquois and Algonquian lands.

- Label Fort Orange and New Amsterdam.

- Give your map a title.

Chapter 4 Review

FOCUS ## Vocabulary Review

Copy the sentences below on a separate sheet of paper. Use the list of vocabulary terms to fill in the blanks.

ally	surplus
packet boat	tax

1. A _____ is money citizens pay to support public services.

2. To have more than enough of something is to have a _____.

3. A _____ is a ship that carried mail and other cargo.

4. A friend or partner is called an _____.

5. **Test Preparation** A _____ is a group of government officials that makes laws.

   (A) **legislature**   (C) **slavery**
   (B) **market economy**   (D) **manor**

FOCUS ## Comprehension Check

6. Why was New Netherland renamed New York?

7. What brought colonists to the New York colony?

8. What country did Great Britain defeat in the 1700s?

9. Why was New York City one of the largest cities in the British colonies during the 1700s?

10. How were farm life and city life the same and different in New York colony?

11. **Critical Thinking** In what way did the end of the French and Indian War lead to the American Revolution?

12. **Critical Thinking** Why do you think Iroquois leaders might have sided with the British during and after the French and Indian War?

FOCUS ## Use the Time Line

Use the time line below to answer each question.

13. How many years after the French and Indian War began did the war end?

14. Was John Peter Zenger tried before or after the New York Assembly was first chosen?

1680	1700	1720	1740	1760
1683 New York Assembly chosen for the first time	1707 England and Scotland join to form Great Britain	1735 John Peter Zenger is tried in New York court	1754 The French and Indian War begins in North America	1763 French and Indian War ends

Historical Maps

Write a complete sentence to answer each question.

15. What colony is east of New Netherland?

16. What colony is south of New Netherland?

17. What clues might make you think this map was made while New Netherland was a Dutch colony?

18. What kinds of information can historians learn from old maps?

CRQ

Constructed Response Questions

Read the document and answer the questions that follow.

> 66 *The carters were driving in every direction; and the sailors and laborers upon the wharfs [docks] . . . were moving their [heavy loads] from place to place. Everything was in motion; all was life, bustle, and activity.* 99

19. What kinds of activities are described?

20. What do you think the writer is describing?

21. **Make a Monument** Work in small groups to design a monument that will show the importance of the trial of John Peter Zenger. Think about what your monument will show. Write a paragraph that could be put on your monument to explain its importance to viewers.

22. **Persuasive** Suppose you are a New York colonist sent to talk to Native Americans about becoming allies of the British. Write a speech in which you explain why they should join the British.

LOG ON For help with the process of writing, visit: www.macmillanmh.com

Unit 2 Review and Test Prep

Comprehension and Critical Thinking Check

Write one or more sentences to answer each question.

1. If a **Northwest Passage** had been found, how would it have helped Europeans?

2. What made New Netherland a **colony**?

3. Why were **investors** important to the Dutch West India Company?

4. What did colonial New York farmers do with their **surplus** crops?

5. Why did New Yorkers demand a **legislature**?

6. What kinds of products did New York colonists **import**?

7. Why did Great Britain want to **tax** the American colonies after 1763?

8. What does it mean to say that colonial New York had a **market economy**?

9. **Critical Thinking** How did a policy of **tolerance** help New Netherland?

10. **Critical Thinking** Compare and contrast the life of an **indentured servant** with the life of an enslaved African.

Reading Skills Check

Summarize

Copy this graphic organizer. Reread "John Peter Zenger" on page 111. Use the graphic organizer to summarize this reading selection. Then answer the questions.

11. What did you look for to summarize the passage?

12. Would you include the statement, "his case helped create freedom of the press in America" in your summary? Why or why not?

13. What is a summary?

1.	1.
2.	2.
3.	3.
4.	4.

Base your answers to questions 14 and 15 on the graph below.

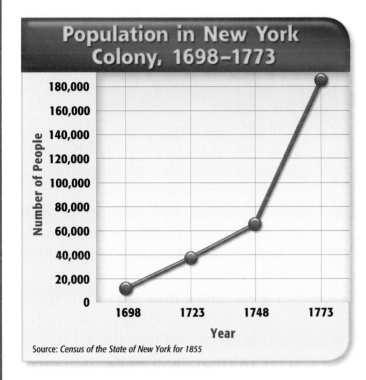

Population in New York Colony, 1698–1773

Number of People

180,000
160,000
140,000
120,000
100,000
80,000
60,000
40,000
20,000
0

1698   1723   1748   1773

Year

Source: *Census of the State of New York for 1855*

14. What was the approximate population of New York colony in 1750?

(A) 38,000

(B) 58,000

(C) 65,000

(D) 100,000

15. Between which years did the population of New York colony increase most rapidly?

(A) 1698–1723

(B) 1723–1748

(C) 1748–1773

(D) 1698–1748

Write About History

16. Letter Write a letter as if you are an indentured servant. In your letter to your family, explain your situation, the kind of work you do, and your hopes for the future.

17. Expository Write a short essay explaining some of the Dutch traditions from New Netherland that became important parts of the American government.

18. Summary Think about the importance of the French and Indian War. Write a one paragraph summary of the causes of the war. Then write a one paragraph summary of the results of the war.

LOG ON For help with the process of writing, visit: www.macmillanmh.com

What happens when different peoples first meet?

Write About the Big Idea

Narrative Essay

Think about what happened as Europeans began to meet the native peoples in New York. Then complete the graphic organizer. Add details about how each new group that came to New York affected the Native Americans.

Use your graphic organizer below to help you write a narrative essay. In your narrative tell a story of what happened when European explorers and settlers met the Native Americans who lived in New York.

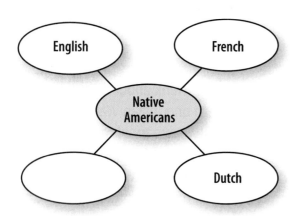

Write a Narrative Essay

- Writing a narrative essay takes planning. Review the following steps to help you.

1. Plan

- To begin you need to decide what your topic is. Here the topic has already been assigned.
- Next develop a plan. Your narrative should relate the main ideas you are describing. It should also provide a background to these events. Details are also important. In telling the story of these events, you should show the reader why these events are worth remembering.

2. Write a First Draft

- Decide on the main ideas that your readers need to know and write background information about them.
- List details you would like to include in your narrative.
- State why you think these events are worth remembering while writing your narrative.

3. Revise and Proofread

- Read your narrative essay and be sure you included the main ideas.
- Be sure you included details.
- Proofread your essay, fixing any errors and checking spelling, capitalization, and punctuation.
- Rewrite your essay neatly before you give it to your teacher.

ACTIVITY

Speak About the Big Idea

An Interview

Recall the people you read about in Unit 2. Create an interview. For example, you might interview a Native American about life before and after the arrival of the Europeans.

Prepare Work in pairs. One person will be interviewed. The other will conduct the interview. Prepare a list of questions and answers. Gather information from your textbook and other research. Practice your interview.

Present The interviewer should introduce his or her guest. Then partners should take two or three minutes to act out their interviews for the rest of the class.

Allow time for your classmates to ask questions. Ask classmates to summarize what they heard.

LAUNCH PAD For help with the Big Idea activity, visit: www.macmillanmh.com

Read More About the Big Idea

Colonial Times: 1600–1700

by Joy Masoff Learn about life in colonial America, illustrated with photographs of re-enactors. There are even colonial crafts you can try at home.

Life in New Amsterdam

by Laura Fischer A description of the arrival of the Dutch in New Amsterdam with maps, pictures and diagrams, with a list of other books about the Dutch colony.

The New York Colony

by Dennis B. Fradin Traces the history of the colony beginning with Native Americans and continuing until New York became the eleventh state. Includes biographies of Hiawatha, Peter Minuit, and Captain Kidd.

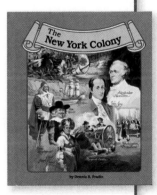

Unit 3

A Time of Change

The Revolution was in the minds and hearts of the people . . . This radical change in the principles, opinion, sentiments, and affections of the people, was the real American Revolution.

— John Adams, Second American President

◄ Cannons on the walls of Fort Ticonderoga, New York

EXPLORE
THE BIG IDEA

Why do people take risks?

In Unit 3, you will read about how the colony of New York became New York State. You will also find out about the risks people took to make this happen.

As you read the chapters in this unit, look for the kinds of risks people were willing to take in order to help New York become a state. Identify reasons why these people or groups took these risks.

Copy and complete the graphic organizer below as you read the unit. Think about the events that changed New York from a colony into a state. Complete the graphic organizer. The first one has been started for you.

New Settlers	American Soldiers	Native Americans
1. wanted land	1.	1.
2. wanted a new start	2.	2.
3.	3.	3.
4.	4.	4.

People Who Made a Difference

Joseph Brant
about 1742–1807

Joseph Brant was a Mohawk chief whose Iroquois forces helped the British in the American Revolution. (page 151)

Mary Jemison
about 1743–1833

Mary Jemison was a white woman who was captured by Shawnee during a raid. She was raised by a Seneca family and chose to live her life according to Native American traditions. (page 174)

1750   1770   1790

1758
Mary Jemison is captured by Shawnee

1775
Joseph Brant leads the Mohawk to join the British

LOG ON For more biographies, visit: www.macmillanmh.com

Washington Irving
1783–1859

Washington Irving wrote the popular short stories "Rip Van Winkle" and "The Legend of Sleepy Hollow" set in New York's Hudson Valley. He has been called "The Father of the American Short Story." (page 190)

Peter Cooper
1791–1883

Peter Cooper was an inventor and manufacturer who built the first American locomotive. He also built the Cooper Union to educate working people. (page 185)

1810   1830   1850

1797
Mary Jemison attends the meeting at Big Tree

1819
Washington Irving writes "Rip Van Winkle"

1830
Peter Cooper starts railroad in Maryland

The Arrow over the Door

Selection from **The Arrow over the Door** by **Joseph Bruchac**

Samuel Russell belongs to the Society of Friends, or Quakers. The Friends are neutral; they will not take sides in a war. However, the American Revolution is coming to Saratoga, New York, and young Samuel sees signs of war all around him.

Things were so confused now, in the summer of 1777. Samuel knew there were some families besides the Friends who were neutral. Yet at times it seemed as if everyone was at war with everyone else. Some neighbors were Loyalists and said they would fight to defend King George. The Patriots said they would fight for freedom from the king. Only a few seasons ago those people had been friends. Now they were ready to kill each other, even their blood relatives. They called each other Tories,

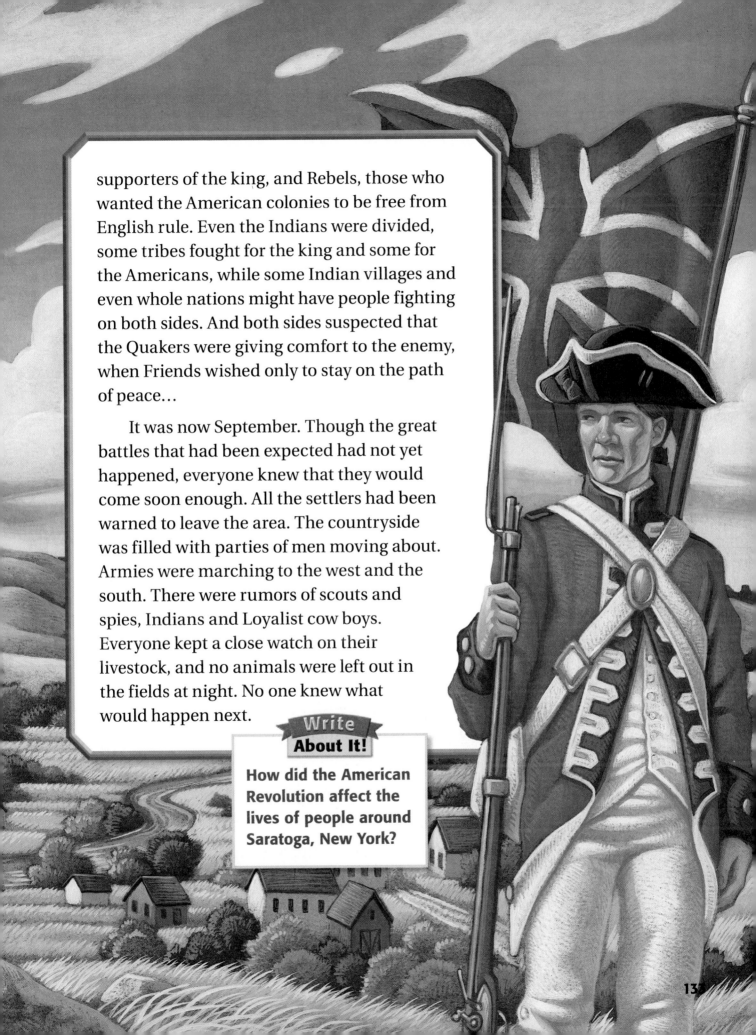

supporters of the king, and Rebels, those who wanted the American colonies to be free from English rule. Even the Indians were divided, some tribes fought for the king and some for the Americans, while some Indian villages and even whole nations might have people fighting on both sides. And both sides suspected that the Quakers were giving comfort to the enemy, when Friends wished only to stay on the path of peace…

It was now September. Though the great battles that had been expected had not yet happened, everyone knew that they would come soon enough. All the settlers had been warned to leave the area. The countryside was filled with parties of men moving about. Armies were marching to the west and the south. There were rumors of scouts and spies, Indians and Loyalist cow boys. Everyone kept a close watch on their livestock, and no animals were left out in the fields at night. No one knew what would happen next.

Write About It!

How did the American Revolution affect the lives of people around Saratoga, New York?

Sequence Events:
War in New York

In this unit, you will read about important events before and during the American Revolution in New York. When you read, think about the order in which these events happened. This order is called the sequence of events. Sequencing events will help you understand and remember what you read.

 Learn It

- Look for clue words such as *first, next, then, after, finally,* and *last.* These words show the order of events.

- Look for dates that tell you exactly when things happened. These are also clue words.

- Now, read the paragraph below. Look for the sequence of events.

Clue Words
These words give clues about the sequence of events.

Events
These tell about the events in the paragraph.

After the French and Indian War, the British government needed money to pay for its army in North America. In 1765, the British government issued the Stamp Act placing taxes on items such as newspapers in the colonies. Then a few years later the British put taxes on more items including tea. After these new taxes in 1773 some colonists dumped 342 boxes of tea into Boston Harbor in an event now called the Boston Tea Party. The last tea party happened in New York City when in 1774 angry Patriots dumped tea into New York Harbor.

 **Try It**

Copy and complete the chart below. Fill in the chart by recording the events in the paragraph on page 134 in the correct sequence.

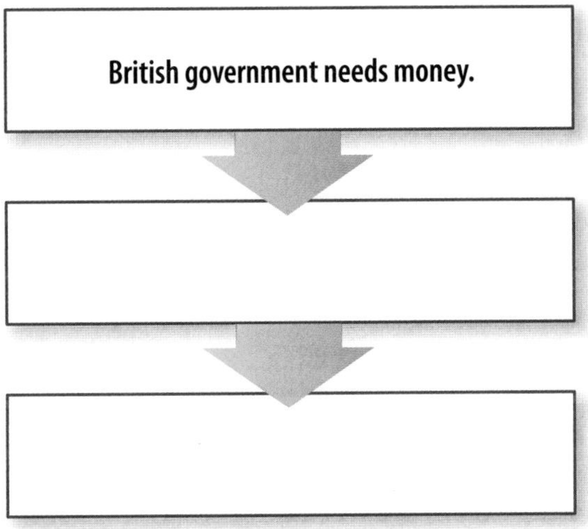

British government needs money.

⬇

⬇

How did you figure out the sequence of events?

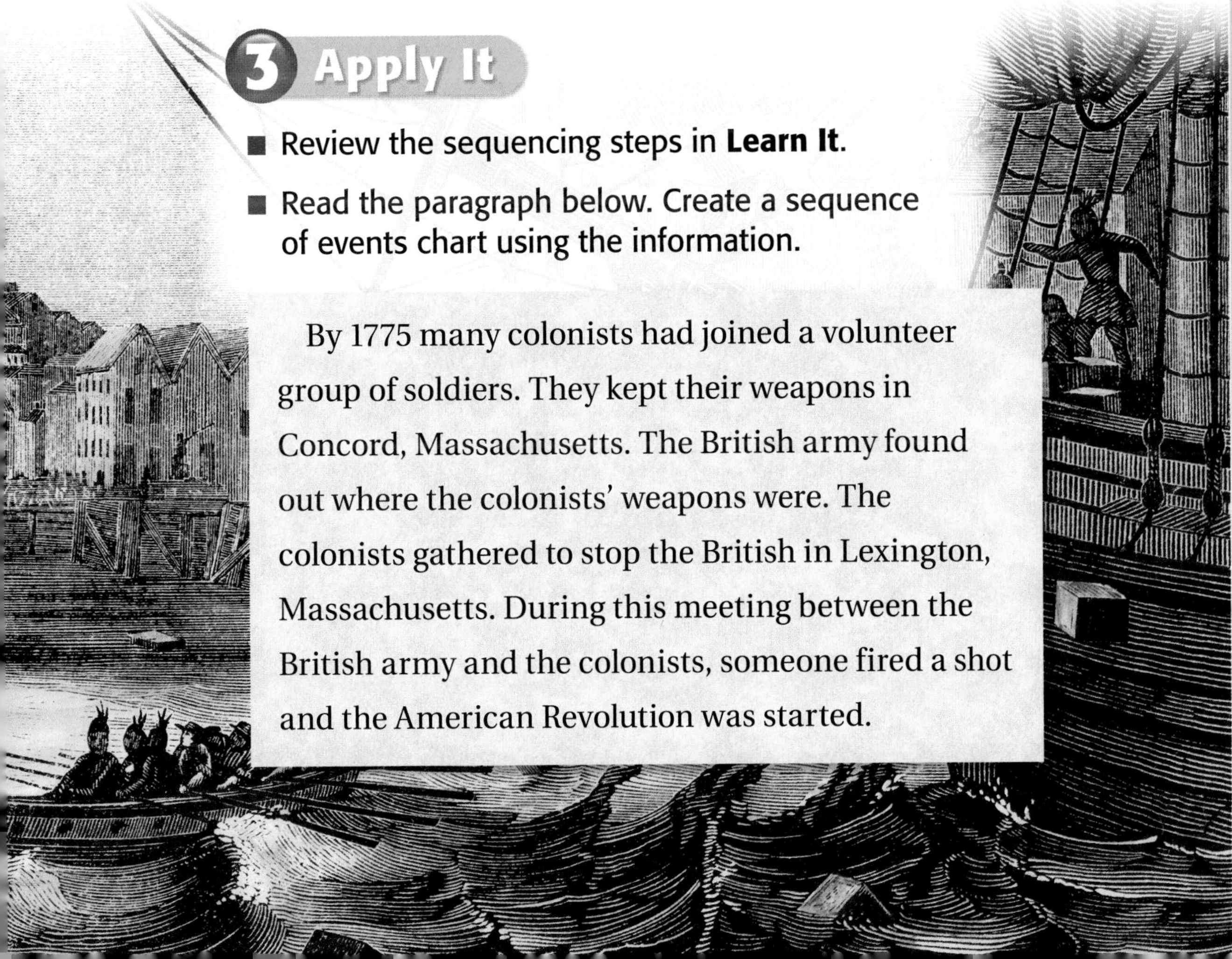

3 Apply It

■ Review the sequencing steps in **Learn It**.

■ Read the paragraph below. Create a sequence of events chart using the information.

By 1775 many colonists had joined a volunteer group of soldiers. They kept their weapons in Concord, Massachusetts. The British army found out where the colonists' weapons were. The colonists gathered to stop the British in Lexington, Massachusetts. During this meeting between the British army and the colonists, someone fired a shot and the American Revolution was started.

Chapter 5

The American Revolution

You Are There

During the summer of 1776, representatives from each colony signed the Declaration of Independence. The new nation had to fight for the freedom it had declared. At first, things did not go well for the American army. John Jay, a New York leader, wrote to the soldiers under George Washington's command:

"If success crown your efforts, all the blessings of Freedom will be your reward."

A Continental soldier ▶

Chapter Events   1750   1760

1
1755
The British capture Fort Ticonderoga during the French and Indian War

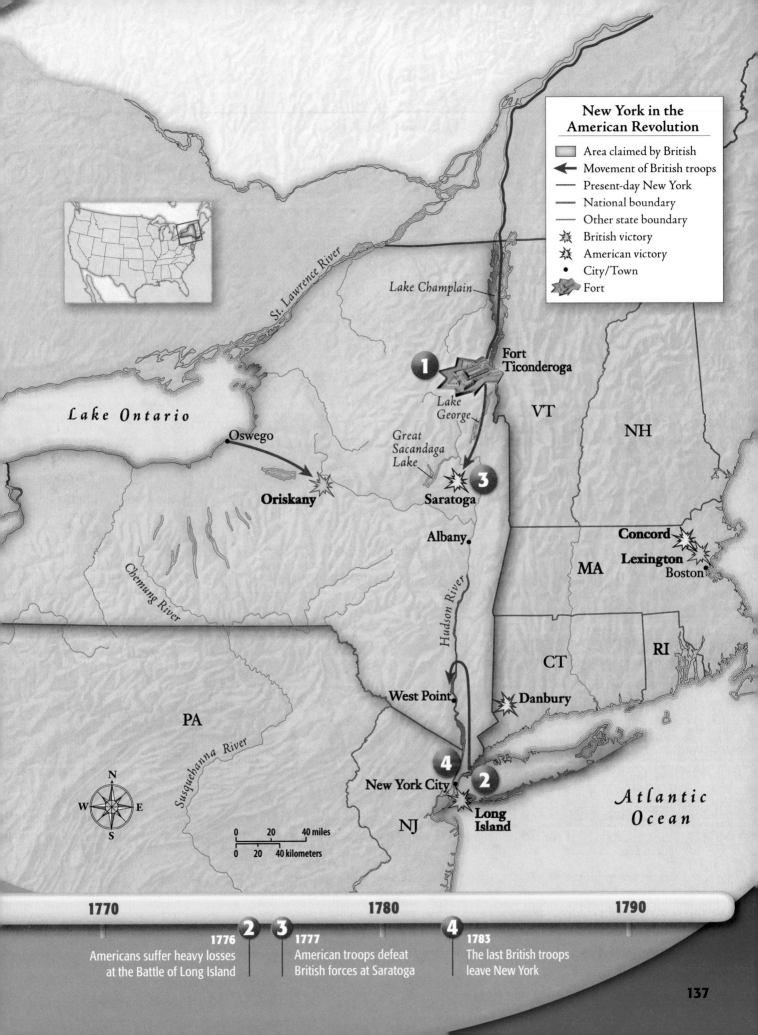

New York in the American Revolution

- Area claimed by British
- → Movement of British troops
- —— Present-day New York
- —— National boundary
- —— Other state boundary
- ✶ British victory
- ✶ American victory
- • City/Town
- 🏰 Fort

St. Lawrence River

Lake Champlain

Lake Ontario

1 Fort Ticonderoga

Lake George

Oswego

Oriskany

Great Sacandaga Lake

3 **Saratoga**

VT

NH

Albany

Concord
Lexington
Boston

MA

Chemung River

Hudson River

RI

CT

West Point

✶ **Danbury**

PA

Susquehanna River

4
New York City

2

NJ

Long Island

Atlantic Ocean

N W E S

0 20 40 miles
0 20 40 kilometers

1770   1780   1790

2 **1776** Americans suffer heavy losses at the Battle of Long Island

3 **1777** American troops defeat British forces at Saratoga

4 **1783** The last British troops leave New York

Why did American colonists declare independence from Great Britain?

VOCABULARY

Stamp Act
Patriot
Loyalist
militia
revolution
delegate
Continental Congress

VOCABULARY STRATEGY

Suffixes The suffix **–ist** means "one who is or does." **Loyalist** means "one who is loyal." What other words use **-ist**?

READING STRATEGY

Sequence Events Use the chart below to list the order of events that caused the American Revolution.

NEW YORK STANDARDS

1.1, 1.2, 1.3, 1.4, 5.1, 4.1

Trouble in the Colonies

Canassatego, an Iroquois, advised British colonists to work together if they hoped to be strong and to earn respect. He told them about the experience of the Iroquois League.

> *Our wise forefathers established Union and Amity [friendship] between the Five Nations. This had made us formidable [strong]; this has given us great Weight and Authority with our neighboring Nations . . . never fall out with one another.*

Sir William Johnson awards medals to Iroquois leaders at his home in upstate New York in 1772. ▼

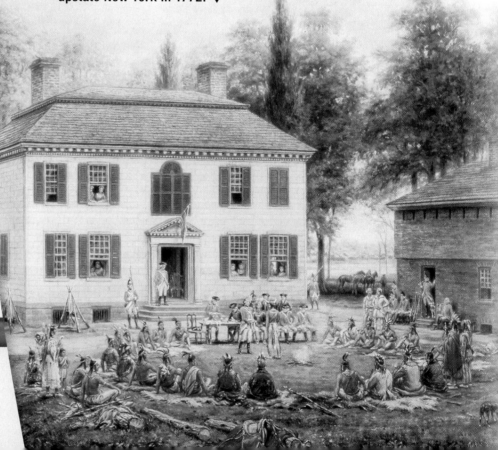

1750	1760	1770	1780

1754
French and Indian War begins

1765
British pass the Stamp Act

1773
Boston Tea Party occurs

A The French and Indian War

For more than 70 years France and Great Britain, with their Native American supporters, battled for control of North America. Chapter 3 told how the French explorer Samuel Champlain helped the Algonquians against the Iroquois. This made the Algonquians friends of the French, but it made the Iroquois their enemy. They sided with the British.

In 1754, British colonists met with the Iroquois League to strengthen their relationship. Colonists, like Benjamin Franklin, were influenced by the Iroquois system of government.

The French and Indian War also began in 1754. British settlers outnumbered the French in North America, but as you have read, the French had a powerful and well-trained army.

British Victory

Many of the battles of the French and Indian War were fought in the New York colony. Sir William Johnson led the British to victory at the Battle of Lake George in 1755. Victories at Fort Niagara and Fort Ticonderoga followed.

British and colonial forces surprised the French at Quebec in 1759.

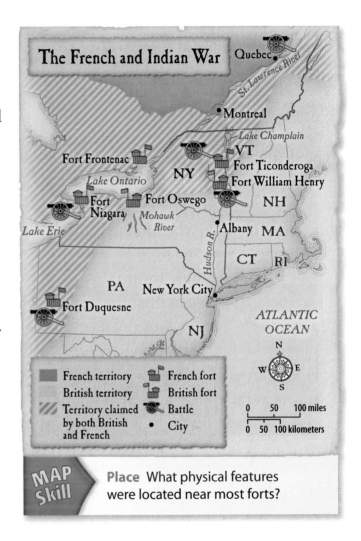

MAP Skill **Place** What physical features were located near most forts?

Soldiers scrambled silently up cliffs that the French thought were impossible to climb. A year later the British also captured Montreal. In 1763, the Treaty of Paris gave the British control of all of French Canada. Great Britain had won the war and much of eastern North America.

✓ **QUICK CHECK** What events led to Britain's control of eastern North America?
Sequence Events

139

B More Troubles in New York

By the time of the French and Indian War, some British settlers had crossed the Appalachian Mountains and tried to settle there. These lands to the west were home to Native Americans, and they were prepared to fight for them.

The British government supported the Native American claims. Great Britain created a boundary line along the Mohawk and Hudson rivers, roughly following the line of the Appalachian Mountains. The lands to the west of this line belonged to the Native Americans. Colonists who had settled there were forced to move out.

This boundary line angered many colonists. They believed they had a right to land they had helped win from France. They thought Britain should be supporting them, not the Native Americans.

▲ A stamp issued under the Stamp Act

New Yorkers pull down the statue of King George III in 1776. ▼

Colonists Grow Angry

Other issues increased the colonists' anger. The French and Indian War was expensive, and Britain needed money to pay these costs. Britain also needed to pay the soldiers who continued to protect the colonies in America. The British thought the colonists ought to pay part of these costs. In 1765 the British government passed the **Stamp Act**, a law that placed a tax on paper sold in the colonies.

As you read in Chapter 4, citizens of the colonies could not vote for members of the British Parliament. Some colonists refused to pay taxes if they could not vote in these elections. These colonists were called **Patriots**. Those who remained loyal to Britain were called **Loyalists**. Ben Franklin, an early Patriot, warned the Loyalists, "Any society that would give up a little liberty to gain a little security will deserve neither and lose both."

Two Tea Parties

Because of the protests, Parliament ended the Stamp Tax, but it still tried to collect taxes on manufactured goods, such as glass and paint. Finally, Parliament passed a special tax on tea. On December 16, 1773, Patriots in Boston boarded British ships and dumped 342 chests of tea into Boston Harbor. This protest became known as the Boston Tea Party. In 1774, Patriots in New York had a "tea party" of their own. They dumped chests of tea into New York Harbor.

As anger with Britain grew, local towns organized groups of citizens who would fight to defend their communities. These citizen armies, or **militias**, included farmers, business owners, and both free and enslaved African Americans.

On April 19, 1775, Patriots in Massachusetts heard of a British plan to seize colonial military supplies in Concord. Local militia fired on the British troops. The **revolution**, or the colonists' fight for freedom, had begun!

Choosing Freedom

Patriots in the thirteen colonies sent **delegates**, people chosen to represent a group, to Philadelphia, Pennsylvania. The group became known as the **Continental Congress**. They met first in September of 1774.

During the second meeting of the Continental Congress, the delegates

PRIMARY SOURCES

From the
Declaration of Independence,
by Thomas Jefferson and other delegates to the Continental Congress, July 1776

"*We hold these truths to be self evident, that all men are created equal, that they are endowed by their Creator with certain unalienable [permanent] Rights, that among these are Life, Liberty and the pursuit of Happiness.*"

Write About It! What rights did the delegates believe they had?

voted to break away from Great Britain. Thomas Jefferson, a delegate from Virginia, wrote the Declaration of Independence to explain the colonists' decision to become independent.

QUICK CHECK Why did Patriots dump tea into harbors? *Make Inferences*

C Birth of a Country

The Declaration of Independence was approved by the Continental Congress on July 4, 1776. By early 1777 all 56 delegates, including four New Yorkers, had signed the Declaration of Independence. These signers faced very real danger. The British would surely imprison or hang them if they won the war because they were no longer loyal to the British king.

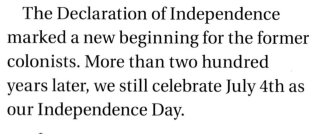

An inkwell from the 1700s ▶

The Declaration of Independence marked a new beginning for the former colonists. More than two hundred years later, we still celebrate July 4th as our Independence Day.

✔ **QUICK CHECK** Why do you think it might have taken so long to get everyone to sign the Declaration? *Draw Conclusions*

What You Learned

A Great Britain's victory in the French and Indian War gave them control of North America.

B After the French and Indian War, Great Britain passed laws that limited settlement and demanded new taxes.

C The Declaration of Independence marked the birth of the New United States.

★ Focus Lesson Review

1. **Focus Question** Why did American colonists declare independence from Great Britain?

2. **Vocabulary** Write about the beginning of the American Revolution using the following vocabulary terms.

delegate	Patriot
Continental Congress	revolution
Loyalist	Stamp Act
militia	

3. **Government** Why did the colonists oppose the new laws passed by Parliament?

4. **Critical Thinking Problem Solving** Why did Great Britain make a boundary along the Mohawk and Hudson rivers?

5. **Reading Strategy Sequence Events** Use the chart to list the order of events leading to the Declaration of Independence.

6. **Write About THE BIG IDEA** Write about the signers of the Declaration of Independence. Why would they risk their lives to sign?

7. **Reading Primary Sources** *"We have always protected the Americans; we may, therefore, subject them to [make them obey] government."* – Samuel Johnson

   How do you think this Englishman felt about the events in this lesson?

Being Informed

Students at a school in Edmeston, near Oneonta, became aware of the problems facing monarch butterflies in Mexico. The students learned that the forests where these butterflies spend the winter are being cut down. Some students wrote letters to the Mexican government. Other students raised money to plant trees.

Read these steps to learn how to become informed.

Build Citizenship

1. **Pick a subject** or an issue that interests you. Make a list of what you already know and what you need to know to understand it.

2. **Identify sources** of information Look for books, newspaper articles, or other sources of information on the topic.

3. **Examine the information** you have gathered.

4. **Apply your knowledge.** Look for ways to share what you have learned.

Think About It

1. What was the issue that interested the students?

2. What are some of the things that students did to help?

3. How did students help others become informed?

4. List some needs in your community.

Write About It!

Pick an issue in your school or community. Explain why you would like to learn more about this issue and list three ways you could become informed.

Fighting in New York

How did the American Revolution affect New York State?

VOCABULARY

retreat
surrender

VOCABULARY STRATEGY

Multiple Meanings
Surrender and **retreat** are words which can be nouns or verbs. You need to read a sentence carefully to know how the word is being used. What other words may be used as nouns or verbs?

READING STRATEGY

Identify Main Idea and Details Use the graphic organizer to show what groups of people supported the Patriot cause.

NEW YORK STANDARDS

1.1, 1.3, 2.2, 3.1, 5.1

It is July 9, 1776, and you are with the Patriot army in New York City. General George Washington sends the following message to the troops. How do you think his words make the soldiers feel?

> " *The General hopes and trusts that every officer and man will endeavor [try] to live and act as becomes a . . . soldier defending the dearest rights and liberties of his country.* "

George Washington directs the escape from Brooklyn during the night. ▼

1774
New Yorkers dump tea
into New York harbor

1776
American soldiers lose the
Battle of Long Island;
Americans leave New York City

1777
Sybil Ludington
rides to warn
the militia

Ⓐ The American Revolution

In 1775 George Washington, a colonel in the Virginia militia, was named Commander in Chief of the Continental army. Washington soon realized that New York would be the key to the fighting. The state lay between colonies in the north and south. If the British captured New York, they could split the young nation in two. Also, New York City's fine harbor would be important to the British for safely unloading troops and supplies.

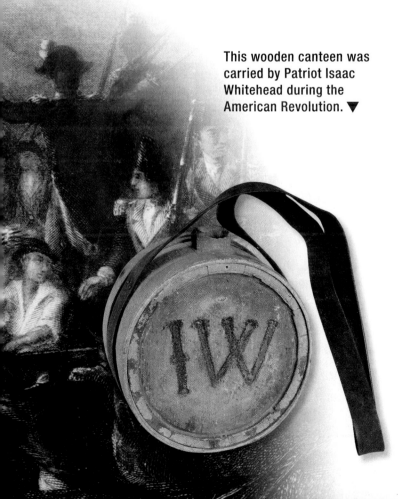

This wooden canteen was carried by Patriot Isaac Whitehead during the American Revolution. ▼

An Important Location

In battle after battle, the British forced the Americans to **retreat**, or give up ground. On August 27, 1776, the Americans lost the Battle of Long Island. Washington's army was trapped in Brooklyn with its back to the East River. The British expected Washington to **surrender**, or give up.

The night of August 29 was very foggy. Fishermen from Massachusetts, including several African Americans, rowed small wooden boats across the river from Manhattan to Brooklyn. Rags were wrapped around the oars to silence them in the water, and orders were given in whispers. More than 9,000 men were transported from Brooklyn back across the river to Manhattan. The next morning the fog lifted. The British were astonished to discover that the American army had escaped!

There was no rest for the small Continental army. The British followed the army and continued to win battles in Manhattan, White Plains, and Peekskill. Washington realized he could not defeat the British army face to face.

QUICK CHECK Why did the British expect Washington to surrender?
Main Idea and Details

145

B Difficult Times

Washington could not afford an all-out battle, but the British could not find his small army to defeat it. On Christmas night, 1776, Washington led the army across the Delaware River and surprised a camp of soldiers in Trenton, New Jersey. This victory at the Battle of Trenton led to another victory at Princeton, New Jersey, in January of 1777. The winter of 1777 was long and cold. The American troops had few supplies and many feared total defeat. The British captured the American capital at Philadelphia in 1778. The British were confident of victory.

Many Kinds of Patriots

Joseph Plum Martin, a teenaged soldier, wrote, about the hardships of life in the Continental army,

" *I endure hardships sufficient to kill half a dozen horses . . . without provisions, without clothing, not a scrap of either shoes or stockings . . .* **"**

There were also female Patriots. Sybil Ludington was a 16-year-old Patriot from a farm near Carmel, New York. She risked her life to warn the local militia about a British attack. You will read more about her on page 147.

QUICK CHECK Why was it so important for the British to capture New York? *Cause and Effect*

What You Learned

Ⓐ The British won the early battles of the American Revolution, including several fought in New York.

Ⓑ The Americans won several battles in the winter of 1777.

Focus Lesson Review

1. **Focus Question** How did the American Revolution affect New York state?

2. **Vocabulary** Write a sentence for each vocabulary word.
   retreat   surrender

3. **Geography** Why was New York's location important to the war?

4. **Critical Thinking** **Sequence Events** Name three battles that took place after the Battle of Long Island.

5. **Reading Strategy** **Identify Main Idea and Details** Use the graphic organizer to tell about the outcome of fighting in New York.

6. **Write About** THE **BIG IDEA** Write about Sybil Ludington or Joseph Plum Martin. Write about why a young person would take such great risks.

7. **Reading Primary Sources** "On becoming soldiers we have not ceased to be citizens."

   What is this Patriot saying about soldiers and citizenship?

Sybil Ludington 1761–1839

Sybil Ludington was the oldest of twelve children. Her father, Colonel Henry Ludington, was commander of the Dutchess County Militia. They lived in Fredericksburg, New York which is now known as Ludingtonville.

On the evening of April 26, 1777, Colonel Ludington learned that a British army was attacking Danbury, Connecticut, about 16 miles away.

Sixteen-year-old Sybil rode at night through rough country, avoiding the British troops and their Loyalist supporters. Sybil rode all night through driving rain, shouting:

> **The British are burning Danbury—muster [gather] at Ludington's!**

Colonel Ludington's militia chased the British troops from the area. Later, Sybil was thanked personally by General George Washington.

 About It! How did Sybil Ludington show courage?

LOG ON For more biographies, visit: www.macmillanmh.com

The Life of Sybil Ludington

1760	1780	1800	1820	1840
1761 Sybil Ludington is born	1777 Sybil makes her dangerous ride	1784 Sybil marries Edward Ogden		1839 Sybil dies in Unadilla, NY

Compare Maps at Different Scales

VOCABULARY

map scale
small-scale map
large-scale map

All maps are drawn to scale. A **map scale** uses a unit of measure, such as an inch, to represent a real distance on earth. A map scale like this one will tell you the size of an area on the map.

A **small-scale map**, such as Map A, covers a large area but cannot include many details. A **large-scale map**, such as Map B, shows many details of a smaller area.

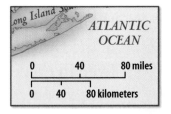

1 Learn It

- If you want to find the routes used by the British troops from New York City, use a small-scale map, or Map A. This map will give you the information you need without many details.

- If you want to know about the area immediately surrounding New York City, you would need the large-scale map, or Map B. It shows a smaller area with many more details and more information.

- Compare the map scales of both maps.

- Map A has a scale of 1 inch = 80 miles. It shows a large area.

- Map B has a scale of 1 inch = 10 miles. It shows a small area.

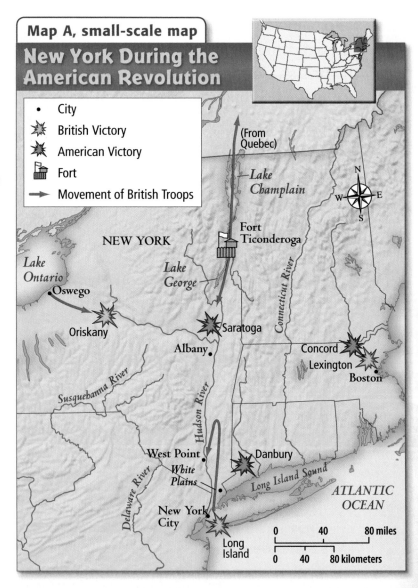

Map A, small-scale map

New York During the American Revolution

- • City
- ✷ British Victory
- ✷ American Victory
- 🏛 Fort
- → Movement of British Troops

2 Try It

- Using the map scale on Map B, find out about how many miles soldiers traveled to get to White Plains from Fort Washington.

- Which map would you use to find the distance between White Plains and the Albany?

- Which map would you use to determine the distance between White Plains and Peekskill?

3 Apply It

- How does a map scale help you to read maps?

- When might you need to compare maps of different scales in your own life?

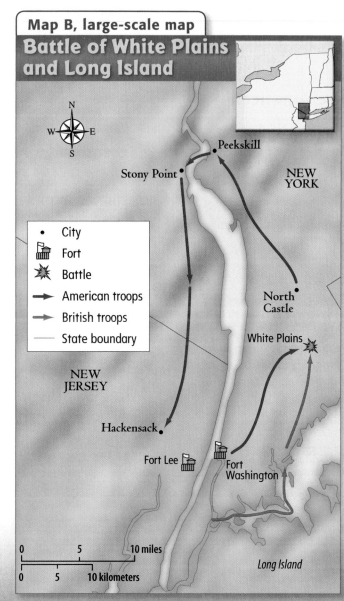

Map B, large-scale map

Battle of White Plains and Long Island

Peekskill

Stony Point

NEW YORK

- • City
- 🏛 Fort
- ✹ Battle
- → American troops
- → British troops
- — State boundary

North Castle

White Plains

NEW JERSEY

Hackensack

Fort Lee

Fort Washington

Long Island

```
0        5        10 miles
0    5    10 kilometers
```

How were American soldiers able to defeat the British army?

VOCABULARY

treaty
traitor

VOCABULARY STRATEGY

Synonyms A treaty is an agreement between nations or groups. What other words mean an agreement?

READING STRATEGY

Summarize Use the chart to summarize the battles at Saratoga.

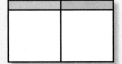

NEW YORK STANDARDS

1.3, 1.4, 3.1

The American Revolution Ends

General Burgoyne was determined to capture New York. He left Canada with a well-supplied army, determined to meet up with the British from New York City. However, things didn't work out as General Burgoyne had planned. How could a small, inexperienced American army defeat this powerful and well organized British force and change the course of American history?

ⓐ New York in the War

After Washington's army escaped to New Jersey, New York City became a British stronghold throughout the remainder of the war. The British hoped to capture the rest of New York and split the 13 states in two.

▼ British uniforms gave their soldiers the nickname "Redcoats."

1775	1778	1781	1784

1777
The Battle of Saratoga

1781
British General Charles Cornwallis surrenders to General Washington

1783
All British soldiers leave New York

The Battle of Saratoga

The British plan was to use two armies, one from New York City, the other from Canada They would join up around Albany.

The British forces from Canada were led by General John Burgoyne (BUR goin). As the British troops moved south into New York, they attacked Fort Stanwix at Rome, New York. American troops rushed to reinforce the troops inside the fort. However, British troops and Iroquois forces led by Joseph Brant defeated the American reinforcements at Oriskany Creek in Oneida County.

General Burgoyne's troops reached Saratoga, New York, in September 1777. They were running out of supplies. They were shocked to learn that the other British army had never left New York City!

On September 19, American General Horatio Gates and his 7,000 Continental soldiers attacked and defeated the British army at Saratoga. Burgoyne tried a second, desperate attack on

▲ This monument in Saratoga shows Benedict Arnold's wounded leg.

October 7. Again, the British were defeated, this time by Patriot General Benedict Arnold.

Burgoyne surrendered. This defeat at Saratoga changed the course of the war. The French king was convinced to sign a **treaty**, or written agreement between two countries. France agreed to send troops and supplies to help the Americans. This support would save the American cause.

Benedict Arnold

Benedict Arnold wanted glory. He was to become America's most famous **traitor**. A traitor is someone who acts against his own country. In 1780, Arnold planned to surrender the important American fortress at West Point, on the Hudson River to the British. Fortunately for the Americans, his plan was discovered, and the fortress at West Point was saved. Arnold fled to England.

QUICK CHECK What events led to the surrender of General Burgoyne? *Summarize*

151

Soldiers of the American Revolution

Use the graphs on this page to learn about the soldiers who fought in the American Revolution. After studying the graphs, answer the questions below.

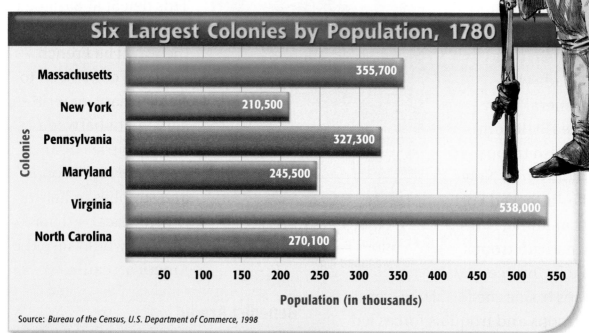

Six Largest Colonies by Population, 1780

- Massachusetts — 355,700
- New York — 210,500
- Pennsylvania — 327,300
- Maryland — 245,500
- Virginia — 538,000
- North Carolina — 270,100

Colonies (y-axis)
Population (in thousands): 50 100 150 200 250 300 350 400 450 500 550

Source: *Bureau of the Census, U.S. Department of Commerce, 1998*

Soldiers in the Patriot Army, 1775 – 1783

- 2% (4,435) Died in Battle
- 3% (6,188) Wounded in Battle
- 10% (20,000) Died from Disease
- 85% (169,377) Returned Home

Source: *United States Department of Defense*

Think About the American Revolution

1. What was the total population of New York colony in 1780?

2. What was the cause of death for most soldiers?

3. Which state would you expect to have sent the most soldiers? Why might this not be true?

B The Battle of Yorktown

In 1781, British attacks moved to the southern states. British General Charles Cornwallis led his army to Yorktown, Virginia, in 1781. He hoped to get supplies from New York City.

The Continental army, led by George Washington and New York's Alexander Hamilton, joined French forces to surround the British army. The French navy blocked supplies to Cornwallis.

On October 19, 1781, General Cornwallis surrendered. The American Revolution was over, and a new nation was born.

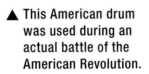

▲ This American drum was used during an actual battle of the American Revolution.

Peace

On September 3, 1783, a treaty called the Peace of Paris officially ended the war. This treaty recognized the independence of the United States.

New York City remained in British hands until November 25, 1783. George Washington watched as the last British soldier boarded his ship, then led his army into the city. New York was an American city at last!

QUICK CHECK Why might Washington have waited to enter New York City? *Make Inferences*

What You Learned

A The American victory at Saratoga was the turning point in the Revolution.

B The British surrendered in 1781; they left New York City in 1783.

✫ Focus Lesson Review

1. **Focus Question** How were American soldiers able to defeat the British army?

2. **Vocabulary** Use the vocabulary words to write two facts about the American Revolution.
   traitor   **treaty**

3. **Citizenship** Why is Benedict Arnold considered a traitor?

4. **Critical Thinking** **Main Idea and Details** How did British General John Burgoyne plan to take control of New York State?

5. **Reading Strategy** **Summarize** Use the two-column chart to summarize this lesson.

6. **Write About** **THE BIG IDEA** Why would General Burgoyne risk two battles with the American army?

7. **Reading Primary Sources** *"Then join hand in hand, brave Americans all, By uniting we stand, by dividing we fall."* – Passage from Liberty Song

   What do the words of this song tell Americans they should do?

Chapter 5 Review

FOCUS Vocabulary Review

Match each vocabulary word to its definition. Write the vocabulary word and definition on your paper.

Patriot	**revolution**
retreat	**treaty**

1. A formal agreement between nations

2. A colonist who was opposed to British rule

3. the colonial fight for freedom

4. give up ground

5. **Test Preparation** A _____ is someone who betrays his or her county.

   (A) **delegate**   (C) **Loyalist**

   (B) **traitor**   (D) **militia**

FOCUS Comprehension Check

6. What Native American group had a government that impressed Benjamin Franklin?

7. Why did Great Britain need to collect money from the colonists?

8. What was the Stamp Act?

9. Why was New York an important location during the American Revolution?

10. Who surrendered his army at Yorktown?

11. **Critical Thinking** Why did the Patriots at first use a militia instead of a regular army?

12. **Critical Thinking** How do you think Patriots might have felt about Benedict Arnold?

FOCUS Use the Time Line

Use the time line below to answer each question.

13. Which happened first, Sybil Ludington's night ride or the surrender of Cornwallis?

14. What happened ten years before British troops left New York?

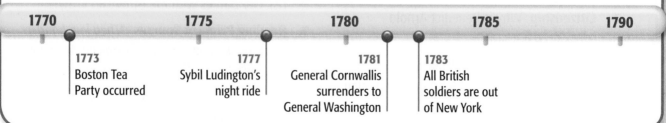

1770	1775	1780	1785	1790

1773
Boston Tea Party occurred

1777
Sybil Ludington's night ride

1781
General Cornwallis surrenders to General Washington

1783
All British soldiers are out of New York

Map and Globe Skills: Compare Maps at Different Scales

Write a complete sentence to answer each question.

15. What is the map scale for this map?

16. Is this a large-scale or small-scale map?

17. **Test Preparation** A _____ uses a unit of measure to show real distance on Earth.

   (A) **large-scale map**   (C) **compass**
   (B) **small-scale map**   (D) **map scale**

18. **Test Preparation** A _____ covers a large area, but has few details.

   (A) **large-scale map**   (C) **compass**
   (B) **small-scale map**   (D) **map scale**

Battle of Saratoga

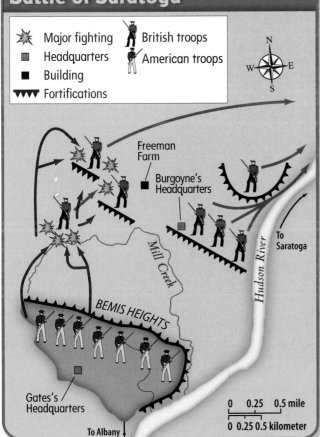

Legend:
- ✳ Major fighting
- ▪ Headquarters (gray)
- ■ Building
- ▼▼▼ Fortifications
- British troops
- American troops

Freeman Farm
Burgoyne's Headquarters
Mill Creek
Hudson River
To Saratoga
BEMIS HEIGHTS
Gates's Headquarters
To Albany

0 0.25 0.5 mile
0 0.25 0.5 kilometer

Constructed Response Questions

Read this selection. Answer the questions below.

From *The Diary of Private Joseph Plumb Martin*:

❝ *We were strictly enjoined [ordered] not to speak, or even cough, while on march. All orders were given from officer to officer, and communicated to the men in whispers.*❞

19. Give two reasons why the British did not realize the Americans were escaping from Long Island.

20. Why do you think this way of leading an army is unusual?

21. **Write a Song** Work in groups to write a song about how the colonists feel about the Stamp Act.

22. **Persuasive** Write a short speech to convince colonists to join in the fight for freedom.

 LOG ON   For help with the process of writing, visit: www.macmillanmh.com

Chapter 6

A New State

You Are There

New York Patriot John Jay wanted to begin building a strong nation. What kind of nation would it be? What would be New York's place in this nation? There were many ideas, and many arguments. The difficult business of hammering out the new government had to begin quickly.

" The first thing . . . to be done is to [build] good and well-ordered governments in all the colonies. "

Lake Erie

New York Patriot John Jay ▶

Chapter Events

1784	1786	1788

1
1784
First Bank of
New York opens

2
1789
George Washington becomes
first President of the United States

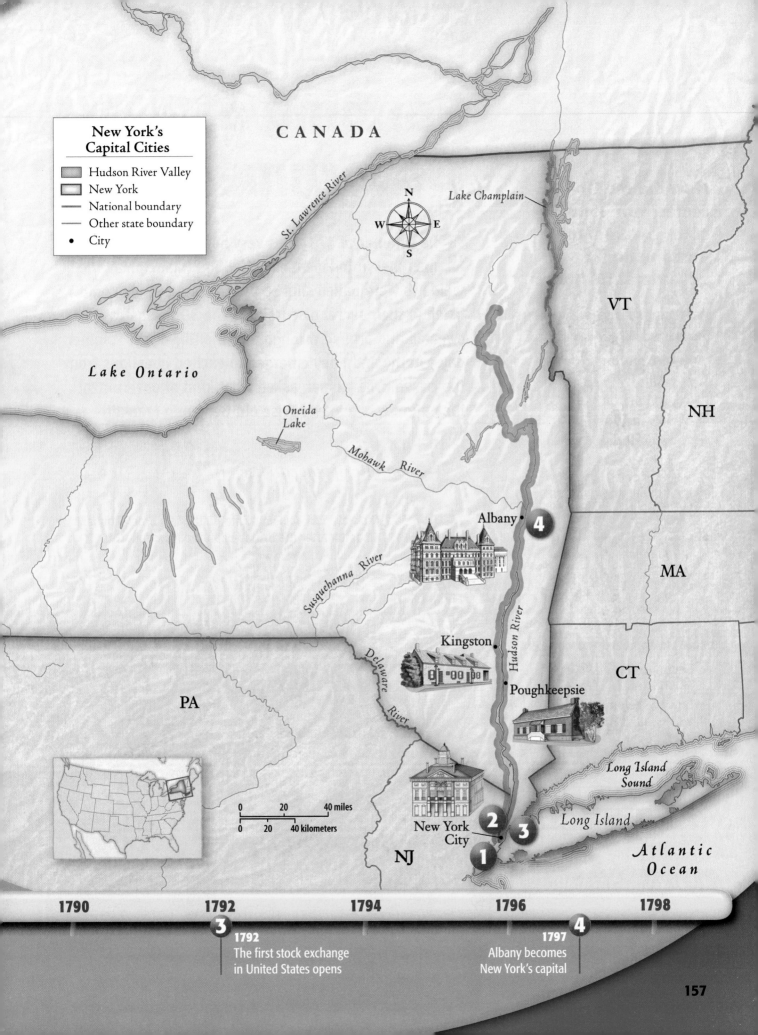

New York's Capital Cities

- Hudson River Valley
- New York
- National boundary
- Other state boundary
- City

CANADA

St. Lawrence River

Lake Champlain

N
W · E
S

VT

NH

Lake Ontario

Oneida Lake

Mohawk River

Albany **4**

MA

Susquehanna River

Hudson River

Kingston

Poughkeepsie

CT

PA

Delaware River

New York City

2
3

Long Island Sound

Long Island

1

NJ

Atlantic Ocean

0   20   40 miles
0   20   40 kilometers

| 1790 | 1792 | 1794 | 1796 | 1798 |

3 1792
The first stock exchange
in United States opens

4 1797
Albany becomes
New York's capital

Forming a Government

How did the United States form new state governments and a national government?

VOCABULARY

convention
capital
representative
constitution
amendment
ratify

VOCABULARY STRATEGY

Synonyms Ratify means to officially approve laws. What other words might be synonyms for approve?

READING STRATEGY

Sequence Events Use the chart below to explain how the colony of New York became a state.

NEW YORK STANDARDS

1.1, 1.2, 1.3, 1.4, 5.1, 5.2, 5.3, 5.4

The summer of 1787 was very hot. A group of men met in Independence Hall in Philadelphia. The windows were nailed shut so that no one outside could listen to their secret discussions. The 39 delegates sweated and argued through four months of hot summer days. In the end, they emerged to excited questions from the crowd. One woman asked what kind of government the nation was to have. Wise old Benjamin Franklin answered,

❝*A republic, if you can keep it.*❞

The New York Assembly met in the Ten Broek house in Kingston after the British captured New York City. ▼

1787
Representatives write the
United States Constitution

1789
New York City becomes the
capital of the United States

1797
Albany becomes
New York's capital

Ⓐ Creating Governments

Independence! The 13 colonies had become 13 independent states, each with its own traditions, history, and economy. Each state needed to create a government of its own. To do this, each state called a **convention**, or a formal meeting held for a special purpose.

Setting Up a State Government

In 1777, New York Patriots met to work out a plan for the new state government. At that time, Kingston was New York's **capital** because the British army controlled New York City. A capital is the place where government leaders meet. The capital had earlier also been located at White Plains and Fishkill.

Representatives, people elected to speak or vote for others, gathered in Kingston for the convention. John Jay led the work of writing the state's **constitution** (kahn sti TOO shun), or plan of government.

✓ QUICK CHECK What did states have to do after ending their connections to the British government? *Sequence Events*

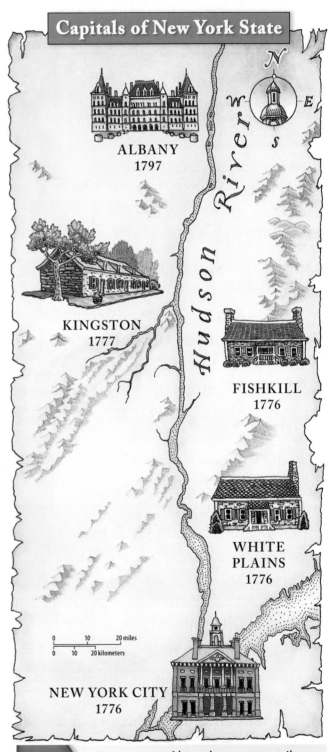

Capitals of New York State

ALBANY
1797

KINGSTON
1777

Hudson River

FISHKILL
1776

WHITE
PLAINS
1776

NEW YORK CITY
1776

| 0 | 10 | 20 miles |
| 0 | 10 | 20 kilometers |

MAP Skill **Movement** About how many miles north was the capital at Albany from the capital at Fishkill?

▲ George Washington takes the oath of office as the first President.

Ⓑ A Young New York

Since British officials were no longer running New York, there were many issues to discuss. The new state government had to work out treaties with Native Americans, end trade disputes, and settle land claims. The state of New York was lucky to have many talented leaders.

Local elections were held to choose representatives from each area of New York. In 1797, the capital moved north from Kingston to Albany. Albany was more centrally located for all New Yorkers.

A National Government

Many Americans wanted to be part of one nation. A nation is the people of an area who live under one government and share a history and culture.

The Articles of Confederation, the first national plan, passed the Congress in 1777. However, the national government quickly showed weaknesses. In May 1787, representatives from 12 states came together in Philadelphia. You read about their work at the beginning of this lesson. Some delegates remembered the rules of the Iroquois League. They hoped for a similar form of government. Through the hot summer months, the delegates argued.

Creating a Constitution

In September 1787, the new national Constitution was finally accepted by the delegates. The United States Constitution is a set of rules that explains how power is distributed across the branches of the national government, and between national and state governments.

The authors of the Constitution also included a way to change the Constitution when necessary. **Amendments** are these changes or additions to the Constitution. Many delegates, including ones from New York, wanted to add amendments before they would sign the new Constitution.

James Madison, John Jay, and Alexander Hamilton wrote essays to persuade people to accept the new Constitution. Their essays are now called *The Federalist Papers*.

In July 1788, New York became the eleventh state to **ratify**, or approve, the Constitution. Some Americans insisted that the new Constitution must protect the rights of ordinary citizens. The first ten amendments to the Constitution are called the Bill of Rights. They were approved in 1791. You can see all of these at the back of the book on page C23.

Bill of Rights

Freedom of Speech
Every American has the right to say what he or she feels about our country.

Freedom of the Press
Every American has the right to write and publish opinions about our country.

Freedom of Assembly
Every American has the right to peacefully gather in groups.

Freedom of Religion
Every American has the right to practice his or her own religion.

▲ Some American freedoms are protected by the Bill of Rights.

George Washington

In 1789 George Washington became the first President of the United States. New York City was chosen as the nation's capital. Washington was sworn in at Federal Hall in New York City on April 30, 1789.

✓ **QUICK CHECK** Why did state governments resist the new Constitution? *Summarize*

What You Learned

A The state of New York formed its own government and wrote its first constitution in 1777.

B When the Articles of Confederation proved too weak, representatives from 12 states met in Philadelphia to write the Constitution of the United States.

Focus Lesson Review

1. **Focus Question** How did the United States form new state governments and a national government?

2. **Vocabulary** Write a summary of Lesson 1. Use these vocabulary words.
   amendment   ratify
   capital   representative
   constitution
   convention

3. **Citizenship** How did the writers of the constitution display good citizenship?

4. **Critical Thinking Problem Solving** How did people make sure the new Constitution protected the rights of citizens?

5. **Reading Strategy Sequence Events** Use the chart to show how New York played a part in the signing of the Constitution.

6. **Write About THE BIG IDEA** Why were people willing to risk weakening their states to get a stronger national government?

7. **Reading Primary Sources** *"Should the States reject this excellent Constitution . . . an opportunity will never again . . . [occur] in peace—the next will be drawn in blood."*
   – George Washington, 1787

   What do you think George Washington hoped to persuade people to do in 1787?

Identify Fact and Opinion

VOCABULARY

fact

opinion

In Lesson 1, you read about the creation of the United States Constitution. Most sentences in the lesson contained **facts**. A fact is a statement that can be proven true. You could prove a fact, for example, by checking it in an encyclopedia.

Other statements are **opinions**. An opinion tells what someone believes or feels. Opinions cannot be proven true or false.

1 Learn It

- Facts can be proven true. Statements with dates and amounts are often facts.

- Opinions state feelings and beliefs. Words like *better, probably, should,* and *believe* signal opinions.

- Now look for facts and opinions in this paragraph.

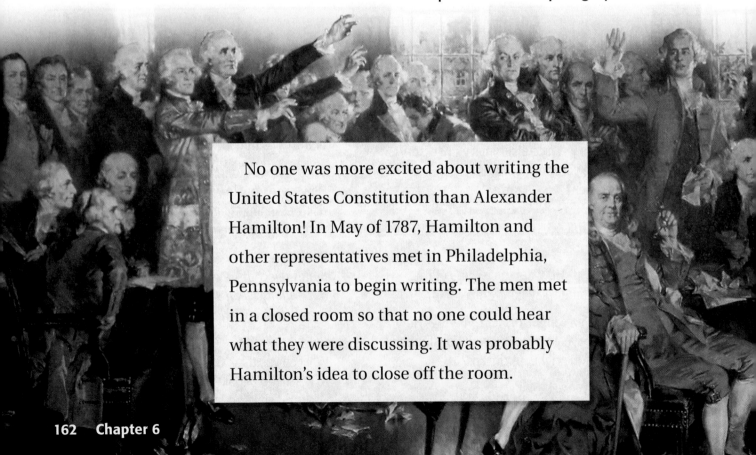

No one was more excited about writing the United States Constitution than Alexander Hamilton! In May of 1787, Hamilton and other representatives met in Philadelphia, Pennsylvania to begin writing. The men met in a closed room so that no one could hear what they were discussing. It was probably Hamilton's idea to close off the room.

2 Try It

Read the paragraph about writing the Constitution again. Answer the questions.

- Is the first sentence a fact or an opinion? How do you know?

- Is the second sentence a fact or an opinion? How do you know?

- Would you be able to prove the third sentence? Explain.

- Why is the last sentence an opinion?

3 Apply It

- Write two statements of fact about your school or classroom.

- Write two statements of opinion.

- Share your facts and opinions with classmates.

The Economy of the New State

How did New York's economy develop in the 1780s and 1790s?

VOCABULARY

entrepreneur
free enterprise
bank
stock
stock exchange

VOCABULARY STRATEGY

Compound Words The word free in **free enterprise** means "without limits." What other words use free, meaning "without limits."

READING STRATEGY

Sequence Events Use the chart below to show how colonial New York's economy developed.

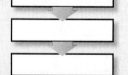

NEW YORK STANDARDS

4.1, 4.2

Robert Morris was a man with an idea. In February of 1784, his ship *Empress of China* sailed for China. More than a year later, the *Empress* returned, loaded with treasures — spices, silks in brilliant colors, delicate china painted with elegant scenes of Chinese daily life, carved ivories and beautifully made boxes and chests. In his own words, Morris's idea would

66 *encourage others in the adventurous pursuit of commerce.* 99

Products like this plate and ivory dominoes were imported to the busy port of New York City [below] in the 1790s. ▶

1780	1785	1790	1795	1800

1784
First Bank of
New York opens

1785
Empress of China
returns to New York

1792
Buttonwood
Agreement signed

1803
First Bank in
Albany opens

A New Ways of Doing Business

Before the American Revolution, most goods sold in New York were carried to the colony by ships from Europe. By the 1780s, New York merchants were looking for new ways to bring goods to New York. The *Empress of China* was one of the first ships to open up trade between the young United States and ancient empire of China. Trade is the buying and selling of goods. When the wonderful goods, such as silk, tea, and china, poured out of the *Empress of China*, people realized what money could be made in trade. Many Americans became **entrepreneurs**, people who start and run their own businesses. Entrepreneurs work in all walks of life—from shopkeeping to shipbuilding.

A system in which business flows freely is known as **free enterprise**. In free enterprise, the government does not try to control what can be bought or sold or who can start a business.

Merchants, even wealthy ones, needed money to pay for their goods and start their businesses. Often they borrowed the money they needed. They paid it back over time as people bought their goods. This led to the founding of **banks**. A bank is a business that helps people borrow and save money.

QUICK CHECK What were the events that helped the United States economy grow? *Sequence Events*

Then and Now

Wall Street

THEN At one time Wall Street had a real wall! It was the last street in Dutch New Amsterdam and ran east to west along the wooden wall of the village. George Washington was sworn in as President of the United States at Federal Hall, at the northeast corner of Wall and Broad Streets.

NOW Federal Hall National Museum is in the old United States Sub-Treasury building, on the site of the original Federal Hall. Diagonally across the street is the New York Stock Exchange, where more than one billion shares of stock are sold daily.

Write About It! What is the difference between Wall Street then and Wall Street now?

B Business in New York

On February 24, 1784, business leaders, including Alexander Hamilton, started the Bank of New York. Each man was an investor. Investors are people who put money into a business to make more money. These investors gave the bank enough money to loan to businesses immediately. The Bank of New York opened on June 9, 1784.

Elkanah Watson was a merchant and land owner in Albany. He decided to try his hand at banking, and in September of 1803, the State Bank of Albany opened its doors in Albany.

Its first loan was a "sum of four thousand dollars for the use of the Great Western Turnpike Company." The road later became U.S. Route 20.

The Buttonwood Agreement

When companies need money, they sell **stock**. A stock is a share of a company and the money it makes. Starting in 1792, the Bank of New York began to raise money by selling stocks. In May 1792, 24 people met under a buttonwood tree in New York City. They signed an agreement called the Buttonwood Agreement. This agreement set up the first **stock exchange** in the United States. A stock exchange is an organized market for buying and selling stocks. Their stock exchange became the New York Stock Exchange, "one of the world's largest money marketplaces."

QUICK CHECK How did the stock exchange begin? *Sequence Events*

What You Learned

A After the American Revolution, New York merchants began trading with China; Alexander Hamilton and other New Yorkers founded banks.

B The stock exchange began as a way to help companies raise money; the Bank of New York and the New York Stock Exchange were founded on Wall Street.

◄ Early American investors met at the Tontine Coffee House

Focus Lesson Review

1. **Focus Question** How did New York's economy develop in the 1780s and 1790s?

2. **Vocabulary** Write a paragraph that uses the following vocabulary terms.
   bank   stock
   entrepreneur   stock exchange
   free enterprise

3. **Culture** How did American merchants and their businesses change the way Americans lived?

4. **Critical Thinking** **Problem Solving** Why did New York merchants sign the Buttonwood Agreement?

5. **Reading Strategy** **Sequence Events** What events helped to make New York into a financial leader after the American Revolution?

6. **Write About** THE **BiG** IDEA What do people risk by starting new businesses?

7. **Reading Primary Sources** *"I remained alone in the society of Washington, for two of the richest days of my life."* Elkanah Watson wrote of his visit to Washington's home at Mt. Vernon. What did Watson mean?

Chapter 6 Review

FOCUS Vocabulary Review

Copy the sentences below on a separate sheet of paper. Use the list of vocabulary terms to fill in the blanks.

amendment   ratify
free enterprise   stock exchange

1. A _____ is an organized market for buying and selling stock.

2. Each _____ changes the Constitution.

3. _____ is a system in which people can run their own businesses.

4. New York voted to _____ the United States Constitution in September 1788.

5. **Test Preparation** The young _____ started a shop with a small loan.

   (A) stock   (C) representative
   (B) entrepeneur   (D) nation

FOCUS Comprehension Check

6. Who were three American leaders who helped convince New York to ratify the Constitution?

7. What effect did the arrival of ships from China have on trade?

8. Why did New York's capital move to Albany?

9. What developments helped New York entrepreneurs to borrow money?

10. Why did the Bill of Rights become part of the United States Constitution?

11. **Critical Thinking** Why was it important for New Yorkers to ratify the U.S. Constitution?

12. **Critical Thinking** What was the purpose of the Buttonwood Agreement?

FOCUS Use the Time Line

Use the time line below to answer each question.

13. When was George Washington elected President?

14. How many years passed between the Buttonwood Agreement and the move of the capital to Albany?

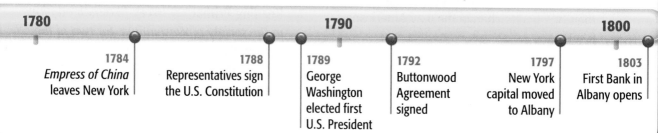

1780	1790	1800

1784 *Empress of China* leaves New York

1788 Representatives sign the U.S. Constitution

1789 George Washington elected first U.S. President

1792 Buttonwood Agreement signed

1797 New York capital moved to Albany

1803 First Bank in Albany opens

Critical Thinking: Identify Fact and Opinion

Decide if each sentence is a fact or an opinion. Explain your answer. Write a complete sentence to answer each question.

15. George Washington is the only President elected in an odd-numbered year.

16. We believe that entrepreneurs have a lot of courage.

17. **Test Preparation** The Buttonwood Agreement was not _____.

   (A) **necessary for business**
   (B) **made by entrepreneurs**
   (C) **a way to cooperate**
   (D) **provided by government**

18. **Test Preparation** When trade with China began, New York's _____.

   (A) **laws changed**
   (B) **economy grew**
   (C) **businesses suffered**
   (D) **leaders met**

Constructed Response Questions

Study the cartoon and answer these questions. Write a complete sentence for each answer.

19. What is the main idea in this political cartoon? How do you know?

20. Why do you think the cartoonist used a snake? Explain your opinion.

21. **Prepare and Perform a Skit** Work in a small group to write a short skit about the signing of the Constitution. Make sure you show how important compromise was. Perform the skit for the class.

22. **Expository** Write a brief essay to describe the New York Stock Exchange. You will need to use reference sources from the school library or the Internet for your research.

 For help with the process of writing, visit: www.macmillanmh.com

New Yorkers Move West

You Are There

Edwin Scrantom belonged to the first family to settle in Rochester. He welcomed new people to the area, and the city grew quickly. It was a time of great change in our state.

" ... master builders ... worked night and day, [but] could not keep the demand for dwellings, and frequently families would bivouac [camp] one, two, or three weeks in their covered wagons before they could find a place ... "

A farmer in western New York ▶

Chapter Events

	1780	1790	1800

1797
Big Tree Treaty
1

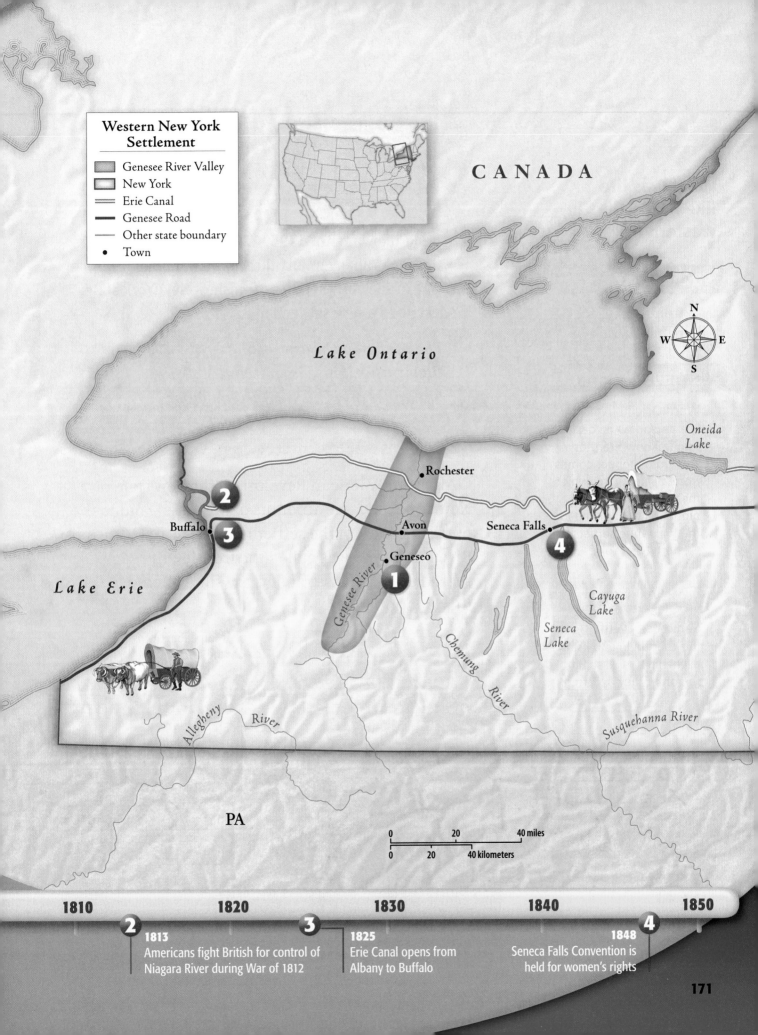

Western New York Settlement

- Genesee River Valley
- New York
- Erie Canal
- Genesee Road
- Other state boundary
- • Town

CANADA

Lake Ontario

Oneida Lake

Rochester

Buffalo

Avon

Seneca Falls

Geneseo

Lake Erie

Cayuga Lake

Seneca Lake

Chemung River

Allegheny River

Susquehanna River

PA

0   20   40 miles

0   20   40 kilometers

1810   1820   1830   1840   1850

2 **1813**
Americans fight British for control of Niagara River during War of 1812

3 **1825**
Erie Canal opens from Albany to Buffalo

4 **1848**
Seneca Falls Convention is held for women's rights

What was life like for settlers in western New York?

VOCABULARY

frontier
pioneer

VOCABULARY STRATEGY

Word Origins A **pioneer** is a person who goes into unknown territory. The word pioneer comes from a Latin word, which means "foot." Why is pioneer a good name for the first white settlers in western New York?

READING STRATEGY

Sequence Events Use the chart below to list the events in this lesson in the order they occurred.

NEW YORK STANDARDS

1.1, 1.2, 1.3, 1.4
3.1, 4.1

The Life of Settlers

During the winter of 1795, 1200 sleds carried settlers through Albany in just three days. Chipman P. Turner was one of the early settlers of western New York state. He described a new settler's life:

" The roof of his house is elm bark . . . The floor of his house is split logs . . . Miles and miles off is his nearest neighbor."

Ⓐ Settling Western Land

After the American Revolution, the new state of New York had large amounts of unsettled land to the north and west of the settlements along the Hudson River. This land was called the **frontier**, the edge of a settled area. To raise money, the state offered to sell this land to settlers.

Pioneer log cabins were simple inside and out. ▼

1797
Iroquois sell land under the Big Tree Treaty

1800
About 15,000 people live in Genesee Country

1812
War of 1812 begins

1814
War of 1812 ends

A **pioneer** is a person who is among the first of non-native people to settle a region. Among the pioneers was Enos Stone, who wrote:

> " . . . *we were from Thursday morning until Sunday evening without having the pleasure of tasting food.* "

The Genesee Valley

During the 1780s, investors set up land companies to buy western land. They then sold small plots to individual settlers.

To attract settlers, land companies built roads such as the Genesee Road. The Genesee Road was once a trail used by Native Americans.

During the 1790s, it led thousands of American settlers to western New York. These settlers came largely from New England. About 15,000 people had settled in Genesee Country by 1800.

The Iroquois League, who were allies of the British, lost almost all of their territory after the American Revolution. By 1800, there was little Native American land left in the state.

QUICK CHECK What events led up to the Iroquois League losing most of their land? *Sequence Events*

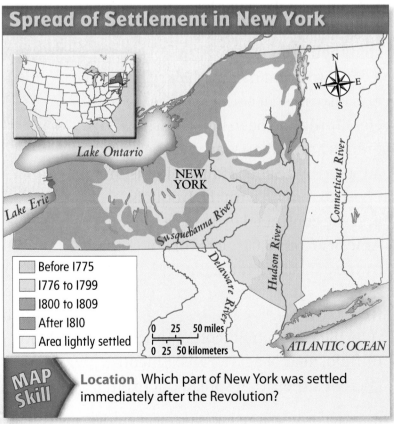

Spread of Settlement in New York

Lake Ontario

Lake Erie

NEW YORK

Susquehanna River

Delaware River

Hudson River

Connecticut River

ATLANTIC OCEAN

Before 1775
1776 to 1799
1800 to 1809
After 1810
Area lightly settled

0   25   50 miles
0 25 50 kilometers

MAP Skill

Location Which part of New York was settled immediately after the Revolution?

173

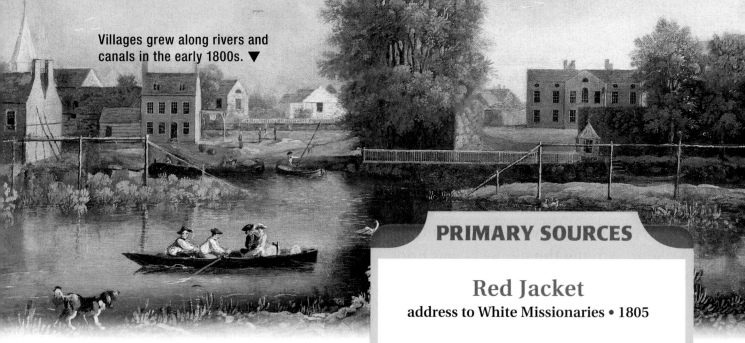

Villages grew along rivers and canals in the early 1800s. ▼

B The Big Tree Treaty

In 1797 representatives of the Holland Land Company and the Seneca leaders met at the village of Big Tree called Geneseo today. Segoyewatha (seg oy uh WAH thuh), or Red Jacket, was a Seneca leader. He opposed the sale of any land to settlers. You can read part of his protest on this page. In spite of his speech, the Seneca sold their land.

A white woman named Mary Jemison was also present at the Big Tree Council. Her family had been killed during the French and Indian War, and she was adopted by a Seneca family. Jemison chose to remain with the Iroquois, and she continued to live as a Native American on 18,000 acres of land kept by the Seneca after the Big Tree Treaty.

New Cities

In 1804, Joseph Ellicott planned Buffalo, near Niagara Falls. Ellicott laid out streets that spread out from the city's center. The village had several log houses, a tavern, and an inn. By 1811, there were about 1,000 people in Buffalo.

Rochester was also settled in the early 1800s. Colonel Nathaniel Rochester settled near the Genesee River and settlers like the Scrantom family joined him.

PRIMARY SOURCES

Red Jacket
address to White Missionaries • 1805

❝ *Brothers, our seats were once large, and yours were small. You have now become a great people, and we have scarcely a place left to spread our blankets.* ❞

Write About It!

How does Red Jacket describe what has happened to the Iroquois?

Red Jacket ▲

The War of 1812

From 1790 to 1820, Great Britain and France were at war. The British navy needed sailors. British ships began stopping American ships and forcing American sailors to serve in the British navy. Angry Americans protests were ignored. At the same time, Americans wanted to drive the British out of Canada. In June of 1812, the United States declared war on Great Britain.

The American army invaded Canada in December 1813. They burned its capital, York, which is now Toronto. The British, in turn, attacked American cities across the Niagara River.

The Battle of Lake Champlain

The Battle of Lake Champlain in September 1814 was an important turning point in the war. Sir George Prevost and 11,000 British soldiers crossed Lake Champlain on several ships. About 1,500 American soldiers led by Brigadier General Alexander Macomb and a small fleet led by Commodore Macdonough defeated this larger British force, stopping their invasion and forcing the British to withdraw to Canada. Soon after this battle, a peace agreement was reached, ending the war.

QUICK CHECK Why did the United States declare war on Great Britain?
Main Idea and Details

What You Learned

A Pioneers moved to western New York and settled the frontier.

B The Battle of Lake Champlain in 1814 was one of the American victories during the War of 1812.

Focus Lesson Review

1. **Focus Question** What was life like for settlers in western New York?

2. **Vocabulary** Write a paragraph describing how people settled in western New York. Use the vocabulary words below.
   frontier   pioneer

3. **Geography** Why was New York the scene of many important battles of the War of 1812?

4. **Critical Thinking Making Inferences** Why do you think the Seneca Indians ended up selling their land to the Americans?

5. **Reading Strategy Sequence Events** List three events from the War of 1812 in the order in which they occurred.

6. **Write About THE BIG IDEA** Why did the United States risk a war with Great Britain?

7. **Reading Primary Sources** *"Next morning the snow was apparently a foot deep, [we did not see] an ounce of butter or tea . . . during nearly the whole time."*

   What challenges faced settler Edwin Scrantom in western New York?

A Young Person's Life on the Frontier

Boys and girls living on the frontier helped their parents with many everyday tasks. Girls helped their mothers manage the house and tend to the other children. Boys helped their fathers work in the fields and bring food home for everyone to eat. One day a week all the families in the area would come together for meetings or worship.

▲ This schoolhouse in Austerlitz, New York was built more than 100 years ago.

▼ Butter was made by hand by pounding the paddle inside this wooden barrel.

◀ Dolls were made from corn husks, the green leaves which wrap ears of corn.

Schoolchildren wrote on slates, a kind of stone that could be wiped off and used again. ▼

Write About It!

Write a paragraph about how a young person's life on the frontier was similar or different from your own.

LOG ON For more about about young people in history, visit: www.macmillanmh.com

Use Special Purpose Maps: Population Maps

VOCABULARY

population density

When you need to know the number of people who live in a place, you would look at a population map. Most population maps show population density. **Population density** measures how many people live within a certain area. Population density can change from place to place within a country or a region. A population density map shows you these differences.

The map on this page shows you where most of the people were living in New York during the 1790s.

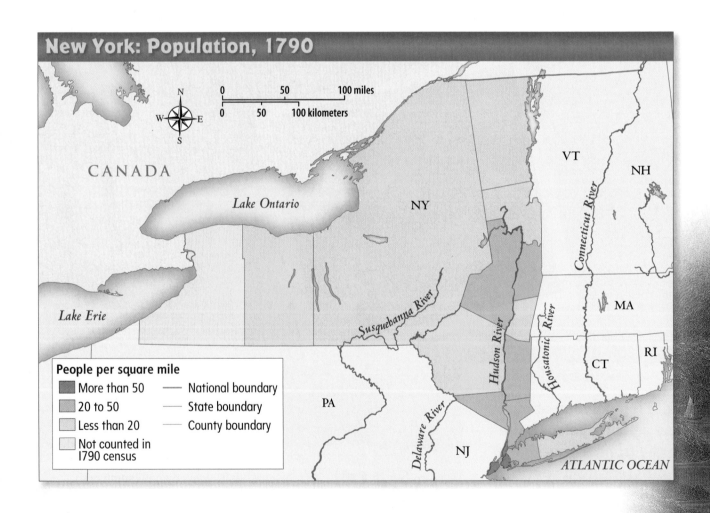

New York: Population, 1790

0   50   100 miles
0   50   100 kilometers

CANADA

Lake Ontario

Lake Erie

NY

VT

NH

Connecticut River

MA

Housatonic River

Hudson River

CT

RI

Susquehanna River

PA

Delaware River

NJ

ATLANTIC OCEAN

People per square mile

- More than 50
- 20 to 50
- Less than 20
- Not counted in 1790 census

— National boundary
— State boundary
— County boundary

1 Learn It

- Look at the map on page 178. Read the title. This map shows the population of New York state in 1790.

- Study the map key. This map key tells you that most people still lived along the Hudson River in 1790.

▲ New York City street in the 1800s

2 Try It

Look at the map on page 178 to answer these questions.

- What was the population per square mile of most of the state in 1790?

- Most of the 1790 population was centered around what two New York cities?

- Why was western New York probably not counted in the 1790 census?

3 Apply It

- How might a population map of 1850 look different from the map on page 178?

- What information about population would not be shown on a population map?

▼ The Hudson River about 1840

New Ways to Travel

How did new ways of travel change life in New York?

VOCABULARY

canal
lock
tow-path
toll
boomtown
locomotive

VOCABULARY STRATEGY

Compound Words
Boomtown is a compound of the words boom and town. You might know that boom means "sudden, rapid growth." What do you think a boomtown is?

READING STRATEGY

Identify Cause and Effect List two effects of the building of the Erie Canal on New York.

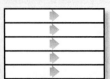

Nathaniel Mack, a young man passing through New York decided on an adventure. He took a trip on the first American steamboat one August day in 1807:

> *66 . . . people lined the banks along the river . . . the engine when in motion made a rattling noise similar to half a dozen wagons . . . but before running any great distance a part of the machinery gave way. The boat returning to the city for repairs, a great many left, fearing to return to resume the trip. 99*

1807
Robert Fulton tests his steamboat

1817
Work begins on the Erie Canal

1825
The Erie Canal opens from Buffalo to Albany

1831
The first railroad in New York is built

Ⓐ Fulton's Dream

Even as a boy, Robert Fulton was a talented artist and designer. He did not design the first steamboat, but his steamboat was the first that was useful for transporting goods and people. The boat made its first journey up the Hudson River from New York City to Albany on a hot August day in 1807. Fulton himself described this first journey:

> *... the success of my experiment gives me great hopes that such boats may be ... of great importance to my country ...*

Suddenly, life began to move at a faster pace. Within a month of its first trip, Fulton's vessel carried passengers from New York to Albany three times per week at a fare of $7.00, about $70.00 today.

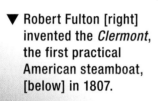

▼ Robert Fulton [right] invented the *Clermont*, the first practical American steamboat, [below] in 1807.

The *Clermont*

Robert Fulton named his boat *Clermont*. During its first voyage, the *Clermont* traveled about 4.5 miles per hour. Onlookers were impressed and afraid. One described the boat

> *as a monster, moving on the waters, defying wind and tide, and breathing flames and smoke.*

QUICK CHECK What effect did Fulton's steamboat have on travel in New York? *Cause and Effect*

181

ⓑ Connecting East to West

The steamboat was only one part of the "transportation revolution" of the early 1800s. It is called a revolution because changes were rapid and completely changed travel.

In 1817, Governor DeWitt Clinton wanted to dig a **canal**, an inland waterway built by people for transportation or irrigation, from Albany to Buffalo. This canal would make it possible to ship farm products from the Great Lakes area to the port of New York City.

Clinton's canal would be 363 miles long. The task seemed impossible, and people called it "Clinton's Ditch."

However, Governor Clinton managed to convince enough people to begin.

Building Challenges

Building the Erie Canal was not easy. Experts had to design a machine to remove tree stumps and to clear the route for the canal. Moreover, the digging was done with shovels by thousands of workers, mostly new arrivals from Ireland.

The canal was four feet deep and forty feet wide. To raise and lower water levels to go over hills and valleys, workers built **locks**. A lock is a kind of water elevator that moves boats within a canal to higher or lower levels. Look at the diagram to see how a lock works.

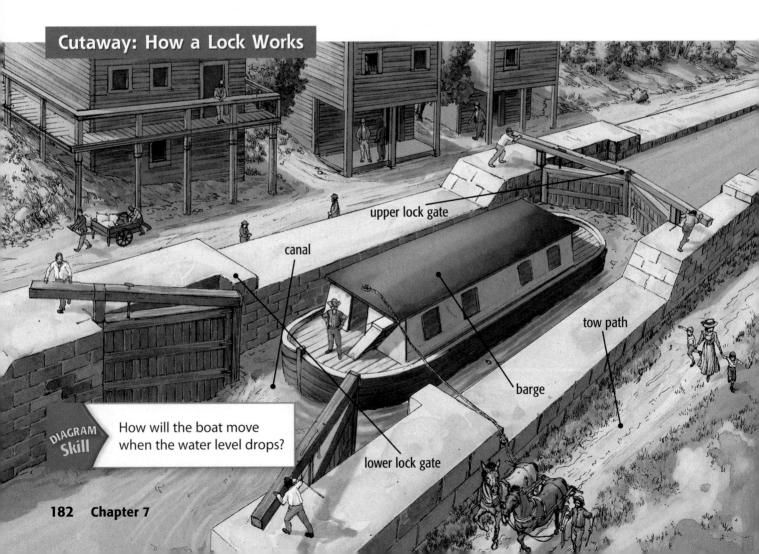

Cutaway: How a Lock Works

upper lock gate

canal

tow path

barge

lower lock gate

DIAGRAM Skill How will the boat move when the water level drops?

A Great Success

After eight years of hard work, the canal was finally finished. Governor Clinton and his wife rode on the first canal boat, the *Seneca Chief,* from Lake Erie to New York Harbor on October 26, 1825. The governor poured a barrel of Lake Erie water into the Atlantic Ocean, calling the ceremony "the Wedding of the Waters."

The Erie Canal made travel between the Great Lakes and New York City much easier. It was still a slow trip. Oxen or mules pulled the boats on a **tow-path**, a path that ran along the side of the canal.

Traffic on the canal grew quickly. Crops and raw materials could be shipped easily from Great Lakes farmers. Manufactured goods from the east could be carried cheaply to the same farmers. Over the next ten years the cost of transporting these goods fell from about $100 per ton to just $6.

Within a year of its completion, more than 350,000 tons of cargo moved through the Erie Canal. New York City became America's leading port and largest city.

People using the canal had to pay a **toll**. A toll is a small fee people pay to use a canal, bridge, or road. The $7 million borrowed to build the canal was quickly repaid. Even today you may cross bridges or use roads that charge tolls.

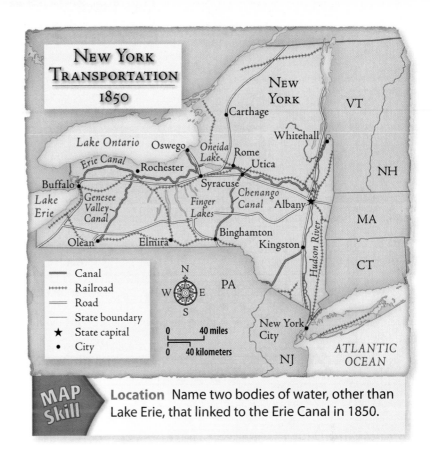

NEW YORK TRANSPORTATION 1850

Legend:
— Canal
+++ Railroad
= Road
— State boundary
★ State capital
• City

MAP Skill **Location** Name two bodies of water, other than Lake Erie, that linked to the Erie Canal in 1850.

The Growth of Towns

The Erie Canal resulted in the growth of several cities. Buffalo's population grew and its port traffic increased. The small frontier settlement became a major city. Rochester became the first **boomtown**, a city that grows rapidly in a short period of time. The city also became the top flour-milling center in the country. Utica, a town about halfway between New York and Buffalo, also grew in population and industry.

QUICK CHECK In what ways did New York State change due to the building of the Erie Canal? *Cause and Effect*

Erie Canal

American Work Song

Verse

Freely

I got a mule, her name is Sal, Fif-teen miles on the E-rie Ca-nal!_ She's a good old work-er and a good old pal, Fif-teen miles on the E-rie Ca-nal!_ We've hauled some barg-es in our day, Filled with lum-ber, coal and hay, And we know ev'-ry inch of the way From Al-ba-ny___ to___ Buf-fa-lo.___

Refrain

Low bridge, ev'-ry-bod-y down, Low bridge, 'cause we're com-ing to a town; And you'll al-ways know your neigh-bor, You'll al-ways know your pal, If you ev-er nav-i-gat-ed on the E-rie Ca-nal.___

What facts does the song give about the Erie Canal?

C The First Train

Another transportation first occurred in the early 1830s. The **locomotive** improved transportation on land just as the steamboat changed transportation on water. A locomotive is a steam-powered engine that pulls railroad cars.

A New York businessman named Peter Cooper started a railroad in Baltimore, Maryland in 1830. The *DeWitt Clinton*, the first steam train in New York, was named for the Governor. It traveled between Albany and Schenectady. Since trains could go anywhere tracks were laid, railroads soon replaced canals as the most common means of transportation.

QUICK CHECK Why do you think the first train might have started at Albany?
Make Inferences

What You Learned

A The steamboat improved travel by water in New York.

B The Erie Canal connected the Great Lakes to the Atlantic Ocean.

C The railroad replaced canals and improved transportation.

The first locomotive to run on the Mohawk Valley Railroad in 1831 ▼

Focus Lesson Review

1. **Focus Question** How did new ways of travel change life in New York?

2. **Vocabulary** Write about the transportation revolution using each vocabulary word.
   boomtown   locomotive
   canal   toll

3. **Technology** How did new transportation methods make New York a national leader?

4. **Critical Thinking** **Make Inferences** What effect might canals and railroads have had on the towns that were located along their routes?

5. **Reading Strategy** **Identify Cause and Effect** What was the effect of the Erie Canal on New York City?

6. **Write About** THE **BiG** IDEA Why would investors risk their money on new inventions?

7. **Reading Primary Sources** *"When the steamboat came so near that the machinery and paddles were heard, the crews in some instances shrunk beneath the decks from the terrific sight."*

   What is this sailor describing?

The **LIBRARY** *of* **CONGRESS**

VOCABULARY

political cartoon

Understand Political Cartoons

Did you know that the song *Yankee Doodle Dandy* was first sung by British soldiers in 1775? They sang this song to make fun of the colonists.

The Americans sang the song with different words. A small group of untrained farmers, "Yankee Doodles," had just defeated the British.

What is a Political Cartoon?

Political cartoons are another way to make people understand an issue. A political cartoon uses pictures to tell readers about events or people in the news.

Patriot Paul Revere was a silversmith, but he also made political cartoons. His cartoon below shows the Patriot version of the Boston Massacre.

1 Learn It

Use these steps to "read" political cartoons.

■ Look at the main characters in the cartoon. What clues does the artist give you about their identity?

■ Scan the cartoon for symbols. A symbol is a picture that stands for something else.

■ Decide the artist's opinion. Do you think Paul Revere supported British troops in Boston?

THE HORSE AMERICA, *throwing his Master.*

2 Try It

Look at the cartoon above.
Answer the questions that follow.

■ Who is the main character in the cartoon?

■ What is the name of the horse? What does this tell you?

■ Do you think this artist liked King George III? Explain your opinion.

3 Apply It

■ Find a political cartoon in a newspaper or magazine.

■ Write a paragraph explaining the meaning of the cartoon. Be sure to explain your opinions.

What were the effects of industry and settlement on New York State?

VOCABULARY

industry
tanning
Industrial
 Revolution
immigrant
famine

VOCABULARY STRATEGY

Word Origins Famine
is from the Latin *fames*,
which means "hunger."
What do you think
famine means?

READING STRATEGY

Compare and Contrast
Use the graphic organizer
below to compare and
contrast New York in 1810
and New York in 1860.

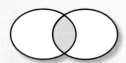

NEW YORK STANDARDS

1.3, 3.1, 4.1, 4.2

New York Grows and Changes

New York was becoming a center of manufacturing and trade. It was a time of change. Georgianna Halloran was a young girl in upstate New York in the late 1800s. Her uncle owned a glove factory.

> *Uncle George was a glove manufacturer. At the time he first started in this business, Johnstown and Gloversville were largely engaged in the manufacture of gloves and mittens. All manufacturing was by means of small scale operations; the cities were filled with small factories, and practically everyone over twelve years of age was engaged in the glove business in some way or another.*

Workers stand in front of the Daniel Hays Glove Factory in Gloversville, New York, in the 1800s ▼

DANIEL HA
MANUFACTURER OF PLYMOUTH GLOVES, WAXED T

1825
Thomas Cole begins a style of painting called the Hudson River School

1845
Great Hunger begins in Ireland

1848
First women's rights convention is held in Seneca Falls

1853
Compulsory education begins in New York

Ⓐ New York Business

All over New York State, new **industries** were growing during the 1800s. Industry is all the companies that make one kind of goods or provide one kind of service. For example, Syracuse quickly became the center of the salt industry in New York. Many factories processed the salt and other companies shipped it out along the Erie Canal.

The Leather Capital

Another growing industry was glove-making. Leather for gloves and shoes comes from animal skins.

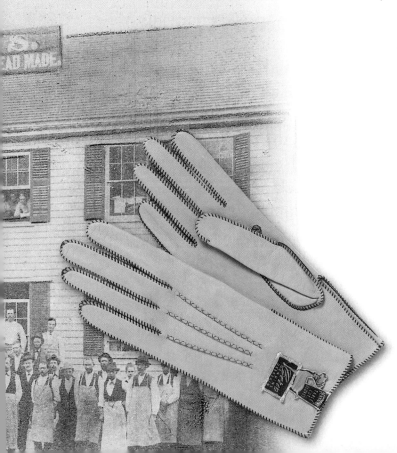

The skins have been treated by **tanning**, a method of scraping and soaking animal skins to make them soft and workable. In 1821, factories in Fulton County, New York, made thousands of pairs of gloves. By 1900, more than 90% of American gloves were made in Fulton County.

New Factories

Almost every industry was changed from handwork in homes to machine work in factories during the 1800s. This is part of what is called the **Industrial Revolution**.

Like the Transportation Revolution, the Industrial Revolution was a quick and complete change in the way things were done.

New inventions changed the way New Yorkers lived and worked. In 1850 Isaac Singer invented the first practical sewing machine, and in 1851 founded a company to manufacture his invention. Many factories began using his sewing machines to make clothes faster and cheaper. Making clothes became one of New York's main industries.

QUICK CHECK How did the Industrial Revolution change the work place? *Compare and Contrast*

189

▲ Thomas Cole painted this view of the Catskill Mountains in 1837.

Ⓑ Life in New York

Life in New York was changing in other ways as well. There were new writers, new painters and new styles of art.

American Writers and Artists

James Fenimore Cooper wrote stories about life on the New York frontier in the 1700s. Washington Irving, another writer, would take walks and write about what he saw. Two of Irving's most famous short stories, "The Legend of Sleepy Hollow" and "Rip Van Winkle," became American classics.

In the 1820s, New York painters Thomas Cole and Frederick Church developed a beautiful style of painting landscapes—paintings that show the landforms of an area. These artists often painted along the Hudson River, so their style became known as the Hudson River School of painting.

You can still visit Olana, Frederick Church's home on the Hudson River.

Looking for a Better Life

After the American Revolution, many **immigrants**—people who come to a new country to live—came to the United States. Before the 1840s, most of these new Americans were from Great Britain or Germany. After 1845, immigrants came from Ireland because of a **famine**. A famine is a time of widespread hunger caused by a crop failure or a shortage of food. A plant disease destroyed the potato crop in Ireland in 1845. Great Britain ruled Ireland at that time. The Irish people had no other food, and the British government would not help. Almost one million people died during "The Great Hunger." Some left Ireland, looking for a better life. Between 1846 and 1851, more than 500,000 Irish immigrants arrived in New York City.

Education

It was not until 1853 that the state began compulsory education, a law requiring all children to go to school. Lawmakers hoped that children would go to school rather than work in factories. People also hoped to "Americanize" immigrants, or help them learn American ways.

Women's Rights

Women in the early 1800s did not have the right to vote. The women's rights movement started in the 1840s. Two leaders were Elizabeth Cady Stanton and Lucretia Mott. They helped to organize the first women's rights convention at Seneca Falls in 1848. You will read more about this convention in the Readers' Theater that follows this lesson.

QUICK CHECK Why did immigrants come to the United States? *Summarize*

Outside an Irish immigrant office in New York City ▶

What You Learned

A New York industries grew in the 19th century, including the salt industry in Syracuse, the leather industry in Fulton County, and the clothing industry in New York City.

B Canals made transporting goods easier by connecting many towns in New York.

C New York became a center for the arts and writing, as well as a place for immigrants to begin new lives.

Focus Lesson Review

1. **Focus Question** What were the effects of industry and settlement in New York State?

2. **Vocabulary** Write a summary of life in New York in the 1800s using these terms.
   immigrant   **Industrial Revolution**

3. **Technology** How did Isaac Singer change life in the 1800s?

4. **Critical Thinking Problem Solving** Why did New Yorkers want compulsory education for all children?

5. **Reading Strategy Compare and Contrast** How did the immigrant population of New York change after the 1840s?

6. **Write About THE BIG IDEA** Why might immigrants risk starting life in a new country?

7. **Reading Primary Sources** *"We live more on the best of every thing here, because we have it so very cheap."* How did this immigrant feel about life in New York?

READERS' THEATER presents

The Call for Women's Rights

Characters

First Narrator	Mrs. Ida Sinclair
Second Narrator	John Sinclair
Beth Sparks	Ella Sinclair
Tom Wilson	Elizabeth Cady Stanton

First Narrator: On July 9, 1848, five women, including Lucretia Mott and Elizabeth Cady Stanton, announced a public meeting, or convention, to discuss women's rights. It would take place at a Seneca Falls church in upstate New York on July 19th and 20th.

Second Narrator: The weather on July 19th was blazing hot. Soon the dusty road leading to the Seneca Falls Church was crowded with wagons carrying people from nearby towns. Many people walked. The large crowd waited quietly for the first women's rights convention in history to begin.

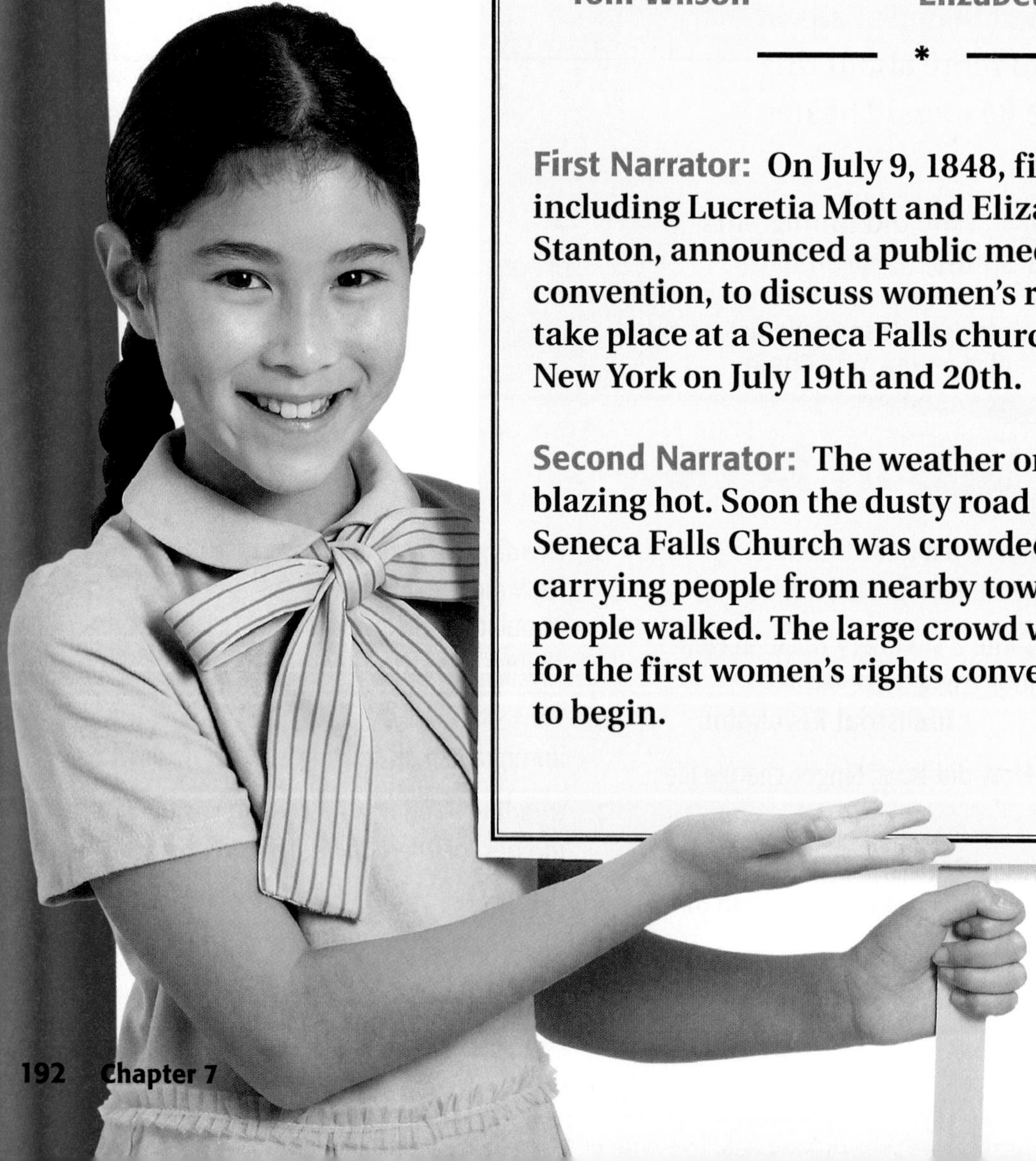

First Narrator: Mrs. Ida Sinclair and her children, nine-year-old John and fourteen-year-old Ella, found seats in the back of the church. Tom Wilson and Beth Sparks were seated on the same bench.

Beth Sparks: I'm so excited about being here. I hardly slept for the last two nights. As soon as I read the notice in the *Seneca County Courier*, I ran and told all my friends about it.

Tom Wilson: Mrs. Sinclair, my brother owns the store next to your husband's law office. He sent me a telegram in Rochester about this convention. As soon as I heard the news, I closed my shop and came down here.

Beth Sparks: Rochester! Why, that's fifty miles away.

Tom Wilson: What is it that you do, miss?

Beth Sparks: Like all my friends, I make gloves for companies here in Seneca Falls.

Ella: That sounds like fun. Do you work in a big factory?

Beth Sparks: No, I work in the kitchen in my parents' house. If I had my choice, I'd do something else – but making gloves is all there is for me. That's why I came to this convention. I'd like some choices.

Tom Wilson: Why, look over there. I see Frederick Douglass!

ELIZABETH CADY STANTON
PROMOTER OF THE FIRST WOMAN'S RIGHTS CONVENTION LIVED HERE, CONVENTION WAS HELD ACROSS THE RIVER
STATE EDUCATION
DEPARTMENT 1932

Ella: Who is he?

Tom Wilson: A famous writer and public speaker. He lives in New York and he wants to end slavery.

Mrs. Sinclair: Quiet, everyone! The meeting is starting.

First Narrator: In a clear voice, Mrs. Stanton explained the purpose of the convention. Mrs. Mott encouraged all the women to take part in the discussion. And *ONLY* women! On that first day men weren't allowed to speak.

John: What's happening now, mama?

Mrs. Sinclair: Mrs. Stanton is starting to read an important document. It's

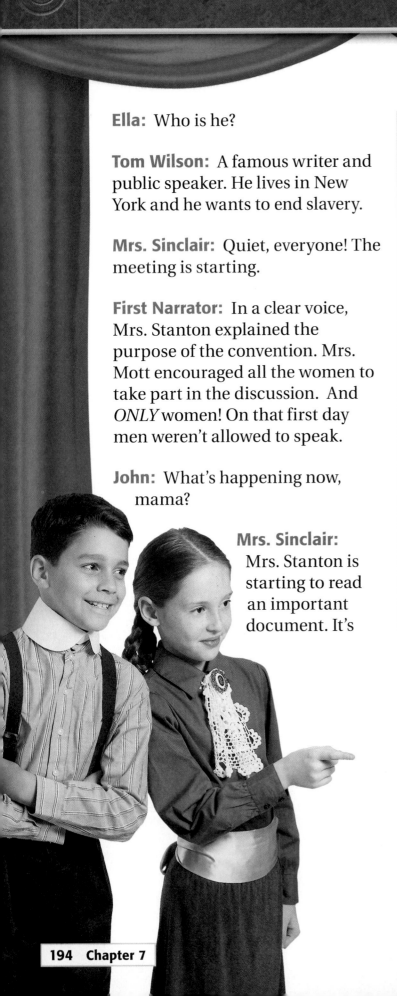

about the rights of all women. Listen carefully.

Elizabeth Cady Stanton: "We hold these truths to be self-evident; that all men *and women* are created equal."

Beth Sparks: Why, it sounds just like the Declaration of Independence.

Mrs. Sinclair: *(with a slight smile)* Not quite, dear. I believe the Declaration says that only "men are created equal."

Second Narrator: Everyone listened carefully, as Elizabeth Stanton read the document, which was called the "Declaration of Sentiments."

Tom Wilson: I like these "sentiments," Mrs. Sinclair. I have to say that I support women's rights.

Beth Sparks: So do I! I've had to give every cent of my wages to my father.

First Narrator: The convention met again the next day to vote on the ideas to be included in the Declaration. People were asked to show their support by signing the document.

Ella: There's Amelia Bloomer, Mama. Isn't her husband the editor of our paper?

Mrs. Sinclair: That's right. I'm sure he'll write something about the convention for the paper.

Beth Sparks: Today we'll be talking about giving women the right to vote. And Mr. Stanton left. He won't have anything to do with that.

First Narrator: The crowd became silent. James Mott, Lucretia Mott's husband, called the convention to order.

John: What's happening now?

Beth Sparks: We going to vote on a list of beliefs about women's rights.

Ella: What do all those statements mean, Mama?

Mrs. Sinclair: That women should have the same rights as men.

Beth Sparks: I am all for that.

Tom Wilson: So am I, ma'am.

First Narrator: On the second day of the convention men were allowed to speak. Tom Wilson stood to talk.

Tom Wilson: I just want to say I think it's shameful only one college in America allows women to attend classes. I hope that changes soon.

Second Narrator: Many people applaud. They voted to pass all the statements except the one that calls for women to have the right to vote.

Ella: I don't understand, mama. Why shouldn't we vote just like Papa does?

Beth Sparks: Just listen to what some people here are saying. They don't want women to take part in our government at all.

Tom Wilson: Now I understand why Mr. Stanton would have nothing to do with this.

Beth Sparks: You surprise me, Mr. Wilson! I thought you believed in women's rights.

Tom Wilson: Well, I do. But it's one thing to get a college education or be able to speak at a public gathering. Voting is something else.

Mrs. Sinclair: I don't think I can agree with you, Mr. Wilson. Voting is a basic right. Without it, women will have no power. But listen to what Mrs. Stanton is saying.

Elizabeth Cady Stanton: *Strange as it may seem to many, we now demand our right to vote, according to the declaration of the government under which we live. Have it we must! Use it we will!**

* These two speeches are the actual words of Elizabeth Cady Stanton.

First Narrator: Frederick Douglass asks for permission to speak.

Ella: What is he saying?

Beth Sparks: He says that women need to vote so we can change laws that treat us unfairly. There is no reason why we shouldn't have a say in making the laws and carrying them out, too.

Second Narrator: Frederick Douglass's words changed many minds. People voted to pass the resolution.

Mrs. Sinclair: Will you sign the document, Miss Sparks?

Beth Sparks: I certainly will!

Mrs. Sinclair: What about you, Mr. Wilson?

Tom Wilson: I must say no, Mrs. Sinclair. I am in favor of women's rights… but not the right to vote.

First Narrator: One hundred people signed the Declaration of Sentiments; 68 women and 32 men, including Frederick Douglass.

Second Narrator: A few days later Frederick Douglass wrote an editorial in his newspaper, *The North Star*, praising the convention. Elizabeth Cady Stanton would not give up.

Elizabeth Cady Stanton: *It will start women thinking, and men too. And when men and women think about a new question, the first step is taken. The great fault of mankind is that it will not think.**

Write About It!

Write your own Readers' Theater play about the second women's rights convention, which took place two week later, in Rochester, New York.

Chapter 7 Review

FOCUS Vocabulary Review

Copy the sentences below on a separate sheet of paper. Use the vocabulary terms.

frontier   **Industrial Revolution**
immigrant   **lock**

1. The edge of a settled area is the
_____.

2. The _____ moves boats within a canal to higher or lower levels.

3. Hoping for a better job, the _____ went to a new country to live.

4. The period of major change in which power-driven machines replaced hand tools is called the _____.

5. **Test Preparation** What is an inland waterway built for transportation called?

 (A) **ditch**   (C) **tow-path**

 (B) **canal**   (D) **toll**

FOCUS Comprehension Check

6. What was the importance of the Genesee Road?

7. Why was the Battle of Lake Champlain important during the War of 1812?

8. Where did Robert Fulton's steamboat go on its first trip?

9. Why did people think Governor Clinton's plan to build the Erie Canal was impossible?

10. How did the transportation revolution change New York?

11. **Critical Thinking** What were some of the major changes in how New Yorkers lived in the 1800s?

12. **Critical Thinking** Many Irish immigrants came to the United States to escape a potato famine. Why might other immigrants have come here?

FOCUS Use the Time Line

Use the time line below to answer each question.

13. What event on the time line involves transportation?

14. What event happened in 1853?

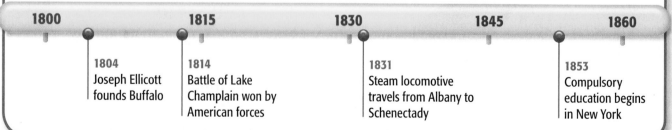

1800	1815	1830	1845	1860
1804 Joseph Ellicott founds Buffalo	**1814** Battle of Lake Champlain won by American forces	**1831** Steam locomotive travels from Albany to Schenectady		**1853** Compulsory education begins in New York

Write a complete sentence to answer each question.

15. What does this map show?

16. What do you know about the areas in red?

17. **Test Preparation** Which place has the greatest population per square mile?

   (A) **Rome**   (B) **Utica**
   (C) **Camden**   (D) **Sherrill**

18. **Test Preparation** What population range was the most common in Oneida County in 2000?

   (A) **less than 500**   (B) **1,000–2,000**
   (C) **500–999**   (D) **more than 2,000**

Oneida County Population, 2000

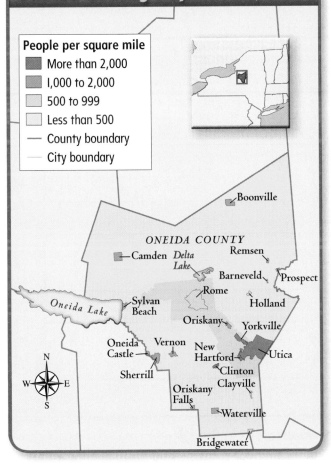

People per square mile

- More than 2,000
- 1,000 to 2,000
- 500 to 999
- Less than 500
- — County boundary
- — City boundary

Constructed Response Questions

Read the letter written by Robert Fulton in 1807. Answer the questions.

> ❝*The signal was given and the boat moved on a short distance . . . She continued to move on. All were still incredulous [disbelieving]. None seemed willing to trust the evidence of their own senses.*❞
> — Robert Fulton, 1807

19. Why was the crowd surprised when the boat moved?

20. How did the people react to the sight of the *Clermont?*

Hands-on Activity

21. **Canal Boat Advertisement** You and some others want to start a business. You will carry goods and people on the Erie Canal. Make a poster advertising your new service. List the fares to each stop you will make. Make your poster colorful to attract business.

Write About History

22. **Come to New York!** You are an immigrant living in New York State in 1850. Write a persuasive letter to your relatives explaining why they should come to New York.

 LOG ON For help with the process of writing, visit: **www.macmillanmh.com**

Comprehension and Critical Thinking Check

Write one or more sentences to answer each question.

1. Why did colonists oppose the **Stamp Act**?

2. Why did **Loyalists** believe that Britain had the right to tax the colonies?

3. What important ideas were expressed by the **Continental Congress** in the **Declaration of Independence**?

4. What caused the British to **surrender** at Yorktown?

5. What did the colonists gain from the 1783 **treaty**, the Peace of Paris?

6. What was the job of the **representatives** who gathered in Kingston, New York, in 1777?

7. What kind of challenges were faced by **pioneers** in New York?

8. Why were Buffalo, Rochester, and Utica considered **boomtowns**?

9. **Critical Thinking** How might the success of an **entrepreneur** depend on **banks**?

10. **Critical Thinking** Why did people think that compulsory education would "Americanize" **immigrants**?

Reading Skills Check

Sequence Events

Copy this graphic organizer. Reread "British Victory" on page 139. Use the graphic organizer to help you order the sequence of events. Answer the questions.

11. What is a sequence of events?

12. How did you figure out the sequence of events?

13. How did you decide what to put in the last box?

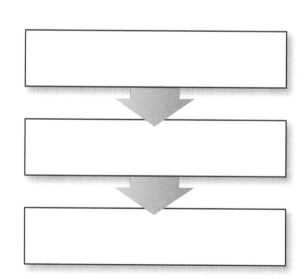

Base your answers to questions 14 and 15 on this map of New York State.

14. About how long is the Erie Canal?

   (A) 500 miles

   (B) 250 miles

   (C) 200 miles

   (D) 300 miles

15. Which route connected Olean to Rochester, New York?

   (A) Erie Canal

   (B) Chenango Canal

   (C) Genesee Valley Canal

   (D) Hudson River

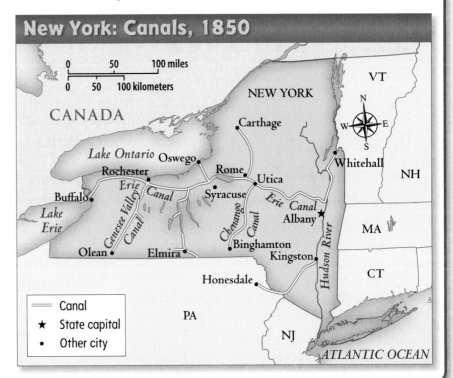

New York: Canals, 1850

16. **Letter** Suppose you are an entrepreneur in New York in the 1790s. Write a letter to a friend telling him about events in New York that have helped your business.

17. **Expository** Some historians have called the War of 1812 America's "Second War of Independence." Write a brief essay explaining why it has this name.

18. **Narrative** Write a letter from the perspective of an Irish immigrant to New York in 1846. Write two or three diary entries to describe his or her experiences.

 LOG ON
For help with the process of writing, visit: www.macmillanmh.com

Unit 3

REVIEW

THE BIG IDEA

Why do people take risks?

Write About the Big Idea

Journal Entry

Think about the events you read about as New York grew and became a state. Then, complete the graphic organizer.

Now, suppose that you are on the frontier in western New York in the early 1800s. Use information from your graphic organizer and from your textbook to write a journal entry about your life on the frontier. Describe the risks you face and explain why you are willing to take them.

New Settlers	American Soldiers	Native Americans
1. wanted land 2. wanted a new start 3. 4.	1. 2. 3. 4.	1. 2. 3. 4.

Write a Journal Entry

1. Plan

- Choose one group from the graphic organizer. Pretend that you live with them.
- List details about your life, including the risks you face.

2. Write a First Draft

- Write the story of a day in your life in early New York. Include details that will be interesting and important to others.
- Use the word "I" as you tell about your life.

3. Revise and Proofread

- Read your journal entry. Did you write about a typical day in your life?
- Proofread your entry. Be sure you spelled words correctly. Check capitalization and punctuation.
- Rewrite your journal entry neatly before handing it in.

ACTIVITY

Speak About the Big Idea

Stories of Experience

Describe stories about the dangers of life in early New York.

Prepare Work with other students who have written journal entries about the same group from the graphic organizer. Use your journal entries, information in Unit 3, and other sources to learn more about life and events on the frontier. Work together to create a story about these events. Practice to make your stories short and interesting.

Present Have each member of the group tell his or her story. Have one person from the group summarize the information from your group.

LAUNCH PAD

For help with the Big Idea activity, visit: www.macmillanmh.com

Read More About the Big Idea

Redcoats and Petticoats

by Katherine Kirkpatrick
The true story of a Long Island family of spies who sent secret messages to George Washington when they hung the family laundry!

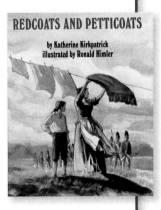

Shh! We're Writing the Constitution

by Jean Fritz
A fact-filled description of the events in Philadelphia in 1787 that led to the signing of the United States Constitution.

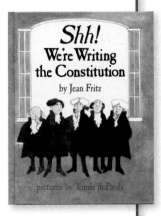

The Amazing Impossible Erie Canal

by Cheryl Harness
Learn how and why the Erie Canal was built, and how the canal helped New York and the United States to grow.

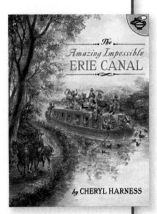

Unit 4

The Empire State

"I pray . . . that your state, as the present seat of empire, may set . . . examples of wisdom and liberality [generosity]. . . . [to] strengthen . . . the Union. . . ."

— George Washington, 1784,
naming New York "The Empire State"

▼ Midtown Manhattan at night

How does technology change people's lives?

In Unit 4, you will read about new inventions and technologies that changed the lives of New Yorkers. You will also read about the many people who helped bring these changes to New York State.

Copy the graphic organizer below. As you read the chapters in this unit, look for information about improvements in transportation, communication, farming, and industry.

Fill in the details about the information you find. The first one has been started for you.

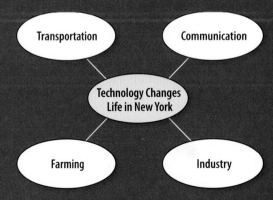

Transportation

Communication

Technology Changes Life in New York

Farming

Industry

Unit 4

People Who Made a Difference

Frederick Douglass
1817–1895

Frederick Douglass escaped from slavery. His autobiography described the harsh conditions enslaved people had to face in the South. He also gave powerful speeches against slavery.
(page 216)

Harriet Tubman
1820–1913

Harriet Tubman escaped slavery and guided people to freedom along the Underground Railroad. In the Civil War, she was a Northern spy and worked as a teacher and nurse.
(page 217)

Samuel Gompers
1850–1924

Samuel Gompers worked as a cigar maker before becoming a leader of the labor movement. He helped found the American Federation of Labor (AFL) and encouraged workers to join unions. (page 233)

1800	1830	1860	1890

1848
Frederick Douglass founds *The North Star* in Rochester, New York

1857
Harriet Tubman helps her parents escape to Auburn, New York

1886
Samuel Gompers helps found the American Federation of Labor

LOG ON

For more biographies, visit:
www.macmillanmh.com

George Eastman
1854–1932

Rochester resident George Eastman simplified how people used photography. His camera, the Kodak, was the first camera to use film on paper rolls.
(page 234)

Herman Badillo
1929–

Herman Badillo served as Bronx Borough President. In 1970 he was the first person born in Puerto Rico to be elected to the United States Congress. (page 264)

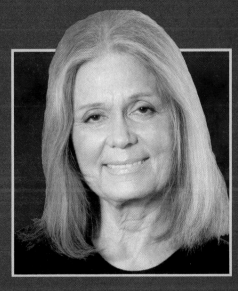

Gloria Steinem
1934–

Gloria Steinem founded the magazine called *Ms.* in 1972. She has written many essays and books that argue for the equal rights of women.
(page 264)

1920   1950   1980   2010

1900
George Eastman's company develops the Brownie camera

1970
Herman Badillo becomes the first Puerto Rican in Congress

1972
Gloria Steinem and others found *Ms.* magazine

In the 1920s, many African American writers and artists lived in Harlem, in New York City. During this time these artists and writers produced many important works. You can read poems by four of these writers on these pages.

Dreams

by Langston Hughes

Hold fast to dreams
For if dreams die
Life is a broken-
    winged bird
That cannot fly.

Hold fast to dreams
For when dreams go
Life is a barren field
Frozen with snow.

Lift Every Voice and Sing

by James Weldon Johnson

Lift every voice and sing
Till earth and heaven ring,
Ring with harmonies
    of Liberty;
Let our rejoicing rise
High as the listening skies,
Let it resound loud as the
    rolling sea.
Sing a song full of the faith that
    the dark past has taught us,
Sing a song full of hope that the
    present has brought us,
Facing the rising sun of our new
    day begun
Let us march on till
    victory is won.

If You Should Go
by Countee Cullen

Love, leave me like the light,
The gently passing day;
We would not know, but for the night,
When it has slipped away.

Go quietly, a dream,
When done, should leave no trace
That it has lived, except a gleam
Across the dreamer's face.

People
by Jean Toomer

To those fixed on white,
White is white,
To those fixed on black,
It is the same,
And red is red,
Yellow-yellow –
Surely there are such sights
In the many colored world,
Or in the mind.
The strange thing is that
These people never see themselves
Or you, or me . . .

O people, if you but used
Your other eyes
You would see beings.

Write About It!

What are the subjects of these Harlem writers' works? Explain your answer.

Compare and Contrast:
Inventions in New York

In this unit, you will learn about inventions that changed the way people lived in New York and in the United States. Comparing is noting how things are similar or alike. Contrasting is noting how they are different. Comparing and contrasting will help you understand the people and events you read about in social studies.

1 Learn It

- To compare two things, note how they are similar.

- To contrast two things, note how they are different.

- Now read the passage below. Think about how you would compare and contrast George Eastman's invention with the cameras you use today.

Find Differences
One main difference is that modern cameras do not use film.

Find Similarities
Film is still sent away to be developed.

A roll of film in the Kodak camera took 100 black and white pictures before it was sent back to the factory where the film was developed. Today, many cameras do not even use film. With modern cameras and computers, you can see the picture you have just taken. There are still cameras that can be sent back to get the film developed, however.

2 Try It

Copy and complete the diagram below. Fill in the diagram with details from the paragraph on page 210.

COMPARE AND CONTRAST DIAGRAM

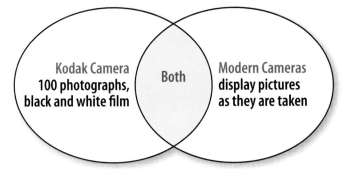

Kodak Camera
100 photographs, black and white film

Both

Modern Cameras
display pictures as they are taken

What did you look for to compare and contrast?

3 Apply It

- Review the steps for comparing and contrasting in Learn It.

- Read the passage below. Use a diagram to show how the Eastman camera and film changed photography.

An advertisement (above) for one of the first Kodak cameras, 1888 (below). ▼

Eastman's invention of celluloid film was important. Before his invention, photographs had to be taken on large glass plates. These glass plates were heavy and fragile, and they broke or scratched easily. Glass plate cameras were large and heavy. They were difficult to move from place to place. George Eastman's celluloid film made it possible for ordinary people to take pictures. The small kodak box camera went on family vacations and to family picnics.

Chapter 8

The Civil War

You Are There

The issue of slavery was on a course to divide the United States and cause a bloody war. One dark night in 1849, a young enslaved woman named Harriet Tubman escaped to freedom. Frightened and excited, she looked at her hands:

"When I found I had crossed the line, I looked at my hands to see if I were the same person . . ."

Harriet Tubman ▶

Chapter Events	1800	1810	1820

1820
Missouri admitted as a slave state;
Maine admitted as a free state

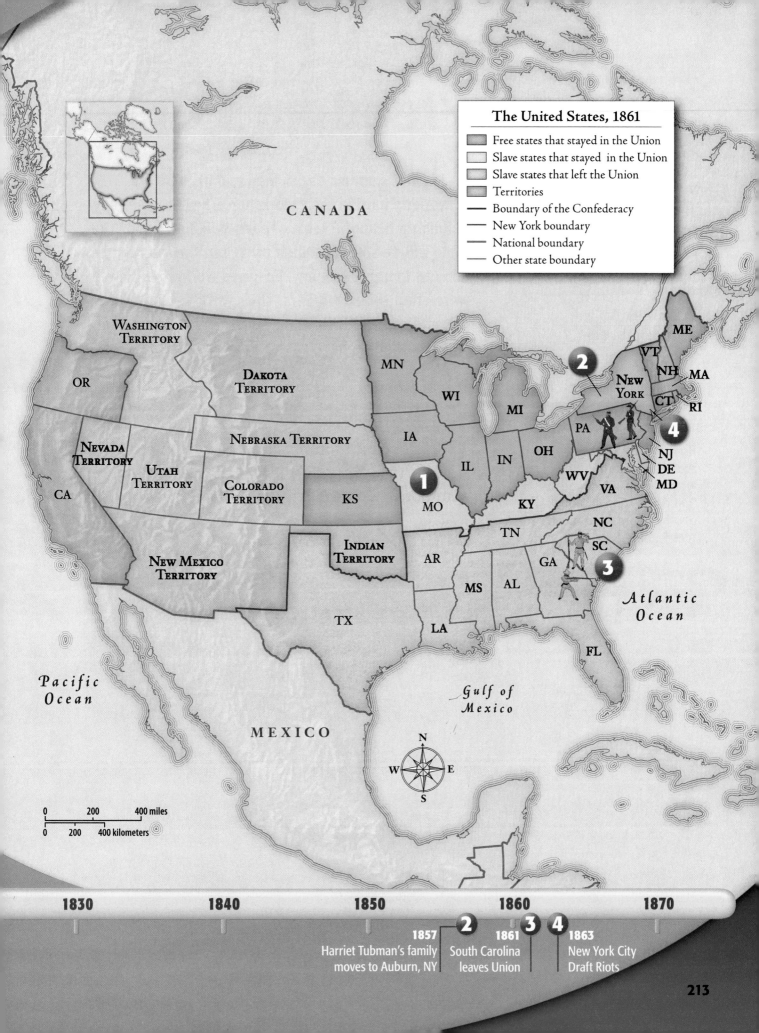

The United States, 1861

- Free states that stayed in the Union
- Slave states that stayed in the Union
- Slave states that left the Union
- Territories
- Boundary of the Confederacy
- New York boundary
- National boundary
- Other state boundary

CANADA

WASHINGTON TERRITORY

OR

DAKOTA TERRITORY

MN

WI

NEVADA TERRITORY

UTAH TERRITORY

NEBRASKA TERRITORY

IA

MI

2

ME

VT

NEW YORK

NH

MA

CA

COLORADO TERRITORY

KS

1

MO

IL

IN

OH

PA

CT

RI

4

NJ

DE

MD

NEW MEXICO TERRITORY

INDIAN TERRITORY

AR

KY

WV

VA

NC

3

WASHINGTON

TN

SC

TX

MS

AL

GA

LA

FL

Atlantic Ocean

Pacific Ocean

MEXICO

Gulf of Mexico

N
W E
S

0   200   400 miles
0   200   400 kilometers

1830   1840   1850   1860   1870

1857
Harriet Tubman's family moves to Auburn, NY

2 **1861**
South Carolina leaves Union

3 **4** **1863**
New York City Draft Riots

Freedom's Call

How did slavery affect New Yorkers in the 1800s?

VOCABULARY

abolitionist
Underground
    Railroad
secede

VOCABULARY STRATEGY

Root Words The word **abolition** is a form of the word **abolish**, which means "get rid of." Can you think of other words that mean "get rid of"?

READING STRATEGY

Summarize Use the chart below to summarize how New Yorkers worked to end slavery.

NEW YORK STANDARDS

1.1, 1.3, 4.1, 5.1

It is a hot summer day. A man and his wife are working hard in their workshop. They are carefully building a beautiful table of dark, polished wood. The table will be sold for a high price, but they will not be allowed to get the money. Enslaved workers in New York were often skilled workers. Their work was sold for high prices. However, their money was given to the person who enslaved them.

Ⓐ Slavery in New York

New York had more enslaved workers than any other state north of Virginia until 1827. Slavery was more common in workshops in New York's cities. New York

Enslaved New Yorkers often made fine products in workshops. ▼

1800	1820	1840	1860

1799
First bill to end slavery passed in New York

1808
Slave trading outlawed in the United States

1820
Missouri Compromise is passed

1850
Fugitive Slave Law passes

1860
Abraham Lincoln elected President

farms were usually small and did not produce large cash crops, as on Southern plantations. New York farmers could not feed and clothe many enslaved workers. Still, the work of enslaved people enriched the state's economy.

The Move to End Slavery

Slavery was legal in all thirteen of the original states. Vermont became a state in 1791. Slavery was illegal in the new state. Other Northern states also began to forbid slavery.

Alexander Hamilton was one of the early **abolitionists**. Abolitionists were people who worked to end slavery. New York's first abolition group was formed in 1784. The abolitionists argued for slavery to be outlawed, and the first law to limit slavery in New York passed in 1799. This law applied only to children of enslaved workers. However, these children would not actually be freed until they became adults. Slavery was outlawed in New York in 1827.

QUICK CHECK Why did more enslaved workers in New York work in cities than on farms? *Compare and contrast*

Populations of Seven States, 1860

State	Total Population* *(includes all groups)	White Population	Free Africans	Enslaved Africans
New York	3,880,735	3,831,590	49,005	None
Massachusetts	1,231,066	1,221,432	9,602	None
Pennsylvania	2,906,215	2,849,259	56,949	None
Georgia	1,057,286	591,550	3,500	462,198
Mississippi	791,305	353,899	773	436,631
South Carolina	703,708	291,300	9,914	402,406
Virginia	1,596,318	1,047,299	58,042	490,865

Source: *U.S. Census of Population and Housing, 1860*

B North and South

Congress passed a series of laws known as the Missouri Compromise in 1820. When Missouri, a slave territory, asked for statehood, the Northern states objected, because there would be more slave states than free states. It was only by agreeing to admit Maine as a free state that the balance was kept. Slavery was dividing the United States in two.

Two African Americans, Samuel Cornish and John Russwurm, started *Freedom's Journal*, an abolitionist newspaper, in 1827. In 1831 William Lloyd Garrison started *The Liberator*, which became the nation's best-known antislavery newspaper. Later, an enslaved African named Frederick Douglass escaped to Rochester, New York. He began his newspaper, *The North Star*, in 1847. There were also abolitionist newspapers in Syracuse and Troy.

Harriet Tubman had escaped from slavery in 1849. Her family settled in Auburn, New York. She returned to the South and helped more than 300 enslaved Africans escape to freedom.

Southern slaveholders were angry. They said each state had the right to make its own laws about slavery. Some New Yorkers wanted to please the South. Many merchants and bankers in New York were making profits on crops from the South. Cotton planters sold their crops through banks and businesses in New York.

By 1850 California wanted to become a state. The Compromise of 1850 was

A "conductor" led escaping Africans to the next "station," often a farmhouse, on the Underground Railroad. ▼

an attempt to avoid violence. California became a free state. The territories of Utah and New Mexico could choose to be slave states or free states. The compromise also included the harsh Fugitive Slave Law. This law made it illegal to help enslaved people as they escaped to freedom.

Abolitionists were angry about the Compromise of 1850. They refused to obey the Fugitive Slave Act. Men were hired to capture people who had escaped from the South. There were fights in Northern cities when these men tried to capture escaped Africans.

Escape to Freedom

Many enslaved Africans escaped through the **Underground Railroad**. The Underground Railroad were actually groups of people who helped escaping Africans along a secret route to freedom. Routes were called "lines." Hiding places were called "stations." Guides were called "conductors."

The Underground Railroad created risks for escaping Africans and their protectors. The Africans had to keep out of sight of men paid to recapture them. Helping slaves escape was a federal crime. Conductors and owners of Underground Railroad stations could be sent to prison.

QUICK CHECK What did people do to fight against slavery? *Main Idea and Details*

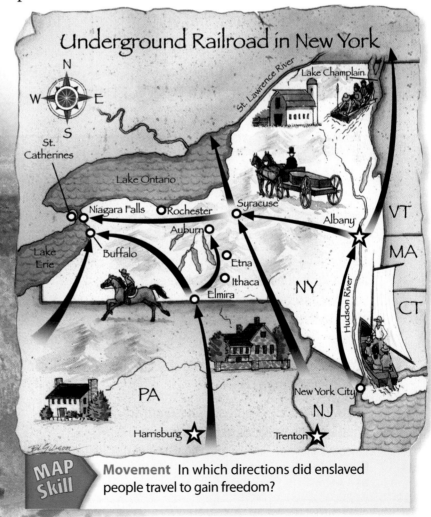

Underground Railroad in New York

MAP Skill

Movement In which directions did enslaved people travel to gain freedom?

▲ Abraham Lincoln in 1858.

ⓒ The Crisis

Abraham Lincoln was elected President in 1860. Lincoln agreed to leave slavery alone in states where it already existed. However, Lincoln opposed slavery in any new territories.

Before Lincoln took the Presidential oath, seven Southern states voted to **secede,** or break away, from the United States. President Lincoln and others worked to avoid fighting. On April 12, 1861, South Carolina troops opened gunfire on Fort Sumter, a federal fort in Charleston harbor. The Civil War had begun.

✓ **QUICK CHECK** What did Abraham Lincoln want to do about slavery in the United States? *Summarize*

What You Learned

Ⓐ In New York, slavery was legal until 1827; many enslaved Africans were skilled craft workers.

Ⓑ Abolitionists worked to end slavery; others helped escaping Africans to freedom.

ⓒ War broke out when Abraham Lincoln took office in 1861.

Focus Lesson Review

1. **Focus Question** How did slavery affect New Yorkers in the 1800s?

2. **Vocabulary** Write a paragraph about the 1850s in the United States. Use each vocabulary term.
   **abolitionist   Underground Railroad
   secede**

3. **Economics** In what ways did slavery affect the New York economy?

4. **Critical Thinking Compare and Contrast** What was the major difference between Lincoln's view of slavery and the views of the leaders of the South?

5. **Reading Strategy Summarize** Summarize the contributions of New Yorkers to the abolition movement.

6. **Write About** THE BIG IDEA Why do you think that abolitionists used railroad terms, like Underground Railroad?

7. **Reading Primary Sources** Abraham Lincoln said, "As I would not be a slave, so I would not be a master. This expresses my idea of democracy." What did Lincoln mean by this statement?

Sojourner Truth 1797–1883

Sojourner Truth was born in Ulster County, New York. Her enslaved parents worked for a wealthy Dutch family named Baumfree, and she was named Isabella.

In 1827, Isabella escaped to New York City. As a free woman she chose the name Sojourner Truth. In the 1840s, she joined a group of abolitionists in Massachusetts. Crowds gathered to hear her speak against slavery and in favor of women's rights.

> *Look at me! Look at my arm! I have ploughed and planted, and gathered into barns, and no man could head me [do better]! And ain't I a woman?*

Sojourner Truth worked to help African American soldiers and newly freed people after the Civil War. Later she retired with her family to Michigan.

Write About It! How did Sojourner Truth use her freedom to help others?

LOG ON For more biographies, visit: www.macmillanmh.com

The Life of Sojourner Truth

1770	1800	1830	1860	1890
	1797 Born in Ulster County New York	1827 Gains her freedom	1843 Changes her name	1861-1865 Helps the Union in the Civil War	1883 Dies in Michigan

Understand Photographs

The **LIBRARY** *of* **CONGRESS**

The first photographs were taken in the 1840s. Photographs help historians to see real life at a particular moment in history.

Look at the photograph on this page. The subject is Julia Ward Howe. What can you tell about Howe from her photograph? Look at details such as her cane and her clothing for clues.

1 Learn It

Read the steps below to help you find information in photographs.

- ■ **Look at the photograph carefully.** Look for details that might tell you where and when the photograph was taken.

- ■ **Try to identify the purpose of the photograph.** Decide why the photographer took this picture.

- ■ **Read the captions.** Captions can provide useful and important information about photographs.

◄ Born in New York, Julia Ward Howe was a leading abolitionist who wrote the words to the *Battle Hymn of the Republic*.

2 Try It

Look at the photograph of Niagara Falls, New York in 1854.

▲ Platt Babbitt built the first photographic studio at Niagara Falls in 1853. By 1900, Niagara Falls was the most photographed location in the United States.

- Why do you think this photo was taken?
- What details in the photo tell you about the time when the photo was taken?
- What can you learn from the caption?

3 Apply It

- Find a photograph from a book, magazine, or from your family's photo albums.
- Write a paragraph describing the photograph. Think about what historians might say about the photograph in the future. Use details to support your opinions.

New York and the Union

VOCABULARY

Civil War
Union
Confederacy
draft
emancipation

VOCABULARY STRATEGY

Multiple Meanings
Draft can mean "a system to choose people for an army." What other meanings does the word draft have?

READING STRATEGY

Identify Main Idea and Details Use the chart below to show how New Yorkers contributed to the Union during the Civil War.

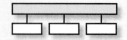

NEW YORK STANDARDS

1.3, 1.4, 4.1, 5.2, 5.3

It is the early morning of Monday, July 13, 1863. You wake up in your house in New York City. You hear angry voices and the sound of breaking glass . . . and gunshots! What is going on? Has an army attacked New York?

New York's poor, many of them recent arrivals in New York, were desperate. Men were being taken into the army while wealthy New Yorkers were able to buy their way out of military service. For three days and three nights, New York City was the scene of fighting, explosions, and fear. What had caused these terrible times?

A reenactment of the Battle of Gettysburg. This photograph shows Southern troops attacking Union soldiers ▼

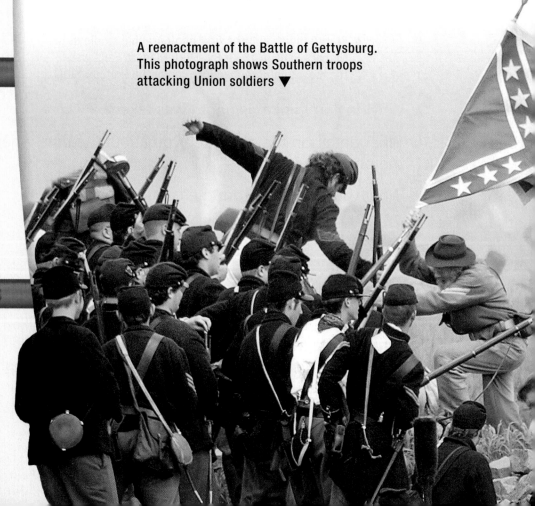

1860	1861	1862	1863	1864	1865

1860
Abraham Lincoln
elected President

1861
Southern states
form new nation

1863
Outbursts in
New York City

1865
Civil War
ends

Ⓐ New York Volunteers

You have read how the **Civil War** began in 1861. A civil war is a war between two regions or groups within a country. On one side were the Northern states, called the **Union**, because they wanted to keep the United States as one united country. The Southern states worked to form their own nation, the Confederate States of America. For this reason, they were called the **Confederacy**.

The new President, Abraham Lincoln, asked for 75,000 soldiers to fight for the Union. New York sent the most soldiers and supplies. New Yorkers also helped by loaning money to the national government.

Great Britain and France were the biggest buyers of Southern cotton. Union leaders were afraid that these European countries would help the Confederacy to win its independence. Lincoln's Secretary of State was a former governor of New York named William Seward. Seward was able to convince Europeans to withhold support for the Confederacy.

QUICK CHECK What did New York do to support the Civil War?
Main Idea and Details

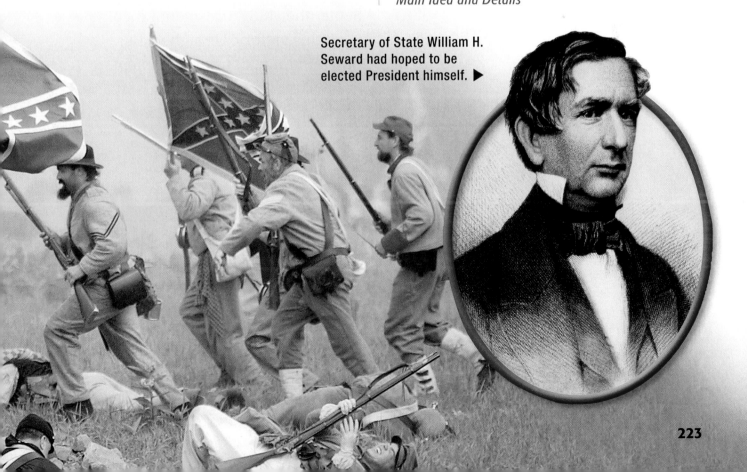

Secretary of State William H. Seward had hoped to be elected President himself. ▶

223

B New York Goes to War

The first battle of the Civil War was at a small creek in Virginia called Bull Run. Union leaders were so sure Union troops would win that they brought their families out from Washington, D.C. to watch the battle. Some even brought picnic lunches.

The battle was a Confederate victory. The Union soldiers, their leaders, and their families had to race for their lives, leaving their picnic baskets behind.

The war continued badly for the Union. Confederate armies led by Robert E. Lee won victories at Fredericksburg and Chancellorsville, Virginia. Union generals seemed unable to win a single battle.

A New Kind of Army

In 1863 the Union army began using the **draft**. A draft is system for forcing people to serve in the army. The idea was not popular. Some people said the government had no right to draft soldiers. Others complained because only the rich could afford to pay a fee of $300 and avoid the draft.

New Yorkers and the War Effort

New Yorkers supported the Union. Wall Street banks raised money for the government. New York factories produced uniforms, boots, guns, and canned foods for the Union troops. New Yorker Elizabeth Blackwell was the first woman doctor in the United States. She and her sister, Emily, trained nurses for Union hospitals.

Calling for Freedom

Some people wanted the war to end with **emancipation**, freeing all enslaved Africans. The Union won a battle at Antietam, Maryland, in September 1862. President Lincoln used this victory. He signed a proclamation, or announcement,

This display at the Lincoln Presidential Library shows Abraham Lincoln and his advisors discussing the Emancipation Proclamation. ▼

on New Year's Day in 1863. The Emancipation Proclamation called for ending slavery throughout the Confederacy.

Gettysburg

In the summer of 1863, Robert E. Lee's Confederate army marched into Pennsylvania. Beginning on July 1, his army fought Union troops at a small town named Gettysburg. Both sides suffered huge losses. The Union army won after three days of terrible fighting. The battle was the turning point of the war.

▲ People burned and looted neighborhoods to protest the draft.

Outrage in New York

By the summer of 1863, the draft law had deeply angered poor men who could not pay the fee to get out of the draft. The war was also causing food and other prices to rise. Uprisings, or riots, took place across the city on July 11. For three days, mobs attacked draft offices, newspapers, and the homes of wealthy New Yorkers.

The crowd blamed the African Americans for their problems. They attacked any African American they saw, including children. They burned an African American orphanage. The uprisings continued until President Lincoln sent in troops. These terrible events, called the New York Draft Riots, remain the worst rioting in American history.

QUICK CHECK Why did President Lincoln decide that September 1862 was the right time to issue the Emancipation Proclamation? *Cause and Effect*

PRIMARY SOURCES

Excerpt from

The Emancipation Proclamation

Issued by Abraham Lincoln,
January 1, 1863

❝ *I do order and declare that all persons held as slaves . . . shall be free; and that the . . . government of the United States, including the military and naval authorities, will recognize and maintain the freedom of said persons.*

I recommend to them [freed people] *that . . . they labor faithfully for reasonable wages.* ❞

Write About It! What did Lincoln expect of the enslaved Africans once they were freed?

DATAGRAPHIC

New York Civil War Soldiers

Beginning with President Lincoln's call for volunteers, New Yorkers led the nation in supporting the war. How many New Yorkers joined the army? The charts below show how New Yorkers served the Union in the Civil War.

New Yorkers in the Union Military

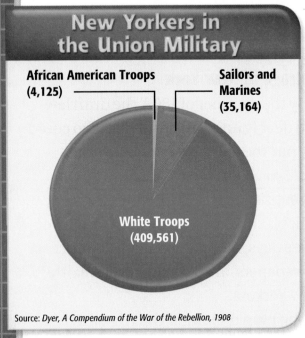

African American Troops (4,125)

Sailors and Marines (35,164)

White Troops (409,561)

Source: *Dyer, A Compendium of the War of the Rebellion, 1908*

How New York Troops Served in the Union Army

- Light Artillery Companies: 66
- Infantry Regiments: 254
- Cavalry Regiments: 32
- Heavy Artillery: 16

Number of Military Groups

Kind of Military Groups

Source: *Dyer, A Compendium of the War of the Rebellion, 1908*

Think About the Civil War

1. How many sailors and marines did New York State supply?

2. How many more cavalry regiments than heavy artillery companies were there?

3. Write a description of the most common New York soldier.

The War Ends

By 1864 Lincoln had at last found strong generals. Ulysses S. Grant led Union armies into Virginia to capture the Confederate capital at Richmond, Virginia. At the same time, General William T. Sherman led Union troops across Georgia in his "March to the Sea." Sherman's troops destroyed resources the Confederacy needed.

In April 1865, General Lee surrendered to General Grant at Appomattox Court House, Virginia. General Grant followed Lincoln's orders to be generous with his surrender terms.

General Ely S. Parker ▶

Lee accepted his offer. Ely S. Parker, a Seneca leader from New York, wrote and corrected the final treaty to end the war. The Civil War was over. Amendments to the Constitution passed after the war gave African American males legal rights.

QUICK CHECK What events led to the Union victory in the Civil War?
Cause and Effect

What You Learned

A New York State contributed the most soldiers and the most money to the Union during the Civil War.

B Anger about the draft and high prices led to riots in New York City in 1863.

C Union generals Grant and Sherman forced an end to the Civil War.

Focus Lesson Review

1. **Focus Question** How did New Yorkers help win the Civil War?

2. **Vocabulary** Write a paragraph about the Civil War. Use the following vocabulary words.
   Confederacy   emancipation
   draft   Union

3. **Economy** How did New York's economic strength help the Union?

4. **Critical Thinking Cause and Effect** How did keeping European countries out of the war help the Union?

5. **Reading Strategy Identify Main Idea and Details** Use the graphic organizer to describe New York's role in the Civil War.

6. **Write About THE BIG IDEA** How did Northern factories and banks help the Union win the Civil War?

7. **Reading Primary Sources** Reread the Primary Source on page 225. What do you think President Lincoln hoped would happen after the war?

Chapter 8 Review

Vocabulary Review

Copy the sentences below on a separate sheet of paper. Use the list of vocabulary words to fill in the blanks.

emancipation	draft
secede	Union

1. Abraham Lincoln led the _____ during the Civil War.

2. Abolitionists wanted _____ of all enslaved Africans.

3. When Lincoln was elected, Southern states began to _____.

4. Riots broke out in New York City in 1863 because of the military _____.

5. **Test Preparation** The _____ helped enslaved Africans escape to freedom.

   (A) **Confederacy**   (C) **draft**
   (B) **abolitionists**   (D) **Underground Railroad**

Comprehension Check

6. What battle was the turning point of the Civil War?

7. Who was William Lloyd Garrison?

8. How did the Underground Railroad help escaping people?

9. What did Congress do in 1820 to keep the balance between free and slaveholding states?

10. Why did Southern states secede in 1860 and 1861?

11. **Critical Thinking** What advantages helped the Union win the Civil War?

12. **Critical Thinking** Why do you think New Yorkers worked so hard for the Union cause?

Use the Time Line

Use the time line below to answer each question.

13. How many years did the Civil War last?

14. How many years after the Missouri Compromise was the Fugitive Slave Act passed?

1820	1830	1840	1850	1860	1870

1820 Congress passes Missouri Compromise

1840 Isabella Baumfree changes her name to Sojourner Truth

1850 Fugitive Slave Act passed

1861 Civil War begins

1865 Civil War ends

Understand Photographs

Write a complete sentence to answer each question.

15. When do you think this photograph was taken? Explain your answer.

16. Who do you think the people in the photograph might be? Explain your answer.

17. **Test Preparation** Historians study photographs to find

   (A) **exact historical dates.**
   (B) **the age of the people.**
   (C) **details about daily life.**
   (D) **the importance of the people.**

18. **Test Preparation** Which primary source would show you the location of the first European settlements in New York?

   (A) **artifacts**   (C) **historical maps**
   (B) **political cartoons** (D) **photographs**

Constructed Response Questions

***Winona Daily Republican,* July 3, 1863
News by Telegraph The Latest
Transmitted To The *Winona Republican***
New York, July 3—The Herald's *Harrisburg Dispatch* says: A column of 25,000 rebels passed through Billsbury yesterday in the direction of Gettysburg. Another account from a gentleman connected with the press, . . . represents the condition of affairs at the close of the fight on Wednesday evening to have been still more favorable and promising of a successful issue [victory].

19. How did the *Winona Daily Republican* receive this information?

20. Do you think this is from a Northern newspaper? Explain your answer.

Hands-on Activity

21. **Create a Poster** Work in groups to make a poster. Your poster should encourage New Yorkers to work for a Union victory.

Hands-on Activity

22. **Expository** Write a short essay describing life in New York City during the Civil War. Be sure to include facts and descriptions of important events.

LOG ON For more about the process of writing, visit: www.macmillanmh.com

Life Changes in New York

You Are There

Many New Yorkers still lived on farms in the late 1800s and early 1900s when a woman in New York spoke the words below:

"We bought a 11-acre farm; my husband was a good dairyman and a first class butter maker, but we could scarcely pay taxes and interest and live . . . the strain was too great, and overwork ruined my health. I have had only one new hat in eight years and one secondhand dress . . ."

In this chapter you will learn how business grew in New York after the Civil War and why many people left their farms and moved to the cities to find jobs in factories.

Buffalo

Lake Erie

2

◀ **A New York farm woman**

Chapter Events 1850 1860 1870

1 **2**

1867
Work begins on the new
State Capitol Building

1873
The Grange forms in
Chautauqua County

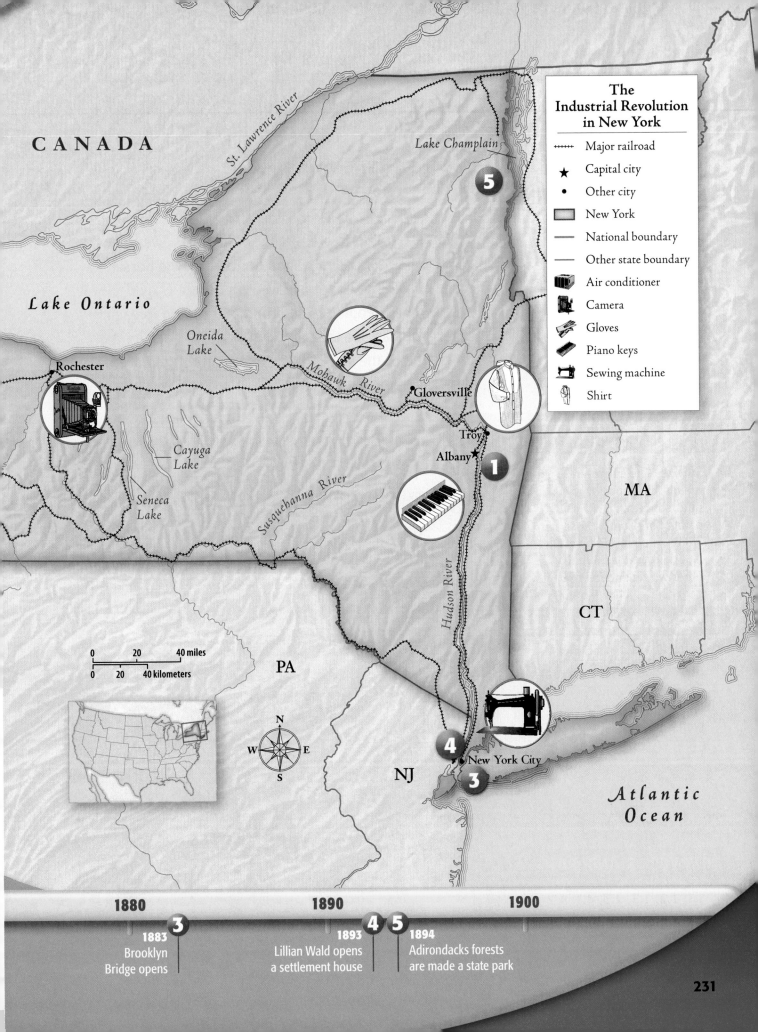

The Industrial Revolution in New York

Legend

- ┅┅┅ Major railroad
- ★ Capital city
- • Other city
- ▭ New York
- ─ National boundary
- ─ Other state boundary
- Air conditioner
- Camera
- Gloves
- Piano keys
- Sewing machine
- Shirt

CANADA

St. Lawrence River

Lake Champlain

5

Lake Ontario

Oneida Lake

Mohawk River

Gloversville

Troy

Albany ★ **1**

Rochester

Cayuga Lake

Seneca Lake

Susquehanna River

Hudson River

MA

CT

PA

NJ

New York City

4

3

Atlantic Ocean

0   20   40 miles
0   20   40 kilometers

N · E · S · W

Timeline

1880 — 1890 — 1900

3 1883
Brooklyn Bridge opens

4 1893
Lillian Wald opens a settlement house

5 1894
Adirondacks forests are made a state park

Inventions and Industries

Why did New York become a business center after the Civil War?

VOCABULARY

manufacturer
employer
labor union
strike

VOCABULARY STRATEGY

Suffixes The suffix **-er** means "someone who does something." A **painter** paints, for example. Use a dictionary to learn what an **employer** does. What other words end in **-er**?

READING STRATEGY

Compare and Contrast Use the diagram below to compare and contrast the life of Samuel Gompers with the life of George Eastman.

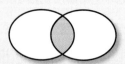

NEW YORK STANDARDS

1.1, 1.2, 1.3, 2.3, 4.1, 4.2

You are trying to cross a street in 1880. Every few seconds a wooden wagon pulled by large horses rushes past. The street is paved, but there is mud everywhere. People are shouting and calling to each other. You can see the store you want to reach on the other side of the street, but you are afraid to move. How will you ever get there?

▼ An elevated railroad in New York City in 1879

Ⓐ New York Becomes a Financial Center

New York's **manufacturers**, people who produce goods in factories, needed money to pay for new inventions and the factories that made them.

Millionaires and Labor Leaders

Some manufacturers borrowed money from New York bankers, such as J.P. Morgan and August Belmont. Others raised money by selling stock, or shares of ownership, in their companies.

When a company succeeds, its stock becomes more valuable. People make money by buying and selling stocks. In the late 1800s, a woman named Hetty Green bought and sold stocks on Wall Street. She was worth $100 million when she died.

Madame C. J. Walker was the first African

◀ A political cartoon of a dishonest New York City politician in 1871

American millionaire. She built a country house on the Hudson River where her daughter supported African American artists, poets, and dancers.

Labor Leaders

Samuel Gompers came from Great Britain. He worked in a cigar factory. Many **employers**, or business owners, made workers spend long days in dangerous conditions for low wages. Samuel Gompers helped organize **labor unions**, groups of workers who try to get better working conditions. He and his followers often used **strikes** when employers would not negotiate with them. A strike is a refusal of all the workers in a business to work until the owners meet their demands. In 1886 Samuel Gompers helped form the American Federation of Labor, or AFL. It was an organization of skilled workers in many industries.

✓ **QUICK CHECK** How was New York's economy different before and after the Civil War? *Compare and Contrast*

233

Electric lights were still new when they were used to outline the building at Luna Park, an early amusement park.

ⓑ An Age of Inventions

During the late 1800s and early 1900s many new inventions changed the way people traveled, communicated, and lived in New York.

Inventors

Alexander Graham Bell was an immigrant from Scotland. Bell taught deaf students to speak. In 1876 he invented the telephone. By 1884 the first long distance phone calls could be made between New York and Boston.

The most famous inventor in American history was Thomas Alva Edison. He invented more than 1,000 practical inventions.

Edison is best remembered for his development of the electric light

New York Inventors	
Inventor	Invention
John Hyatt	Developed celluloid, an early form of plastic
Lewis Latimer	Improved the electric light bulb
Jan Ernst Matzeliger	Invented an automatic shoemaking machine
Elijah McCoy	Invented an automatic lubricating device to oil machinery
Elisha Graves Otis	Invented safety brakes for elevators
Eliphalet Remington	Produced typewriters
Madame C. J. Walker	Developed beauty products
George Westinghouse	Invented air brakes for railroads

CHART Skill Which inventions improved other forms of technology?

bulb. Edison built an electric power station in New York City in 1882. The first light bulbs cost one dollar each. Today that would be about fifty dollars!

Lewis Latimer was an African American who improved the light bulb by inventing the carbon filament.

The Eastman Camera

George Eastman, from Rochester, New York, invented a paper-backed film for cameras. People could carry the Eastman camera, a small wooden box. Eastman made the film out of a form of plastic, called celluloid. Each roll of film took 100 pictures. The camera made an unusual clicking sound when you took a picture, and Eastman

▲ New Yorker Lewis Latimer, inventor

named the camera after this sound. The first "Kodak" camera was born.

Eastman used his profits to build schools, parks, and other benefits for Rochester.

Look at the chart on page 234. You can see inventions of other famous New Yorkers.

QUICK CHECK How did the inventions of the 1800s change the way we live today? *Draw Conclusions*

What You Learned

Ⓐ New York was a center of finance and industry.

Ⓑ Many inventions of the time changed the way people lived.

★ Focus Lesson Review

1. **Focus Question** Why did New York become a center of business after the Civil War?

2. **Vocabulary** Write a news story about Samuel Gompers using the following vocabulary terms.
   employer   **strike**
   labor union

3. **Economics** Why might inventors and business people have come to New York after the Civil War?

4. **Critical Thinking Cause and Effect** How did factory conditions lead to the rise of labor unions?

5. **Reading Strategy Compare and Contrast** Use a Venn Diagram to compare and contrast the life before and after the age of invention.

6. **Write About** THE **BIG IDEA** Choose one invention mentioned in this lesson and write a paragraph explaining how the invention has changed peoples lives.

7. **Reading Primary Sources** "Necessity [need] is the theme and the inventress [female inventor] . . . " What do you think the inventor who said this means?

What was life like for immigrants in New York?

VOCABULARY

tenement
settlement house
social worker

VOCABULARY STRATEGY

Suffixes The suffix **-ment** is a noun ending that can mean "a place where." What do you think a **settlement** is?

READING STRATEGY

Identify Main Idea and Details Use the graphic organizer to show why immigrants came to America.

NEW YORK STANDARDS

1.1, 1.2, 1.3, 2.1, 2.3, 4.1, 5.2, 5.3

Coming to the United States

The huge steel ship slices through the Atlantic waves. The cold wind hurts your cheeks. You pull your thin woolen coat tighter. Other people from your village crowd around you looking for their first view of their new lives. Eagerly you and your friends crowd the rail. Who will be first to see your new home?

Ⓐ New Americans

The United States grew rapidly after the Civil War. People arrived from Europe and other areas in the busy cities of New York. Some people hoped to make a fortune. Some wanted to escape from harsh governments. Others were

1886
Charles B. Stover opens
the first settlement house

1893
Lillian Wald founds
a settlement house

looking for adventure. The United States was a land of opportunity for the immigrants. After 1892 many of these immigrants landed at Ellis Island in New York Harbor.

Finding a Home

Tickets to the United States were very expensive. Immigrants had little money when they arrived. Few of them spoke English. They tried to live near people who spoke their language and shared their customs. Whole neighborhoods became small versions of the home country.

Buffalo had a Polish neighborhood and an Italian neighborhood. Each neighborhood had familiar shops, restaurants, and churches. New York City's Chinatown had one of the largest Chinese communities.

Finding Work

Everyone in an immigrant family worked so they could buy food and pay the rent. They were crowded into

▲ Large families often lived in crowded tenement apartments.

tenements—crowded apartment buildings. Cities offered little help to these neighborhoods. Disease and crime flourished.

Immigrants had to work hard. Even children your age went to work. This is called child labor. Children worked long hours in dangerous conditions among loud machines. There was a constant threat of injury.

Many factories were dangerous places to work. Workers fell into the machinery or were injured in other ways. Workers did not receive sick pay or vacations. If workers were too sick to work, they lost their jobs.

✔ **QUICK CHECK** What details tell you more about the lives of immigrants in New York? *Main Idea and Details*

◄ Immigrant families, like the one on the left, watched for the Statue of Liberty as their ship entered New York Harbor.

237

B Fixing Problems

Tenements were noisy and unhealthy. Many children died from accidents or diseases.

New Yorkers Help

In 1886, Charles B. Stover founded the first settlement house in New York City. A **settlement house** was a place that tried to help immigrants.

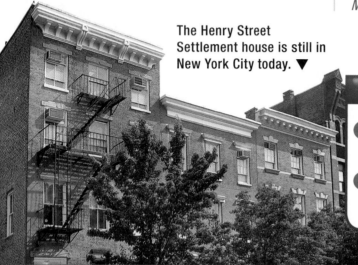

The Henry Street Settlement house is still in New York City today. ▼

Settlement houses offered English classes, entertainment, and helped immigrants find work.

In 1893, Lillian Wald opened the Henry Street Settlement in New York City. Her settlement house employed **social workers**, people who provide services to people in need.

✓ **QUICK CHECK** Why might someone open a settlement house in New York City?
Make Inferences

What You Learned

Ⓐ Immigrants worked long hours for low wages.

Ⓑ People helped the immigrants by building settlement houses.

★ Focus Lesson Review

1. **Focus Question** What was life like for immigrants in New York?

2. **Vocabulary** Write a paragraph about New York in 1900. Use these vocabulary terms.
   settlement house
   social worker
   tenement

3. **Culture** Why do you think immigrants settled near people from their old countries?

4. **Critical Thinking Problem Solving** How did settlement houses help immigrants solve problems?

5. **Reading Strategy Identify Main Idea and Details** Use the graphic organizer for details about this main idea: Immigrants faced many challenges.

6. **Write About** THE **BiG** IDEA Write a paragraph that explains how factories were good and bad for immigrants.

7. **Reading Primary Sources** "Over broken asphalt, over dirty mattresses and heaps of refuse we went. . . . There were two rooms and a family of seven not only lived here but shared their quarters with boarders."

   What is Lillian Wald describing? Explain your answer.

Lillian Wald 1867–1940

Lillian D. Wald was born in Cincinnati, Ohio. When Wald was a young girl, her family moved to Rochester, New York. She did very well in school. Wald graduated from high school when she was only 15 years old.

After becoming a nurse in 1891, Wald volunteered to provide immigrants in New York's tenements with nursing care.

> **Never in all the years have we on Henry Street doubted . . . our belief in the essential dignity of man and the obligations of each generation to do better for the oncoming generation.**

She opened the Henry Street Settlement in 1895. Wald spent the rest of her life caring for and educating people in immigrant neighborhoods. She was also a leader in organizing school health programs, improvements in factories, and child labor laws. Lillian Wald died in 1940 but much of her work still lives on today.

 Write About It! How did Lillian Wald show that she was a responsible citizen?

 LOG ON For more biographies, visit: www.macmillanmh.com

The Life of Lillian Wald

1865	1885	1905	1925
1867 Born in Cincinnati, Ohio	**1891** Became a nurse	**1895** Opened the Henry Street Settlement	**1902** Worked to have nurses in all public schools	**1910** Worked for safer factories

Growth and Change

How did the growth of industries and cities change New York?

VOCABULARY

capitol
suspension bridge
skyscraper

VOCABULARY STRATEGY

Multiple Meanings
The word **capitol** means "a building where a government meets." A **capital** is "a city where a government meets."

READING STRATEGY

Sequence Events Use the chart to list the events in the building of the Statue of Liberty.

NEW YORK STANDARDS

1.1, 1.2, 1.3
2.1, 5.3

In 1986, the Statue of Liberty in New York Harbor was 100 years old. President Ronald Reagan said,

" *. . . We applaud those immigrants who . . . passed through this harbor, went by this lady, looked up at her torch . . . We are the keepers of the flame of liberty. We hold it high for the world to see, a beacon of hope . . .* "

▲ Fireworks celebrate the 100th birthday of the Statue of Liberty.

1860	1865	1870	1875	1880	1885

1867
New state capitol is
begun in Albany

1885
Adirondacks
forests become
a state park

1883
Brooklyn Bridge opens

Ⓐ The Statue of Liberty

The people of France planned a gift to mark the 100 years since the Declaration of Independence was signed in 1776. They decided to send the world's tallest statue. It was designed by Frederic Auguste Bartholdi. You can read about France's gift in Primary Sources on this page.

Work began in 1875. However, the statue was not completed until 1884. The statue was built first in France, then it was taken apart and the pieces were shipped to the United States.

Ordinary American citizens donated money for a base for the statue. School children collected pennies. In the end, Americans raised $250,000 for the base of the statue.

The United States threw a huge party on October 28, 1886. There was a great parade through Manhattan. Office workers on Wall Street threw ticker tape from machines that printed out stock prices. The "ticker tape" parade became a New York tradition.

Today the Statue of Liberty is a symbol of freedom for the entire world.

✓ QUICK CHECK What were the events that led to the opening of the Statue of Liberty in 1886? *Sequence Events*

PRIMARY SOURCES

The New Wonder of the World

From the *Elizabethtown Post*, May 21, 1885

66 *This new Wonder of the World, which is now being loaded on the French transport (ship that carries goods) Isere for shipment to this country, is the largest statue in the world. Some idea of its magnitude (size) may be obtained from the fact that 40 persons found standing room within the head. A six-foot man standing on the level of the lips only just reached the eyebrow.* 99

About It!

Explain how this article gives you an understanding of the size of the Statue of Liberty.

241

B Building New York

After the Civil War, new buildings went up in all New York cities.

A New Building in Albany

One of the most famous buildings of this time is our State **Capitol** in Albany. A capitol is a building where governments meet and laws are made.

Thomas Fuller and Augustus Laver designed our capitol. It took more than 30 years to finish the building. The Capitol opened in 1899. The Capitol is 400 feet long and 300 feet wide. It has five floors, a basement and an attic. Some of the walls are over 16 feet thick!

The Brooklyn Bridge

At about the same time the Capitol was being built, there was a need for a bridge to connect Brooklyn to Manhattan. However, the bridge would have to stand up to the strong East River currents and be high enough for ships to sail underneath it. Such a task seemed impossible.

John Roebling drew up plans for a **suspension bridge**. A suspension bridge hangs, or is suspended, from cables stretched between strong towers. Roebling had already invented the cables he would need. He was ready to build the bridge.

Construction began in 1869 and continued for 13 years. John Roebling died before it was finished. His son, Washington Roebling, took over the job. Washington was badly injured while working on the bridge. His wife, Emily, studied engineering and worked to complete the bridge. On May 23, 1883, Emily Roebling was the first person to cross the Brooklyn Bridge.

The City Goes Up and Up

By 1880, many cities were becoming overcrowded. Most people had to walk to work. In 1904 New York opened its first workable subway, which allowed people to get from their homes to their jobs quickly. As the subway trains moved swiftly under the streets, the city began to grow.

Buildings in the cities were still small and crowded. Two inventions allowed

The roadway of the Brooklyn Bridge is suspended on steel cables. ▼

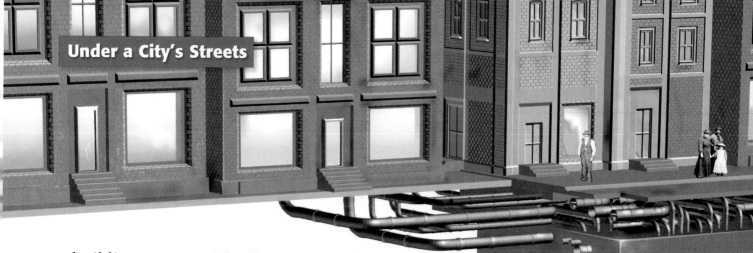

buildings to grow. The first were steel beams, which could support the weight of many floors in a building. The steel beams acted like a skeleton, and buildings grew taller.

With taller buildings came a second problem: getting to the higher floors. New Yorker Elisha Otis solved this problem with the safety elevator. The first elevator was installed in 1857 in a building in New York City.

These tall buildings were called **skyscrapers**. Skyscrapers like the Guaranty Building and Ellicott Square Building in Buffalo opened in 1896. Soon Albany, Rochester, and Syracuse also had skyscrapers, though they were not as tall as skyscrapers today.

The Woolworth Building in New York City opened in 1913. Until 1930, it was the tallest building in the world. The Empire State Building was finished in 1931 and is still the tallest building in New York State. Today, the Albany Mall is also famous for its skyscrapers.

QUICK CHECK What inventions changed cities after 1860? *Summarize*

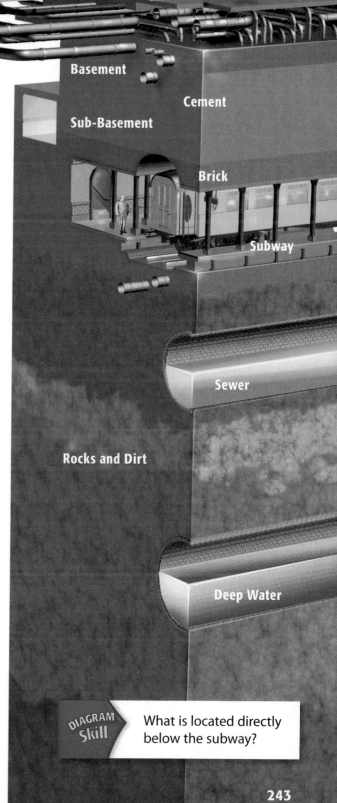

Basement

Cement

Sub-Basement

Brick

Subway

Sewer

Rocks and Dirt

Deep Water

DIAGRAM Skill What is located directly below the subway?

C Saving the Wild Lands

New Yorker Theodore Roosevelt became President in 1901. Roosevelt felt strongly about conservation, or protection, of our natural resources. He wanted to protect the country's natural beauty and land for future Americans.

Roosevelt said:

" *To waste, to destroy, our natural resources, to skin and exhaust the land . . . will result in undermining* [weakening] *. . . our children . . .* "

Theodore Roosevelt poses in a national park. ▶

In 1905, President Roosevelt worked with Congress to establish the U.S. Forest Service. He also set aside more land for preservation than all previous presidents.

QUICK CHECK Explain how President Roosevelt felt about preserving land. *Main Idea and Details*

What You Learned

A The Statue of Liberty is an engineering marvel and a great symbol of freedom, given to the United States by France.

B Many new structures were built in New York cities in the late 1800s and early 1900s, including the state capitol, skyscrapers, and the Brooklyn Bridge.

C People began working toward conserving America's natural resources.

Focus Lesson Review

1. **Focus Question** How did the growth of industries and cities change New York?

2. **Vocabulary** Write a paragraph about new buildings in New York using the following vocabulary terms.
   **capitol   suspension bridge
   skyscraper**

3. **Government** What did the national government do to protect our natural resources?

4. **Critical Thinking Make Inferences** Why do you think people in the 1880s might have been surprised to see Emily Roebling directing work on the Brooklyn Bridge?

5. **Reading Strategy Sequence Events** Use the chart to show the order of events in building the Brooklyn Bridge.

6. **Write About THE BiG IDEA** How did new technology lead to the creation of skyscrapers?

7. **Reading Primary Sources** "Here at our sea-washed, sunset gates shall stand a mighty woman with a torch . . . From her beacon-hand Glows world-wide welcome . . . " What is Emma Lazarus describing in this passage?

Cooperation

Helen Keller was blind and deaf. Annie Sullivan came to teach her. When Keller decided to work with, or cooperate, with Sullivan, she quickly understood that she could learn to read, and express her ideas.

Read these steps to learn why it is important for good citizens to cooperate to reach their goals.

Build Citizenship

1. **Identify the problem** or the issue.

2. **Express points of view.** Discuss some reasons that people disagree.

3. **Look for common goals or interests.** Think about possible solutions.

4. **Find ways that everyone can gain from cooperation.** Look for a solution that will satisfy everyone.

Think About It

1. What did Annie Sullivan want Helen Keller to do?

2. Could Helen Keller have learned to read and speak without cooperating?

Write About It!

Write a paragraph describing a time when you had to cooperate with your classmates to accomplish a goal.

Helen Keller learned to read and write (above) with her teacher Annie Sullivan (right).

What kinds of jobs did New Yorkers do around 1900?

VOCABULARY

- urban
- rural
- Grange
- reform
- sweatshop

VOCABULARY STRATEGY

Prefixes The prefix **re-** means "do again," so the word **reform** means "form again" or "improve." What other words use the prefix **re-?**

READING STRATEGY

Summarize Use the chart to summarize how farm life changed during the Industrial Revolution.

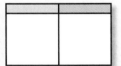

NEW YORK STANDARDS

1.3, 2,1, 3.1, 4.1, 4.2
5.1, 5.3

New York Goes to Work

You wake up on a summer morning in 1900 on a quiet farm. At first all you can hear are crickets and birds singing. Suddenly there is a new sound, growing closer—the sound of a puffing steam engine.

You leap out of bed. Today you and your family will begin the harvest. Everyone has a lot of work to do!

Ⓐ Changes on New York Farms

You have read about the Industrial Revolution. During the 1800s, power–driven machines changed **urban**, or city, life. **Rural** life on farms and in small villages changed, too.

Farm Life

Steam-driven machines began to do farm work in the 1800s. The steam-driven combine could harvest crops and get them ready for market. Farmers no longer needed so many helpers. The number of people in rural areas began to drop.

1860	1880	1900	1920

1867
The Grange is founded

1885
Samuel Gompers helps found the AFL

1902
President Roosevelt ends a coal miners' strike

1911
Triangle Shirtwaist Factory fire

Even with machines, everyone in a farm family had to work. Even the children collected eggs, carried water, and tended animals.

Neighbors often lived far apart. Most social life took place at the one-room schoolhouse or at the local church. Families had to make their own music, stories, and games.

The Grange

Oliver Hudson Kelley started a farm movement called the **Grange** in 1867. The first New York chapter of the Grange was founded in Chautauqua County in 1873. Soon, 17,000 farmers had joined the Grange in New York State.

The Grange began as a way to provide education and a social life in farm areas. Later, its members worked for political and economic changes. The railroads were the main target of Grange protests. Sometimes railroad companies charged very high rates for transporting crops. The Grangers demanded that the rates be made fair. Grange protests helped to create the Interstate Commerce Act in 1887, making railroad rates fairer. Grange members also worked to **reform**, or change, the way taxes were collected. The Grange also supported women in their fight for the right to vote.

QUICK CHECK How did the Grange change life for farmers? *Summarize*

Teams of horses pulled large machinery through fields, replacing many human workers. ▼

This poster encouraged farmers to join the Grange. ▲

247

Then and Now

How Factory Environments Have Changed

THEN Sweatshops were crowded, dirty, and unsafe. Workdays were long and pay was low. Even children had to work so families could survive.

NOW Modern factories are much safer. Inspectors make sure that workers' health is protected. Workers receive a minimum wage and must be paid overtime for longer hours.

Write About It! Write a paragraph that explains how factories have improved since 1900.

ⓑ Factories Change

In America's cities, there was also a demand for reform. People worried about the poor who were living in crowded unhealthy slums. People wanted reforms to improve American cities and industries.

The Triangle Fire Brings Reforms

Some industries produced their work in **sweatshops**, dark and dirty workshops where immigrant workers were paid low wages and worked long hours.

On March 25, 1911, a fire broke out at the Triangle Shirtwaist Factory in New York City. Most of the immigrant workers were Jewish and Italian teenagers. These women made shirtwaists, a popular type of women's blouse. Flames and smoke spread quickly through the crowded building. The owners of the factory had locked the doors because they thought their workers were stealing from them.

Some of the terrified young women ran for a fire escape, but it was poorly maintained and it fell to the street, nine stories below. Others broke windows and climbed onto high ledges to escape the flames. Some of them leaped to their deaths on the streets below; others fell when faced by the flames. Many more were lost in the fire. The fire was put out quickly, but 146 women were dead. People were angry and demanded factory reforms.

The Labor Movement Grows

The period of the early 1900s is called the Progressive Era, or time, because Americans worked for social and economic progress, or improvements.

You read about Samuel Gompers. The AFL was an all-male trade union for skilled workers. Women and unskilled workers had no voice in this union.

Workers strike in front of a shop in 1937. ▼

Later they formed the CIO. In 1955 the two labor groups formed the AFL-CIO.

When Theodore Roosevelt became President, he continued to lead the Progressive Movement. In 1902, he helped end a strike by coal mine workers. He also worked for improvements for workers in many industries.

✓ **QUICK CHECK** Why do you think some factories were called sweatshops? *Make Inferences*

What You Learned

Ⓐ Machines made farm work easier, while the Grange worked for rural reforms.

Ⓑ Unfair and unsafe urban conditions led to the reforms of the Progressive Movement.

★ Focus Lesson Review

1. **Focus Question** What kinds of jobs did New Yorkers do around 1900?

2. **Vocabulary** Write a summary of what you learned in this lesson using the following vocabulary words.
   Grange   rural
   reform   sweatshop

3. **Technology** How did the Industrial Revolution change farming?

4. **Critical Thinking Fact and Opinion** Write one fact and one opinion about the Triangle Shirtwaist Fire.

5. **Reading Strategy Summarize** Use a chart to tell what you learned about the Triangle Shirtwaist Fire.

6. **Write About THE BIG IDEA** Write a paragraph to answer this question: Does technology always change people's lives for the better?

7. **Reading Primary Sources** "The workroom was crowded and hot . . . The [medical] examination revealed the fact that she ['Sadie G.'] had lead poisoning . . .

   What does the passage describe? Explain your answer.

Chapter 9 Review

FOCUS Vocabulary Review

Copy the sentences below on a separate sheet of paper. Use the list of vocabulary words to fill in the blanks.

employer	rural
tenement	suspension bridge

1. The Brooklyn Bridge is a _____ .

2. _____ areas are made up mostly of farms.

3. _____ hire people to work in their businesses.

4. Many immigrants lived in _____ .

5. **Test Preparation** A _____ is a factory where workers are paid low wages and work in unhealthy conditions.

   (A) **settlement house**   (C) **tenement**

   (B) **labor union**   (D) **sweatshop**

FOCUS Comprehension Check

6. Name two ways businessmen could get money to finance their businesses.

7. Why did Lillian Wald found a settlement house?

8. Why did the French give the Statue of Liberty to the United States?

9. Why might workers want to start a union?

10. What was the Progressive Movement?

11. **Critical Thinking** Why did the Grange want to keep railroad rates low?

12. **Critical Thinking** Why did immigrants agree to work long days in sweatshops?

FOCUS Use the Time Line

Use the time line below to answer each question.

13. Which event occurred after 1900?

14. Which was started first, the Grange, or settlement houses?

1870	1880	1890	1900	1910	1920

1873
The Grange started in Chautauqua County in New York

1882
Edison builds the first electric power station

1886
Charles B. Stover opens the first settlement house in New York

1911
Triangle Shirtwaist Factory fire

Understand Photographs

Write a complete sentence to answer each question.

15. When do you think this picture was taken? Explain your answer.

16. Where do you think this picture was taken? Explain your answer.

17. **Test Preparation** Which kind of primary source would express an opinion about a historical event?

    (A) **artifact**   (C) **political cartoon**
    (B) **historical map** (D) **photograph**

18. **Test Preparation** Which of these items is not an artifact?

    (A) **the first photograph**
    (B) **an encyclopedia**
    (C) **an Iroquois basket**
    (D) **a songbook from the Civil War**

Constructed Response Questions

19. What is this primary source describing?

20. Do you think the writer is an American or an immigrant? Explain your choice.

At Liberty's Gate

New York – Five thousand "seekers of liberty" are pouring through the gates of Ellis Island every 24 hours these days. They come from almost every quarter of Europe, Asia, and Africa . . .

21. **Have a Celebration of Culture** Find out about different cultures. Learn about the food, music, or games of one particular country. Each student can share something from his or her country with the class.

22. **Expository** Write a paragraph about how people's lives were changed by one of the inventors discussed in this chapter.

 LOG ON For more about the process of writing, visit: www.macmillanmh.com

Chapter 10

New York in the 20th Century

You Are There

President Theodore Roosevelt described his ideas of what the United States should be in a 1903 speech:

"*Let the watchwords of all our people be the old familiar watchwords of honesty, decency, fairdealing, and common sense . . . The welfare of each of us is dependent . . . upon the welfare of all of us.*"

Theodore Roosevelt ▶

Lake Erie

②
•Buffalo

| Chapter Events | 1900 | 1920 | 1940 |

①
1933
Governor Franklin Roosevelt becomes President

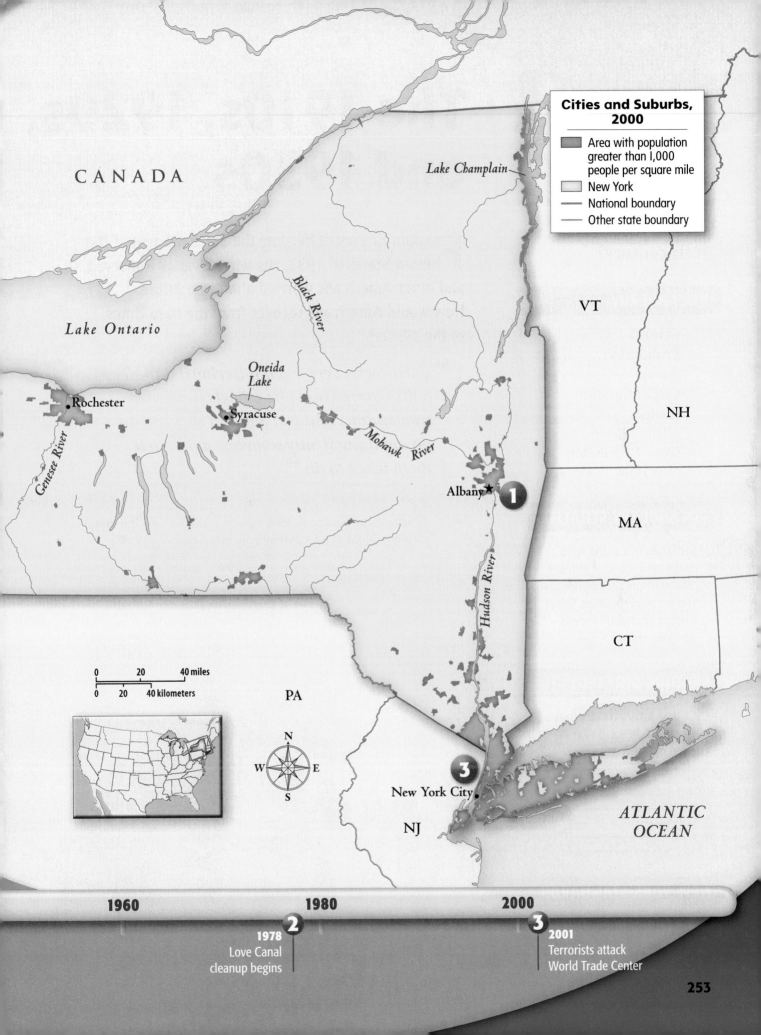

CANADA

Lake Ontario

Lake Champlain

Black River

Oneida Lake

Genesee River

•Rochester

•Syracuse

Mohawk River

Albany ★ **1**

VT

NH

MA

Hudson River

CT

Cities and Suburbs, 2000

Area with population greater than 1,000 people per square mile

New York

National boundary

Other state boundary

0   20   40 miles

0   20   40 kilometers

PA

N
W   E
S

3

New York City•

NJ

ATLANTIC OCEAN

1960

1980

2000

2
1978
Love Canal cleanup begins

3
2001
Terrorists attack World Trade Center

The 1910s, 1920s, and 1930s

How did New Yorkers face the challenges of the 20th century?

VOCABULARY

- neutral
- Prohibition
- repeal
- Great Migration
- Harlem Renaissance
- Great Depression
- New Deal

VOCABULARY STRATEGY

Suffixes The suffix **-tion** makes a verb into a noun. The verb **prohibit** becomes the noun **prohibition**. What other vocabulary words use this suffix?

READING STRATEGY

Cause and Effect What effects did World War I have on New York?

	▶
	▶
	▶
	▶
	▶

NEW YORK STANDARDS

1.1, 1.2, 1.3, 2.2
4.1, 4.2, 5.1, 5.2, 5.3

Franklin Roosevelt became the 31st President of the United States in 1933. His wife, Eleanor Roosevelt, and other Americans worried about the future. How would Americans recover from the hard times of the 1930s?

❝*It was very, very solemn [serious] and a little terrifying. The crowds were so tremendous and you felt that they would do anything if only someone would tell them what to do.*❞

A ticker-tape parade in 1931 celebrates the round-the-world airplane flight of pilots Wiley Post and Harold Gatty. ▼

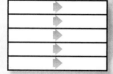

1910	1920	1930	1940

1917
United States enters
World War I

1929
Stock Market crash ends
Roaring Twenties

1933
New York's Franklin
Roosevelt becomes
President

1939
New York hosts
World's Fair

Ⓐ A Time of Changes

At the beginning of the century, people wanted to make the United States and New York State a better place. They worked to reform industry, politics, and society. They wanted to make factories safer, shorten the work week, and improve pay. Others worked to open government to new voters. Still others worked for women's rights. These people who worked for a better society were called reformers.

Changing the Constitution

The Constitution originally said that United States senators should be chosen by each state's government. Reformers wanted to change this so that people could elect their senators themselves. In 1913, the 17th Amendment allowed the direct election of senators.

You may remember from the Readers' Theater in Chapter 7 that women could not vote in the United States. Carrie Chapman Catt, Susan B. Anthony, and many other women and men worked for women's right to vote. After 70 years, they succeeded when the 19th Amendment passed in 1920.

▲ New York City women demand the right to vote.

The first leaders of the women's voting movement gave speeches and marched for their cause. During World War I, more than one million women in New York signed a petition asking for the right to vote.

When the 19th Amendment passed Carrie Chapman Catt gave this speech of victory:

❝ *The vote is the emblem [symbol] of your equality, women of America, the guaranty of your liberty. . . . That vote has been costly. Prize it!*❞

QUICK CHECK What was the effect of changes that took place in American life in the early 1900s? *Cause and Effect*

255

ⓑ Rich and Poor

World War I broke out in Europe in 1914. The Allies—Great Britain, France, and Russia—fought against the Central Powers—Germany, Austria-Hungary, and Turkey.

The United States Enters the War

At first, the United States tried to remain **neutral**. Neutral means not taking sides. It was not easy staying neutral. In 1915, a German submarine sank the passenger ship *Lusitania*, killing over 100 Americans. In 1917, the British intercepted a German telegram. It promised American territory if Mexico would join the Central Powers. Many Americans saw the telegram as an attack on the United States. President Woodrow Wilson called for war.

▲ This cartoon shows the lively spirit of the 1920s.

The United States declared war on Germany on April 6, 1917. The arrival of American troops quickly brought victory to the Allies. The Treaty of Versailles ended the war in 1919.

The Roaring Twenties

In the years after the war, the stock market and the economy grew rapidly. Radio and movies became popular. Famous people included pilot Charles Lindbergh and actress Mary Pickford.

In 1920, the 18th Amendment to the Constitution established **Prohibition**, making it illegal to buy or sell alcoholic drinks. (In 1933, the 21st Amendment **repealed**, or cancelled, the 18th Amendment.)

The 1920s were a time of wealth and leisure. Langston Hughes and Zora Neale Hurston (inset) were among Harlem writers and artists. ▼

◀ Men without jobs line up for a meal at a "soup kitchen."

Moving North

Hoping to find better jobs, many African Americans moved from rural areas in the South. This is known as the **Great Migration**. The Great Migration led to African American communities in Northern cities, such as Harlem in New York City.

A number of African American artists lived in Harlem. Poet Langston Hughes, musician Duke Ellington, and writer W.E.B. Du Bois were all part of the **Harlem Renaissance**—a time of creativity in the 1920s. Harlem became a center for African American culture.

Crash!

Many people bought stocks, hoping to get rich. On October 29, 1929, the stock market "crashed." Prices fell to record lows. The crash ended the Roaring Twenties. It started a period in the 1930s called the **Great Depression**. Many people have no jobs or money during a depression.

A Plan to End the Great Depression

In 1932, New York Governor Franklin Roosevelt was elected President. In his first speech as President, Roosevelt boldly declared, "the only thing we have to fear is fear itself." His first act was to call for a "bank holiday." Banks were closed for three days to stop people from removing all of their money at once.

President Roosevelt's plan was called the **New Deal**. Social Security was established to provide income to retired Americans. Other programs paid for new roads and to bring electricity to rural areas. These projects provided jobs and improved life for New Yorkers and other Americans.

QUICK CHECK How did the stock market affect the 1920s and 1930s? *Cause and Effect*

C Troubled Times

In the 1930s, there was trouble in Europe again. Americans disagreed about what role the United States should play in Europe's troubles. Some people wanted to ignore Europe while others felt the nation should try to help. The United States planned to remain neutral if another war started in Europe.

▲ A poster shows the New York World's Fair of 1939.

The World of Tomorrow

In 1939, New York opened a world's fair. A world's fair is an exhibition of displays from many countries. The fair's theme in 1939 was "The World of Tomorrow." The planners wanted to celebrate the inventions and ideas that would make a better world possible.

In September 1939, the lights on the Polish building at the fair were turned off. The German army had attacked Poland. World War II had begun.

QUICK CHECK What event started World War II?
Cause and Effect

What You Learned

A In the early 1900s, the Progressive Era brought about many changes.

B An economic boom in the 1920s was followed by the Great Depression.

C Another world war broke out in 1939.

Focus Lesson Review

1. **Focus Question** How did New Yorkers face the challenges of the 20th century?

2. **Vocabulary** Write a description of life after World War I using the following vocabulary terms.
   Great Depression   **Prohibition**
   Harlem Renaissance

3. **Economics** Why did Franklin Roosevelt close the banks for three days?

4. **Critical Thinking Make Inferences** Why did President Roosevelt warn Americans about "fear itself?"

5. **Reading Strategy Cause and Effect** How did the stock market crash affect New York?

6. **Write About THE BIG IDEA** How did new inventions like airplanes and movies change people's lives?

7. **Reading Primary Sources**
   "August 26th will be remembered as one of the great days in the history of the women of the world and in the history of this republic. "

   What is the *New York Times* article describing? Why do you think so?

Langston Hughes 1902–1967

Langston Hughes began writing poetry in the eighth grade. In his high school, he was elected class poet. Hughes continued writing as an adult in New York City. He spent a lot of time in Harlem jazz clubs. Jazz music gave his writing a special rhythm.

Hughes wrote poems, essays, books, and plays. A few of his best poetry collections include *The Weary Blues* (1926) and *Shakespeare in Harlem* (1942). Hughes was proud of his background. He said:

> **No great poet has ever been afraid of being himself... We... now intend to express our individual dark-skinned selves without fear or shame.**

Hughes inspired other African American writers. After he died in 1967, his Harlem home was turned into a New York City landmark, or place of historic interest.

Write About It! How do you think music can influence someone's poetry?

LOG ON For more biographies, visit:
www.macmillanmh.com

The Life of Langston Hughes

1900	1920	1940	1960	1980

1902 James Langston Hughes is born in Joplin, Missouri

1923 Travels to Africa and Europe

1926 Publishes first book of poems

1943 Writes a column for a Chicago Newspaper

1967 Langston Hughes dies

How did life change after World War II?

VOCABULARY

ration
suburb
commute
United Nations
civil rights
pollution

VOCABULARY STRATEGY

Prefixes The prefix **sub-** means "beneath" or "secondary." **Urb** comes from a word meaning "city." What do you think **suburb** means?

READING STRATEGY

Sequence Events Choose four events from this lesson and put them in the order in which they occurred.

NEW YORK STANDARDS

1.2, 1.3, 2.1, 2.2, 3.1, 4.1, 5.1, 5.3

World War II and the American Century

On December 8, 1941, a grim-faced President Franklin Roosevelt asked Congress for a declaration of war:

> "*Yesterday, December 7, 1941—a date which will live in infamy [shame]—the United States of America was suddenly and deliberately attacked by naval and air forces of the Empire of Japan.*"

Damaged battleships burn after the Pearl Harbor attack on December 7, 1941. ▼

1940	1950	1960	1970	1980

1941
America enters World War II

1945
World War II ends; United Nations is founded

1962
Telstar, the first communications satellite, is launched

1965
Civil Rights Act passes

1978
Residents of Love Canal fight to clean up community

Ⓐ Another World War

By 1941, most of the countries of Europe and Asia were involved in World War II. President Roosevelt tried to keep Americans out of the war, but Japan attacked the United States at Pearl Harbor on December 7, 1941.

The United States at War

The United States again joined the Allies—Great Britain, France, and the Soviet Union—in the war against Germany, Italy, and Japan.

New Yorkers pitched in to win the war. Nearly two million New Yorkers served in the military. Many soldiers sailed to Europe from New York Harbor. New York City mayor Fiorello LaGuardia organized civilian defense. Factories in Buffalo, Rochester, Syracuse, and other cities produced war supplies. The Brooklyn Navy Yard built warships. One factory on Long Island turned out more planes than any other factory in the world!

The Home Front

Everyone helped with the war effort. Some people held scrap drives to collect metal and rubber to make into war supplies. People also **rationed**, or used less of, gasoline, rubber, certain foods and other supplies. Americans were encouraged to "make do with less" so troops could have more food, equipment, and supplies. New York farmers grew food for the Allies. Even city residents grew "victory gardens" to increase food production.

Bond drives raised money to pay for the war. A bond is a kind of loan. The buyer of a bond is paid back in a certain amount of time. Bondholders also get interest, a percentage of the loan as a reward for loaning the money.

The war came to an end in August 1945. The war was over, but America faced a new enemy—the Soviet Union.

QUICK CHECK How did New York contribute to winning World War II?
Sequence Events

Children collected old metal during scrap iron drives. ▼

Levittown, New York, (above) was one of the earliest suburbs. Families (right) watched television together in their new suburban homes.

Ⓑ A New Way of Life

A new kind of American town developed after World War II. It was called a **suburb**—a smaller community very close to a larger city. People moved to the suburbs because houses were affordable and there were open places for children to play. One of the first suburban housing areas was called Levittown, on Long Island. Houses in Levittown were exactly alike, built on an assembly-line system.

Suburbs

Families and children were an important part of life in the suburbs. Schools, shopping centers, and parks were built to meet the needs of families. People who lived in the suburbs depended on automobiles because distances between homes, schools, and shops were longer than in the city. People also used automobiles to **commute**, or travel regularly to work. American life changed as more and more people settled in suburbs.

Television

Can you imagine a world without television? The first televisions were sold in stores just after World War II. Television soon became the main source of news and entertainment for most people. In the 1950s New York City became a center for television and it remains a broadcasting center today.

A War Without Guns

The United States faced a new enemy in the 1950s. Its wartime ally, the Soviet Union, became an enemy because its armies threatened western Europe. This period of time is called the Cold War. A Cold War is a war of suspicion and angry words. The Soviet Union and the United States acted like countries at war.

At the end of World War II, an organization called the **United Nations**, or UN, was set up to help keep peace in the world. It met at Lake Success, on Long Island, from 1946 to 1950. In 1952 the UN moved into its new headquarters in Manhattan. The UN continues to work for peace and equality around the world.

▲ Schoolchildren seek shelter under their desks during Cold War drills for attacks by Soviet bombers.

QUICK CHECK What was one effect of the growth of suburbs in the 1950s? *Cause and Effect*

The flags of every member nation fly in front of UN headquarters in New York City. ▼

New Yorkers Make a Difference

During the 1960s, many groups of Americans demanded equal opportunities and **civil rights**. Civil rights are the rights of all citizens to be treated equally under the law.

Equal Treatment

The National Association for the Advancement of Colored People, or NAACP, began in New York in 1909. It worked to end discrimination against African Americans. The movement for civil rights took hold in 1955 in Montgomery, Alabama. One of the leaders of this movement was Martin Luther King, Jr., of Atlanta, Georgia.

A famous New York leader of the civil rights movement was Malcolm X. He gave many speeches demanding equal rights for African Americans. He also encouraged African Americans to build and own their own businesses.

▲ Bella Abzug and Gloria Steinem marching for women's rights.

Other New Yorkers worked for equality and civil rights in Congress. Herman Badillo, from the Bronx, became the first person born in Puerto Rico to serve in Congress in 1971.

Women's Rights

Women wanted equal opportunities as well. In 1966, the National Organization for Women (NOW) was formed.

Gloria Steinem moved from Ohio to New York in 1960. She founded *Ms.* magazine, to publicize the women's rights movement.

Bella Abzug was another New York leader of the women's movement. She represented New York in Congress during the 1970s.

◀ Malcolm X speaks in New York.

Protecting the Environment

Pollution is anything that dirties the air, soil, or water. In the 1970s, residents of a neighborhood called Love Canal near Niagara Falls, New York, began to fight pollution in their neighborhood. Led by Lois Gibbs, they forced the owners of the polluted land to clean up their neighborhood. Later, other New Yorkers stopped another company from emptying chemicals into the Hudson River.

These cleanup operations show that New Yorkers are working to make their state a safer and more beautiful place to live. Conservation and strong laws against pollution will continue to protect the environment of New York.

QUICK CHECK How did people work to make New York a better place to live? *Main Idea and Details*

◄ A volunteer plants trees on Earth Day, April 22.

What You Learned

A New Yorkers worked together to win World War II.

B Suburbs developed after World War II; The United Nations began to meet in New York.

C New Yorkers worked together to promote equal rights, and protect the environment.

☆ Focus Lesson Review

1. **Focus Question** How did life change after World War II?

2. **Vocabulary** Use the vocabulary words below to write a summary of what you learned in this lesson.
   commute   ration
   pollution   suburb

3. **Culture** How did television change American life in the 1950s and 1960s?

4. **Critical Thinking** **Problem Solving** How did residents of Love Canal fix the pollution in their community?

5. **Reading Strategy** **Sequence Events** List three events of the Equal Rights movement and the order in which they occurred.

6. **Write About** THE **BIG IDEA** Write a paragraph about how the automobile changed life.

7. **Reading Primary Sources** Look at the photograph of the family on page 262. What can you tell about life in the 1950s from this photograph?

A Young Person's Life in the 1950's

American life changed in the 1950s. After the hard times of the Depression and the sacrifices of World War II, Americans were ready to relax and have fun. The 1950s began a time of "fads," trends or activities that were wildly popular for a short period of time.

Portable record players played 78s, 45s, and the new LPs (long-playing) records. ▶

◀ This boy is bouncing his "pogo stick" a popular toy of the 1950s.

Classic American cars surround a drive-in restaurant. ▼

Picnics were popular with families in the 1950s. ▶

Americans enjoyed new technology. This audience is wearing special glasses to see a three-dimensional, or "3-D," movie. ▼

◀ This girl spins a hula hoop, one of the earliest and most popular fads of the 1950s.

Write About It!

Choose one fad or trend from the 1950s. Write a paragraph comparing it to a similar fad or trend today.

LOG ON

For more about young people in history, visit: www.macmillanmh.com

Write an Outline

VOCABULARY

outline

You have read about New Yorkers during World War II. Writing an **outline** will help you group facts to write answers and study for tests. An outline is a plan that presents ideas about a subject in an organized way.

1 Learn It

Use the following steps when you create an outline, such as the one below.

- Identify the topic. The topic is "The Effects of World War II on New York"

- Identify the main ideas.
  - ◆ People want to help their country win the war.
  - ◆ Many New Yorkers serve in the military.
  - ◆ New Yorkers at home recycle and go to work in factories to make weapons.

- Include supporting details and facts in your outline.
  - ◆ Look at page 261. The first idea is "Another World War." A supporting detail would be "The United States at War."
  - ◆ Organize the information.

When you create an outline, start with Roman numerals to show the sequence of the main ideas. Under each of your main ideas, group the facts that support it. Place a capital letter beside each fact.

World War II and New York

I. Another World War
   A. The United States at War
      1. The United States joined the Allies
      2. New Yorkers worked to win
   B. The Home Front
      1. Civilians helped the war effort
      2. There were scrap drives and rationing
      3. Bond drives raised money
      4. The war ended in 1945

② Try It

Read the following article about women during the war. Take notes as you read.

Many American women worked to help in World War II.

Women who worked during the war often had two jobs. One job might be to work in factories making war supplies, or in hospitals. The other job was working at home.

During the war, many women worked six days a week at their paying job. In the evenings and during whatever free day they had, many also had the job of taking care of their children and homes.

Now, create an outline organizing the information found in the article. Include a topic and supporting detail for each of the main ideas. Use your outline to answer the following questions.

■ What is the topic of the article?

■ How did you decide which statements were main ideas and which were supporting details?

③ Apply It

■ How can writing outlines help you better understand what you read?

■ Reread page 264. Write an outline about what you've read. Use the outline to write a report about the Equal Rights Movement.

Workers building warplanes at a New York factory during World War II ▼

A New Century

What are the challenges facing New York in the twenty-first century?

VOCABULARY

terrorism
global trade

VOCABULARY STRATEGY

Suffixes The suffix **-ism** means "the idea or organization of" something. **Terrorism** means "the organization of terror." What other words end in **-ism**? What does each word mean?

READING STRATEGY

Identify Main Idea and Details Use a chart to find the main idea and details about the challenges facing New York.

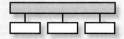

NEW YORK STANDARDS

1.2, 1.3, 2.1, 4.1

A year after the attacks on the World Trade Center in New York City, the Voice of America, a radio station, said:

> ❝ *The events of September eleventh did not only affect Americans. The attacks united people around the world in sympathy for the families and friends of those who were killed. Millions of people in all areas of the world were touched by the events of that terrible day.* ❞

©2001 The Record (Bergen Co., N.J.), Thomas E. Franklin, Staff Photographer.

2000   2001   2002   2003   2004   2005

2001
World Trade
Center attacked

2003
Blackout cuts electricity
across New York State

Ⓐ September 11, 2001

September 11, 2001, was a cloudless day. Around 9 A.M. people around the world were shocked to learn that two airplanes had crashed into the towers of the World Trade Center in Manhattan. Police and firefighters rushed to the scene. Then the towers collapsed. Almost 3,000 people were killed in the worst terrorist attack in American history.

This attack was an act of **terrorism**— the use of violence and fear for political reasons. New York City Mayor Rudolph Guiliani reminded New Yorkers and the world,

> 66 *New York is still here. We've suffered terrible losses and we will grieve for them, but we will be here, tomorrow and forever.* 99

A New World Trade Center

New Yorkers wanted to replace the buildings that were destroyed. Everyone agreed that there should be something built to remember the people who were killed in the attack. A competition was held to choose the best design. A design called "Reflecting Absence" was chosen. The plan will include two reflecting pools on the ground where the two towers once stood. In addition, a Freedom Tower was planned to replace the World Trade Center. It would be 1,776 feet high. What is the significance of the number 1776?

✔ **QUICK CHECK** What is an act of terrorism? *Main Idea and Details*

▼ Twin beams of blue light called the "Tribute in Light," mark the spot of the World Trade Center attacks.

◀ New York City firefighters raise the American flag at the site of the World Trade Center, September 11, 2001.

271

ⓑ Challenges

New York State is facing other challenges as well. New York's factories have to compete with factories in other countries. Some of these countries can manufacture products for much less money than New Yorkers can. This is one result of **global trade**. Global trade means that products are bought and sold across national boundaries.

The population of New York in 1990 was around 18 million. Today it is more than 19 million. New York's citizens must be aware of their changing needs as the population grows. They will need to protect their environment as more people place more demands on resources.

QUICK CHECK How is the population of New York changing? *Main Idea and Details*

What You Learned

ⓐ Terrorist attacks on the World Trade Center in New York City killed nearly 3,000 people.

ⓑ New Yorkers face new challenges in the 2000s.

Focus Lesson Review

1. **Focus Question** What are the challenges facing New York in the twenty-first century?

2. **Vocabulary** Write one sentence for each of the following vocabulary terms.
   global trade   **terrorism**

3. **Economics** How does global trade change the way products are manufactured?

4. **Critical Thinking Make Inferences** Why do you think New Yorkers want to replace the World Trade Center?

5. **Reading Strategy Identify Main Idea and Details** What was the effect of the attack on the World Trade Center on New Yorkers?

6. **Write About** THE **BiG** IDEA How can technology help New Yorkers deal with new challenges?

7. **Reading Primary Sources** Read the quote below and answer the following question.
   "It is a memorial that expresses both the . . . loss of life and its consoling renewal, a place where all of us come together to remember from generation to generation."

   Why is it important to build a memorial at the World Trade Center site?

Steven Chu 1948–

Steven Chu grew up in Garden City, New York. As a child he learned how to build things. First he built plastic model airplanes and ships. Then he moved on to constructions that often filled up the living room in his house. As an older boy, he learned about chemistry and experimented with homemade rockets.

After college, Chu became a scientist. With the help of coworkers, he built a machine that slows down atoms by making them very, very cold. For his work, he was awarded the Nobel Prize in Physics in 1997. This is a very important scientific and cultural award.

Today, Chu is a college professor, teaching young scientists. He encourages them to use their knowledge to build things, just as he did as a young man.

❝ *You have to look and be able to see things that other people looked at and didn't see before.* ❞

Write About It! How does Steven Chu continue to show leadership?

LOG ON For more biographies, visit: www.macmillanmh.com

The Life of Steven Chu

1945	1955	1965	1975	1985	1995	2005
1948 Born in St. Louis	**1950** Moves to Garden City		**1976** Earns Ph.D. from University of California	**1985** With coworkers, traps atoms using lasers		**1997** Awarded Nobel Prize in Physics

Chapter 10 Review

FOCUS Vocabulary Review

Copy the sentences. Use the list of vocabulary terms to fill in the blanks.

Great Migration	**New Deal**
neutral	**ration**

1. President Franklin Roosevelt's plan was the _____ .

2. The United States remained _____ for the first three years of World War I.

3. During the _____ , African Americans moved from the South to the North.

4. To help with the war effort, people on the home front had to _____ goods.

5. **Test Preparation** A _____ is a community located near a big city.

   (A) **neutral**　　(C) **terrorism**
   (B) **suburb**　　(D) **pollution**

FOCUS Comprehension Check

6. Name two events that led to the United States entering World War I.

7. What was the 19th Amendment to the Constitution?

8. What was the Harlem Renaissance?

9. Why was tax money spent on building projects during the Great Depression?

10. How did people in New York during World War II contribute to the war effort?

11. **Critical Thinking** Compare the Progressive Era with the equal rights movement. How were they similar and different?

12. **Critical Thinking** How was the American involvement in World War I different from American involvement in World War II?

FOCUS Use the Time Line

Use the time line below to answer each question.

13. Was the World's Fair in New York before or after the end of World War II?

14. How many years passed between women gaining the right to vote and the Civil Rights Act?

1920 | 1940 | 1960 | 1980

1920 Women gain right to vote

1932 New York Governor Franklin Roosevelt elected President

1939 New York hosts World's Fair

1945 World War II ends; Cold War tensions begin

1965 Civil Rights Act passes

Write an Outline

Write a complete sentence to answer each question.

Read the selection below and use it to answer the following questions.

The 1939 World's Fair in New York was one of the largest world fairs of all time. Countries from around the world participated in the biggest international event since World War I. Forty-five million people came to see the fair from April 20, 1939, to October 27, 1940.

The theme of the fair was "The World of Tomorrow." It was divided into different zones like the Communication Zone, the Transportation Zone, and the popular Amusement Area, which included a Futurama ride.

15. What is the main idea of the first paragraph?

16. What is a supporting detail of the second paragraph?

17. **Test Preparation** What is the topic of this passage?

    (A) the development of amusement parks
    (B) the construction of a Futurama ride
    (C) the history of New York
    (D) the 1939 World's Fair in New York

18. **Test Preparation** Which detail supports the main idea from the first paragraph?

    (A) the fair closed in 1940
    (B) forty-five million people came to see the fair
    (C) the fair opened in 1939
    (D) The Amusement Area was popular.

Constructed Response Questions

Read the statement by Harry Truman who became President after the sudden death of Franklin Roosevelt in 1945.

> " *I don't know if any of you fellows [newspaper reporters] ever had a load of hay fall on you, but when they told me yesterday what had happened [Roosevelt's death], I felt like the moon, the stars, and all the planets had fallen on me.* "

19. What is President Truman talking about in this statement?

20. Why do you think Truman felt "that the moon, the stars, and the planets" had fallen on him?

21. **Suffrage Skit** Write and perform a short skit about a women's suffrage demonstration. Make a poster to carry and write a speech about why women should have the right to vote.

22. **Narrative** Write a one-page short story about living in Harlem during the Harlem Renaissance. Describe what you see and hear around you.

 LOG ON For more about the process of writing, visit: www.macmillanmh.com

Comprehension and Critical Thinking Check

1. What was the goal of the **abolitionists**?

2. Why did some states **secede** from the Union to form the **Confederacy**?

3. What caused the New York City **Draft** Riots in 1863?

4. Why would an **employer** resist a **labor union**?

5. How did **settlement houses** help people in **urban** areas?

6. What inventions made **skyscrapers** possible?

7. What were some of the political **reforms** that occurred during the Progressive Era?

8. What did people do to gain **civil rights** for all Americans?

9. **Critical Thinking** How did the New Deal help American workers and improve the country during the **Great Depression**?

10. **Critical Thinking** How have New Yorkers demonstrated the importance of fighting **pollution** from the late 1800s up to recent times?

Reading Skills Check

Compare and Contrast

Copy this graphic organizer. Recall what you have read about immigrants who came to New York from overseas. Reread the information of the Great Migration found on page 257. Use the graphic organizer to help you compare and contrast these movements of people to New York.

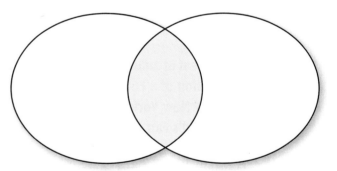

11. Where did most of the overseas immigrants come from?

12. Where did the people come from who took part in the Great Migration?

13. How were the reasons for each group coming to New York similar and how were they different?

Base your answers to questions 14 and 15 on the advertisement below.

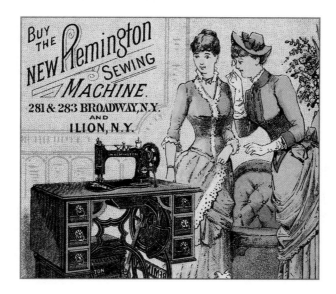

14. Where could you buy this sewing machine?

    (A) Albany, NY

    (B) Chicago, Illinois

    (C) Baltimore, Maryland

    (D) Ilion, New York

15. Why do you think the manufacturer created this advertisement?

    (A) to show many features of the sewing machine

    (B) to show how the machine was better than other sewing machines

    (C) to make readers want to use this sewing machine

    (D) to advertise that the machine is made in New York

16. Letter Suppose you are a young New York soldier serving in the Union army. Write a letter home describing your life as a soldier.

17. Expository Write a brief essay discussing how technology changed rural life in New York.

18. Summary Think about how New York contributed to winning World War II. Write a one-paragraph summary of your ideas.

For more about the process of writing, visit: **www.macmillanmh.com**

REVIEW THE BIG IDEA

How does technology change people's lives?

Write About the Big Idea

A Letter of Request

Recall some of the changes in technology you learned about in this unit. Complete the graphic organizer. Add details about each type of technology.

Choose one type of technology. Use information from your graphic organizer to write a letter to an organization or to a professional person. Request information about someone who brought that type of technology to New York.

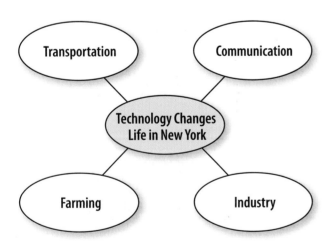

Write a Letter of Request

1. Plan

- Decide what you want to know.
- Think about the body of your letter. Specify exactly what information you are requesting. Explain when you need it.

2. Write a First Draft

- Include your address and a greeting. Remember your signature.
- Use language that is friendly, yet formal. State your request clearly in simple language.

3. Revise and Proofread

- Be sure the information you are requesting is clear.
- Check the tone of your language. Remember to thank the person who will receive your letter for his or her help.
- Combine related sentences.
- Proofread your letter. Be sure you have all parts of a letter. Be sure you have used correct punctuation.
- Ask your teacher to review your letter. Rewrite it neatly.

ACTIVITY

Speak About the Big Idea

Presenting Ideas

Choose a person you read about in Unit 4. Think about that person's contribution to New York. The person may have invented a new kind of technology. The person may have contributed to reforms for people who live and work in New York.

Prepare Take the role of the person to explain what he or she contributed to New York. Prepare notes that give details and examples. You can dress in clothing similar to what the person would have worn. Use information from Unit 4, your graphic organizer, and information you received in response to your letter of request.

Present Present the ideas of the person. Explain his or her contribution to technology that changed New York.

For help with the Big Idea activity, visit: www.macmillanmh.com

Read More About the Big Idea

Her Story, Her Words

by Frances E. Ruffin The true story of Sojourner Truth, who escaped from slavery in New York. She became a well-known abolitionist and supporter of women's rights.

The Story of the Statue of Liberty

by Betsy and Giulio Maestro A beautifully illustrated description of the building of one of the most famous symbols of the United States.

Dreaming of America

by Eve Bunting The true story of 15-year-old Annie Moore, the first immigrant to land at Ellis Island in 1892.

Unit 5

A Changing New York

"*Without leaps of imagination, or dreaming, we lose the excitement of possibilities. Dreaming, after all, is a form of planning.*"

— Gloria Steinem

What causes a society to grow?

In Unit 5, you will read about the structure of government on local, state, and national levels. You will also learn about the people, celebrations, and activities of New York.

Copy the chart below. As you read the chapters in this unit, fill in the chart with information about what caused New York to grow and the effects of that growth. The first cause has been filled in for you.

Cause		Effect
Local Governments		

◀ The Nelson A. Rockefeller Empire State Plaza in Albany, New York

People Who Made a Difference

Oscar Garcia Rivera
1900–1969

Oscar Garcia Rivera moved from Puerto Rico to New York to fight for the rights of poor people. He organized unions and was elected to the New York State Assembly. (page 301)

Shirley Chisholm
1924–2005

Shirley Chisholm was the first African-American woman to be elected to Congress. She fought for the rights of women and the poor, and ran for President in 1972.
(page 309)

Daniel Patrick Moynihan
1927–2003

Daniel Patrick Moynihan served New York as Senator for over 20 years. He was also Ambassador to India and a presidential advisor to Presidents Kennedy and Nixon.
(page 308)

| 1930 | 1940 | 1950 | 1960 |

1937
Oscar Rivera is elected
to New York Assembly

LOG ON

For more biographies, visit:
www.macmillanmh.com

Ruth Bader Ginsburg
1933–

Ruth Bader Ginsburg was one of the first female law professors in the country before becoming the second woman to serve on the Supreme Court in 1993. (page 308)

Tania León
1943–

Tania León moved to New York from Cuba and became one of the first female symphony orchestra conductors. She also writes music and has received many awards for her talent. (page 323)

Lois Gibbs
1951–

Lois Gibbs began her fight to clean up Love Canal in 1976. Her work led to the creation of the Superfund, national money to clean up pollution sites across the United States. (page 326)

1971
Tania León conducts her first orchestra

1976
Lois Gibbs works for Love Canal cleanup

1970   1980   1990   2000

1968
Shirley Chisholm elected to U.S. Congress

1976
Daniel Patrick Moynihan is elected to the Senate

1993
Ruth Bader Ginsburg appointed to Supreme Court

I Want to Be a Fisherman

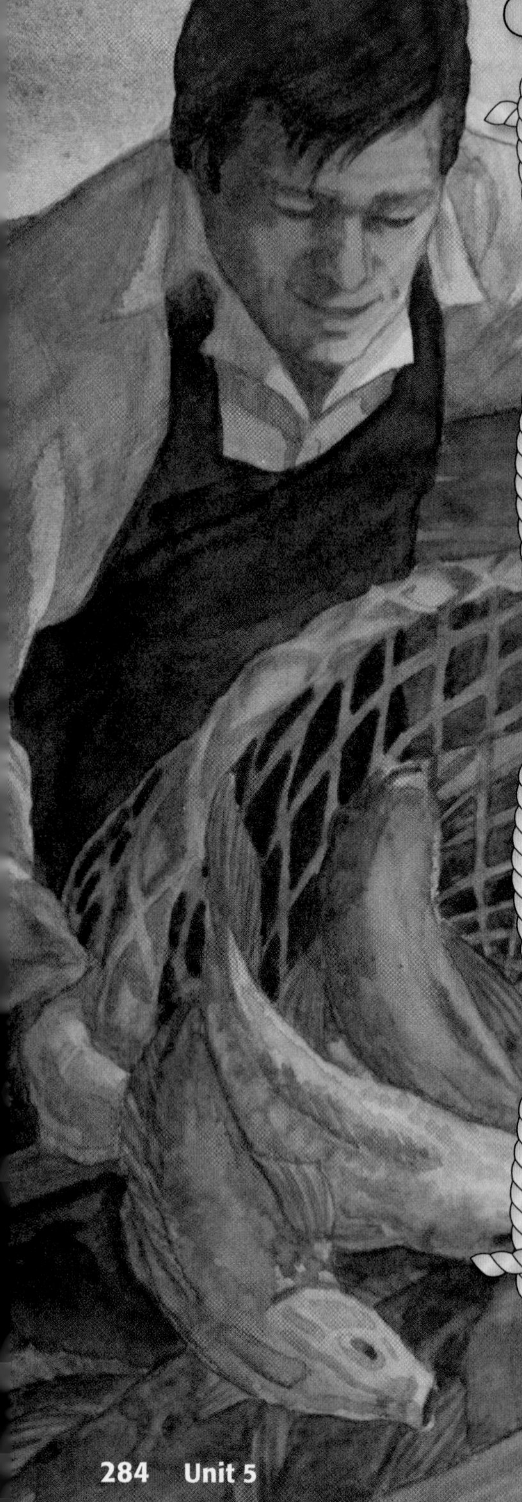

by Sandra Weiner

In this selection, New Yorker Christine Vorpahl tells why she wants to be a trap fisherman like her father when she grows up.

My father is Stuart Vorpahl, Jr.,
and I am Christine.
I want to be a trap fisherman like him
when I grow up.
His father and grandfather
were fishermen, too . . .
Trap fishing is a very old way of catching fish.
We learned how to do it
from the American Indians . . . you've got to
get to those nets – rain, wind, or storm.
We are always worrying about bad weather.
All fishermen do . . .
When there are no fish to sell,
there is no money to buy food or pay bills . . .
I love the summer . . .
I can go fishing every day.

My father wakes me around six
in the morning . . .
My father and I pile the lunch
into the back of the truck . . .
Neither of us is saying anything,
but inside me,
I wonder if the water will be rough
or if there will be any fish in the traps.
I know my father
thinks about that all the time.
When there are no fish
or hardly enough to sell,
he is very quiet.
When the nets are full,
he whistles or hums . . .
I feel the same way he does about fishing.
It's something about the sea.
When you are away from it,
you can't wait to get back.

Write About It!

Write an essay about
what you would like to
do when you grow up.

Identify Cause and Effect:
New York's Government

In this unit, you will read about New York's government. Thinking about cause and effect will help you understand how and why New York's government has changed. A cause is an event that makes something happen. An effect is what happens. When one thing causes another thing to happen, they have a cause-and-effect relationship.

1 Learn It

- When you read, ask yourself what happened. This will help you find an effect.

- Ask why this effect happened. This will help you find a cause.

- Look for the words *because*, *therefore*, *so*, and *as a result*. These clue words point to causes and effects.

- Read the paragraph below. Look for causes and effects.

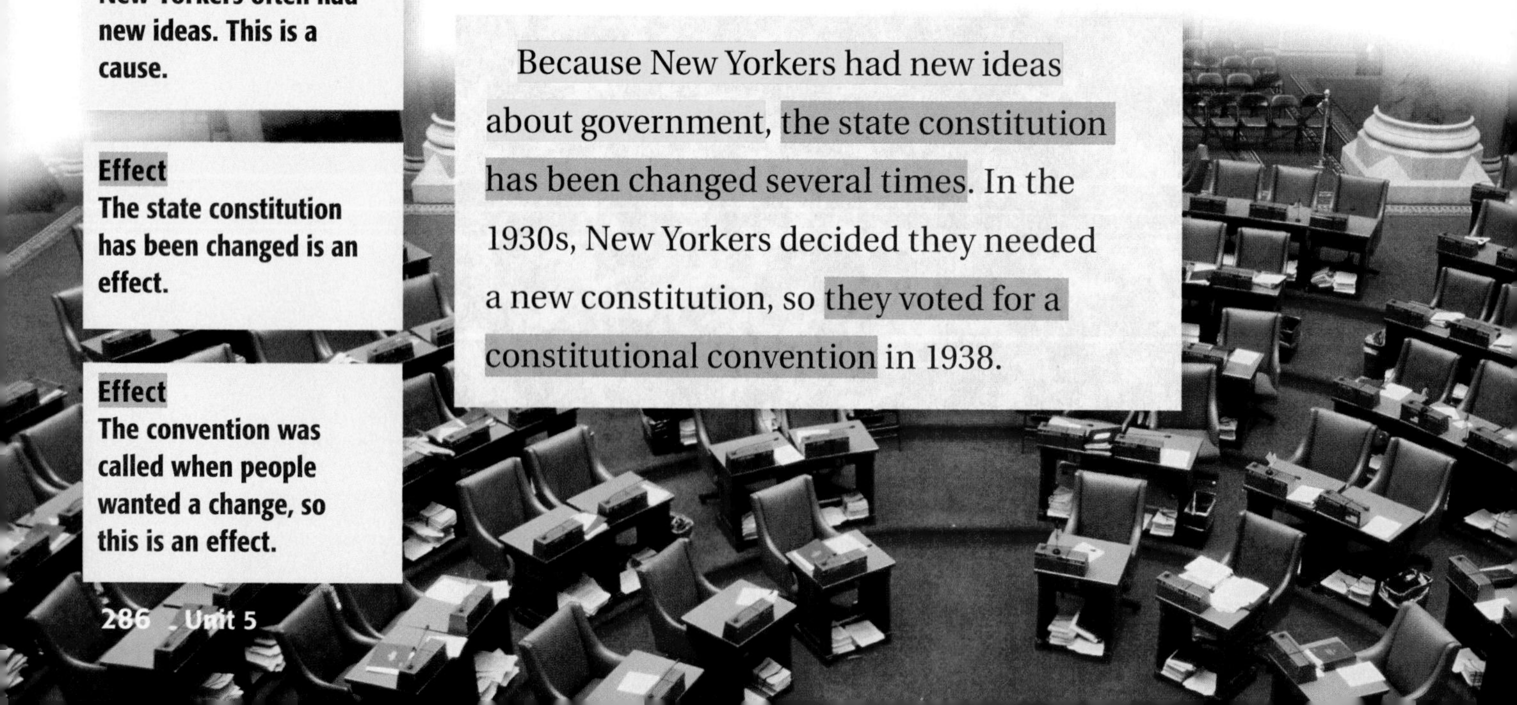

Cause
New Yorkers often had new ideas. This is a cause.

Effect
The state constitution has been changed is an effect.

Effect
The convention was called when people wanted a change, so this is an effect.

Because New Yorkers had new ideas about government, the state constitution has been changed several times. In the 1930s, New Yorkers decided they needed a new constitution, so they voted for a constitutional convention in 1938.

 **Try It**

Copy the cause-and-effect chart below. Fill in the chart with causes and effects from the paragraph on page 286.

CAUSE-AND-EFFECT CHART

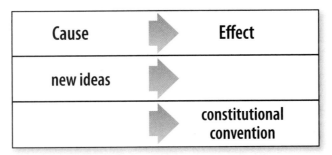

Cause		Effect
new ideas		
		constitutional convention

What words help you identify cause and effect?

3 Apply It

- Review the steps for understanding cause and effect in Learn It.

- Read the paragraphs below. Create a cause-and-effect chart using the information.

New Yorkers can change their constitution in two ways. A change can be made at any time if the government branch called the legislature passes it. Then, at the next election, the new legislature must vote for the change, too. After the change is passed by both the old and the new legislatures, it becomes a law.

The writers of the 1938 Constitution wanted to be sure that New Yorkers would be able to make changes. So, voters are asked every 20 years if they want any change. If they vote for a change, a new constitutional convention must be called. The last call was in 1997. There won't be another call until the year 2017.

Governing New York

You Are There

Lake Superior

Lake Michigan

"*In winter, citizens ... don't like slippery streets or sidewalks in front of their homes. In summer, they don't want smelly garbage piling up on their curbs. They expect fires to be put out quickly and criminals taken off the streets.*"

When William Johnson was Mayor of Rochester he listed some tasks that New York citizens expect from their governments. In this chapter, you will learn what some of the jobs of a government are and why they are needed.

◀ Mayor William Johnson

1 New York State Court of Appeals

2 New Americans at Ellis Island

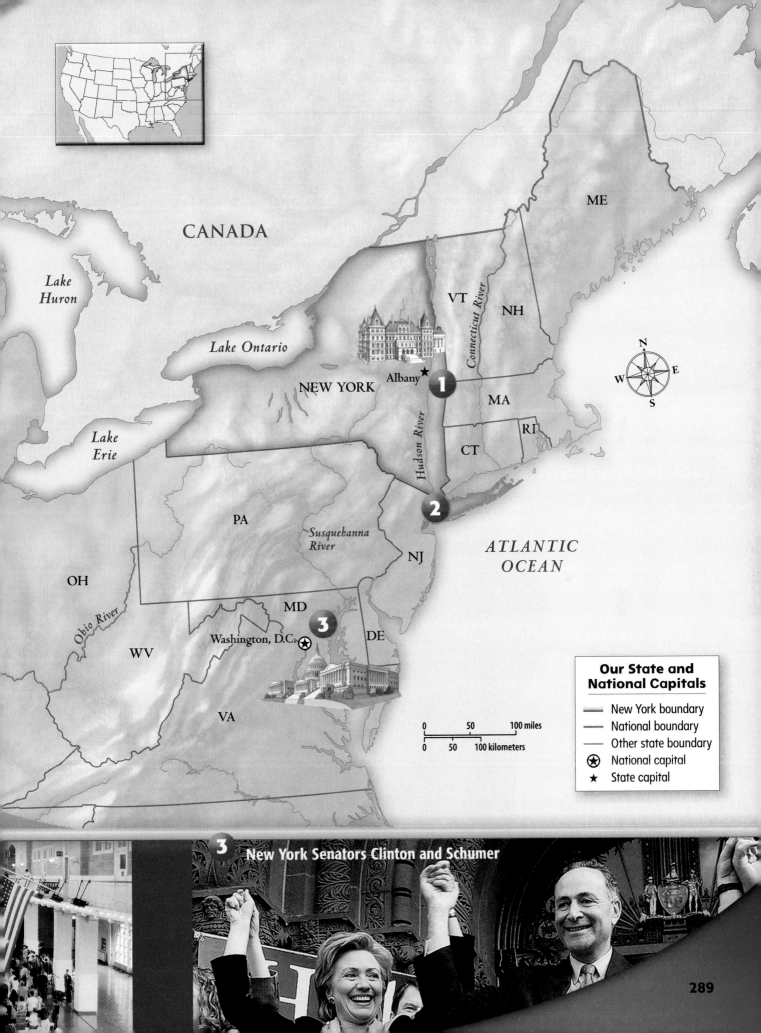

CANADA

Lake Huron

Lake Ontario

Lake Erie

NEW YORK

Albany ★ **1**

VT

NH

ME

Connecticut River

MA

RI

CT

Hudson River

2

ATLANTIC OCEAN

PA

Susquehanna River

NJ

OH

Ohio River

WV

MD

3

Washington, D.C. ⊛

DE

VA

Our State and National Capitals

— New York boundary
— National boundary
— Other state boundary
⊛ National capital
★ State capital

0   50   100 miles
0   50   100 kilometers

3 **New York Senators Clinton and Schumer**

VOCABULARY

government
municipal
 government
elect
mayor
city council
city manager
county

VOCABULARY STRATEGY

Compound Words An open compound word has a space between the two words. What are the three open compounds in the vocabulary list?

READING STRATEGY

Identify Cause and Effect In what ways does local government touch the lives of citizens? Complete this cause and effect chart to list your answers.

Local Government

In 2002 Michael Bloomberg became mayor of New York City. He is one of many people working in local government in the state of New York. This is how Mayor Bloomberg describes his job:

" I've got the greatest job in the world. There's no other job in government where cause and effect is so tightly coupled where you can make a difference every day in so many different ways and in so many different people's lives. It's a great challenge. "

Local workers, like this crossing guard, provide government services every day. ▼

Ⓐ How Government Works

Government is the laws and people that run a country, state, or town. **Municipal government**, the local government of a city, town, or village, looks after a small area. Local government is New York's smallest division of government. What do you know about your local government?

Local Governments

Local governments have many responsibilities. They run the police and fire departments. They take care of streets and sidewalks. They give permission to builders to build new buildings. Some local governments also run libraries and public parks.

Some of the people who work for local government are **elected**. To elect means to choose by voting. Other people who work for local government are hired. These people usually do the daily business of local government. Look at the chart to see how local government is organized.

Municipal Governments

Usually, a **mayor** is the head of a municipal government. There is also a **city council**, or a group of people who meet to make decisions for the city. In Ithaca, for example, the mayor works with a ten-member Common Council. Both the mayor and the city council members are elected.

In small towns or villages, the mayor and council members may not work full-time. They may have other jobs when there is no local government business.

A **city manager** is an expert hired to run the daily business of a city. Some cities, such as Watertown and Elmira, have city managers.

New York City is the biggest city in the state. In fact, it is the largest city in the United States. Because it is so large, New York City has a special kind of government. New York City has five divisions called boroughs (BU rowz). Each borough has an elected borough president. Voters from all five boroughs elect a mayor and city council members to deal with issues that affect the entire city.

✔️ **QUICK CHECK** Why is the structure of New York City local government different from other cities in New York State? *Cause and Effect*

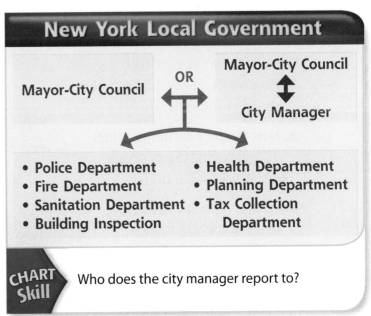

New York Local Government

Mayor-City Council **OR** Mayor-City Council ⇕ City Manager

- Police Department
- Fire Department
- Sanitation Department
- Building Inspection
- Health Department
- Planning Department
- Tax Collection Department

CHART Skill Who does the city manager report to?

Local Government Statistics

Each year, governments have to decide how to spend the money they collect as taxes and fees. Look at the two graphs below and answer the questions about how the city of Rochester spends its money.

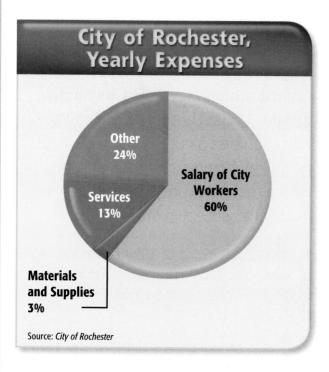

City of Rochester, Yearly Expenses

Other 24%

Salary of City Workers 60%

Services 13%

Materials and Supplies 3%

Source: *City of Rochester*

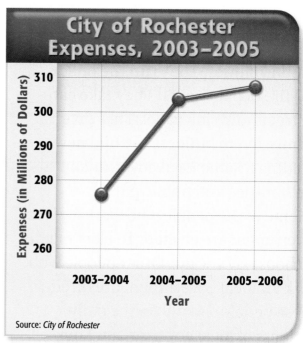

City of Rochester Expenses, 2003–2005

Expenses (in Millions of Dollars)

Year

2003–2004 2004–2005 2005–2006

Source: *City of Rochester*

Think About Local Government Spending

1. How much money did Rochester spend in 2004–2005?

2. How much of Rochester's total budget is used to pay people who work for the city?

3. What is probably happening to the amount of money Rochester spends on city workers each year?

B Governing Larger Areas

A **county** is a political division of a state. There are 62 counties in New York State. Counties include cities, towns, and open areas. Look at the map on page A14 of your textbook. What is the name of your county?

Every county has a government to care for roads and to protect people. Some counties have other responsibilities, too. Montgomery County cares for 171 miles of snowmobile trails. Seneca County has a historian of its early newspapers. Other counties manage museums and libraries.

Special Districts

New York has special districts, or government areas. A school district, for example, is an area that includes several schools. A board of education runs all the schools in a district. School board members are usually elected. How are schools in your district alike and different?

The board of education decides how to spend the district's money. It also makes decisions about how the schools will be run.

QUICK CHECK Name one duty of county government. *Main Idea and Details*

What You Learned

A Local governments run cities and towns. Some people working in local government are elected, and others are hired.

B Counties are divisions of states; school districts run the schools of an area.

⭐ Focus Lesson Review

1. **Focus Question** What does a local government do?

2. **Vocabulary** Use the vocabulary terms below to write a paragraph about local government.
   city council   elect
   county   mayor

3. **Government** What are some responsibilities of a municipal government?

4. **Critical Thinking Make Decisions** You are the mayor of a city in New York State. You have very little money this year. How will you spend the city's money?

5. **Reading Strategy Identify Cause and Effect** Use the chart to answer this question: If a city lowers taxes, what might happen to the services the city provides?

6. **Write About THE BiG IDEA** Write a paragraph explaining how government might help a city to grow.

7. **Reading Primary Sources** *"The job is most time-consuming . . . There are tough . . . decisions that only the Mayor can make."*

   What problems does Mayor Johnson of Rochester face?

Use the Internet

The **World Wide Web** is a collection of information on the Internet. The Web has about three billion **Web sites**, or locations were you can find information. The New York government has its own Web site. So do most New York companies, cities, and schools.

You can use a search engine to help you sort through the sites. A search engine is a computer program that finds information on the Web.

VOCABULARY

World Wide Web
Web site
Keyword
URL

1 Learn It

- Type in a **keyword** in a search engine to start a search. A keyword is a topic word that helps you find information. For example, the keyword "Cooperstown" helps you find information about Cooperstown, New York.

- Your search engine will then give you a list of Web sites that match your search. Read the Web sites' titles and descriptions to see if they have information you might want.

- Look at the **URL**, or web address, for each site. The last three letters in each URL give you an idea of the type and quality of the information of each site.

- The URL for government sites will always be ".gov." The URL for private companies is ".com." Schools use ".edu," and research organizations and charity groups are listed as ".org."

- Always find at least two sources for your information. This will allow you to compare what one site says against what the other says.

Jackie Robinson began playing for the Brooklyn Dodgers in 1947. ▶

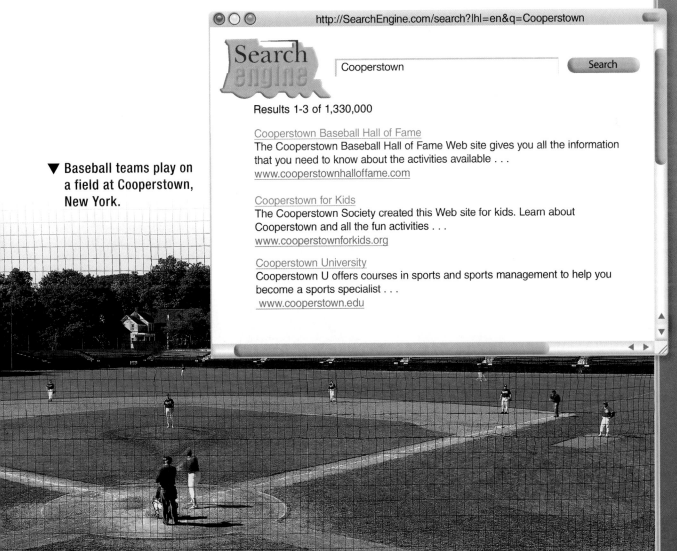

2 Try It

Use the sample search engine page below to answer the following questions.

- What is the keyword for this search?

- What is the URL for Cooperstown University?

- Which site do you think would have the most accurate information about the Baseball Hall of Fame at Cooperstown?

3 Apply It

Do an Internet search to answer these questions.

- Use an Internet search engine to find Web sites about baseball in New York.

- What keyword or keywords might help you to find specific information about New York baseball teams?

- Start with a general keyword, such as "New York Baseball." Narrow your search by using additional keywords, such as "New York baseball teams."

▼ Baseball teams play on a field at Cooperstown, New York.

http://SearchEngine.com/search?lhl=en&q=Cooperstown

Search engine

Cooperstown   [Search]

Results 1-3 of 1,330,000

Cooperstown Baseball Hall of Fame
The Cooperstown Baseball Hall of Fame Web site gives you all the information that you need to know about the activities available . . .
www.cooperstownhalloffame.com

Cooperstown for Kids
The Cooperstown Society created this Web site for kids. Learn about Cooperstown and all the fun activities . . .
www.cooperstownforkids.org

Cooperstown University
Cooperstown U offers courses in sports and sports management to help you become a sports specialist . . .
www.cooperstown.edu

What does New York State government do?

VOCABULARY

democracy
checks and balances
budget
legislative branch
bill
veto
executive branch
judicial branch

VOCABULARY STRATEGY

Root Words The root words of **democracy** mean "rule of or by the people." Why do people call the United States government a democracy?

READING STRATEGY

Summarize Use the chart below to list the three branches of government and the jobs each branch does.

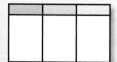

NEW YORK STANDARDS

1.2, 1.3, 1.4, 3.1, 3.2, 5.1, 5.2, 5.3, 5.4

State Government

Some day soon, you will be a New York State voter! This is one of a citizen's most important responsibilities. You will have to decide who will get your vote to represent you on your city council and in Albany. What qualities would a person need to earn your vote?

Ⓐ Making New York Work

The first New York State constitution was approved in 1777. The state constitution in use today was written in 1938 and changed in 2002. Our state government is a **democracy**, a system in which citizens vote for their government representatives.

The state government is made up of three parts. Each part, or branch, has different duties and powers. No branch has all the power. This system is called **checks and balances**. The power of each branch of government is checked, or stopped, and balanced by the powers of the other parts.

How State Government Works

The state government provides services to all people in New York. For example, a driver's license comes from the state government. The main offices of all state services are located in Albany, the state capital. However, most state offices have branches in every county and in large cities.

In 2005 New York State spent almost 120 billion dollars. This money paid for services, programs, workers, parks, highways, and other state expenses. Most of the money comes from taxes paid by New Yorkers. The government makes a **budget** (BUJ it), or plan for spending its money. The chart below shows you how New York spent some of its budget in 2005.

QUICK CHECK Why must the state government be careful about the amount of money it spends? *Make Inferences*

◀ New Yorkers march for a cause in front of the State Capitol building in Albany.

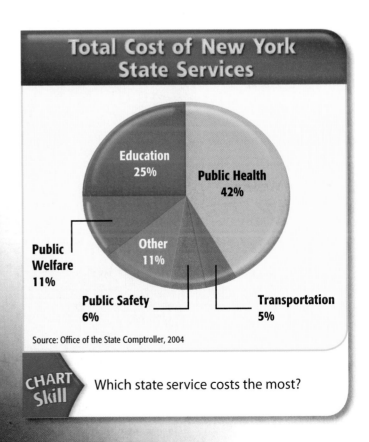

Total Cost of New York State Services

- Public Health 42%
- Education 25%
- Public Welfare 11%
- Other 11%
- Public Safety 6%
- Transportation 5%

Source: Office of the State Comptroller, 2004

CHART Skill Which state service costs the most?

❶ The Three Branches of State Government

Three branches of government in New York work together to run the state. One branch makes the laws, another branch carries out the laws, and the third branch interprets, or makes decisions about which laws fit within the state constitution.

Making Laws

The **legislative** (LEJ is lay tiv) **branch** makes the laws. It is made up of two parts: the State Senate, which has 62 members; and the State Assembly, which has 150 members. Voters elect both state senators and assembly members. All state lawmakers are elected every two years.

Although it is the job of the state legislature to make laws, anyone can suggest a law—the governor, members of the state legislature, or citizens of New York. Each suggestion must be turned into a **bill**, or a written idea for a law. The bill is introduced to the state legislature. Only members of the Senate or the Assembly can introduce a bill. After a bill is introduced and discussed, the Senate and the Assembly vote. If the bill is passed by both parts of the legislative branch, it goes to the governor. The governor can sign the bill and make it a law, or the governor can **veto** the law. Veto means to refuse to approve a bill. Two-thirds of the members of both houses of the

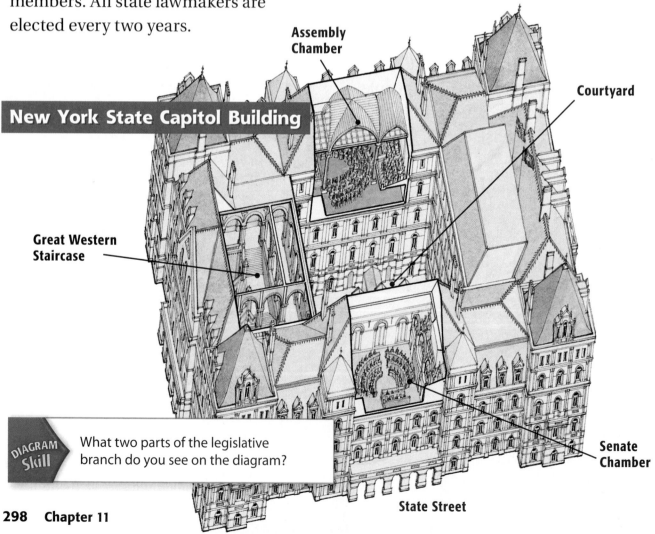

New York State Capitol Building

Assembly Chamber

Courtyard

Great Western Staircase

Senate Chamber

State Street

DIAGRAM Skill What two parts of the legislative branch do you see on the diagram?

from the speech by Nancy Calhoun • August 1, 2005

<u>Preserving</u> Our History, <u>Ensuring</u> Our Future

" . . . New York has a rich and diverse history . . . Our local governments and communities are the backbone of this system, and the grants announced today ensure our history will be properly saved and stored for use by future generations. "

preserve to keep
ensure to make sure of

Write About It! Why does Nancy Calhoun think it is important to protect local records in New York State?

▲ Assemblywoman Nancy Calhoun

---

legislature would have to pass the law again to overcome the governor's veto.

Look at the Primary Source above. Assembly member Nancy Calhoun explains her bill to help local governments protect their records, which became a state law in 2005.

Carrying out Laws

The **executive** (eg ZEK yoo tiv) **branch** is the part of government that makes sure that laws are followed. It also plans the state's budget. The executive branch has different departments. The Department of Education licenses teachers, tests students, and decides where to open new schools.

The head of the executive branch is the governor, who is elected every four years. Being governor is hard work. Mario Cuomo served as governor of

New York from 1983 until 1994. In his first seven days in office he had:

" . . . given two major speeches, met personally with record numbers of visitors and legislators, . . . appointed a Court of Appeals judge, . . . and begun the hard process of preparing a budget. . . . "

Interpreting the Laws

The **judicial** (joo DI shul) **branch** decides whether someone has broken the law. It also interprets the laws of New York State.

QUICK CHECK What are the three branches of government and what does each one do? *Summarize*

© Explaining the Law

The judicial branch works for justice. This means that judges uphold the law and try to be fair in the way people are treated and decisions are made.

State Courts

The most powerful court in New York is the Court of Appeals. It is made up of seven judges who serve for fourteen years. Decisions made by a judge in a lower court, can be reviewed by the Court of Appeals. Judges in the Court of Appeals decide whether decisions made in lower courts are correct.

The Court of Appeals judges are picked by the governor and approved by the Senate. This is a good example of the system of checks and balances. If the Senate doesn't approve the governor's selection, he or she must choose again. Lower court judges are elected to their positions.

Courts often reach decisions with the help of a **jury.** A jury is a group of twelve ordinary citizens who are chosen to decide on a case in a court of law. More than 600,000 people serve as jurors each year in New York. The jury system is one of the important traditions of American democracy.

✓ **QUICK CHECK** What is one example of the system of checks and balances in action? *Main Idea and Details*

What You Learned

A New York State has three branches of government in Albany.

B The three branches of state government are the executive, legislative, and judicial branches.

C The courts and juries work for justice.

⭐ Focus Lesson Review

1. **Focus Question** What does New York State government do?

2. **Vocabulary** Write about the job of the governor of New York using the vocabulary terms below.
   bill   executive branch
   budget   veto

3. **Citizenship** What are two ways citizens can help their state government?

4. **Critical Thinking** **Make Inferences** Why might it be difficult for state leaders to make a budget?

5. **Reading Strategy** **Summarize** Describe three powers of the New York State governor.

6. **Write About** THE **BiG** IDEA Write a paragraph describing how state government can help a state to grow.

7. **Reading Primary Sources**
   "Should things go wrong at any time, the people will set them to rights by the peaceable exercise of their elective rights."
   – Thomas Jefferson

   Who does Jefferson believe will direct the government?

Oscar Garcia Rivera 1900–1969

Oscar Garcia Rivera was born in Mayaguez, Puerto Rico. He was the top student at his junior high school and was the president of his high school class.

Although Rivera had a comfortable life in Puerto Rico, he moved to New York in 1926 to become a lawyer. He wanted to bring justice to poor people.

He graduated from St. John's University School of Law in Queens, New York. He opened three law firms in New York City, including one that offered free legal services. Rivera helped Spanish-speaking employees of the City Hall Post Office to join their union. He spent his life defending the rights of New York workers.

Rivera became the first Puerto Rican elected to public office in the United States. He was elected to the New York State Assembly in 1937. He got government services for an area of New York City called Spanish Harlem, which other representatives had ignored.

"*History is our best teacher. We have no way of foreseeing [knowing] the future except by studying the events of the past.*"

 Write About It! Why did Oscar Garcia Rivera want to move to New York?

 LOG ON For more biographies, visit: www.macmillanmh.com

The Life of Oscar Garcia Rivera

1900	1915	1930	1945	1960	1975
1900 Born in Puerto Rico	**1917** Puerto Ricans are granted citizenship	**1926** Moves to New York	**1930** Graduates from law school	**1937** Elected to the New York State Assembly	**1969** Dies in Puerto Rico

Field Trip to _____

ALBANY
NEW YORK

Albany has been New York's capital city since 1797. You can see much of New York's history in Albany's buildings and museums today. Many of these buildings are located around the Nelson A. Rockefeller Empire State Plaza.

Albany

1 ## The New York State Museum ▼

The New York State Museum faces the Capitol building from the other end of the mall. The building contains the state library, the state archives, and collections of artifacts from New York State history.

2 ## The Performing Arts Center ▼

The Performing Arts Center has been called the "Egg" because of its unusual shape. Inside are two auditoriums facing each other.

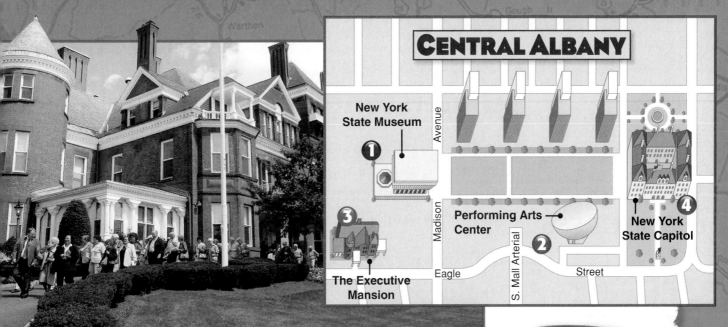

CENTRAL ALBANY

New York State Museum ❶

Madison Avenue

Performing Arts Center

The Executive Mansion ❸

Eagle

S. Mall Arterial

Street ❷

New York State Capitol ❹

ALBANY

❸ The Executive Mansion ▲

The Executive Mansion has been the home of New York's governors since 1877. The original house has been remodeled and expanded several times since the state bought the property.

ACTIVITY

Choose one of the buildings on the Field Trip. Do some research before you write several paragraphs telling more about the building.

❹ The New York State Capitol ▼

The New York State Capitol took 32 years to complete (1867-1899.) The building is well known for its beautiful rooms. The final cost was $25 million dollars (about half a billion dollars today!).

LOG ON For virtual field trips, visit:
www.macmillanmh.com

Understand Letters

The LIBRARY of CONGRESS

A letter is a written message between two people. Letters are important primary sources because they often contain information that helps historians to understand a specific time or place better.

A Letter from Theodore Roosevelt to His Son

Theodore Roosevelt was governor of New York and President of the United States. In 1890, he worked for the national government in Washington, D.C. He wrote the letter on these pages to his son, Ted, who was at home in New York.

▲ President Theodore Roosevelt and his sons Theodore, Jr., Quentin, Kermit, and Archibald.

1 Learn It

Read the steps below to locate information in letters.

- Think about the letter and its writer. Predict the kind of information you expect to find in the letter.

  - Look for the date and the place where the letter was written.

  - Scan the letter to find details about events or background information.

  - Read more carefully to find out why the letter was written.

  - Look up unfamiliar words or places as you read.

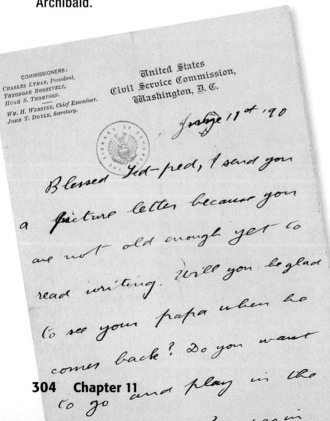

◀ This is the first page of Theodore Roosevelt's letter to his son.

2 Try It

Roosevelt's letter is rewritten below. Read the letter. What information can you learn from it?

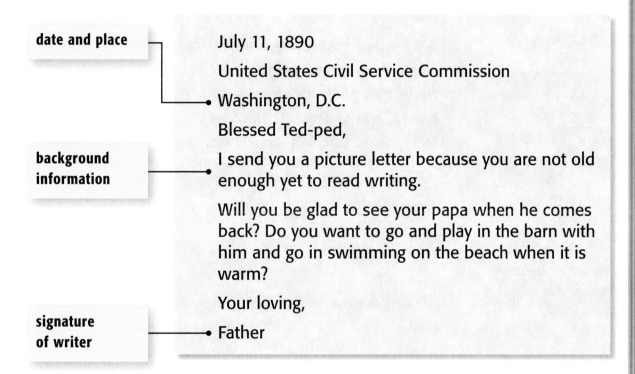

date and place

July 11, 1890

United States Civil Service Commission

Washington, D.C.

Blessed Ted-ped,

background information

I send you a picture letter because you are not old enough yet to read writing.

Will you be glad to see your papa when he comes back? Do you want to go and play in the barn with him and go in swimming on the beach when it is warm?

Your loving,

signature of writer

Father

3 Apply It

Write a letter to a friend or family member. Describe the activities you enjoy when you are together. Use descriptive language as Roosevelt did.

Roosevelt drew pictures on the second page of his letter so his young son could understand the story. ▶

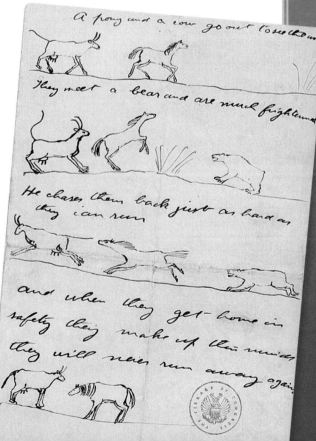

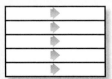

What does the national government do?

VOCABULARY

citizen
democratic republic
Congress
House of
  Representatives
Senate
Supreme Court

VOCABULARY STRATEGY

Root Words Republic comes from two words meaning "the public thing." What do you think a **democratic republic** might be?

READING STRATEGY

Identify Cause and Effect Use the chart to explain how each branch of government deals with the other branches of government.

	▷
	▷
	▷
	▷

NEW YORK STANDARDS

1.1, 5.1, 5.2, 5.3, 5.4

Our National Government

You have probably heard that "the people" control the government of the United States. How does this work? Can you think of some ways that our government is owned "by the people"? How does our government live up to Abraham Lincoln's famous words,

> *". . . government of the people, by the people, for the people . . ."*

Ⓐ Our National Government

The government of the United States is called the national, or federal, government. It provides services to people in all fifty states. Among these federal services are the American army, navy, air force, and coast guard. The federal government also prints money and postage stamps, and makes sure that food and drugs are safe for people to use.

A **citizen** is a person who is born in a country or who has earned the right to become a member of the country by law. Citizens of the United States have rights guaranteed by the Bill of Rights. These are the first ten amendments to the United States Constitution. For example, we can talk freely about our ideas and practice any religion. American citizens also have responsibilities, such as voting, following the laws, and paying taxes.

Our nation's capital city is Washington, D.C. The United States is a **democratic republic**. This means citizens elect representatives to make decisions for them. We also choose the President in national elections. The national government has the same three branches as New York State: legislative, executive, and judicial.

The President of the United States

The executive branch makes sure the laws are carried out. The President of the United States heads the executive branch. The President also serves as the commander-in-chief of the military. He or she appoints a cabinet, or group of advisors, such as the Secretary of State and the Secretary of Defense. The President can veto laws.

The President has a four-year term of office and can be elected only twice. So far, there have been six Presidents from New York State.

QUICK CHECK How do the people control the government of the United States? *Cause and Effect*

President George Washington laid the cornerstone of the United States Capitol in 1793. ▼

B An Idea Becomes a Law

The legislative branch of our national government is the **Congress**. Congress has two parts. The **House of Representatives** has 435 members from every state, decided by state population. New York has 29 representatives.

Each state elects two senators to the **Senate**. Senators pass laws, approve treaties, and federal judges, cabinet officers, and ambassadors. Former New York Senator Daniel Patrick Moynihan was also a cabinet officer and an Ambassador to India.

The Judicial Branch

The **Supreme Court** is the highest federal court. It interprets laws and decides if they agree with the United States Constitution.

Supreme Court judges, or justices, are chosen by the President and approved by the Senate. They serve for life. The first Chief Justice of the Supreme Court was New Yorker John Jay in 1789. Thurgood Marshall became the first African American justice in 1967. Sandra Day O'Connor was the first woman on the Supreme Court. New York's Ruth Bader Ginsburg became the second in 1993.

QUICK CHECK How have New Yorkers served in the national government? *Compare and Contrast*

What You Learned

A The United States is a democratic republic.

B A bill becomes a law when it is passed by Congress and signed by the President.

Focus Lesson Review

1. **Focus Question** What does the national government do?

2. **Vocabulary** Write a paragraph describing the three branches of national government. Use the vocabulary terms listed below.
   Congress   **Senate**
   House of Representatives   **Supreme Court**

3. **Citizenship** Name three responsibilities of United States citizens.

4. **Critical Thinking** **Making Inferences** Which person in the national government has the most power?

5. **Reading Strategy** **Identify Cause and Effect** Why do you think the writers of the Constitution might have divided powers among the three branches of government?

6. **Write About** **THE BIG IDEA** Write a paragraph explaining how citizens can contribute to their national government.

7. **Reading Primary Sources** *"We serve only the public interest as we see it, guided by the Constitution and by our own consciences."*

   How does former Chief Justice Earl Warren see his job?

Shirley Chisholm 1924–2005

Shirley Chisholm was born in Brooklyn, New York, but she lived on the Caribbean island of Barbados until she was 11. Her father taught her to challenge people who did not treat others fairly.

Chisholm was always a leader. In 1960 she started a Harlem, New York, political club to encourage African American and Spanish-speaking citizens to vote.

In 1964 Chisholm was elected to the New York State Assembly. She was elected to the United States Congress in 1968. She worked to improve education, civil rights, women's rights, and to help the poor. Chisholm said:

> **We Americans have a chance to become someday a nation in which all . . . classes can exist in their own selfhoods, but meet on a basis of respect and equality . . .**

Shirley Chisholm ran for President of the United States in 1972.

 Write About It! What causes did Shirley Chisholm support?

 LOG ON For more biographies, visit: www.macmillanmh.com

The Life of Shirley Chisholm

1920	1940	1960	1980	2000
1924 Born in Brooklyn	**1946** Graduated from Brooklyn College with honors	**1964** Elected to New York State Assembly	**1968** Elected to Congress **1972** Runs for President	**2005** Dies in Florida at age 80

CITIZENSHIP
POINTS OF VIEW

Who Can Be President?

Every year immigrants become American citizens, called naturalized citizens. The Constitution today does not allow naturalized citizens to become President of the United States.

Read below to find out about three different points of view on who should be allowed to run for President of the United States.

❝ *If a grown-up came to the United States and became an American citizen, then it wouldn't be okay for them . . . The Constitution says a person must be native-born to be President and you should think carefully before changing the law.* ❞

David Bernstein
Seatucket, New York
From an interview, 2005

❝ *A naturalized citizen might be a better leader even though he or she was born in another country. If naturalized citizens serve in the army, they should be allowed to run for the nation's highest office.* ❞

Katherine Yom
Yonkers, New York
From an interview, 2005

❝ *If a person shows that he or she is loyal and loves this country and wants to make it a good place to live, they should be allowed to run. We have changed our Constitution many times before.* ❞

Alex Woodard
Fairport, New York
From an interview, 2005

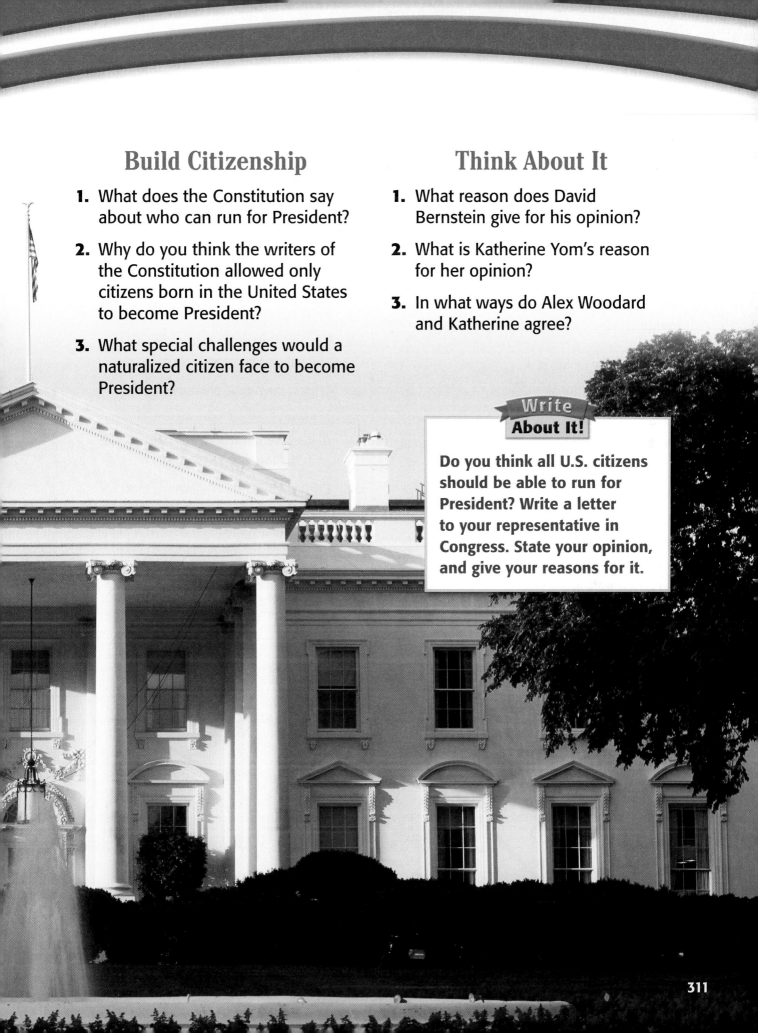

Build Citizenship

1. What does the Constitution say about who can run for President?

2. Why do you think the writers of the Constitution allowed only citizens born in the United States to become President?

3. What special challenges would a naturalized citizen face to become President?

Think About It

1. What reason does David Bernstein give for his opinion?

2. What is Katherine Yom's reason for her opinion?

3. In what ways do Alex Woodard and Katherine agree?

Write About It!

Do you think all U.S. citizens should be able to run for President? Write a letter to your representative in Congress. State your opinion, and give your reasons for it.

Chapter 11 Review

FOCUS Vocabulary Review

Copy the sentences below on a separate sheet of paper. Use the list of vocabulary words to fill in the blanks.

bill   budget
county   mayor

1. A plan for using money is a _____.

2. A _____ is the head of a municipal government.

3. A written idea for a law is a _____.

4. A _____ is one of the areas into which a state is divided.

5. **Test Preparation** The _____ is the part of government that makes laws.

   (A) **checks and balances**
   (B) **judicial branch**
   (C) **executive branch**
   (D) **legislative branch**

FOCUS Comprehension Check

6. Name two things that local governments do.

7. What is the difference between a mayor and a city manager?

8. What is a borough?

9. What do the executive branches of state and national governments do?

10. What is the capital of New York State?

11. **Critical Thinking** How does the power of the governor "check and balance" the power of the state legislature?

12. **Critical Thinking** What would most likely happen if representatives in the government started to pass laws that the majority of the voters did not support?

FOCUS Use the Time Line

Use the time line below to answer each question.

13. How many years did New York's first constitution last?

14. How old is New York's most recent constitution?

1750	1800	1850	1900	1950

1777
New York's first constitution

1823
New York adopts a new constitution

1846
New York writes its third constitution

1895
New York's fourth constitution is adopted

1938
New York adopts its current constitution

Use the Internet

Write a complete sentence to answer each question.

15. What is a keyword for a search?

16. What is the URL for the official City of Albany Web Site?

17. **Test Preparation** Which site would most likely have the most reliable information about how the city government of Albany works?

(A) www.albany.gov
(B) www.albanycitymaps.com
(C) www.albanytravelguide.org
(D) www.albanycollege.edu

18. **Test Preparation** Which site lists places to stay in Albany?

(A) www.albany.gov
(B) www.albanycitymaps.com
(C) www.albanytravelguide.org
(D) www.albanycollege.edu

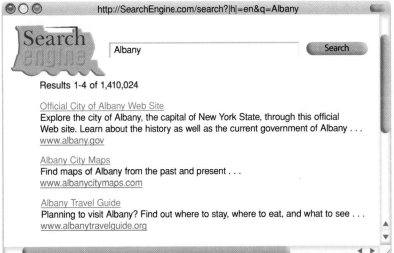

http://SearchEngine.com/search?|h|=en&q=Albany

Search Engine

Albany   [Search]

Results 1-4 of 1,410,024

Official City of Albany Web Site
Explore the city of Albany, the capital of New York State, through this official Web site. Learn about the history as well as the current government of Albany . . .
www.albany.gov

Albany City Maps
Find maps of Albany from the past and present . . .
www.albanycitymaps.com

Albany Travel Guide
Planning to visit Albany? Find out where to stay, where to eat, and what to see . . .
www.albanytravelguide.org

Using Primary Sources **CRQ**

Constructed Response Questions

Read the quote below and answer the questions that follow.

> *You don't make progress by standing on the sidelines . . . You make progress by implementing [acting on] ideas.*
> — Representative Shirley Chisholm

19. What does Shirley Chisholm think citizens should do?

20. How does Chisholm say progress is made?

Write About History

21. **Persuasive** Your city is about to pass a law requiring grade school children to stay at home after 8 P.M. on weeknights or to have adult supervision. Write a letter to the editor of your local newspaper supporting or criticizing this law.

 LOG ON For help with the process of writing, visit: www.macmillanmh.com

New York Today

You Are There

"Americans need New York because New York . . . allows difference to be celebrated, . . . allows people to reach their full potential. And that's . . . what drives freedom, what moves us forward, and what is really the hope of the future."

Historian Kenneth T. Jackson wrote these words about New York.

In this chapter you will read about the people who live in New York today. You will also learn about the challenges they face in the new century.

Fort Niagara State Park

Lake Erie

3

Lake Erie State Park

Allegany State Park

◀ Kenneth T. Jackson

1 **Pakistani Americans celebrate**

2 Warren Street, Hudson, New York

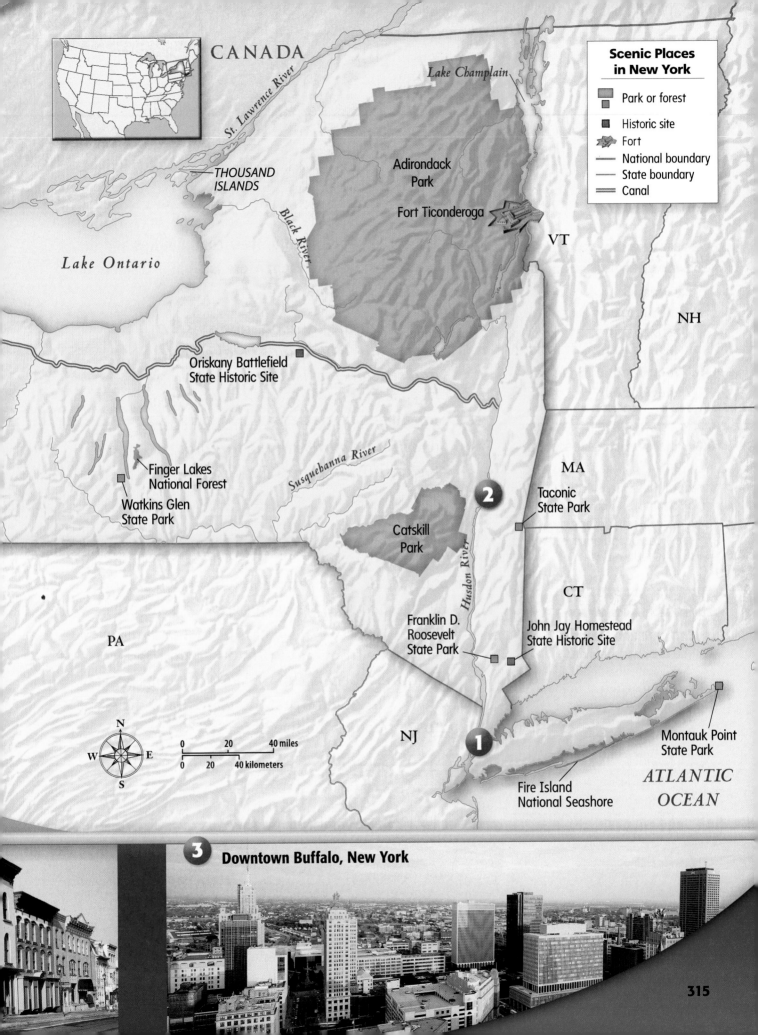

CANADA

St. Lawrence River

THOUSAND ISLANDS

Lake Ontario

Black River

Adirondack Park

Fort Ticonderoga

Lake Champlain

VT

NH

Oriskany Battlefield State Historic Site

Susquehanna River

MA

Finger Lakes National Forest

Watkins Glen State Park

Catskill Park

Taconic State Park

Hudson River

CT

PA

Franklin D. Roosevelt State Park

John Jay Homestead State Historic Site

2

1

NJ

Montauk Point State Park

Fire Island National Seashore

ATLANTIC OCEAN

Scenic Places in New York

- Park or forest
- Historic site
- Fort
- National boundary
- State boundary
- Canal

N W E S

0   20   40 miles

0   20   40 kilometers

3 **Downtown Buffalo, New York**

Who are the people of New York today?

VOCABULARY

diversity
ethnic group
citizenship
urbanization
metropolitan area
megalopolis

VOCABULARY STRATEGY

Prefixes *Polis* is a Greek word that means "city or city-state (a city that governs itself)." Can you see two vocabulary words that include *polis*?

READING STRATEGY

Compare and Contrast Use the chart below to show how city life is the same and different from life in rural New York.

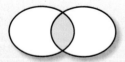

NEW YORK STANDARDS

1.1, 1.2, 1.3, 1.4, 2.1, 3.1, 4.1, 5.1, 5.3

The World of New York

New Yorkers are proud of their communities and the people who live in them. Here is what a resident of Skaneateles, New York, said:

> *What can you say about upstate? Everything. Thousands of lakes, rivers and streams for fishing and boating. Gorgeous mountains and rolling green hills. You can be in most upstate cities one minute and be in the tranquil [peaceful] wilderness the next.*

Ⓐ E Pluribus Unum

E pluribus unum is a Latin phrase that means "out of many, one." It is our national motto, or saying, but it also perfectly describes New York. There is no such thing as a typical New Yorker because New Yorkers come from many different countries and backgrounds. Because of this, our state has great **diversity**. This means that there are many different groups of people who live here.

All these different New Yorkers have become part of the American culture. As you have learned, culture is the way of life shared by a group of people, including their language, beliefs, music, foods, and holidays. Although New Yorkers are Americans, this does not mean that they have forgotten the customs of their ancestors. Many **ethnic groups**, or groups of people whose ancestors are from the same country or area, keep their special customs alive. This makes for a rich and exciting society. Throughout the year, New Yorkers can go to events all around the state to experience this variety of cultures.

Albany hosts an African American Arts and Culture Festival each year.

The Iroquois Arts Festival is held in Howe's Cave, New York. In Buffalo you can choose summer festivals or parades celebrating countries such as Italy, Lebanon, Poland, and Scotland.

Many people who move to New York hope to become American citizens. The United States government has rules about how to earn American **citizenship**. People must live in the United States for five years and be able to read, write, and speak English. They must know United States history and also understand the Constitution. Finally, they must promise to be loyal to the United States.

QUICK CHECK How have immigrants affected New York in the past and today? *Compare and Contrast*

Vineyards near the Finger Lakes and the Tulip Festival in Albany (right) are reminders of two of New York's ethnic groups. ▼

Large cities like Schenectady (above) are surrounded by suburbs (right). ▲

❸ How New Yorkers Live

New Yorkers live in cities, suburbs, and rural areas. Cities, or urban areas, are very large towns with many people. Suburbs are communities just outside of large cities. Rural areas are in the countryside.

Cities

As cities grew, they spread out into rural areas. This is called **urbanization**. Many cities are the center of a **metropolitan area**, meaning a large city and its surrounding suburbs. New York City is the largest city in New York. It is also part of a **megalopolis**, a series of almost continuous metropolitan areas running into each other. The megalopolis that includes New York City runs from Boston, Massachusetts, to Washington, D.C.

Metropolitan areas vary in size. More than one million people live in the Buffalo metropolitan area. Buffalo's downtown area has skyscrapers, colleges, and cultural sites, as well as arenas for professional sports. The surrounding suburbs have homes for Buffalo's office workers and shopping for their families.

Suburbs

Suburbs are smaller than nearby cities. Many houses have yards and garages for cars. Because suburbs are spread out over larger areas, people who live in the suburbs depend on cars to get around and to go to work.

Many people live in the Albany suburbs of Colonie and Delmar, for example. These suburban residents travel to work in Albany each day. Colonie is proud to be a town of neighborhoods, "each with [its] own distinctive personality," one resident says.

Rural Areas

Life in most rural areas of New York depends on agriculture or tourism. The town of Lowville in Lewis County, for example, has one of the largest milk collection centers in the United States as well as a large cheese factory. Dairy farms around Lowville provide the milk for these centers.

The town of Saranac Lake, in the Adirondacks, offers many outdoor activities to visitors. Many people in this rural town work in the tourist industry, working in shops or restaurants, or acting as guides.

Rural New Yorkers often travel long distances to shop or to go to nearby towns. Families in some rural communities have lived in the same area, even on the same farm, for many generations.

✓ **QUICK CHECK** What is one reason people in rural and suburban areas need cars? *Cause and Effect*

What You Learned

Ⓐ People in New York come from around the world, with many different customs and traditions.

Ⓑ New Yorkers live in cities, suburbs, and rural areas.

★ Focus Lesson Review

1. **Focus Question** Who are the people of New York today?

2. **Vocabulary** Write a paragraph about New Yorkers today. Use each vocabulary term.
   citizenship   ethnic group
   diversity   urbanization

3. **Government** What role does the United States government play in becoming a citizen?

4. **Critical Thinking** **Problem Solving** How do people adapt to their region in the work they do?

5. **Reading Strategy** **Compare and Contrast** Use the diagram to show how life in New York's types of communities is different or the same.

6. **Write About** THE **BIG** IDEA Write a newspaper article that describes why a new suburb has grown quickly.

7. **Reading Primary Sources** Compare this quote from the *Memphis Flyer* to the one about upstate New York on page 316.

   "The last thing I did was walk over the Brooklyn Bridge. After all these years, it's still awesome . . . The buildings are immense [huge], but the beauty . . . is in the details."

What do New Yorkers do in their leisure time?

VOCABULARY

historic site
recreation

VOCABULARY STRATEGY

Word Origins The word **recreation** comes from a word which means "to create anew," or "to refresh or restore". Can you think what the word recreation means?

READING STRATEGY

Identify Main Idea and Details Use the chart below to show what role sports play in the life of New Yorkers.

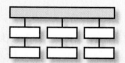

NEW YORK STANDARDS

1.1, 1.2, 1.3, 1.4, 3.1, 4.1, 5.1

Leisure Time in New York

New York is a wonderful place for visitors and citizens alike. There are historical locations where visitors can learn about New York's role in our nation's history. New Yorkers can cheer their favorite sports teams, or they can hike or ski in the beautiful natural areas of our state. Here is what one visitor to the Baseball Hall of Fame in Cooperstown said:

> **"** *One of the things that gave me chills . . . was a tribute to Ebbets Field and the old Brooklyn Dodgers. We passed . . . through the actual turnstile from Ebbets Field to enter the room that was made to look like we were really entering the ballpark.* **"**

Ⓐ The Arts

Tourism is one of New York's most important industries. New York City is world famous for its museums and its Broadway theaters. There are other

museums and theaters throughout our state. Cooperstown hosts the Glimmerglass Opera Festival. Saratoga has a summer performing arts festival, and Syracuse has a Shakespeare festival. Arts and performances can be found in every part of our state.

Historic Sites

New York is also rich in **historic sites**, places where something important happened in the past. At Fort Niagara, you can learn about military life in the past. Other preserved or recreated forts show life on the frontier in New York. You can even visit historic village museums at places like Bethpage, Monroe, and Genesee Village.

QUICK CHECK What is the difference between historical and cultural sites? *Main Idea and Details*

▼ A jazz entertainer performs at the Syracuse Jazzfest.

Then and Now

Taking Vacations

THEN In 1900, only wealthy New Yorkers could afford to take vacations. Most people traveled by carriage or train. Many people visited resorts such as Saratoga Springs.

NOW Today, many people take time for vacations. Some New Yorkers take their vacations within New York. Here they can visit theme parks, national parks, historic sites, or beach areas.

Write About It! What has changed about New Yorkers' vacations since 1900?

B New York Sports

New Yorkers often look to sports for **recreation**. Recreation means the things people do to relax or to play. Both summer and winter sports are popular in New York. Sports and recreation are important industries in New York's economy.

New York has two major league baseball teams as well as many farm teams. In 1846 the first professional baseball game was played between two teams from New York, the New York Nine and the Knickerbockers. Knickerbocker is a nickname for the early Dutch settlers of New York. The professional basketball team in New York is still named the Knickerbockers, or "Knicks."

New York has three National Football League teams: the New York Jets, the New York Giants, and the Buffalo Bills.

The New York Islanders play hockey on Long Island, the New York Rangers in New York City.

Many New Yorkers take part in winter sports on the mountains of upstate New York. Lake Placid, in the Adirondack Mountains, was the site of the 1932 and 1980 Winter Olympics. This area continues to attract visitors.

QUICK CHECK Explain why cultural activities and recreation are important New York industries. *Make Inferences*

What You Learned

A New York has many cultural events and historic sites that people can visit, and is also a home to the arts.

B New Yorkers spend a lot of time playing sports and watching a variety of professional sports.

Focus Lesson Review

1. **Focus Question** What do New Yorkers do in their leisure time?

2. **Vocabulary** Write a paragraph using the following vocabulary terms to describe a fun weekend in New York State.
   historic site   **recreation**

3. **Geography** What is one way that geography affects the sports New Yorkers enjoy?

4. **Critical Thinking Problem Solving** How might a New Yorker looking for peace and quiet spend a vacation in New York?

5. **Reading Strategy Identify Main Idea and Details** Use the chart to list how people use free time in New York.

6. **Write About** THE **BiG** IDEA Write why the arts and sporting events draw people to New York.

7. **Reading Primary Sources** The title of a news story about the move of the Brooklyn Dodgers to California was "They Took Our Hearts, Too." How do you think the writer felt about the team's move?

Tania León 1943–

Tania León was born in Havana, Cuba. As a child, León learned to play the piano and violin. In 1967, she moved to New York City. Two years later, she started the music department and orchestra for the Dance Theater of Harlem.

In 1971, León was asked to conduct, or lead, an orchestra.

❝ . . . *I had never done it in my life. It was my very first time, but I picked up the baton, and I conducted the performance.*❞

After that 1971 performance, she began to study conducting. León has led orchestras all over the world. She also continues to compose music.

In 1998, León was presented with the New York Governor's Lifetime Achievement Award.

 How has Tania León shown courage in her life?

▲ Tania León (top) began conducting for the Dance Theater of Harlem (below).

LOG ON For more biographies, visit: www.macmillanmh.com

The Life of Tania León

1940	1950	1960	1970	1980	1990	2000

1943 Born in Havana, Cuba

1967 Comes to New York City

1971 Conducts an orchestra for first time

1998 Awarded New York Governor's Lifetime Achievement Award

READ ROAD MAPS

There are thousands of roads throughout New York. Some began as trails made by Native Americans, others are carefully planned **interstate highways**. An interstate highway has two or more lanes and goes across two or more states. You use a **road map** to see where the roads in a certain area go. By reading a road map you can figure out how to get from one place to another.

VOCABULARY

interstate highway
road map
route

1 Learn It

- Map A has several different kinds of roads. The thick green lines are interstate highways. Interstate highways run through major cities across the United States.

- Study the map key. A purple line identifies a state highway. State highways are highways that run within a state.

- The "name" of each interstate and state highway is a number. Notice the different symbols for each of the three kinds of highways. Which highway runs from Watertown to Canton?

- Remember this fact: Odd-numbered interstate highways generally run north and south. Even-numbered highways usually run east and west. This numbering can help drivers when they are lost.

2 Try It

- Look at Map A. How is Interstate Highway 81 different from State Highway 20?

- What **route** would you take to get from West Point to Utica? A route is the course you take to get somewhere.

Map A

New York State

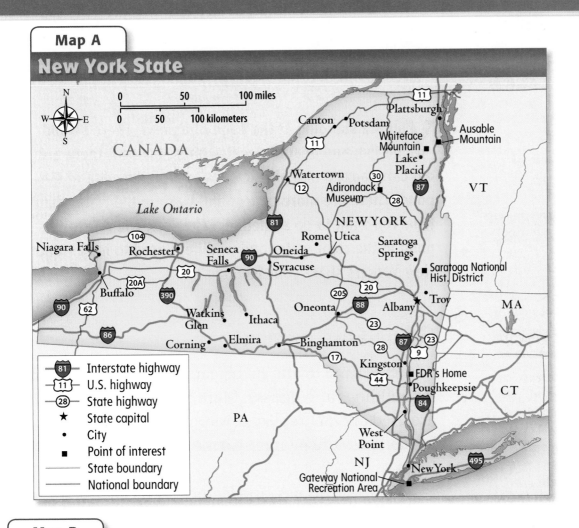

0   50   100 miles
0   50   100 kilometers

CANADA

Lake Ontario

NEW YORK

VT

MA

CT

NJ

PA

Plattsburgh
Canton   Potsdam
Whiteface   Ausable
Mountain   Mountain
Lake
Placid
Watertown
Adirondack
Museum
Rome Utica
Saratoga
Springs
Niagara Falls   Rochester   Seneca   Oneida
Falls
Syracuse
Saratoga National
Hist. District
Buffalo
Watkins   Ithaca   Oneonta   Albany   Troy
Glen
Corning   Elmira   Binghamton
Kingston
FDR's Home
Poughkeepsie
West
Point
Gateway National
Recreation Area
New York

Legend
- 81 Interstate highway
- 11 U.S. highway
- 28 State highway
- ★ State capital
- • City
- ■ Point of interest
- State boundary
- National boundary

Map B

Niagara Falls, New York

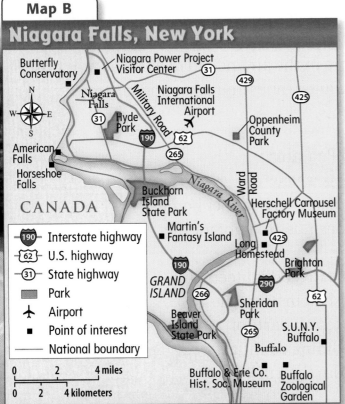

Butterfly
Conservatory
Niagara Power Project
Visitor Center
Niagara Falls
International
Airport
Niagara
Falls
Hyde
Park
Oppenheim
County
Park
American
Falls
Horseshoe
Falls
CANADA
Buckhorn
Island
State Park
Niagara River
Ward Road
Herschell Carrousel
Factory Museum
Martin's
Fantasy Island
Long
Homestead
Brighton
Park
GRAND
ISLAND
Sheridan
Park
Beaver
Island
State Park
S.U.N.Y.
Buffalo
Buffalo
Buffalo & Erie Co.
Hist. Soc. Museum
Buffalo
Zoological
Garden
Military Road

Legend
- 190 Interstate highway
- 62 U.S. highway
- 31 State highway
- Park
- ✈ Airport
- ■ Point of interest
- National boundary

0   2   4 miles
0   2   4 kilometers

3 Apply It

Road maps can also be useful for smaller areas. You may need to know how different streets connect. Look at Map B of downtown Niagara Falls.

■ How would you get from Sheridan Park to the Niagara Falls International Airport without traveling on interstate highways?

■ What are some major highways where you live? What streets are around your school?

Challenges

What challenges face New Yorkers in the new century?

VOCABULARY

congestion
public
   transportation

VOCABULARY STRATEGY

Prefixes The prefix **trans-** means "across, beyond, or through." **Transportation** means "carrying goods or people across a region." What are some other words beginning with **trans-**?

READING STRATEGY

Summarize Use the chart below to summarize how New Yorkers are trying to reduce pollution.

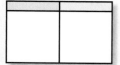

NEW YORK STANDARDS

1.4, 3.1, 4.1, 4.2, 5.3

You are standing at the edge of a pond. There should be fish and beautiful water birds. Instead, there are old cars, boxes, and plastic bags around the edge of the pond. There are more papers and trash in the water than fish. You want to do something. How can you return this pond to the clear water and wildlife it used to have? Many New Yorkers share your feelings.

Ⓐ The Environment

As cities and towns get bigger, they need more land for buildings and houses. More and more resources are used and not replaced. More garbage needs to be hauled. More people also means more cars and highways.

All of these homes, and factories, and automobiles create air pollution. One result of air pollution is acid rain. Factories and power plants burn coal and release chemicals into the air. These chemicals mix with moisture in the air and fall to earth as acid rain. Acid rain pollutes rivers and lakes and destroys fish and plants.

Cleaning Up Pollution

Lois Gibbs is a New Yorker who fought to clean up pollution near her home. Today she continues to fight for the environment.

The Buffalo River–Eighteen Mile Creek Watershed in western New York takes up parts of Erie and Wyoming counties. There are more than 900

farms and 55,700 acres of pasture within the watershed. Federal and state government agencies worked with the local towns to fix and secure river and stream banks. They also treat the water to make it safe and clean.

Local, state, and federal governments work to pass laws to protect our environment and keep people safe.

QUICK CHECK How do large populations of people affect the environment? *Summarize*

Volunteers of the Onondaga Nation clean up roadsides each year [top], while city residents turn vacant lots into gardens [below]. ▼

I Love New York

Lyrics and Music by Steve Karmen

Refrain

I____ love New York.____ I____ love New York.____

Verse

There is-n't an-oth - er like it no mat-ter where

you go, and no-bod - y can com - pare it,

it's win and place and show, you know. New York is spe-

cial, you know. New York is diff - 'rent 'cause there's

no place else on earth quite like New York.____ And that's why

Refrain

I____ love New York.____ I____ love New York.____

What are some of the things that make New York different?

B Work and Travel

New York's growing population needs transportation. Most people drive cars. More cars on the roads lead to **congestion**, or crowded conditions on roads and highways. You already know about congestion if you have ever sat in a traffic jam!

Many New Yorkers now live in suburbs. Usually **public transportation** systems, such as buses, subways, and trains, are found only in larger cities. People in smaller towns have to use cars to get to work or to shop. Congestion and air pollution are two of the problems this creates.

New York is trying to clean up its air and water, but this requires every New Yorker to do his or her part. Do you know what you can do to help?

QUICK CHECK How can public transportation help fix one of New York's problems? *Problem Solving*

What You Learned

A New York faces many environmental challenges in this century, in part because of its growing population.

B New Yorkers are working together to solve the problems of pollution of air and water.

Focus Lesson Review

1. **Focus Question** What challenges face New Yorkers in the new century?

2. **Vocabulary** Write a paragraph using the following terms.
   congestion
   public transportation

3. **Government** How does the government help protect the environment?

4. **Critical Thinking Problem Solving** How could people solve the problem of traffic congestion?

5. **Reading Strategy Summarize** Use a chart to summarize some of the challenges that New York faces.

6. **Write About** THE **BIG** IDEA
   Write a short report that describes what could happen if too many people move into a town.

7. **Reading Primary Sources** " . . . *winds bring power plant emissions from outside New York into the Adirondacks . . . 80 percent of the lush red spruce and balsam fir forests have turned brown and died . . .*" – Bryan Houseal

   What makes acid rain difficult to fix?

Chapter 12 Review

FOCUS Vocabulary Review

Copy the sentences below on a separate sheet of paper. Use the list of vocabulary terms to fill in the blanks.

congestion	diversity
historic site	ethnic group

1. Any _____ is a group of people whose ancestors are from the same area.

2. _____ means variety or differences.

3. Any _____ is a place where something important happened in the past.

4. _____ means crowded conditions.

5. **Test Preparation** A _____ is an area that includes a city and its suburbs.

   (A) **metropolitan area**   (C) **citizenship**
   (B) **culture**   (D) **recreation**

FOCUS Comprehension Check

6. What do historical sites teach us?

7. What kind of diversity are found in New York's recreational sites?

8. How would public transportation help with congestion?

9. How are suburbs a part of urbanization?

10. What are the causes and effects of acid rain?

11. **Critical Thinking** Why is it important that governments plan for the growth of cities?

12. **Critical Thinking** Why do you think many New Yorkers choose to visit other parts of their state?

FOCUS Use the Time Line

Use the time line below to answer each question.

13. How many years after the first permanent assembly met in New York City was Albany chosen as the home of the New York State Legislature?

14. What was the name of the settlement built near present-day Albany?

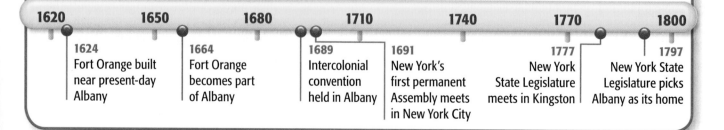

| 1620 | 1650 | 1680 | 1710 | 1740 | 1770 | 1800 |

1624 Fort Orange built near present-day Albany

1664 Fort Orange becomes part of Albany

1689 Intercolonial convention held in Albany

1691 New York's first permanent Assembly meets in New York City

1777 New York State Legislature meets in Kingston

1797 New York State Legislature picks Albany as its home

Skills Check

Read Road Maps

Write a complete sentence to answer each question.

15. What does the road map below show?

16. Which state highway is also Chili Avenue?

17. **Test Preparation** The Interstate Highway which makes a circle around downtown Rochester is ______?

18. **Test Preparation** Interstate ______ goes past the Greater Rochester International Airport.

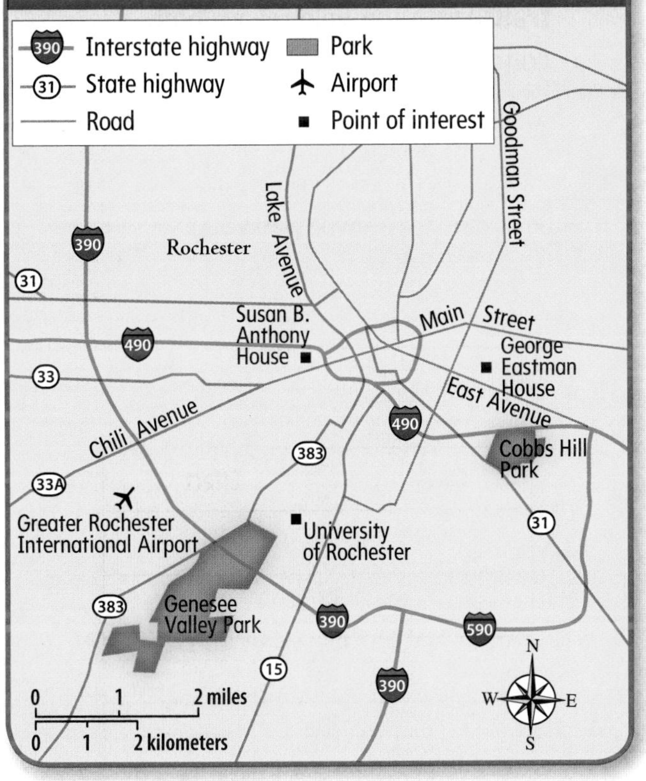

Rochester, New York
390 Interstate highway
31 State highway
Road
Park
Airport
Point of interest
Rochester
Lake Avenue
Goodman Street
Main Street
Susan B. Anthony House
George Eastman House
East Avenue
Chili Avenue
Cobbs Hill Park
Greater Rochester International Airport
University of Rochester
Genesee Valley Park
390
490
590
31
33
33A
383
15
0 1 2 miles
0 1 2 kilometers
N
S
E
W

Using Primary Sources CRQ

Constructed Response Questions

Read the passage and answer the questions.

> *"Walking into H.W. Smith Elementary School [in Syracuse] feels like entering the United Nations . . . In grades kindergarten through six, more than 250 students representing nearly 40 countries speak more than 20 different languages . . ."*

19. What does this source tell you about cultural diversity in Syracuse?

20. Do you think that Syracuse is unusual in this ethnic variety? Explain your answer.

Hands-on Activity

21. **Make a Brochure** Work in groups to create a brochure that answers the following question:

What is fun to see and do in your area of New York?

Write About History

22. **Descriptive** Suppose that you want visitors to come to a historic site in New York. Write a poem or song that describes the site and tells people why they should visit.

LOG ON For help with the process of writing, visit: **www.macmillanmh.com**

Comprehension and Critical Thinking Check

Write one or more sentences to answer each question.

1. What are some services that both a local **government** and a **municipal government** might provide?

2. How is the our state government a **democracy**?

3. How is the state **legislative branch** similar to the federal legislative branch?

4. How does the Court of Appeals show the system of **checks and balances**?

5. What are some examples of New York's **diversity**?

6. How do **ethnic groups** make life here more rich and interesting?

7. What might New Yorkers and visitors to our state do for **recreation**?

8. How is a **metropolitan area** different from a **megalopolis**?

9. **Critical Thinking** Why is serving on a **jury** an example of citizenship?

10. **Critical Thinking** How can **public transportation** help relieve both **congestion** and pollution?

Reading Social Studies Check

Identify Cause and Effect

Copy this graphic organizer. Reread "The Environment" on page 326. Use the graphic organizer to help you figure out the effects of certain kinds of pollution.

11. How do you know what is a cause and what is an effect?

12. What are some of the causes of pollution in our state?

13. What are some effects of air pollution on the environment?

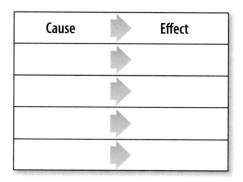

Cause		Effect

Use the diagram to answer questions 14 and 15 below.

How a Bill Becomes a Law

1 Citizens develop an idea for a bill.

2 Members of the State Assembly or the Senate propose the bill.

3 Both houses of the legislature vote to approve the bill.

5 If the bill is vetoed, another vote can be taken. If 2/3 of the Assembly and Senate votes to approve it, the bill becomes a law.

4 The governor signs the bill or the governor vetoes the bill.

14. Who does NOT have a chance to approve a bill?

(A) the governor

(B) the citizens

(C) the Assembly

(D) the Senate

15. What happens when the governor vetoes a bill?

(A) A vote of 2/3 of the Assembly and Senate can overturn the veto.

(B) The bill becomes a law.

(C) The bill cannot be discussed again.

(D) Citizens can express their disappointment.

Write About Government

16. Letter Write a letter to your local government or to the state legislature explaining an idea for improving New York State's schools.

17. Expository Write a short essay that explains how a bill becomes a law in our state government.

18. Summary Think about how diversity has affected life in New York. Write a one paragraph summary of your ideas.

 LOG ON For help with the process of writing, visit: www.macmillanmh.com

Unit 5

What causes a society to grow?

Write About the Big Idea

Reports

Think about all the changes you read about in Unit 5. Complete the graphic organizer below. Add causes, or reasons, for each effect.

Use information from your graphic organizer and other sources to write a report. Your report should end up being several paragraphs. The topic of your report will be why New York grew.

Cause		Effect
	➤	
	➤	
	➤	
	➤	

Write a Report

1. Plan
- Choose a reason why New York grew.
- Use the Internet to find more information about your topic. Remember that your purpose is to give information.

2. Write a First Draft
- In the first paragraph of your report introduce your topic.
- Add paragraphs that give facts, details, and examples of what caused New York's growth.
- In your final paragraph write a conclusion.

3. Revise and Proofread
- Read your report. Be sure your sentences and paragraphs tell about your topic.
- Check that your first paragraph makes a good introduction. Edit your final paragraph to make a good summary of your reasons.
- Proofread your report. Did you indent all your paragraphs?
- Rewrite your report neatly before handing it in to your teacher.

ACTIVITY

Speak About the Big Idea

Newscasts

Suppose you are a television reporter telling about something that caused New York to grow. Use your graphic organizer and your report for ideas.

Prepare Work with a partner. You and your partner will be "co-anchors" of a nightly news program. Rehearse your presentation of your topic.

Present Each pair of broadcasters will report on the news of New York. Be sure to report on what each change is and what caused the change. You might want to express an opinion about whether the change has been good or bad for New York. Be sure it is clear to your listeners when you are giving your own opinion.

LAUNCH PAD For help with the Big Idea activity, visit: www.macmillanmh.com

Read More About the Big Idea

Vote!

by Eileen Christelow Explore the role of a good citizen. Learn how citizens vote and why each vote makes a difference.

A Very Important Day

by Maggie Rugg Herold Join Kiki Soutsos, Miguel Huerta, Veena Patel and other New Yorkers as they hurry through a snowstorm to become new American citizens. Cheerful illustrations accompany this story of America's newest immigrant groups.

The Voice of the People

by Betsy Maestro and Giulio Maestro A colorfully illustrated book explaining the American electoral system with real examples from America's history.

Citizenship Handbook

Good citizens know the Founding Documents of the United States – the Declaration of Independence and the Constitution of the United States.

- The **Declaration of Independence** describes the ideas of our country, the beliefs that support our nation.
- The **Constitution** tells the rules for how our nation will be governed.
- **Amendments**, or changes, to the Constitution show how American ideas about government have changed over the years.
- The first ten amendments, the **Bill of Rights**, list the rights of every American citizen.

This Citizenship Handbook includes explanations of the Founding Documents. Use the blue explanations to help you understand what it means to be an American citizen.

Being a Good Citizen

In your textbook, you have read biographies of people from New York. On each BIOGRAPHY page you saw one of the eight words below. These words help define what it means to be a good citizen, and they are the qualities people look for in their leaders. These words describe how to be a good citizen in your home, school, community, state, and country.

COURAGE being brave in the face of difficulty

FREEDOM making choices and holding beliefs of one's own

HONESTY telling the truth

JUSTICE working toward fair treatment for everyone

LEADERSHIP showing good behavior that others will follow

LOYALTY showing support for people and one's country

RESPECT treating others as you would like to be treated

RESPONSIBILITY being worthy of trust

The *Declaration of Independence*

By the summer of 1776, American colonists had been at war with Great Britain for 14 months. During that time colonists debated whether they were fighting to gain more rights from Great Britain or for independence. As the fighting went on, more and more colonists argued that peace with Britain was no longer possible. In June 1776 members of the Second Continental Congress asked Thomas Jefferson (1743–1826) of Virginia to write a statement explaining why the colonies ought to be independent. Read the Declaration of Independence that Jefferson wrote and the notes of explanation beside it. Notice Jefferson's ideas about government, rebellion, and people's rights. Notice also what unjust acts he accuses King George III of Great Britain of having committed against the colonists. How do King George's actions take away the rights that Jefferson believes people and governments should have?

The Preamble
Sometimes a people needs to break away from their home country and form their own country.

A Declaration of Rights
We believe that all people are created equal and have basic rights that can never be taken away. They are the right to live, to be free, and to look for happiness.

People create governments to preserve these basic rights.

When in the course of human events, it becomes necessary for one people to dissolve the political bands which have connected them with another, and to assume, among the Powers of the earth, the separate and equal station to which the Laws of Nature and of Nature's God entitle them, a decent respect to the opinions of mankind requires that they should declare the causes which impel them to the separation.

We hold these truths to be self-evident, that all men are created equal, that they are endowed by their Creator with certain unalienable Rights, that among these are Life, Liberty, and the pursuit of Happiness.

That, to secure these rights, Governments are instituted among Men, deriving their just Powers from the consent of the governed.

That, whenever any Form of Government becomes destructive of these ends, it is the Right of the People to alter or to abolish it, and to institute new Government, laying its foundation on such Principles, and organizing its powers in such form, as to them shall seem most likely to effect their Safety and Happiness.

Prudence, indeed, will dictate that Governments long established should not be changed for light and transient causes; and, accordingly all experience hath shown, that mankind are more disposed to suffer, while evils are sufferable, than to right themselves by abolishing the forms to which they are accustomed. But, when a long train of abuses and usurpations, pursuing invariably the same Object, evinces a design to reduce them under absolute Despotism, it is their right, it is their duty, to throw off such Government, and to provide new Guards for their future security.

Such has been the patient sufferance of these Colonies; and such is now the necessity which constrains them to alter their former Systems of Government. The history of the present King of Great Britain is a history of repeated injuries and usurpations, all having in direct object the establishment of an absolute Tyranny over these States.

To prove this, let Facts be submitted to a candid world.

He has refused his Assent to Laws the most wholesome and necessary for the public good.

He has forbidden his Governors to pass Laws of immediate and pressing importance, unless suspended in their operation till his Assent should be obtained; and when so suspended, he has utterly neglected to attend to them.

He has refused to pass other Laws for the accommodation of large districts of People, unless those People would relinquish the right of Representation in the Legislature, a right inestimable to them and formidable to tyrants only.

He has called together legislative bodies at places unusual, uncomfortable, and distant from the depository of their Public Records, for the sole purpose of fatiguing them into compliance with his measures.

People have the right to change their government, get rid of it, and form a new one if their government does not preserve their basic rights.

People should not change governments except for important reasons, such as the misuse of power. When this happens, people have the right and duty to form a new government.

A List of Abuses

It is time for the colonies to break away. For years King George III of Great Britain has ruled the colonies badly while he was trying to gain control over them.

He has:

• refused to sign needed laws passed by the colonists or to allow his governors in America to pass important laws.

• refused to recognize large voting districts unless the people living in them give up their right to be represented in the legislature, or lawmaking body.

• ordered lawmakers in the colonies to meet in unusual or hard to get to places to try to get them to accept his rule.

He would not allow colonists to:

- meet in legislatures or hold new elections.

- settle the West or emigrate.

- create courts in some places.

The king also:

- forced colonial judges to obey him.

- sent officials to the colonies who mistreated people and demanded unfair taxes.

- kept soldiers in the colonies in times of peace and tried to give them power over colonial legislatures.

- with other British officials, passed laws for the colonies that the colonists did not want.

- forced colonists to house and feed British soldiers.

- protected soldiers who murdered colonists by not punishing them or giving them fake trials.

- cut off American trade.

- demanded taxes the colonists never agreed to.

- would not allow colonists accused of crimes to be tried by jury.

He has dissolved Representative Houses repeatedly, for opposing, with manly firmness, his invasions on the rights of the people.

He has refused for a long time, after such dissolutions, to cause others to be elected; whereby the Legislative Powers, incapable of Annihilation, have returned to the People at large for their exercise; the State remaining in the mean time exposed to all the dangers of invasion from without, and convulsions within.

He has endeavoured to prevent the Population of these States; for that purpose obstructing the Laws of Naturalization of Foreigners; refusing to pass others to encourage their migration hither, and raising the conditions of new Appropriations of Lands.

He has obstructed the Administration of justice by refusing his Assent to Laws for establishing judiciary Powers.

He has made judges dependent on his Will alone, for the tenure of their offices, and the amount and payment of their salaries.

He has erected a multitude of New Offices, and sent hither swarms of Officers to harass our People, and eat out their substance.

He has kept among us, in times of Peace, Standing Armies, without the Consent of our legislature.

He has affected to render the Military independent of and superior to the Civil Power.

He has combined with others to subject us to a jurisdiction foreign to our constitution, and unacknowledged by our laws; giving his Assent to their Acts of pretended Legislation:

For quartering large bodies of armed troops among us:

For protecting them, by a mock Trial, from Punishment for any Murders which they should commit on the Inhabitants of these States:

For cutting off our Trade with all parts of the world:

For imposing Taxes on us without our Consent:

For depriving us, in many cases, of the benefits of Trial by jury:

For transporting us beyond Seas to be tried for pretended offences:

For abolishing the free System of English Laws in a neighbouring Province, establishing therein an Arbitrary government, and enlarging its Boundaries, so as to render it at once an example and fit instrument for introducing the same absolute rule into these Colonies:

For taking away our Charters, abolishing our most valuable Laws, and altering fundamentally the Forms of our Governments:

For suspending our own Legislatures, and declaring themselves invested with Power to legislate for us in all cases whatsoever.

He has abdicated Government here, by declaring us out of his Protection and waging War against us.

He has plundered our seas, ravaged our Coasts, burnt our towns, and destroyed the Lives of our People.

He is at this time transporting large Armies of foreign Mercenaries to compleat the works of death, desolation and tyranny, already begun with circumstances of Cruelty & perfidy scarcely paralleled in the most barbarous ages, and totally unworthy the Head of a civilized nation.

He has constrained our fellow Citizens taken Captive on the high Seas to bear Arms against their Country, to become the executioners of their friends and Brethren, or to fall themselves by their Hands.

He has excited domestic insurrections amongst us, and has endeavoured to bring on the inhabitants of our frontiers, the merciless Indian Savages, whose known rule of warfare, is an undistinguished destruction of all ages, sexes and conditions.

In every stage of these Oppressions We have Petitioned for Redress in the most humble terms: Our repeated Petitions have been answered only by repeated injury. A Prince, whose character is thus marked by every act which may define a Tyrant, is unfit to be the ruler of a free People.

- brought colonists falsely accused of a crime to Great Britain to be put on trial.

- ended British laws in the Ohio River Valley and recognized this area as French territory (forcing the colonists living there to obey harsh French laws).

- taken away important laws and the charters that made our governments legal and changed our governments.

- ended our legislatures and claimed to have the right to pass laws for us.

King George III gave up his right to rule the colonies when he failed to protect us and went to war against us.

He has:

- robbed American ships at sea, forced captured sailors to join the British navy, and burned down our towns.

- brought foreign soldiers to the colonies to commit cruel acts against us.

- tried to persuade enslaved people in the colonies to rebel and Native Americans to fight the colonists.

Statement of Independence

For years we have asked King George III to correct these problems, without success. The king is an unfair ruler who is not fit to rule a free people.

We have told the British about our problems and about the unfair laws passed by their government. We hoped they would help us because they believe in justice, are related to us, and have much in common with us. We were wrong. We must, therefore, break away from Great Britain and create our own country.

Nor have We been wanting in attention to our British brethren. We have warned them from time to time of attempts by their legislature to extend an unwarrantable jurisdiction over us. We have reminded them of the circumstances of our emigration and settlement here. We have appealed to their native justice and magnanimity, and we have conjured them by the ties of our common kindred to disavow these usurpations, which, would inevitably interrupt our connections and correspondence. They too have been deaf to the voice of justice and of consanguinity. We must, therefore, acquiesce in the necessity, which denounces our Separation, and hold them, as we hold the rest of mankind, Enemies in War, in Peace Friends.

We, therefore, the Representatives of the United States of America, in General Congress Assembled,

Signers

Button Gwinnett (Ga.)
Lyman Hall (Ga.)
George Walton (Ga.)

William Hooper (N.C.)
Joseph Hewes (N.C.)
John Penn (N.C.)
Edward Rutledge (S.C.)
Thomas Heyward, Jr. (S.C.)
Thomas Lynch, Jr. (S.C.)
Arthur Middleton (S.C.)

John Hancock (Mass.)
Samuel Chase (Md.)
William Paca (Md.)
Thomas Stone (Md.)
Charles Carroll of Carrollton (Md.)
George Wythe (Va.)
Richard Henry Lee (Va.)
Thomas Jefferson (Va.)
Benjamin Harrison (Va.)
Thomas Nelson, Jr. (Va.)
Francis Lightfoot Lee (Va.)
Carter Braxton (Va.)

appealing to the Supreme judge of the world for the rectitude of our intentions, do, in the Name, and by Authority of the good People of these Colonies, solemnly publish and declare, That these United Colonies are, and of Right ought to be Free and Independent States; that they are Absolved from all Allegiance to the British Crown, and that all political connection between them and the State of Great Britain, is and ought to be totally dissolved; and that as Free and Independent States, they have full Power to levy War, conclude Peace, contract Alliances, establish Commerce, and to do all other Acts and Things which Independent States may of right do. And for the support of this Declaration, with a firm reliance on the protection of divine Providence, we mutually pledge to each other our Lives, our Fortunes and our sacred Honour.

In the name of the American people, we, members of the Continental Congress, state that the United States is no longer a colony of Great Britain. Instead, it is an independent country. This gives it the right to make war and peace, make agreements with other countries, trade with them, and do all the things that free countries do. We support this Declaration of Independence by promising each other our lives, our fortunes, and our honor.

Robert Morris (Pa.)	William Floyd (N.Y.)	Josiah Bartlett (N.H.)
Benjamin Rush (Pa.)	Philip Livingston (N.Y.)	William Whipple (N.H.)
Benjamin Franklin (Pa.)	Francis Lewis (N.Y.)	Samuel Adams (Mass.)
John Morton (Pa.)	Lewis Morris (N.Y.)	John Adams (Mass.)
George Clymer (Pa.)	Richard Stockton (N.J.)	Robert Treat Paine (Mass.)
James Smith (Pa.)	John Witherspoon (N.J.)	Elbridge Gerry (Mass.)
George Taylor (Pa.)	Francis Hopkinson (R.I.)	Stephen Hopkins (R.I.)
James Wilson (Pa.)	John Hart (N.J.)	William Ellery (R.I.)
George Ross (Pa.)	Abraham Clark (N.J.)	Roger Sherman (Conn.)
Cæsar Rodney (Del.)		Samuel Huntington (Conn.)
George Read (Del.)		William Williams (Conn.)
Thomas McKean (Del.)		Oliver Wolcott (Conn.)
		Matthew Thornton (N.H.)

The Constitution of The United States

Explanation and Summary

The following text explains the meaning of the Constitution and its Amendments. Crossed out sentences are no longer in effect.

Preamble

The people of the United States make this Constitution to form a stronger nation; to ensure peace, justice, and liberty; to defend its citizens; and to improve the lives of its people.

Article 1

Congress has the power to make laws. It is made up of the Senate and the House of Representatives.

1. Members of the House of Representatives are elected every two years by voters in each state.

2. A member of the House of Representatives must be at least 25 years old, a U.S. citizen for at least seven years, and live in the state he or she represents.

3. The number of Representatives for each state is based on the number of people who live in that state. Every ten years a census, or count, must be taken to determine the population of each state. (This census included indentured servants but not most Native Americans. Each enslaved person was counted as three-fifths of a free person. Today all people are counted equally.)

Preamble

We the people of the United States, in order to form a more perfect Union, establish justice, insure domestic tranquility, provide for the common Defense, promote the general welfare, and secure the blessings of liberty to ourselves and our posterity, do ordain and establish this Constitution for the United States of America.

Article 1. The Legislative Branch

Section 1. The Congress

All legislative powers herein granted shall be vested in a Congress of the United States, which shall consist of a Senate and House of Representatives.

Section 2. The House of Representatives

1. The House of Representatives shall be composed of members chosen every second year by the people of the several states, and the electors in each state shall have the qualifications requisite for electors of the most numerous branch of the state legislature.

2. No person shall be a Representative who shall not have attained to the age of twenty-five years, and been seven years a citizen of the United States, and who shall not, when elected, be an inhabitant of that state in which he shall be chosen.

3. Representatives and ~~direct taxes~~ shall be apportioned among the several states which may be included within this Union, according to their respective numbers, ~~which shall be determined by adding to the whole number of free persons, including those bound to service for a term of years, and excluding Indians not taxed, three-fifths of all other persons.~~ The actual enumeration shall be made within three years after the first meeting of the Congress of the United States, and within every subsequent term of ten years, in such manner as they shall by law direct. The number of Representatives shall not exceed one for every 30,000, but each state shall have at least one Representative; ~~and until~~

~~such enumeration shall be made, the state of New Hampshire shall be entitled to choose three, Massachusetts, eight, Rhode Island and Providence Plantations, one, Connecticut, five, New York, six, New Jersey, four, Pennsylvania, eight, Delaware, one, Maryland, six, Virginia, ten, North Carolina, five, South Carolina, five, and Georgia, three.~~

4. When vacancies happen in the representation from any state, the executive authority thereof shall issue writs of election to fill such vacancies.

5. The House of Representatives shall choose their Speaker and other officers; and shall have the sole power of impeachment.

4. Special elections called by the state's governor must be held to fill any empty seat in the House of Representatives.

5. Members of the House of Representatives choose their own leaders. Only they have the power to impeach, or accuse, government officials of crimes in office.

Section 3. The Senate

1. The Senate of the United States shall be composed of two Senators from each state, ~~chosen by the legislature thereof,~~ for six years; and each Senator shall have one vote.

1. Each state has two Senators. Each one serves a term of six years and has one vote in the Senate. (State legislatures elected Senators. The Seventeenth Amendment changed this. Senators are now elected directly by the people.)

2. ~~Immediately after they shall be assembled in consequence of the first election, they shall be divided as equally as may be into three classes. The seats of the Senators of the first class shall be vacated at the expiration of the second year, of the second class at the expiration of the fourth year, and of the third class at the expiration of the sixth year, so that one-third may be chosen every second year; and if vacancies happen by resignation, or otherwise, during the recess of the legislature of any state, the executive thereof may make temporary appointments until the next meeting of the legislature, which shall then fill such vacancies.~~

2. One-third of the Senate seats are up for election every two years. (The Seventeenth Amendment changed the way empty seats are filled.)

3. No person shall be a Senator who shall not have attained to the age of thirty years, and been nine years a citizen of the United States, and who shall not, when elected, be an inhabitant of that state for which he shall be chosen.

4. The Vice President of the United States shall be president of the Senate, but shall have no vote, unless they be equally divided.

5. The Senate shall choose their other officers, and also a president pro tempore, in the absence of the Vice President, or when he shall exercise the office of the President of the United States.

3. To be a Senator, a person must be at least 30 years old, a U.S. citizen for at least nine years, and live in the state he or she represents.

4. The Vice President is in charge of the Senate but votes only to break a tie.

5. Senators choose their own leaders. When the Vice President is absent, the Senate leader is called the President pro tempore (prō tem'pə rē), or temporary President.

6. The Senate holds all impeachment trials. When the President is impeached, the Chief Justice of the Supreme Court is the judge for the trial. A two-thirds vote is needed for conviction, or judgment of guilt.

7. Impeached officials convicted by the Senate can be removed from office and barred from serving again in government. Regular courts of law can decide other punishments.

1. State lawmakers make the rules for Congressional elections. Congress can change some of these rules.

2. Congress meets at least once a year, beginning in December. (The Twentieth Amendment changed this date to January 3.)

1. The Senate and House of Representatives decide if their members were elected fairly and are qualified. Half the members of each house of Congress must be present for Congress to do most business. Absent members can be required to attend meetings of Congress.

2. Each house of Congress may set rules and punish members for breaking them. A two-thirds vote is needed to expel, or force out, a member.

3. Each house of Congress keeps and publishes a record of its activities. Secret matters may be left out of this record. If one-fifth of the members demand it, a vote on any matter will be published.

4. During a session of Congress, neither house can stop meeting for more than three days or decide to meet somewhere else unless the other house agrees.

6. The Senate shall have the sole power to try all impeachments. When sitting for that purpose, they shall be on oath or affirmation. When the President of the United States is tried, the Chief Justice shall preside; and no person shall be convicted without the concurrence of two-thirds of the members present.

7. Judgment in cases of impeachment shall not extend further than to removal from office, and disqualification to hold and enjoy any office of honor, trust or profit under the United States; but the party convicted shall nevertheless be liable and subject to indictment, trial, judgment and punishment, according to law.

Section 4. Elections and Meetings of Congress

1. The times, places and manner of holding elections for Senators and Representatives shall be prescribed in each state by the legislature thereof; but the Congress may at any time by law make or alter such regulations, except as to the places of choosing Senators.

2. The Congress shall assemble at least once in every year and such meeting shall be on the first Monday in December, unless they shall by law appoint a different day.

Section 5. Rules of Procedure for Congress

1. Each house shall be the judge of the elections, returns and qualifications of its own members, and a majority of each shall constitute a quorum to do business; but a smaller number may adjourn from day to day, and may be authorized to compel the attendance of absent members, in such manner, and under such penalties as each house may provide.

2. Each house may determine the rules of its proceedings, punish its members for disorderly behavior, and with the concurrence of two-thirds, expel a member.

3. Each house shall keep a journal of its proceedings, and from time to time publish the same, excepting such parts as may in their judgment require secrecy; and the yeas and nays of the members of either house on any question shall, at the desire of one-fifth of those present, be entered on the journal.

4. Neither house, during the session of Congress, shall, without the consent of the other, adjourn for more than three days, nor to any other place than that in which the two houses shall be sitting.

Section 6. Privileges and Restrictions of Members of Congress

1. The Senators and Representatives shall receive a compensation for their services, to be ascertained by law, and paid out of the Treasury of the United States. They shall in all cases, except treason, felony and breach of the peace, be privileged from arrest during their attendance at the session of their respective houses, and in going to and returning from the same; and for any speech or debate in either house, they shall not be questioned in any other place.

2. No Senator or Representative shall, during the time for which he was elected, be appointed to any civil office under the authority of the United States, which shall have been created, or the emoluments whereof shall have been increased during such time; and no person holding any office under the United States, shall be a member of either house during his continuance in office.

1. Each member of Congress receives a salary from the U.S. government. Except for very serious crimes, no member can be arrested in the place where Congress is meeting. Members cannot be arrested for anything they say in Congress.

2. Senators and Representatives may not hold any other job in the federal government while they serve in Congress.

Section 7. How Laws Are Made

1. All bills for raising revenue shall originate in the House of Representatives; but the Senate may propose or concur with amendments as on other bills.

2. Every bill which shall have passed the House of Representatives and the Senate, shall, before it become a law, be presented to the President of the United States. If he approve he shall sign it, but if not he shall return it, with his objections to that house in which it shall have originated, who shall enter the objections at large on their journal, and proceed to reconsider it. If after such reconsideration two-thirds of that house shall agree to pass the bill, it shall be sent, together with the objections, to the other house, by which it shall likewise be reconsidered, and if approved by two-thirds of that house, it shall become a law. But in all such cases the votes of both houses shall be determined by yeas and nays, and the names of the persons voting for and against the bill shall be entered on the journal of each house respectively. If any bill shall not be returned by the President within ten days (Sundays excepted) after it shall have been presented to him, the same shall be a law, in like manner as if he had signed it, unless the Congress by their adjournment prevent its return, in which case it shall not be a law.

3. Every order, resolution, or vote to which the concurrence of the Senate and House of Representatives may be necessary (except on a question of adjournment) shall be presented to the President of the United States; and before the same shall take effect, shall be approved by him, or being disapproved by him, shall be repassed by two-thirds of the Senate and House of Representatives, according to the rules and limitations prescribed in the case of a bill.

1. All money and tax bills must begin in the House of Representatives. The Senate can later pass or change these bills.

2. After a bill, or suggested law, passes both houses of Congress, it goes to the President. If the President signs the bill, it becomes a law. If the President vetoes, or rejects, the bill, it goes back to Congress. A President's veto can be overridden, or upset, if Congress votes again and two-thirds of the members of each house vote in favor of the bill. The bill becomes a law. If the President does not sign or vetoes a bill within ten days (not counting Sundays) of first receiving it, the bill becomes a law. If Congress stops meeting before ten days have passed, however, the bill does not become a law. (This last type of action is called a "pocket veto.")

3. Every act passed by Congress must be given to the President either to sign or veto. The only exception is when Congress votes to adjourn, or stop meeting.

Congress has the power to:

1. raise and collect taxes to pay debts and to protect and serve the country. However, federal taxes must be the same everywhere in the United States;

2. borrow money;

3. control trade with foreign nations, between states, and with Native Americans;

4. decide how people can become U.S. citizens and make laws dealing with people and businesses unable to pay their debts;

5. print money, decide its value, and decide the standards of weights and measures;

6. punish people who make counterfeit, or fake, money and bonds;

7. set up post offices and roads for the delivery of mail;

8. protect the rights and creations of scientists, artists, authors, and inventors;

9. create federal, or national, courts lower than the Supreme Court;

10. punish crimes committed at sea;

11. declare war;

12. form and support an army, but the money set aside to do this can be for no more than two years;

13. form and support a navy;

14. make rules for the armed forces;

15. call the militia (today called the National Guard) to make sure federal laws are obeyed, put down rebellions, and fight invasions;

16. organize, arm, and discipline the National Guard, though states have

Section 8. Powers Granted to Congress

1. The Congress shall have power to lay and collect taxes, duties, imposts and excises, to pay the debts and provide for the common defense and general welfare of the United States; but all duties, imposts and excises shall be uniform throughout the United States;

2. To borrow money on the credit of the United States;

3. To regulate commerce with foreign nations, and among the several states, and with the Indian tribes;

4. To establish a uniform rule of naturalization, and uniform laws on the subject of bankruptcies throughout the United States;

5. To coin money, regulate the value thereof, and of foreign coin, and fix the standard of weights and measures;

6. To provide for the punishment of counterfeiting the securities and current coin of the United States;

7. To establish post offices and post roads;

8. To promote the progress of science and useful arts, by securing for limited times to authors and inventors the exclusive right to their respective writings and discoveries;

9. To constitute tribunals inferior to the Supreme Court;

10. To define and punish piracies and felonies committed on the high seas and offenses against the law of nations;

11. To declare war, grant letters of marque and reprisal, and make rules concerning captures on land and water;

12. To raise and support armies, but no appropriation of money to that use shall be for a longer term than two years;

13. To provide and maintain a navy;

14. To make rules for the government and regulation of the land and naval forces;

15. To provide for calling forth the militia to execute the laws of the Union, suppress insurrections and repel invasions;

16. To provide for organizing, arming, and disciplining, the militia, and for governing such part of them as may be employed in the service of the United States, reserving to the states

respectively, the appointment of the officers, and the authority of training the militia according to the discipline prescribed by Congress;

17. To exercise exclusive legislation in all cases whatsoever, over such district (not exceeding ten miles square) as may, by cession of particular states, and the acceptance of Congress, become the seat of the government of the United States, and to exercise like authority over all places purchased by the consent of the legislature of the state in which the same shall be, for the erection of forts, magazines, arsenals, dockyards, and other needful buildings;—and

18. To make all laws which shall be necessary and proper for carrying into execution the foregoing powers, and all other powers vested by this Constitution in the government of the United States, or in any department or officer thereof.

Section 9. Powers Denied to Congress

1. The migration or importation of such persons as any of the states now existing shall think proper to admit, shall not be prohibited by the Congress prior to the year one thousand eight hundred and eight, but a tax or duty may be imposed on such importation, not exceeding ten dollars for each person.

2. The privilege of the writ of habeas corpus shall not be suspended, unless when in cases of rebellion or invasion the public safety may require it.

3. No bill of attainder or ex post facto law shall be passed.

4. No capitation, or other direct, tax shall be laid, unless in proportion to the census or enumeration herein before directed to be taken.

5. No tax or duty shall be laid on articles exported from any state.

6. No preference shall be given any regulation of commerce or revenue to the ports of one state over those of another; nor shall vessels bound to, or from, one state, be obliged to enter, clear, or pay duties in another.

7. No money shall be drawn from the Treasury, but in consequence of appropriations made by law; and a regular statement and account of the receipts and expenditures of all public money shall be published from time to time.

---

the power to appoint officers and train soldiers in the National Guard;

17. govern the capital and military sites of the United States;

18. make all laws necessary to carry out the powers of Congress. (This is called the "elastic clause" because it stretches the powers of Congress.)

Congress does not have the power to:

1. stop enslaved people from being brought into the United States before 1808. In 1808, the first year trade was allowed, Congress passed a law banning it;

2. arrest and jail people without charging them with a crime, except during a rebellion or emergency;

3. punish a person who has not had a trial or has done something wrong that was not against the law when the person did it;

4. pass a direct tax (such as an income tax) unless it is in proportion to the population. (The Sixteenth Amendment allowed an income tax);

5. tax goods sent out of a state;

6. favor ports of one state over ports of another state; nor can a state tax the ships of another state that enter its borders;

7. spend money without passing a law and keeping a record of what is spent;

8. give someone a title of nobility (such as king or queen); nor may a worker in the federal government accept a gift or title from a foreign government.

State governments do not have the power to:

1. make treaties, print money, or do anything forbidden in Section 9 of the Constitution, above;

2. tax goods sent into and out of a state unless Congress agrees;

3. keep armed forces, go to war, or make agreements with other states or countries unless Congress agrees.

Article 2

1. The President has the power to execute, or carry out, the laws of the United States. The President and Vice President together serve a term of four years.

2. The President is chosen by electors from each state. Today these electors are chosen by the voters and are called the Electoral College. The number of electoral votes for each state is decided by adding up the number of the state's Senators and Representatives.

3. (This part of the Constitution describes the first way the President and Vice President were elected. The Twelfth Amendment changed this method. Originally, the person who

8. No title of nobility shall be granted by the United States; and no person holding any office of profit or trust under them, shall, without the consent of the Congress, accept of any present, emolument, office, or title, of any kind whatever, from any king, prince, or foreign state.

Section 10. Powers Denied to the States

1. No state shall enter into any treaty, alliance, or confederation; grant letters of marque and reprisal; coin money; emit bills of credit; make anything but gold and silver coin a tender in payment of debts; pass any bill of attainder, ex post facto law, or law impairing the obligation of contracts, or grant any title of nobility.

2. No state shall, without the consent of the Congress, lay any imposts or duties on imports or exports, except what may be absolutely necessary for executing its inspection laws; and the net produce of all duties and imposts, laid by any state on imports or exports, shall be for the use of the Treasury of the United States; and all such laws shall be subject to the revision and control of the Congress.

3. No state shall, without the consent of Congress, lay any duty of tonnage, keep troops, or ships of war in time of peace, enter into any agreement or compact with another state, or with a foreign power, or engage in war, unless actually invaded, or in such imminent danger as will not admit of delay.

Article 2. The Executive Branch

Section 1. Office of President and Vice President

1. The executive power shall be vested in a President of the United States of America. He shall hold his office during the term of four years, and, together with the Vice President, chosen for the same term, be elected, as follows:

2. Each state shall appoint, in such manner as the legislature thereof may direct, a number of electors, equal to the whole number of Senators and Representatives to which the state may be entitled in the Congress; but no Senator or Representative, or person holding an office or trust or profit under the United States, shall be appointed an elector.

3. ~~The electors shall meet in their respective states, and vote by ballot for two persons, of whom one at least shall not be an inhabitant of the same state with themselves. And they shall make a list of all the persons voted for, and of the number of votes for each; which list they shall sign and certify, and transmit sealed~~

to the seat of the government of the United States, directed to the president of the Senate. The president of the Senate shall, in the presence of the Senate and House of Representatives, open all the certificates, and the votes shall then be counted. The person having the greatest number of votes shall be the President, if such number be a majority of the whole number of electors appointed; and if there be more than one who have such majority, and have an equal number of votes, then the House of Representatives shall immediately choose by ballot one of them for President; and if no person have a majority, then from the five highest on the list the said House shall in like manner choose the President. But in choosing the President, the votes shall be taken by states, the representation from each state having one vote; a quorum for this purpose shall consist of a member or members from two-thirds of the states, and a majority of all the states shall be necessary to a choice. In every case, after the choice of the President, the person having the greatest number of votes of the electors shall be the Vice President. But if there should remain two or more who have equal votes, the Senate shall choose from them by ballot the Vice President.

received the most electoral votes became President and the person who received the next highest number became Vice President.)

4. The Congress may determine the time of choosing the electors, and the day on which they shall give their votes; which day shall be the same throughout the United States.

4. Congress decides when Presidential electors are chosen and when they vote. Electors vote on the same day throughout the country. (Today people vote for the electors every four years on the Tuesday after the first Monday of November.)

5. No person except a natural born citizen, ~~or a citizen of the United States, at the time of the adoption of this Constitution,~~ shall be eligible to the office of the President; neither shall any person be eligible to that office who shall not have attained to the age of thirty-five years, and been fourteen years a resident within the United States.

5. To be President, a person must be a citizen born in the United States, at least 35 years old, and have lived in the United States for at least 14 years.

6. In case of the removal of the President from office, or of his death, resignation, or inability to discharge the powers and duties of the said office, the same shall devolve on the Vice President, and the Congress may by law provide for the case of removal, death, resignation, or inability, both of the President and Vice President, declaring what officer shall then act as President, and such officer shall act accordingly, until the disability be removed, or a President shall be elected.

6. If the President leaves office or can no longer serve, the Vice President becomes President. If there is no Vice President, Congress may decide who becomes President. (The Twenty-Fifth Amendment changed the way these offices are filled.)

7. The President shall, at stated times receive for his services, a compensation, which shall neither be increased nor diminished during the period for which he shall have been elected, and he shall not receive within that period any other emolument from the United States, or any of them.

7. The President receives a salary that cannot be raised or lowered while in office. The President can receive no other gift or salary from the country or its states while in office.

8. Before taking office, the person elected President takes an oath to carry out the laws of the country and to defend the Constitution.

8. Before he enter on the execution of his office, he shall take the following oath or affirmation:—"I do solemnly swear (or affirm) that I will faithfully execute the office of President of the United States, and will to the best of my ability, preserve, protect and defend the Constitution of the United States."

Section 2. Powers Granted to the President

1. The President is in charge of the armed forces and state militias. The President can demand written advice and opinions of the people in charge of each executive department (the President's Cabinet). The President also has the power to pardon, or free, people convicted of federal crimes, except in cases of impeachment.

1. The President shall be Commander in Chief of the Army and Navy of the United States, and of the militia of the several states, when called into the actual service of the United States; he may require the opinion, in writing, of the principal officer in each of the executive departments, upon any subject relating to the duties of their respective offices, and he shall have power to grant reprieves and pardons for offenses against the United States, except in cases of impeachment.

2. The President has the power to make treaties, but they must be approved by two-thirds of the Senate. The President also has the power to name ambassadors, important government officials, and judges of the Supreme Court and other federal courts, with the approval of the Senate.

2. He shall have power, by and with the advice and consent of the Senate, to make treaties, provided two-thirds of the Senators present concur; and he shall nominate, and by and with the advice and consent of the Senate, shall appoint ambassadors, other public ministers and consuls, judges of the Supreme Court, and all other officers of the United States, whose appointments are not herein otherwise provided for, and which shall be established by law; but the Congress may by law vest the appointment of such inferior officers, as they think proper, in the President alone, in the courts of law, or in the heads of departments.

3. The President has the power to fill empty offices for a short time when the Senate is not meeting.

3. The President shall have power to fill up all vacancies that may happen during the recess of the Senate, by granting commissions which shall expire at the end of their next session.

Section 3. Duties of the President

The President must tell Congress from time to time what the condition of the country is. (This speech is called the State of the Union address and is given once a year, usually in late January.) In this message, the President recommends ways to improve the country. The President can also, in time of emergency, call Congress to meet. When Congress cannot decide whether or not to stop meetings, the President can make this decision. The President receives foreign officials, makes sure the country's laws are carried out, and appoints officers in the armed forces.

He shall from time to time give to the Congress information of the state of the Union, and recommend to their consideration such measures as he shall judge necessary and expedient; he may, on extraordinary occasions, convene both houses, or either of them, and in case of disagreement between them, with respect to the time of adjournment, he may adjourn them to such time as he shall think proper; he shall receive ambassadors and other public ministers; he shall take care that the laws be faithfully executed, and shall commission all the officers of the United States.

Section 4. Removal from Office

The President, Vice President and all civil officers of the United States, shall be removed from office on impeachment for, and conviction of, treason, bribery, or other high crimes and misdemeanors.

Article 3. The Judicial Branch

Section 1. Federal Courts

The judicial power of the United States shall be vested in one Supreme Court, and in such inferior courts as the Congress may from time to time ordain and establish. The judges, both of the Supreme and inferior courts, shall hold their offices during good behavior, and shall, at stated times, receive for their services, a compensation, which shall not be diminished during their continuance in office.

Section 2. Powers of Federal Courts

1. The judicial power shall extend to all cases, in law and equity, arising under this Constitution, the laws of the United States, and treaties made, or which shall be made, under their authority; to all cases affecting ambassadors, other public ministers and consuls; to all cases of admiralty and maritime jurisdiction; to controversies to which the United States shall be a party; to controversies between two or more states; between a state and citizens of another state; between citizens of different states, between citizens of the same state claiming lands under grants of different states, and between a state, or the citizens thereof, and foreign states, citizens or subjects.

2. In all cases affecting ambassadors, other public ministers and consuls, and those in which a state shall be party, the Supreme Court shall have original jurisdiction. In all the other cases before mentioned, the Supreme Court shall have appellate jurisdiction, both as to law and fact, with such exceptions, and under such regulations as the Congress shall make.

3. The trial of all crimes, except in cases of impeachment, shall be by jury; and such trial shall be held in the state where the said crimes shall have been committed; but when not committed within any state, the trial shall be at such place or places as the Congress may by law have directed.

The President, Vice President, and other non-military officials may be impeached, or accused of committing crimes, and removed from office if found guilty.

Article 3
The judicial power, or the power of courts to make decisions, is held by the Supreme Court and by lower federal, or national, courts created by Congress. Supreme Court and other federal judges hold office for life if they act properly. Judges receive a salary that cannot be lowered.

1. Federal courts have authority over:
a) all laws made under the Constitution;
b) treaties with foreign governments;
c) cases involving:
   • matters occurring at sea;
   • the federal government;
   • different states or citizens of different states; and
   • foreign citizens or governments. (The Eleventh Amendment partly limits which cases federal courts can hear.)

2. In cases involving either states or ambassadors and government officials, the Supreme Court only makes a judgment. All other cases begin in lower courts but may later be appealed to, or reviewed by, the Supreme Court.

3. All criminal cases, except those of impeachment, are judged by trial and jury in the state where the supposed crime took place. If a crime occurs outside of any state, Congress decides where the trial takes place.

1. Treason is the crime of making war against the United States or helping its enemies. To be found guilty of treason, a person must confess to the crime or two witnesses must swear to having seen the crime committed.

2. Congress decides the punishment for treason. Relatives of people convicted of treason cannot also be punished for the crime.

Article 4

Each state must respect the laws, records, and court decisions of other states. Congress may pass laws to help carry out these matters.

1. Citizens are guaranteed all their basic rights when visiting other states.

2. A person charged with a crime, who flees to another state, must be returned to the state where the crime took place if the governor of the state demands it.

3. A person enslaved in one state, who flees to another state, is still enslaved and must be returned to the person's owner. (The Thirteenth Amendment, which outlawed slavery, overturned or took away the need for this section of the Constitution.)

1. Congress may let new states become part of the United States. No new state can be formed from another state or by joining parts of other states, unless Congress and the legislatures of the states involved approve.

2. Congress has the power to make laws and rules for territories and government properties of the United States.

Section 3. The Crime of Treason

1. Treason against the United States shall consist only in levying war against them, or in adhering to their enemies, giving them aid and comfort. No person shall be convicted of treason unless on the testimony of two witnesses to the same overt act, or on confession in open court.

2. The Congress shall have power to declare the punishment of treason, but no attainder of treason shall work corruption of blood, or forfeiture except during the life of the person attainted.

Article 4. Relations Among the States

Section 1. Recognition by Each State of Acts of Other States

Full faith and credit shall be given in each state to the public acts, records, and judicial proceedings of every other state. And the Congress may by general laws prescribe the manner in which such acts, records and proceedings shall be proved, and the effect thereof.

Section 2. Rights of Citizens in Other States

1. The citizens of each state shall be entitled to all privileges and immunities of citizens in the several states.

2. A person charged in any state with treason, felony, or other crime, who shall flee from justice, and be found in another state, shall on demand of the executive authority of the state from which he fled, be delivered up, to be removed to the state having jurisdiction of the crime.

3. No person held to service or labor in one state, under the laws thereof, escaping into another, shall, in consequence of any law or regulation therein, be discharged from such service or labor, but shall be delivered up on claim of the party to whom such service or labor may be due.

Section 3. Treatment of New States and Territories

1. New states may be admitted by the Congress into this Union; but no new state shall be formed or erected within the jurisdiction of any other state; nor any state be formed by the junction of two or more states, or parts of states, without the consent of the legislatures of the states concerned as well as of the Congress.

2. The Congress shall have power to dispose of and make all needful rules and regulations respecting the territory or other property belonging to the United States; and nothing in this Constitution shall be so construed as to prejudice any claims of the United States, or of any particular state.

Section 4. Guarantees to the States

The United States shall guarantee to every state in this Union a republican form of government, and shall protect each of them against invasion; and on application of the legislature, or of the executive (when the legislature cannot be convened) against domestic violence.

Article 5. Amending the Constitution

The Congress, whenever two-thirds of both houses shall deem it necessary, shall propose amendments to this Constitution, or, on the application of the legislatures of two-thirds of the several states, shall call a convention for proposing amendments, which, in either case, shall be valid to all intents and purposes, as part of this Constitution, when ratified by the legislatures of three-fourths of the several states, or by conventions in three-fourths thereof, as the one or the other mode of ratification may be proposed by the Congress; provided that no amendment which may be made prior to the year one thousand eight hundred and eight shall in any manner affect the first and fourth clauses in the Ninth Section of the First Article; and that no state, without its consent, shall be deprived of its equal suffrage in the Senate.

Article 6. Debts, Federal Supremacy, Oaths of Office

Section 1. Prior Debts of the United States

All debts contracted and engagements entered into, before the adoption of this Constitution, shall be as valid against the United States under this Constitution, as under the Confederation.

Section 2. The Supreme Law of the Land

This Constitution, and the laws of the United States which shall be made in pursuance thereof; and all treaties made, or which shall be made, under the authority of the United States, shall be the supreme law of the land; and the judges in every state shall be bound thereby, anything in the constitution or laws of any state to the contrary notwithstanding.

Section 3. Oaths of Office

The Senators and Representatives before mentioned, and the members of the several state legislatures, and all executive and judicial officers, both of the United States and of the several states, shall be bound by oath or affirmation, to support this Constitution; but no religious test shall ever be required as a qualification to any office or public trust under the United States.

The federal government guarantees that the people of each state have the right to elect their leaders. It also promises to protect each state from invasion, rebellion, and acts of violence.

Article 5
There are two ways to make amendments, or changes, to the Constitution: two-thirds of each branch of Congress can ask for an amendment; or, two-thirds of the state legislatures can call an official meeting to ask for an amendment. Three-fourths of the state legislatures or three-fourths of special state conventions must approve the suggested amendment for it to become part of the Constitution. No state can be denied its equal vote in the Senate without its approval. No amendment could be made before 1808 that affected either the slave trade or certain direct taxes.

Article 6
The United States government promises to pay back all debts and honor all agreements made by the government under the Articles of Confederation.

The Constitution and all the laws and treaties made under it are the supreme, or highest, law in the United States. If state or local laws disagree with federal law, the federal law must be obeyed.

All officials of the federal and state governments must promise to support the Constitution. A person's religion may never be used to give a person a job in the U.S. government or to take it away.

Article 7

The Constitution will become law when special conventions in 9 (of the 13 original) states approve it.

This Constitution is completed by the agreement of everyone at this convention on September 17, 1787.

The people present have signed their names below.

Article 7. Ratification of the Constitution

The ratification of the conventions of nine states, shall be sufficient for the establishment of this Constitution between the states so ratifying the same.

Done in convention by the unanimous consent of the States present the Seventeenth day of September in the year of our Lord one thousand seven hundred and eighty seven, and of the Independence of the United States of America the Twelfth.

In witness whereof we have hereunto subscribed our names.

George Washington, President and deputy from Virginia

DELAWARE
George Read
Gunning Bedford, Jr.
John Dickinson
Richard Bassett
Jacob Broom

MARYLAND
James McHenry
Daniel of St. Thomas Jenifer
Daniel Carroll

VIRGINIA
John Blair
James Madison, Jr.

NORTH CAROLINA
William Blount
Richard Dobbs Spaight
Hugh Williamson

SOUTH CAROLINA
John Rutledge
Charles Cotesworth Pinckney
Charles Pinckney
Pierce Butler

GEORGIA
William Few
Abraham Baldwin

NEW HAMPSHIRE
John Langdon
Nicholas Gilman

MASSACHUSETTS
Nathaniel Gorham
Rufus King

CONNECTICUT
William Samuel Johnson
Roger Sherman

NEW YORK
Alexander Hamilton

NEW JERSEY
William Livingston
David Brearley
William Paterson
Jonathan Dayton

PENNSYLVANIA
Benjamin Franklin
Thomas Mifflin
Robert Morris
George Clymer
Thomas FitzSimons
Jared Ingersoll
James Wilson
Gouverneur Morris

Attest: William Jackson, Secretary

Amendments to the Constitution

The first ten amendments to the Constitution guarantee basic freedoms and are known as the Bill of Rights.

Amendment 1. Freedom of Religion, Speech, Press, Assembly, and Petition (1791)

Congress shall make no law respecting an establishment of religion, or prohibiting the free exercise thereof; or abridging the freedom of speech, or of the press; or the right of the people peaceably to assemble, and to petition the government for a redress of grievances.

Amendment 1
Under the First Amendment, Congress cannot make laws that:
1) set up an official religion; or prevent people from practicing their religion;
2) stop people from saying what they want;
3) stop people from printing what they want;
4) prevent people from gathering peacefully and asking the government to listen to their problems and to correct them.

Amendment 2. Right to Keep Weapons (1791)

A well-regulated militia being necessary to the security of a free state, the right of the people to keep and bear arms shall not be infringed.

Amendment 2
People have the right to keep weapons and be part of the state militia (today the National Guard).

Amendment 3. Protection Against Quartering Soldiers (1791)

No soldier shall, in time of peace, be quartered in any house, without the consent of the owner, nor in time of war, but in a manner to be prescribed by law.

Amendment 3
During peacetime, people cannot be forced to house and feed soldiers in their homes. During war, Congress may set other rules.

Amendment 4. Freedom from Unreasonable Search and Seizure (1791)

The right of the people to be secure in their persons, houses, papers, and effects, against unreasonable searches and seizures, shall not be violated, and no warrants shall issue, but upon probable cause, supported by oath or affirmation, and particularly describing the place to be searched, and the persons or things to be seized.

Amendment 4
To search a person's home or property, the government must get a search warrant, or special approval, describing exactly what place is to be searched and what items are expected to be found.

Amendment 5. Rights of Persons Accused of a Crime (1791)

No person shall be held to answer for a capital, or otherwise infamous, crime, unless on a presentment or indictment of a grand jury, except in cases arising in the land or naval forces, or in the militia, when in actual service in time of war or public danger; nor shall any person be subject for the same offense to be twice put in jeopardy of life or limb; nor shall be compelled in any criminal case to be a witness against himself, nor be

Amendment 5
A person cannot be charged with a serious crime unless a grand jury (a group of citizens appointed to study criminal evidence) decides that a good reason exists for a trial. (The only exceptions are cases involving people in the armed forces.) A person judged innocent by a court of law cannot be tried again for the same crime.

People on trial cannot be forced to testify, or speak in court, against themselves. A person cannot have life, liberty, or property taken away unless fairly decided by a court of law. If the government takes away property for the use of the public, a fair price must be paid the owner.

Amendment 6

In all criminal cases, a person accused of a crime has the right to a fast, public trial by a fair jury in the place where the crime took place. All persons accused of a crime have the right to:
- know the charges against them;
- hear the evidence and witnesses against them;
- call witnesses in their defense;
- have a lawyer.

Amendment 7

A person has the right to a trial by jury in civil, or noncriminal, cases involving more than $20.

Amendment 8

The government cannot ask for very high bail, or deposit of money, from a person accused of a crime. People convicted of crimes cannot be fined an unfairly high amount, nor be punished in a cruel or unusual way.

Amendment 9

The rights of the people are not limited to those stated in the Constitution.

Amendment 10

Powers not given the U.S. government and not forbidden to the states are left to the states or to the people.

---

deprived of life, liberty, or property, without due process of law; nor shall private property be taken for public use, without just compensation.

Amendment 6. Right to a Jury Trial in Criminal Cases (1791)

In all criminal prosecutions, the accused shall enjoy the right to a speedy and public trial, by an impartial jury of the state and district wherein the crime shall have been committed, which district shall have been previously ascertained by law, and to be informed of the nature and cause of the accusation; to be confronted with the witnesses against him; to have compulsory process for obtaining witnesses in his favor, and to have the assistance of counsel for his defense.

Amendment 7. Right to a Jury Trial in Civil Cases (1791)

In suits at common law, where the value in controversy shall exceed twenty dollars, the right of trial by jury shall be preserved, and no fact tried by a jury shall be otherwise re-examined in any court of the United States than according to the rules of the common law.

Amendment 8. Protection from Unfair Fines and Punishment (1791)

Excessive bail shall not be required, nor excessive fines imposed, nor cruel and unusual punishments inflicted.

Amendment 9. Other Rights of the People (1791)

The enumeration in the Constitution, of certain rights, shall not be construed to deny or disparage others retained by the people.

Amendment 10. Powers of the States and the People (1791)

The powers not delegated to the United States by the Constitution, nor prohibited by it to the states, are reserved to the states respectively, or to the people.

Amendment 11. Limiting Law Cases Against States (1798)

The judicial power of the United States shall not be construed to extend to any suit in law or equity, commenced or prosecuted against one of the United States, by citizens of another state, or by citizens or subjects of any foreign state.

Amendment 12. Election of President and Vice President (1804)

The electors shall meet in their respective states, and vote by ballot for President and Vice President, one of whom, at least, shall not be an inhabitant of the same state with themselves; they shall name in their ballots the person voted for as President, and in distinct ballots the person voted for as Vice President, and they shall make distinct lists of all persons voted for as President, and of all persons voted for as Vice President, and of the number of votes for each, which lists they shall sign and certify, and transmit, sealed, to the seat of government of the United States, directed to the President of the Senate; the President of the Senate shall, in the presence of the Senate and House of Representatives, open all the certificates and the votes shall then be counted; the person having the greatest number of votes for President shall be the President, if such number be a majority of the whole number of electors appointed; and if no person have such majority, then from the persons having the highest numbers not exceeding three on the list of those voted for as President, the House of Representatives shall choose immediately, by ballot, the President. But in choosing the President, the votes shall be taken by states, the representation from each state having one vote; a quorum for this purpose shall consist of a member or members from two-thirds of the states, and a majority of all the states shall be necessary to a choice. And if the House of Representatives shall not choose a President whenever the right of choice shall devolve upon them, before the fourth day of March next following, then the Vice President shall act as President, as in the case of the death or other constitutional disability of the President. The person having the greatest number of votes as Vice President, shall be the Vice President, if such number be a majority of the whole number of electors appointed, and if no person have a majority, then from the two highest numbers on the list, the Senate shall choose the Vice President; a quorum for the purpose shall consist of two-thirds of the whole number of Senators, and a majority of

Amendment 11

A state government cannot be sued in a federal court by people of another state or a foreign country.

Amendment 12

This amendment changed the method of choosing a President and Vice President. The new method is called the Electoral College. Candidates for President and Vice President now run for office together, and each elector casts only one vote. (Before, candidates for President and Vice President ran for office separately, and each elector cast two votes.) Under the Electoral College, people called electors meet in their home states. Electors choose one person for President and a different person for Vice President. (One of the people voted for must be from a different state than the elector.) These electoral votes are then sent to the U.S. Senate where they are counted. The person who receives more than half the electoral votes for President is elected President. The person who receives more than half the electoral votes for Vice President is elected Vice President. If no person receives more than half the electoral votes for President, the House of Representatives chooses the President. A list of the top three vote-getters is sent to the House of Representatives. From this list, each state casts one vote for President. The person who receives more than half the votes in the House of Representatives is elected President. If no person receives more than half the vote, the Representatives vote again. If the Representatives fail to elect a President by March 4 (later changed to January 20), the Vice President serves as President. If no person receives at least half the electoral votes for Vice President, no one becomes Vice President and a list of the top two vote-getters is sent to the Senate. From this list, the Senators then vote for Vice President, with each Senator entitled to one vote. The person who receives more than half the votes in the Senate becomes Vice President. Qualifications for the office of Vice President are the same as those of President.

Amendment 13

1. Slavery is outlawed in the United States.

2. Congress can pass any laws necessary to carry out this amendment.

Amendment 14

1. This amendment made formerly enslaved people citizens of both the United States and the states in which they lived. No state can deny any citizen the basic rights given in the Fifth Amendment. All states must treat people equally under the law.

2. The number of a state's Representatives in Congress can be lowered if the state prevents qualified citizens from voting. (This section aimed to force states in the South to allow African Americans to vote.)

the whole number shall be necessary to a choice. But no person constitutionally ineligible to the office of President shall be eligible to that of Vice President of the United States.

Amendment 13. Slavery Outlawed (1865)

Section 1. Abolition of Slavery

Neither slavery nor involuntary servitude, except as a punishment for crime whereof the party shall have been duly convicted, shall exist within the United States, or any place subject to their jurisdiction.

Section 2. Enforcement

Congress shall have power to enforce this article by appropriate legislation.

Amendment 14. Rights of Citizens (1868)

Section 1. Citizenship

All persons born or naturalized in the United States and subject to the jurisdiction thereof, are citizens of the United States and of the state wherein they reside. No state shall make or enforce any law which shall abridge the privileges or immunities of citizens of the United States; nor shall any state deprive any person of life, liberty, or property, without due process of law; nor deny to any person within its jurisdiction the equal protection of the laws.

Section 2. Representation in Congress

Representatives shall be apportioned among the several states according to their respective numbers, counting the whole number of persons in each state, excluding Indians not taxed. But when the right to vote at any election for the choice of electors for President and Vice President of the United States, Representatives in Congress, the executive and judicial officers of a state, or the members of the legislature thereof, is denied to any of the male inhabitants of such state, being twenty one years of age and citizens of the United States, or in any way abridged, except for participation in rebellion, or other crime, the basis of representation therein shall be reduced in the proportion which the number of such male citizens shall bear to the whole number of male citizens twenty one years of age in such state.

Section 3. Penalties for Confederate Leaders

No person shall be a Senator or Representative in Congress, or elector of President and Vice President, or hold any office, civil or military, under the United States, or under any state, who, having previously taken an oath, as a member of Congress, or as an officer of the United States, or as a member of any state legislature, or as an executive or judicial officer of any state, to support the Constitution of the United States, shall have engaged in insurrection or rebellion against the same, or given aid or comfort to the enemies thereof. But Congress may, by vote of two-thirds of each house, remove such disability.

3. Any Confederate official who took part in the Civil War cannot again hold any federal or state office. But Congress can remove this restriction by a two-thirds vote.

Section 4. Responsibility for Public Debt

The validity of the public debt of the United States, authorized by law, including debts incurred for payment of pensions and bounties for services in suppressing insurrection or rebellion, shall not be questioned. But neither the United States nor any state shall assume or pay any debt or obligation incurred in aid of insurrection or rebellion against the United States ~~or any claim for the loss or emancipation of any slave~~; but all such debts, obligations, and claims shall be held illegal and void.

4. All money borrowed by the U.S. government to fight the Civil War is to be paid back. No debts the Confederate states or the Confederate government made to pay for the Civil War are to be paid back by the federal or state governments. No money would be paid to anyone for the loss of people they once held in slavery.

Section 5. Enforcement

The Congress shall have power to enforce, by appropriate legislation, the provisions of this article.

5. Congress can pass laws needed to carry out this amendment.

Amendment 15. Voting Rights (1870)

Section 1. Black Suffrage

The right of citizens of the United States to vote shall not be denied or abridged by the United States or any state on account of race, color, or previous condition of servitude.

Amendment 15

1. No federal or state government can stop people from voting because of their race or color, or because they were once enslaved. The purpose of this amendment was to give black men the right to vote.

Section 2. Enforcement

The Congress shall have power to enforce this article by appropriate legislation.

2. Congress can pass laws needed to carry out this amendment.

Amendment 16. Income Tax (1913)

The Congress shall have the power to lay and collect taxes on incomes, from whatever source derived, without apportionment among the several states, and without regard to any census or enumeration.

Amendment 16

Congress has the power to collect an income tax no matter what the population of a state is.

Amendment 17

1. Senators are to be elected by the voters of each state. (This amendment changed the method by which state legislatures elected Senators as outlined in Article 1, Section 3, Clause 1, of the Constitution.)

2. Special elections can be held to fill empty seats in the Senate. State legislatures may permit the governor to name a person to fill an empty seat until the next election.

3. This amendment does not affect the election or term of office of any Senator in office before the amendment becomes part of the Constitution.

Amendment 18

1. Making, selling, or transporting alcoholic, or intoxicating, drinks in the United States is illegal. (This amendment was called the Prohibition Amendment because it prohibited, or banned, the use of alcohol.)

2. Both Congress and the states can pass laws needed to carry out this amendment.

3. This amendment is to become part of the Constitution only if it is approved within seven years. (It was repealed, or canceled, by the Twenty-First Amendment.)

Amendment 17. Direct Election of Senators (1913)

Section 1. Method of Election

The Senate of the United States shall be composed of two Senators from each state, elected by the people thereof, for six years; and each Senator shall have one vote. The electors in each state shall have the qualifications requisite for electors of the most numerous branch of the state legislatures.

Section 2. Vacancies

When vacancies happen in the representation of any state in the Senate, the executive authority of such state shall issue writs of election to fill such vacancies: provided that the legislature of any state may empower the executive thereof to make temporary appointments until the people fill the vacancies by election as the legislature may direct.

Section 3. Those Elected under Previous Rules

This amendment shall not be so construed as to affect the election or term of any Senator chosen before it becomes valid as part of the Constitution.

Amendment 18. Prohibition of Alcoholic Drinks (1919)

Section 1. Prohibition

After one year from the ratification of this article the manufacture, sale, or transportation of intoxicating liquors within, the importation thereof into, or the exportation thereof from, the United States and all territory subject to the jurisdiction thereof for beverage purposes is hereby prohibited.

Section 2. Enforcement

The Congress and the several states shall have concurrent power to enforce this article by appropriate legislation.

Section 3. Time Limit on Ratification

The article shall be inoperative unless it shall have been ratified as an amendment to the Constitution by the legislatures of the several states, as provided in the Constitution, within seven years from the date of the submission hereof to the states by the Congress.

Amendment 19. Women's Right to Vote (1920)

Section 1. Women Made Voters

The right of citizens of the United States to vote shall not be denied or abridged by the United States or by any state on account of sex.

Section 2. Enforcement

Congress shall have power to enforce this article by appropriate legislation.

Amendment 20. Terms of Office (1933)

Section 1. Start of Terms of Office

The terms of the President and Vice President shall end at noon on the 20th day of January, and the terms of Senators and Representatives at noon on the 3rd day of January, of the years in which such terms would have ended if this article had not been ratified; and the terms of their successors shall then begin.

Section 2. Meeting Time of Congress

The Congress shall assemble at least once in every year, and such meeting shall begin at noon on the 3rd day of January, unless they shall by law appoint a different day.

Section 3. Providing for a Successor of the President-Elect

If at the time fixed for the beginning of the term of the President, the President-elect shall have died, the Vice President-elect shall become President. If a President shall not have been chosen before the time fixed for the beginning of his term, or if the President-elect shall have failed to qualify, then the Vice President-elect shall act as President until a President shall have qualified; and the Congress may by law provide for the case wherein neither a President-elect nor a Vice President-elect shall have qualified, declaring who shall then act as President, or the manner in which one who is to act shall be selected, and such person shall act accordingly until a President or Vice President shall have qualified.

Section 4. Elections Decided by Congress

The Congress may by law provide for the case of the death of any of the persons from whom the House of Representatives may choose a President whenever the right of choice shall have devolved upon them, and for the case of the death of any of the persons from whom the Senate may choose a Vice President whenever the right of choice shall have devolved upon them.

Section 5. Effective Date

~~Sections 1 and 2 shall take effect on the 15th day of October following the ratification of this article.~~

Amendment 19

1. No federal or state government can stop people from voting because of their sex. This amendment granted women the right to vote.

2. Congress can pass laws needed to carry out this amendment.

Amendment 20

1. The President and Vice President begin their terms on January 20. This date is called Inauguration Day. The terms of members of Congress begin on January 3. (Originally their terms began on March 4.)

2. Congress must meet at least once a year beginning at noon on January 3. However, Congress may pick a different day to first meet.

3. If the person elected President dies before taking office, the Vice President becomes President. If no person is elected President before the term of office begins, or if the person elected President does not have the skills or experience to serve, then the Vice President acts as President until a President is chosen. If both the person elected President and the person elected Vice President are not approved, Congress selects the President.

4. If, during the time Congress is choosing the President and Vice President, one of these two people dies, Congress may pass a law deciding how to choose the President and Vice President.

5. Sections 1 and 2 of this amendment take effect on the fifteenth day of October after this amendment becomes part of the Constitution.

This amendment is to become part of the Constitution only if it is approved within seven years by three-fourths of the state legislatures.

Amendment 21

1. The Eighteenth Amendment is repealed, or no longer in effect.

2. Any state or territory of the United States may pass prohibition laws.

3. This amendment is to become part of the Constitution only if state conventions approve it within seven years.

Amendment 22

1. No person can be elected President more than two times. No person can be elected President more than once who has served more than two years of another President's term. This amendment does not affect any President who is in office when this amendment becomes part of the Constitution.

2. This amendment is to become part of the Constitution only if three-fourths of the state legislatures approve it within seven years.

Section 6. Time Limit on Ratification

~~This article shall be inoperative unless it shall have been ratified as an amendment to the Constitution by the legislatures of three-fourths of the several states within seven years from the date of its submission.~~

Amendment 21. Repeal of Prohibition (1933)

Section 1. Prohibition Ends

The Eighteenth article of amendment to the Constitution of the United States is hereby repealed.

Section 2. Protection of State and Local Prohibition Laws

The transportation or importation into any state, territory, or possession of the United States for delivery or use therein of intoxicating liquors, in violation of the laws thereof, is hereby prohibited.

Section 3. Time Limit on Ratification

~~This article shall be inoperative unless it shall have been ratified as an amendment to the Constitution by conventions in the several states, as provided in the Constitution, within seven years from the date of the submission hereof to the states by the Congress.~~

Amendment 22. President Limited to Two Terms (1951)

Section 1. Limit on Number of Terms

No person shall be elected to the office of the President more than twice, and no person who has held the office of President, or acted as President, for more than two years of a term to which some other person was elected President shall be elected to the office of the President more than once. ~~But this Article shall not apply to any person holding the office of President when this Article was proposed by the Congress, and shall not prevent any person who may be holding the office of President, or acting as President, during the term within which this Article becomes operative from holding the office of President or acting as President during the remainder of such term.~~

Section 2. Time Limit on Ratification

~~This Article shall be inoperative unless it shall have been ratified as an amendment to the Constitution by the legislatures of three-fourths of the several states within seven years from the date of its submission to the states by the Congress.~~

Amendment 23. *Presidential Elections for the District of Columbia (1961)*

Section 1. Presidential Electors in the District of Columbia

The District constituting the seat of Government of the United States shall appoint in such manner as the Congress may direct: A number of electors of President and Vice President equal to the whole number of Senators and Representatives in Congress to which the District would be entitled if it were a State, but in no event more than the least populous State; they shall be in addition to those appointed by the States, but they shall be considered, for the purposes of the election of President and Vice President, to be electors appointed by a State; and they shall meet in the District and perform such duties as provided by the Twelfth article of amendment.

Section 2. Enforcement

The Congress shall have power to enforce this article by appropriate legislation.

Amendment 24. *Poll Tax Ended (1964)*

Section 1. Poll Taxes Not Allowed in Federal Elections

The right of citizens of the United States to vote in any primary or other election for President or Vice President, for electors for President or Vice President, or for Senator or Representative in Congress, shall not be denied or abridged by the United States or any state by reason of failure to pay any poll tax or other tax.

Section 2. Enforcement

The Congress shall have the power to enforce this article by appropriate legislation.

Amendment 25. *Presidential Succession (1967)*

Section 1. Filling the Vacant Office of President

In case of the removal of the President from office or of his death or resignation, the Vice President shall become President.

Section 2. Filling the Vacant Office of Vice President

Whenever there is a vacancy in the office of the Vice President, the President shall nominate a Vice President who shall take the office upon confirmation by a majority vote of both houses of Congress.

Section 3. Disability of the President

Whenever the President transmits to the President pro tempore of the Senate and the Speaker of the House of Representatives his written declaration that he is unable to discharge the powers

---

Amendment 23

1. People living in Washington, D.C. (the District of Columbia), have the right to vote in Presidential elections. The number of electoral votes of Washington, D.C., can never be more than the number of electoral votes of the state with the fewest number of people.

2. Congress can pass any laws necessary to carry out this amendment.

Amendment 24

1. No person can be kept from voting in a federal election for failing to pay a poll, or voting, tax or any other kind of tax.

2. Congress can pass any laws necessary to carry out this amendment.

Amendment 25

1. If the President dies, resigns, or is removed from office, the Vice President becomes President.

2. If the office of Vice President becomes empty, the President names a new Vice President, with the approval of both houses of Congress.

3. If the President is unable to carry out the powers and duties of office, the President may tell the leaders of Congress. The Vice President then serves as Acting President. The

President may return to office only when he or she tells the leaders of Congress that he or she can again carry out the powers and duties of office.

4. If the Vice President and at least half the Cabinet, or a special committee, inform the leaders of Congress that the President cannot carry out the powers and duties of office, the Vice President immediately becomes Acting President. If the President tells the leaders of Congress that he or she is able to serve as President, he or she again becomes President. But if, within four days, the Vice President and at least half the Cabinet (or a special committee) tell the leaders of Congress that the President still cannot carry out the powers and duties of office, the President does not return to office. Instead, Congress must meet within 48 hours. In the next 21 days, Congress must decide if the President is able to carry out the powers and duties of office. If two-thirds of both houses of Congress vote that the President is unable to serve, the President is removed from office and the Vice President becomes Acting President. If two-thirds do not vote this way, the President stays in office.

Amendment 26
1. This amendment gives people who are at least 18 years old the right to vote.

2. Congress can pass laws needed to carry out this amendment.

Amendment 27
There can be no law changing the salaries of members of Congress until after the next election of the House of Representatives.

and duties of his office, and until he transmits to them a written declaration to the contrary, such powers and duties shall be discharged by the Vice President as Acting President.

Section 4. When Congress Designates an Acting President

Whenever the Vice President and a majority of either the principal officers of the executive departments or of such other body as Congress may by law provide, transmit to the President pro tempore of the Senate and the Speaker of the House of Representatives their written declaration that the President is unable to discharge the powers and duties of his office, the Vice President shall immediately assume the powers and duties of the office as Acting President. Thereafter, when the President transmits to the President pro tempore of the Senate and the Speaker of the House of Representatives his written declaration that no inability exists, he shall resume the powers and duties of his office unless the Vice President and a majority of either the principal officers of the executive departments or of such other body as Congress may by law provide, transmit within four days to the President pro tempore of the Senate and the Speaker of the House of Representatives their written declaration that the President is unable to discharge the powers and duties of his office. Thereupon Congress shall decide the issue, assembling within 48 hours for that purpose if not in session. If the Congress, within 21 days after receipt of the latter written declaration, or, if Congress is not in session, within 21 days after Congress is required to assemble, determines by two-thirds vote of both houses that the President is unable to discharge the powers and duties of his office, the Vice President shall continue to discharge the same as Acting President; otherwise, the President shall assume the powers and duties of his office.

Amendment 26. Vote for Eighteen-Year-Olds (1971)

Section 1. Voting Age

The right of citizens of the United States, who are 18 years of age or older, to vote shall not be denied or abridged by the United States or any state on account of age.

Section 2. Enforcement

The Congress shall have the power to enforce this article by appropriate legislation.

Amendment 27. Limits on Salary Changes (1992)

No law, varying the compensation for the services of the Senators and Representatives, shall take effect, until an election of Representatives shall have intervened.

Reference Section

The Reference Section has many parts, each with a different type of information. Use this section to look up people, places, and events as you study.

New York Symbols

STATE SEAL ▲
The state seal has been redesigned five times between 1777 and 1882. The seal also appears on New York's flag.

STATE MOTTO "Excelsior"
The state motto, Excelsior, means "Ever Upward." ▲

STATE FLOWER Rose
The rose, whether wild or from a garden, was made the state flower in 1955. The rose can be any color. ◄

STATE ANIMAL Beaver
The beaver was adopted as the state animal in 1975. The beaver is a symbol of the Dutch colonial fur trade. ▼

STATE BIRD Eastern Bluebird
The Eastern Bluebird was adopted as the state bird in 1970. These songbirds have not been common since the 1950s. ▶

STATE FLAG
The current flag is a modern version of a Revolutionary War flag. The two women represent Liberty and Justice. ▲

STATE TREE Sugar Maple
Maple syrup is made from the sap of Sugar Maples. In the fall, its leaves turn brillant reds and oranges. ▶

EXCELSIOR

Famous New Yorkers

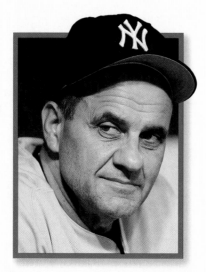

JOE TORRE

Born in Brooklyn in 1940; baseball player and manager; played on All Star teams five years in a row; manager of New York Yankees teams that won the World Series four times

COLIN POWELL

Born in the Bronx in 1937; four-star general; former Chairman of the Joint Chiefs of Staff; Secretary of State

LOIS GIBBS

Born in Niagara Falls in 1951; spokesperson, ecologist, organizer; made Love Canal pollution a public issue; argued for ecology Superfund; Member of Ecology Hall of Fame

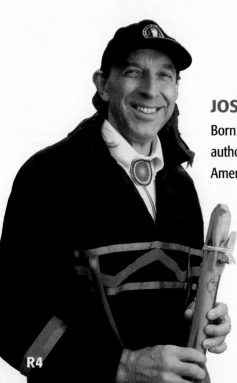

JOSEPH BRUCHAC III

Born in Saratoga Springs in 1942; poet; author; storyteller; publisher of Native American authors

MAURICE SENDAK

Born in Brooklyn in 1928; author, illustrator; known for his books and a Broadway musical of *Where the Wild Things Are*; awarded the National Medal of Arts in 1997

JUDITH JAMISON

Born in Philadelphia in 1943; dancer, teacher, artistic director of the Alvin Ailey American Dance Theater; star of Broadway show *Sophisticated Ladies* (1981); Kennedy Center Award winner (1999)

NYDIA VELAZQUEZ

Born in Puerto Rico in 1953; politician; first Hispanic to serve on New York City Council (1984); first Puerto Rican woman in Congress (1992)

YO YO MA

Born in Paris in 1955; composer, performer, teacher; studied cello at Juilliard Music School in New York City; Grammy Award winner (1999)

DANIEL GOLDIN
Born in the Bronx in 1940; named administrator of NASA (National Aeronautics and Space Administration) in 1992; retired in 2001, having served longer than anyone before

RUTH BADER GINSBERG

Born in Brooklyn in 1993; Law School Professor (1972); Federal Judge (1980); U.S. Supreme Court Justice (1993)

Famous New Yorkers

BURTON RICHTER

Born in New York City in 1931; built a machine that makes atomic particles travel faster; discovered a new subatomic particle; Nobel Prize winner in 1976

E.L. DOCTOROW

Born in New York City in 1931; official New York State Author from 1989 to 1991; his novels are often set in New York locations and use actual events from history; twice won the National Book Award

ALEX RODRIQUEZ

Born in New York City in 1975; youngest major league player to hit 400 home runs; named the American League Most Valuable Player in 2003; today plays for the New York Yankees

MAYA LIN

Born in Athens, Ohio in 1959; architect; judge for the memorial for the victims of the World Trade Center attacks; designed the Vietnam Veterans Memorial as well as other buildings and public areas

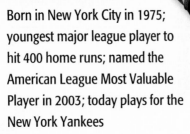

NORAH JONES

Born in New York City in 1979; daughter of Ravi Shankar, a famous musician from India; won eight Grammy awards for her first album

CHRISTOPHER WALKEN

Born in Queens, New York, in 1943; won an Obie for his work in plays and an Oscar for his work in films

ILYASAH SHABAZZ

Born in New York City in 1963; was two years old when her father, Malcom X, was killed; has dedicated her life to education and government; has written and spoken about the importance of each person taking control of his or her life

GRACE PALEY

Born in the Bronx in 1922; official New York State Author from 1986 to 1988; has written poetry and short stories; taught at Syracuse University, Columbia University, and Sarah Lawrence College in Bronxville, New York; recognized by the National Endowment for the Arts in 1987

VERA WANG

Born in Manhattan in 1949; writer, skater, designer; competed in figure skating championships (1968); designed Olympic skating costumes (1994)

DENZEL WASHINGTON

Born in Mount Vernon, New York, in 1954; actor on television, in films, and in plays; Oscar winner in 1989 and 2002; spokesperson for the Boys and Girls' Clubs of America

New York and United States 1500–2005

1500		1600				1700	

New York Events

1570
Iroquois League is formed

1609
Henry Hudson arrives

1625
New Netherland colony is formed

1664
British change New Netherland to New York

1733
Peter Zenger put on trial

1500		1600				1700	

United States Events

1609
Jamestown is founded

1620
Pilgrims land on Plymouth Rock

1673
Jacques Marquette and Louis Jolliet explore the Mississippi Valley

1754
French and Indian War begins

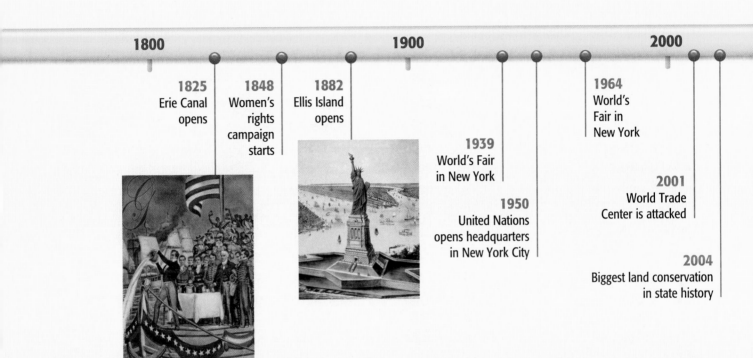

1800

1900

2000

1825
Erie Canal opens

1848
Women's rights campaign starts

1882
Ellis Island opens

1939
World's Fair in New York

1950
United Nations opens headquarters in New York City

1964
World's Fair in New York

2001
World Trade Center is attacked

2004
Biggest land conservation in state history

1800

1900

2000

1776
American Revolution begins

1783
United States gains independence

1787
United States Constitution is signed

1861
Civil War begins

1929
Stock market crash

1941
Pearl Harbor is attacked

1969
Neil Armstrong walks on the Moon

Governors of New York

GOVERNORS OF THE STATE OF NEW YORK	TERM
George Clinton	1777–1795
John Jay	1795–1801
George Clinton	1801–1804
Morgan Lewis	1804–1807
Daniel D. Tompkins	1807–1817
John Tayler (acting)	1817
DeWitt Clinton	1817–1822
Joseph C. Yates	1823–1824
DeWitt Clinton	1825–1828
Nathaniel Pitcher (acting)	1828
Martin Van Buren	1829
Enos T. Throop (acting)	1829–1830
Enos T. Throop	1831–1832
William L. Marcy	1833–1838
William H. Seward	1839–1842
William C. Bouck	1843–1844
Silas Wright	1845–1846
John Young	1847–1848
Hamilton Fish	1849–1850
Washington Hunt	1851–1852
Horatio Seymour	1853–1854
Myron H. Clark	1855–1856
John A. King	1857–1858
Edwin D. Morgan	1859–1862
Horatio Seymour	1863–1864
Reuben E. Fenton	1865–1868
John T. Hoffman	1869–1872
John Adams Dix	1873–1874
Samuel J. Tilden	1875–1876
Lucius Robinson	1877–1879

GOVERNORS OF THE STATE OF NEW YORK	TERM
Alonzo B. Cornell	1880–1882
Grover Cleveland	1883–1884
David B. Hill (acting)	1885
David B. Hill	1886–1891
Roswell P. Flower	1892–1894
Levi P. Morton	1895–1896
Frank S. Black	1897–1898
Theodore Roosevelt	1899–1900
Benjamin B. Odell, Jr.	1901–1904
Frank W. Higgins	1905–1906
Charles Evans Hughes	1907–1910
Horace White (acting)	1910
John Alden Dix	1911–1912
William Sulzer	1913
Martin Glynn (acting)	1913–1914
Charles S. Whitman	1915–1918
Alfred E. Smith	1919–1920
Nathan L. Miller	1921–1922
Alfred E. Smith	1923–1928
Franklin D. Roosevelt	1929–1932
Herbert H. Lehman	1933–1942
Charles Poletti (acting)	1942
Thomas E. Dewey	1943–1954
W. Averell Harriman	1955–1958
Nelson Rockefeller	1959–1973
Malcolm Wilson (acting)	1973–1974
Hugh J. Carey	1975–1982
Mario M. Cuomo	1983–1994
George E. Pataki	1995–2006

Gazetteer

This Gazetteer is a geographical dictionary that will help you to pronounce and locate the places discussed in this book. Latitude and longitude are given for cities and some other places. The letters and numbers tell you where each place first appears on a map (m.) or in the text (t.)

Pronunciation Key

a	at	ē	me	ō	old	ū	use	ng	song
ā	ape	i	it	ô	fork	ü	rule	th	thin
ä	far	ī	ice	oi	oil	u̇	pull	th	this
âr	care	îr	pierce	ou	out	ûr	turn	zh	measure
e	end	o	hot	u	up	hw	white	ə	about, taken, pencil, lemon, circus

A

Adirondack Mountains (ad ə rän' dak moun' tenz) Mountain range in northeastern New York. (m.11, t.13)

Albany (ôl' bə nē) City on the Hudson River; capital of New York State; 43°N, 74°W. (m.11, t.116)

Allegany State Park (al ə gā' nē stāt pärk) Largest New York state park, located in the southwestern part of the state. (m.10, t.14)

Appalachian Plateau (ap ə lā' chən pla tō) Plateau of rolling hills that covers nearly half the state. (m.13, t.13)

Auburn (ô' bərn) City in the Finger Lakes Region; home of Harriet Tubman; 43°N, 77°W. (m.217, t.217)

B

Binghamton (bing' əm tən) County seat of Broome County; population: 53,008; 42°N. 75°W. (m.11)

Buffalo (buf' ə lō) City and port on Lake Erie; endpoint of the Erie Canal; 43°N, 79°W. (m.10, t.174)

C

Catskill Mountains (kat' skil moun' tenz) Mountain range in southeastern New York. (m.11, t.13)

Central New York (sen' trəl nü yôrk) Region of New York State around the joining of the Mohawk and Hudson Rivers; includes the cities of Albany, Schenectady, and Troy. (m.15, t.15)

Cooperstown (kü' pûrz toun) Village southwest of Schenectady; home of the Baseball Hall of Fame and Museum; 42°N, 74°W. (m.15, t.320)

D

Dunkirk (dun' kûrk) City in Chautauqua County; population 13,131; 42°N 70°W. (t.16)

Dutchess Quarry Caves (duch' əs kwôr' ē kāvz) A series of caves located in southeastern New York, near present-day Middletown. (m.45, t. 47)

E

Ellis Island (el' əs ī' lənd) Island in New York Bay; served as an immigration center from 1892 to 1854. (t.237)

Elmira (el mī' rə) City in the Finger Lakes Region; an important stopping point on the Underground Railroad; 42°N, 77°W. (m.11)

Empire State Building (em' pīr stāt bil' ding) New York City's most famous skyscraper; completed in 1931. (m.15, t.243)

Erie Canal (îr' ē kə nal') Canal that runs over 350 miles from Buffalo on Lake Erie to Albany on the Hudson River. (m.21, t. 182)

Etna (et' nə) Town in Tompkins County; a station on the Underground Railroad; 42°N 76°W. (m.217)

Finger Lakes (fin' gər lāks) Group of long narrow lakes arranged like the fingers of a hand; located in the Finger Lakes Region. (m.13, t.13)

Finger Lakes Region (fin' gər lāks rē jən) Region of New York State where the Finger Lakes and Rochester are found. (m.15, t.15)

Fort Niagara (fôrt nī ag' rə) Fort at the mouth of the Niagara River; first built by the French in 1725. (m.139, t.139)

Fort Orange (fôrt är' inj) First Dutch settlement in New York; the location is now Albany. (m.81, t.89)

Fort Ticonderoga (fort tī kän dər ō' gä) Fort built on the waterway linking Lake George and Lake Champlain; named Fort Ticonderoga in 1759. (m.139, t.139)

Genesee Falls (jen ə sē' fôls) Town in Wyoming County; population 460, 42°N 78°W. (m.21)

Genesee River (jen ə sē' ri' vər) River that flows across Western New York into Lake Ontario. (m.21, t.173)

Geneseo (jen ə sē' ō) Village on the Genesee River; location of the Big Tree Treaty in 1797; 43°N, 78°W. (m.171, t.174)

Gloversville (gluv' ərz vil) City in Central New York; a glovemaking center of the United States; 43°N, 74°W. (m.231, t.188)

Great Lakes (grāt lāks) Chain of five lakes (Superior, Michigan, Huron, Erie, & Ontario) in North America along the border between the United States and Canada. (m.22, t.13)

Great Sacandaga Lake (grāt sak ən dä gə lāk) An artificial lake created by the Conklingville Dam. (m.21, t.22)

Harlem (här' ləm) Part of Manhattan; by 1920, it was the largest African American community in the United States. (t.257)

Hudson River (hud' sən ri' vər) River in eastern New York that flows into New York Bay. (m.21, t.21)

Hudson River Valley (hud' sən ri' vər va' lē) Valley that runs north and south between the Catskill Mountains and the Taconic Mountains. (m.13, t.13)

Hudson-Catskill Region (rhud' sən ri' vər va' lē and kat' skil moun' tenz) Region of New York State where the lower Hudson River Valley, Catskill Mountains, and Taconic Mountains are located. (m.15, t.16)

Ithaca (ith' i kə) City in the Finger Lakes Region at the south end of Cayuga Lake; 42°N, 77°W. (m.19, t.291)

Jamestown (jāmz' toun) City in Chautauqua County; population 31,730; 42°N 79°W. (m.51, t.16)

Kingston (king' stən) City on the Hudson River; meeting place of the first state government in 1777; 42°N, 74°W. (m.19, t.159)

Pronunciation Key								
a	at	ē	me	ō	old	ū	use	ng	song
ā	ape	i	it	ô	fork	ü	rule	th	thin
ä	far	ī	ice	oi	oil	ù	pull	th	this
âr	care	îr	pierce	ou	out	ûr	turn	zh	measure
e	end	o	hot	u	up	hw	white	ə	about, taken, pencil, lemon, circus

Lake Champlain (lāk sham plān') Long, narrow lake in northern New York; forms part of the border with Vermont. (m.11, t.22)

Lake Erie (lāk îr' ē) The most southern of the five Great Lakes; forms part of the border between the United States and Canada. (m.10, t.21)

Lake George (lāk jôrj) Lake in northern New York; linked to Lake Champlain. (m.21)

Lake Ontario (lāk on târ' ē ō) The smallest of the five Great Lakes; forms part of the border between the United States and Canada. (m.11, t.21)

Lake Placid (lāk pla' səd) Village southwest of Plattsburgh; Site of the 1932 and 1980 Winter Olympics; population, 2,485; 44°N 74°W. (m.21)

Levittown (lev' ət toun) Long Island community, suburb of New York City built in 1946; 41°N, 74°W. (t.262)

Long Island (lông ī' lənd) Island in the Atlantic Ocean with 280 miles of coastline; the borough of Brooklyn lies on its southern end. (m.13, t.16)

Long Island Sound (lông ī' lənd sound) A narrow part of the Atlantic Ocean that lies between the Connecticut and New York shores to the north and Long Island to the south. (m.13, t.23)

Love Canal (luv kə nal') Town near Niagara Falls; location of environmental cleanup in the 1970s; 43°N, 79°W. (t.265)

Metropolitan New York Region (me trō pol it ən nü yôrk rē jən) Region that includes the most southern and eastern parts of New York State. (m.15, t.16)

Mohawk River (mō' hôk ri' vər) Largest tributary of the Hudson River; located in Central New York. (m.11, t.21)

Montauk Point (mon' tôk point) Tip of Long Island that is the easternmost place in New York. (m.19)

Mount Marcy (moun' t marcy) Called Tawahus, meaning "the Cloud Splitter," by Native Americans; the highest point in New York State. (m.11)

New Amsterdam (nü am' stər dam) Dutch settlement started in 1625 on Manhattan Island, which became New York City. (m.81, t.90)

New Netherland (nü neth' ər lənd) Dutch colony in North American (1624-1664) that included parts of present-day New York, New Jersey, and Delaware. (m.81, t.89)

New Paltz (nü pôlts) Village in the Hudson River Valley first settled by Huguenot immigrants; 42°N, 74°W. (t.115)

New York City (nü yôrk si' tē) City at the mouth of the Hudson River; largest city in the country and an important port and business center; 41°N,74°W. (m.11, t.97)

New York Harbor (nü yôrk bā) Harbor in southern New York at the mouth of the Hudson River; where it flows into the Atlantic Ocean. (m.21, t.23)

Niagara Falls (nī ag' rə fôls) Great falls on the Niagara River, up to 184 feet high. (m.13, t.21)

Niagara River (nī ag' rə ri' vər) River in western New York that connects Lake Erie with Lake Ontario. (m.21, t.21)

Northern New York Region (nor' thərn nü yôrk rē jən) Region of New York State where the Adirondack Mountains and Lake Champlain are located. (m.15, t.15)

Olana (ō la' nə) Home of painter Frederic Edwin Church, located near the town of Hudson, 42°N, 74°W. (t.190)

Oneida Lake (ō nīd' ə lāk) Large lake in Central New York. (m.11)

Oriskany (ô ris ka' nē) Village on the Mohawk River; location of American Revolution battlefield; 43°N, 75°W. (m.148, t.151)

Plattsburgh (plats' bərg) City in Northern New York on the western shore of Lake Champlain; 45°N, 74°W. (m.11)

Potsdam (pots' dam) City in St. Lawrence County; site of Clarkson University and SUNY Potsdam; population 15,957; 44°N 75°W. (m.51, t.16)

Poughkeepsie (pə kip' sē) City in Dutchess County; Site of Vassar College; population 42,777; 41°N 73°W. (m.51)

Quebec (kwi bek') City in Canada on the north bank of the St. Lawrence River; 47°N, 72°W. (m.84, t.84)

Rochester (roch' ə stər) City on the Genessee River and port on the Erie Canal; major New York Center for industry; 43°N, 78°W. (m.11, t.174)

St. Lawrence River (sānt lär' əns ri' vər) River on the border of the United States and Canada that connects the Great Lakes with the Atlantic Ocean. (m.13, t.21)

Saranac Lake (sar' ə nak lāk) Town in Franklin County; population 5,041; 44°N 74°W (m.19)

Saratoga (sar ə tō' gə) Village on the west bank of the Hudson River; now called Schuylerville. Location of British surrender in 1777 after the Battle of Saratoga; 43°N, 74°W. (m.148)

Saratoga Springs (sar ə tō' gə springz) City in Saratoga County; population 26,186; 43°N 74°W. (m.51)

Schenectady (skə nek' tə dē) County seat of Schenectady County; population 61,821; 42°N 73°W. (m.51)

Seneca Falls (sen' i kə fôls) Village in the Finger Lakes Region; location of first women's rights convention in 1848; 43°N, 77°W. (t.191)

Seneca Lake (sen' i kə lāk) The largest of the Finger Lakes and the second deepest lake in the United States. (m.11)

Syracuse (sir' ə kyüs) City in the Finger Lakes Region; an important port on the Erie Canal; 43°N, 76°W. (m.11, t.189)

Taconic Mountains (tə kän' ik moun' tənz) Mountain range along the eastern border of New York. (m.13, t.13)

Thousand Islands (thouz' ənd ī lənds) Group of about 1,700 islands located where the St. Lawrence River meets Lake Ontario. (m.21, t.21)

Ticonderoga (tī kon də rō' gə) Town in Essex County; Site of a fort important in colonial wars and the American Revolution; population 5,167; 44°N 73°W. (m.137, t.16)

Troy (troi) City in Rensselaer County; population 49,170; 43°N 73°W. (m.231)

Utica (yü' ti kə) City on the Mohawk River, important starting point for settlers moving west in early 1800s; 43°N, 75°W. (m.51, t.183)

Verrazano Narrows (ver ə zä' nō na' rōz) A narrow water passage between Staten Island and Brooklyn in New York Harbor. (t.83)

Wall Street (wôl strēt) Street on the southern tip of Manhattan Island; became the business center of New York State and the United States. (t.166)

Pronunciation Key				
a at	ē me	ō old	ū use	ng song
ā ape	i it	ô fork	ü rule	th thin
ä far	ī ice	oi oil	u̇ pull	th this
âr care	îr pierce	ou out	ûr turn	zh measure
e end	o hot	u up	hw white	ə about, taken, pencil, lemon, circus

Washington, D.C. (wä′ shing tən dē sē) Capital of the United States; 39°N, 77°W. (m.289, t.307)

Watertown (wä′ tür toun) City in Jefferson County; population 26,705; 43°N 76°W. (m.11)

Watkins Glen Gorge (wät′ kinz glen gorj) A 2-mile long gorge, 300 feet deep in places; located in the Finger Lakes Region. (m.15, t.8)

West Point (west point) City in Orange County; site of the United States Military Academy; population 7,138; 41°N 74°W. (m.148. t.151)

Western New York (wes′ tərn nü yôrk) Westernmost region of New York State that borders Lake Erie, where Buffalo and Niagara Falls are found. (m.15, t.15)

White Plains (hwīt plānz) City in Westchester County; Site of a battle during the American Revolution; population 53,077; 41°N 74°W. (m.148, t.159)

Whiteface Mountain (hwīt′ fās moun′ tən) Peak in the Adirondack Mountains over 4,800 feet high. (m.11)

Biographical Dictionary

The Biographical Dictionary lists the people you have learned about in this book. The Pronunciation Key tells you how to say their names. The page numbers let you see where each person first appears in the text.

Pronunciation Key

a	at	ē	me	ō	old	ū	use	ng	song
ā	ape	i	it	ô	fork	ü	rule	th	thin
ä	far	ī	ice	oi	oil	ù	pull	th	this
âr	care	îr	pierce	ou	out	ûr	turn	zh	measure
e	end	o	hot	u	up	hw	white	ə	about, taken, pencil, lemon, circus

A

Abzug, Bella (ab' zug), 1920-1998 Women's rights leader and New York congresswoman for 3 terms. (p.264)

Adams, John (ad' əmz), 1735-1826 Patriot; delegate to the Continental Congress; second President of the United States. (p.128)

Adams, Mary (ad' əmz), 1920s-1999 A Mohawk artist and basketmaker. (p.5)

Anthony, Susan B. (an' thə nē), 1820-1906 Abolitionist and women's rights leader. (p.255)

Arnold, Benedict (ärn' əld), American Revolutionary War leader who betrayed his country. (p.151)

B

Badillo, Herman (bə dē' yō), 1929- Politician; the first Puerto Rican person to be elected to the United States House of Representatives. (p.207)

Bartholdi, Frederic Auguste (bär täl' dē), 1834-1904 French sculptor who designed the Statue of Liberty. (p.241)

Bell, Alexander Graham (bel), 1847-1922 Inventor of the telephone. (p.234)

Belmont, August (bel' mont), A New York banker. (p.233)

Blackwell, Elizabeth (blak' wel), 1821-1910 First woman doctor in America; trained nurses during the Civil War. (p.224)

Bloomberg, Michael (blüm' bûrg) 1942- Businessman and Mayor of New York. (p.290)

Brant, Joseph (brant), 1772-1807 Also called Thayendanegea. Mohawk leader who sided with the British in the American Revolution. He fought at the Battle of Oriskany. (p.130)

Burgoyne, John (bər gôyn'), 1722-1792 British general whose defeat at the Battle of Saratoga in 1777 helped convince France to aid the Americans during the American Revolution. (p.151)

Burroughs, John (bûr' ōz), 1837-1921 American nature writer who grew up in the Catskill Mountains. (p.10)

C

Calhoun, Nancy (kal hün') 1944- New York Assembly member from the 96th District since 1990. (p.299)

Canassatego (kan ə sät' ə gō), 1700s? Iroquois Chief who worked with British colonists. (p.138)

Cartier, Jacques (kär tē ā' zhäk), 1491-1557 French explorer who traveled from the Atlantic up the St. Lawrence River. (p.84)

Catt, Carrie Chapman (kat), 1859-1947 Leader in the women's rights movement. (p.255)

Champlain, Samuel de (sham plān'), 1567-1635 French explorer who founded Quebec in 1608 and discovered Lake Champlain in 1609. (p.74)

Chisholm, Shirley (chiz' əm), 1924-2005 Politician; the first African American woman to be elected to the United States House of Representatives. (p.282)

Chu, Steven (chū) 1948- A Nobel prize winning scientist who discovered how to slow atoms down. (p.319)

Church, Frederic Edwin (chərch), 1826-1900 Landscape painter associated with the Hudson River School. (p.190)

Clinton, De Witt (klin′ tən), 1769-1828 New York governor who supported the building of the Erie Canal. (p.182)

Cole, Thomas (kōl), 1801-1848 Painter associated with the Hudson River School. (p.190)

Columbus, Christopher (kə lum′ bəs), 1451?-1506 Italian sea captain and explorer. Hired by Spain's rulers, he reached the Americas in search of a sea route to Asia in 1492. (p.83)

Cooper, James Fenimore (kü′ pər), 1789-1851 New York writer of stories about the frontier. (p.190)

Cooper, Peter (kü′ pər), 1791-1883 Inventor and manufacterer who built the first locomotive in America. (p.131)

Cornish, Samuel (kôr′ nish), 1793-1858 African American abolitionist who, together with John Russwurm, started the first African American newspaper, *Freedom's Journal.* (p.216)

Cornwallis, Charles (kôrn wä ′ ləs), 1738-1805 British General who surrendered at Yorktown, Virginia, leading to the end of the American Revolution. (p.153)

Cullen, Countee (ku′ lən), 1903-1946 Poet of the Harlem Renaissance. (p.209)

Cuomo, Mario (kü ō′ mō), 1932- 56th governor of New York State from 1983-1995. (p.299)

Deganawida (də gän ə wē′ də), 1500s Leader of the Iroquois who helped organize the Iroquois League. (p.4)

Douglass, Frederick (dug′ ləs) 1817-1895 Abolitionist who escaped from slavery and spoke out against slavery. He founded an anti-slavery newspaper in Rochester called *The North Star.* (p.206)

Drisius, Samuel (dris′ ē əs), 1602-1673? Leader of the Dutch Church in New Amsterdam. (p.94)

Du Bois, W.E.B. (dü boyz′), 1868-1963 African American leader who helped to start a magazine called *The Crisis* and helped encourage the Harlem Renaissance. (p.257)

Eastman, George (ēst′ mən), 1854-1932 Inventor of a new kind of film that made it easier to take photographs. (p.206)

Edison, Thomas Alva (ed′ i sən), 1847-1931 America's most famous inventor; inventor of the light bulb. (p.234)

Ellicott, Joseph (e′ lə kət), 1760-1826 Mapmaker for the Holland Land Company; founder of the settlement of Buffalo in 1801. (p.174)

Ellington, Duke (el′ ing tən), 1899-1974 Songwriter, jazz musician, and bandleader whose music was popular during and after the Harlem Renaissance, and is still popular today. (p.257)

Franklin, Benjamin (frang′ klən), 1706 – 1790 American writer, printer, scientist and diplomat. Author of *Poor Richard's Almanac.* (p.139)

Fulton, Robert (ful′ tən), 1765-1815 Builder of the first successful steamboat in 1807. (p.181)

Garrison, William Lloyd (gar′ ə sən), 1805-1879 Abolitionist who started the American Anti-Slavery Society in 1833. (p.216)

Gates, Horatio (gāts), 1728-1806 American general who defeated the British at the Battle of Saratoga in the American Revolution. (p.151)

Gibbs, Lois (gibz), 1951- A resident of Niagara Falls who became an public and environmental activist about the disposal of hazardous waste. (p.283)

Ginsburg, Ruth Bader (gins′ bərg), 1933- Judge; the second woman to serve on the United States Supreme Court. (p.283)

Giuliani, Rudolph (jū lē ä′ nē) 1944- Mayor of New York City from 1994 to 2001. (p.271)

Gompers, Samuel (gom′ pərs), 1850-1924 Labor union leader from New York City who helped form one of the first labor unions in 1873. (p.206)

Grant, Ulysses S. (grant), 1822-1885 Leader of the Union Army during the Civil War and 18th President of the United States, 1869-1877. (p.227)

Green, Hetty (grēn), 1834-1916 Millionaire who made her fortune by buying and selling stocks and land. (p.233)

Hamilton, Alexander (ham' əl tən), 1755-1804 New York representative who signed the United States Constitution; one of the authors of *The Federalist Papers*; first United States Secretary of the Treasury; founder of the New York Stock Exchange and the Bank of New York. (p.166)

Hiawatha (hī ə wä' thə), 1500s Mohawk leader who, with Deganawida, helped organize the Iroquois League. (p.61)

Hogan, Linda (hō' gən) 1947- Native American writer and poet. (p.2)

Hudson, Henry (hud' sən), ?-1611 English sea captain and explorer. Working for the Dutch West India Company, he explored the Hudson River in 1609 as far north as present-day Albany looking for a Northwest Passage. (p.85)

Hughes, Langston (hūz), 1902-1967 Writer and poet who became famous during the Harlem Renaissance. (p.257, 259)

Hutchinson, Anne (huch' ən sən), 1591-1643 An Englishwoman who settled in New Netherland after being forced to leave the New England colonies because of her religious views. (p.74)

Hyatt, John (hī' ət), 1837–1920 Inventor of celluloid, an early form of plastic. (p.234)

Irving, Washington (ûr' ving), 1783-1859 New York writer whose works include *Rip Van Winkle* and *The Legend of Sleepy Hollow*. (p.131)

Jackson, Kenneth T. (jak' sən), 1939- New York historian and professor of history at Columbia University. (p.314)

Jay, John (jā), 1745-1829 Lawmaker who helped write the New York Constitution. He became the first Chief Justice of the United States Supreme Court. (p.159)

Jefferson, Thomas (jef' ər sən), 1743-1826 A Virginian who drafted the Declaration of Independence. He became the third President of the United States, 1801-1809. (p.141)

Jemison, Mary (jem' ə sən), 1743-1833 Settler in the Genesee River Valley after the American Revolution; received land on Gardeau Flats from the Big Tree Treaty. (p.130)

Jikonsahseh (ji kôn' sä sä), 1500s Iroquois woman who helped convince the Seneca to join the great peace. (p.5)

Johnson, James Weldon (jon' sən), 1871-1938 Composer, writer, and poet of the Harlem Renaissance. (p.208)

Johnson, Sir William (jon' sən), 1715-1774 British leader who convinced the Iroquois not to take sides in the French and Indian War. (p.139)

Johnson, William (jon' sən), 1942- 64th Mayor of Rochester. (p.288)

Keller, Helen (kel' ər), 1880-1968 A deaf and blind writer and speaker, who learned to read and write from her teacher, Anne Sullivan. (p.245)

Kennedy, Jr. Robert (ken' ə dē), 1954- Environmentalist, Riverkeeper, environmental activist. (p.35)

King, Jr. Martin Luther (king), 1929-1968 Civil rights leader. (p.264)

Pronunciation Key									
a	at	ē	me	ō	old	ū	use	ng	song
ā	ape	i	it	ô	fork	ü	rule	th	thin
ä	far	ī	ice	oi	oil	ù	pull	th	this
âr	care	îr	pierce	ou	out	ûr	turn	zh	measure
e	end	o	hot	u	up	hw	white	ə	about, taken, pencil, lemon, circus

L

LaGuardia, Fiorello (lə gwär′ dē ə fē ə re′ lō), 1882-1947 Mayor of New York City from 1933-1945. (p.261)

Latimer, Lewis (lat′ i mər), 1848-1928 African American inventor who improved the light bulb by making it last longer. He helped build the nation's first electric power station in Manhattan. (p.234)

Lee, Robert E. (lē), 1807-1870 Commander of the Confederate army during the Civil War. (p.224)

León, Tania (lā ōn′) 1943- Orchestra conductor; founder and musical director of the Dance Theater of Harlem. (p.283)

Lincoln, Abraham (ling′ kən), 1809-1865 16th President of the United States, 1861-1865 and leader of the Union during the Civil War. (p.218)

Ludington, Sybil (lud′ ing tən), 1761-1839 Daughter of a New York militia colonel; warned militia members that the British planned to burn Danbury, Connecticut. (p.146, 147)

M

Marshall, Thurgood (mar′ shəl), 1908-1991 Lawyer and the first African American to serve on the United States Supreme Court, 1967-1991. (p.308)

Minuit, Peter (min′ yə wət), 1580-1638 Dutch colonial governor of New Netherland who bought Manhattan Island from the Lenni Lenape. (p.89)

Morgan, J(ohn).P(ierpont). (môr′ gən), 1837-1913 A banker who made millions of dollars and helped some big businesses grow by lending them money. (p.233)

Morris, Robert (môr′ əs), 1734-1806 Merchant who funded the *Empress of China*. (p.164)

Mott, Lucretia (mot), 1793-1880 Leader in the antislavery and women's rights movement. (p.191)

Moynihan, Daniel Patrick (moi′ nə han), 1927-2003 New York senator who served for over 20 years. (p.308)

N

Nicolls, Richard (nik′ əls), 1624-1672 First British governor of New York, 1664-1668. (p.109)

O

O'Connor Sandra Day (ō kon′ ər), 1930- First woman Justice of the Supreme Court of the United States in 1981. (p.308)

Olmsted, Frederick Law (ōlm′ sted), 1822-1903 Landscape architect who designed parks in Brooklyn, Buffalo, New York City, and Niagara Falls. (p.42)

Otis, Elisha Graves (ō′ təs), 1811-1861 Inventor of mechanical brakes for the elevator. (p.234)

P

Parker, Ely S. (pär′ kər), 1828-1895 Union officer and Seneca chief. (p.227)

Philipse, Frederick (fil′ ips), 1626-1702 Wealthy landowner in New York. He and his wife, Margaret, built Philipsburg Manor. (p.112)

R

Red Jacket (red ja′ kət), 1758?-1830 Also called Sagoyewatha; Seneca leader who did not want to sell Iroquois land to the Holland Land Company. (p.174)

Remington, Eliphalet (rem′ ing tən), 1793-1861 Manufacturer of sewing machines and typewriters. (p.234)

Rivera, Oscar Garcia (äs′ kûr gär sē′ ə rē vâr′ ə), 1900–1969 First Puerto Rican elected to office in continental United States; he served in the New York Assembly 1937–1940. (p.282)

Robinson, Jackie (ro′ bin sən), 1919-1972 First black major league baseball player; began playing for the Brooklyn Dodgers in 1947. (p.294)

Rochester, Nathaniel (ro′ ches tər), 1752-1831 Founder of the settlement of Rochester on the Genesee River in 1803. (p.174)

Roebling, Emily (rōb′ ling), 1843-1903 Wife of Washington Roebling; she managed the construction of the Brooklyn Bridge. (p.242)

Roebling, John (rōb′ ling), 1806-1869 The bridge builder who prepared the plans for the Brooklyn Bridge in 1867. (p.242)

Roosevelt, Eleanor (rō′ zə velt), 1884-1962 The wife of President Franklin Roosevelt; delegate to the United Nations; journalist; author; co-wrote the Universal Declaration of Human Rights. (p. 254)

Roosevelt, Franklin Delano (rō′ zə velt), 1882-1945 The 32nd President of the United States from 1933 to 1945. He was governor of New York from 1928 to 1932. (p.257)

Roosevelt, Theodore (rō′ zə velt), 1858-1919 26th President of the United States from 1901 to 1909; governor of New York from 1899 to 1900. (p.244)

Russwurm, John (rus′ wərm), 1799-1851 Abolitionist who, together with Samuel Cornish, started the first African American newspaper, *Freedom's Journal*. (p.216)

Seward, William (sü′ wûrd), 1801-1872 New York Governor 1839-1843; United States Senator 1849-1861; Secretary of State 1861-1869. (p.223)

Singer, Isaac (sing′ ər), 1811-1875 Inventor of the Singer sewing machine. (p.189)

Stanton, Elizabeth Cady (stan′ tən), 1815-1902 Abolitionist and women's rights leader. (p. 207)

Steinem, Gloria (stīn əm), 1934- Women's rights leader. (p.207)

Stuyvesant, Peter (stī′ və sənt), 1610-1672 Governor of New Netherland from 1647 until 1664, when Great Britain seized the colony. (p.75)

Tammany (ta′ mə nē), 1600s Lenni Lenape leader who is said to have sold the island of Manhattan to Peter Minuit. (p.75)

Toomer, Jean (tü′ mûr), 1894-1967 Harlem Renaissance poet and writer. (p.209)

Truth, Sojourner (trüth), 1797?-1883 Abolitionist who escaped from slavery in 1827 and spoke out for abolition of slavery and for women's rights. (p.219)

Tubman, Harriet (tub′ mən), 1820?-1913 Abolitionist who escaped from slavery in 1849. She became a conductor on the Underground Railroad and made 19 trips to slave states to free others. (p.206)

Verrazano, Giovanni da (ver ə zän′ ō jō vä′ nē də), 1485(?)-1528(?) Italian sea captain and explorer. Sailing for France, he explored New York harbor in 1524. (p.83)

Wald, Lillian (wäld), 1867-1940 Nurse who established Henry Street Settlement House to provide basic health care to immigrants. (p.238, 239)

Walker, C. J. (wä′ kər) Business woman and supporter of the arts; First African-American millionaire. (p.233)

Washington, George (wä′ shing tən), 1732-1799 First President of the United States from 1789 to 1797; fought in the French and Indian War; led the Continental Army during the American Revolution. (p.145)

Watson, Elkanah (wät′ sən), 1758-1842 Businessperson who started Albany's first bank. (p.166)

Westinghouse, George (wes′ ting hous), 1846-1914 Inventor of air brakes for railroads; later helped develop a system to send electric power over long distances. (p.234)

Zenger, John Peter (zen′ gər), 1697-1746 Newspaper printer whose trial in 1734 was an important step toward freedom of the press. (p.111)

Pronunciation Key									
a	at	ē	me	ō	old	ū	use	ng	song
ā	ape	i	it	ô	fork	ü	rule	th	thin
ä	far	ī	ice	oi	oil	ù	pull	th	this
âr	care	îr	pierce	ou	out	ûr	turn	zh	measure
e	end	o	hot	u	up	hw	white	ə	about, taken, pencil, lemon, circus

Glossary

This glossary will help you to pronounce and understand the meanings of the vocabulary terms in this book. The page number at the end of the definition tells where the term first appears.

Pronunciation Key

a	at	ē	me	ō	old	ū	use	ng	song
ā	ape	i	it	ô	fork	ü	rule	th	thin
ä	far	ī	ice	oi	oil	ů	pull	th	this
âr	care	îr	pierce	ou	out	ûr	turn	zh	measure
e	end	o	hot	u	up	hw	white	ə	about, taken, pencil, lemon, circus

A

abolitionist (ab ə lish′ ə nist) A person who works to end slavery. (p. 215)

agriculture (ag′ ri kul chər) The business of growing crops and raising animals. (p. 49)

ally (al′ î) A person or country that joins with another for a common purpose. (p.115)

amendment (ə mend′ mənt) A change or addition to the United States Constitution. (p. 161)

ancestor (an′ ses tər) Someone in your family who came before you. (p. 56)

archaeologist (är kē ol′ ə jist) A scientist who studies artifacts to learn how people lived in the past. (p. 47)

artifact (är′ ti fakt) An object made or used by people who lived in the past. (p. 40)

assembly (ə sem′ blē) A lawmaking body. (p. 110)

B

bank (bank) A business that helps people borrow and save money. (p.165)

bill (bil) A written idea for a law. (p.298)

boomtown (büm′ toun) A town which grows rapidly in a short period of time. (p.183)

border (bôr′ dər) An imaginary line which separates states and countries. (p.22)

boundary (bound′ ə rē) A line or physical feature that shows where one place ends and another begins. (p. 22)

budget (buj′ ət) A plan for using an amount of money for specific purposes. (p.297)

C

canal (kə nal′) An inland waterway built by people for transportation or irrigation. (p.182)

capital (ka′ pə təl) A city where government leaders meet. (p.159)

capitol (ka′ pə təl) A building where governments meet and laws are made. (p.242)

checks and balances (cheks and bal′ ən səz) The system in which the power of each branch of government is balanced by the powers of the other branches. (p.297)

circle graph (sûr′ kəl graf) A graph in the shape of a circle that shoes the sizes of different parts of a whole; also called a pie graph. (p.92)

citizen (sit′ ə zən) A person who is born in a country or who has earned the right to become a member of the country by law. (p.307)

citizenship (sit′ ə zən ship) The condition of being a citizen. (p.317)

city council (si′ tē koun′ səl) A legislative branch of city government; a group of representatives that makes a city's laws and decides how it should spend its money. (p.291)

city manager (si′ tē′ man′ ə gər) A person hired to run the city's daily business. (p.291)

civil rights (siv′ əl rîts) The rights of all citizens to be treated equally under the law. (p.264)

civil war (siv′ əl wôr) A war between regions or groups within a country. (p. 223)

Civil War, The (siv′ əl wôr) The war between the Union states of the North and the Confederate states of the South from 1861 to 1865 (p. 223)

clan (klan) A group of families who share the same ancestors. (p.62)

clan mother (klan mə thər) The head of a clan among the Iroquois people. (p.63)

climate (klī′ mət) The pattern of weather of a certain place over many years. (p.24)

coast (kôst) The land along a body of water. (p.23)

colony (kol′ ə nē) A place that is ruled by another country. (p.84)

commute (kə mût′) To travel a distance each day from one's home to one's workplace. (p.262)

Confederacy (kən fed′ ər ə sē) In the United States, the name adopted by the 11 Southern states during the Civil War. (p. 223)

congestion (kən jes′ chən) Overcrowding of cities or highways. (p.329)

Congress (kong′ ris) The legislative branch of the United States government. (p.308)

consequence (kon′ si kwens) The possible result of a choice or an action. (p.28)

conservation (kon sər vâ′ shən) The careful use of natural resources. (p.35)

constitution (kon sti tü′ shən) A plan of government. (p.159)

continent (kon′ tə nənt) One of Earth's seven great bodies of land–Africa, Antarctica, Asia, Australia, Europe, North America, and South America. (p.13)

Continental Congress (kon tə nen′ təl kong′ ris) A group of colonists who first met in Philadelphia in 1774 to discuss how the colonies should deal with Great Britain. (p.141)

convention A formal meeting held for a special purpose. (p.159)

council (koun′ səl) A group of people who meet to talk and make decisions. (p.63)

county (koun′ tē) One of the sections into which a state or country is divided. (p.293)

culture (kul′ chər) A way of life shared by a group of people. (p.89)

decision (di sizh′ ən) A choice that helps you reach a goal. (p.86)

degree (di grē′) A unit for measuring distance on Earth's surface. (p.18)

delegate (del′ i gât) A person chosen to represent a group. (p.141)

democracy (di mok′ rə sē) A system of government in which the people elect their leaders. (p.297)

democratic republic (dem ə krat′ ik re pub′ lik) A government in which citizens elect representatives to make decisions for them. (p.307)

diversity (di vûr si tē) Variety; differences. (p.316)

draft (draft) A plan to select people to serve in the military. (p.224)

economy (i kon′ ə mē) The way a country or other place uses or produces natural resources, good, and services. (p.37)

elect (ē lekt′) To choose by voting. (p.291)

elevation (el ə vâ′ shən) The height of land above sea level. (p.25)

elevation map (el ə vâ shən map) A map that shows the elevation of an area. (p.50)

emancipation (i man sə pâ′ shən) The act of setting free from slavery or control. (p.224)

Pronunciation Key

a	at	**ē**	me	**ō**	old	**ū**	use	**ng**	song
ā	ape	**i**	it	**ô**	fork	**ü**	rule	**th**	thin
ä	far	**ī**	ice	**oi**	oil	**ù**	pull	**th**	this
âr	care	**îr**	pierce	**ou**	out	**ûr**	turn	**zh**	measure
e	end	**o**	hot	**u**	up	**hw**	white	**ə**	about, taken, pencil, lemon, circus

employer (em ploi′ ər) Someone who has people working for him or her. (p.233)

entrepreneur (än trə prə nûr′) Someone who starts and runs his or her own business. (p.165)

environment (en vî′ rən mənt) The surroundings in which people, plants, or animals live. (p.34)

ethnic group (eth′ nik grüp) A group of people who share the same language, customs, or history. (p.317)

executive branch (eg zek′ yə tiv branch) The branch of government that carries out laws. (p.299)

explorer (ek splôr′ ər) A person who travels to unfamiliar places to find out about them. (p.83)

export (ek′ spôrt) Something sold or traded to another country. (p.106)

fact (fakt) A statement that can be proven true. (p.162)

famine (fa′ mən) A time of widespread hunger caused by a crop failure or a shortage of food. (p.190)

free enterprise (frē en′ tər prîz) The economic system that allows people to decide how to own and run their own businesses. (p.165)

free trade (frē trâd) Trade without restrictions or taxes. (p.97)

frontier (frun tēr′) The edge of a settled area. (p.172)

geography (jē og′ rə fē) The study of Earth and the way people, plants, and animals use it. (p.12)

glacier (glā′ shər) A huge sheet of ice that moves slowly across the land. (p.14)

global grid (glô bəl grid) The crisscrossing lines of latitude and longitude on a map or globe. (p.18)

global trade (glô bəl trād) Trade in which products are bought and sold across national boundaries. (p.272)

goal (gôl) Something that a person wants or tries to get. (p.86)

goods (gůdz) Products which are bought and sold in trade. (p.20)

government (guv′ ərn mənt) The laws and people that run a country, state, county, city, or town. (p.110)

Grange (grânj) An organization that helps farmers and rural communities. (p.247)

graph (graf) A diagram that shows information. (p.92)

Great Depression (grât di presh′ ən) The period of widespread economic hardship in the 1930s. (p.257)

Great Migration (grât mîgrā′ shən) The movement of many African Americans in the early and middle 1900s from rural areas of the Southeast to urban areas of the Northeast and Midwest. (p.257)

harbor (här′ bər) A sheltered body of water along a coast where boats can dock. (p.23)

Harlem Renaissance (här′ ləm ren′ ə säns) A time in the 1920s in Harlem when many important African American works of art and learning were created. (p.257)

heritage (her′ i tij) The history, traditions, beliefs, and customs that a group of people share. (p.52)

historic site (hi stôr′ i kəl sît) A place where something interesting or important happened in the past. (p.321)

House of Representatives (hous uv rep rə sen′ tə tivs) The house of Congress in which each state's number of representatives is determined according to its population. (p.308)

hunter-gatherer (hun′ tər ga′ thər ər) A person who found food both by hunting animals and gathering plants, fruits, and nuts. (p.48)

immigrant (im′ i grənt) A person who comes to a new country to live. (p.190)

import (im′ pôrt) Something brought in from another country for sale or use. (p.106)

indentured servant (in den′ shərd sər′ vənt) A person who works for an employer for a period of time in return for payment of travel expenses. (p.106)

Industrial Revolution (in dus′ trē əl rev ə lü′ shən) The major change, starting in the 1800s, in which power-driven machines replaced hand tools. (p.189)

industry (in′ dus trē) All the businesses that make one kind of goods or provide one kind of service. (p.189)

interstate highway (in′ tər stāt hî′ wâ) A road with at least two lanes of traffic in each direction that connects two or more states. (p.324)

investor (in vest′ ər) A person who puts money into a business and shares the profits. (p.90)

judicial branch (jü dish′ əl branch) The part of government that interprets the laws. (p.299)

keyword (kē′ wûrd) Topic word that you enter into a search engine that helps you find other information. (p.294)

labor union (lā′ bər ûn′ yən) A group of workers in a particular industry or factory who organize to get better working conditions. (p.233)

landform (land′ fôrm) A natural feature on Earth's surface. (p.13)

large-scale map (lärj skāl map) A map that shows many details in a small area. (p.148)

latitude (lat′ i tüd) A measure of the distance on Earth north or south of the equator. (p.18)

league (lēg) An association of people or nations to work for their common interests. (p.61)

legislative branch (lej′ is lā tiv branch) The branch of government that makes laws. (p.298)

legislature (lej′ is lā chər) A group of people elected to makes laws. (p.110)

line graph (līn graf) A graph that shows patterns and amounts of change over time. (p.92)

lock (lok) A kind of water elevator that moves boats within a canal to higher or lower levels. (p.182)

locomotive (lōk ə mō′ tiv) A steam-powered engine that pulls a train. (p.185)

longhouse (lông′ hous) A long wooden building in a Native American village in which many related families lived. (p.53)

longitude (lon′ ji tüd) A measure of distance on Earth east or west of the prime meridian. (p.18)

Loyalist (loi′ ə list) A colonist who remained loyal to Great Britain during the American Revolution. (p.140)

manor (man′ ər) A large piece of land that the owner rents in smaller plots to a number of farmers. (p.105)

manufacturer (man yə fak′ chər er) Someone who produces goods in factories. (p.233)

map (map) A kind of picture of Earth. (p.120)

map scale (map skāl) The measurement a map uses to indicate the real size of a place on Earth. (p.148)

market economy (mär′ kit i kon′ ə mē) An economy in which people decide for themselves what to sell or buy. (p.117)

mayor (mā′ ər) A head of a city government. (p.291)

megalopolis (meg ə lä′ pō lis) A large urban area in which several cities run into each other. (p.318)

merchant (mər′ chənt) A person who buys and sells goods. (p.106)

meridian (mə rid′ ē ən) A line of longitude. (p.18)

metropolitan area (me trō pól itən âr ē ə) A large city and its surrounding suburbs. (p.318)

militia (mi lish′ ə) A group of volunteers who fought in an emergency during the colonial period and the American Revolution. (p.141)

mouth (mouth) The place where a river empties into another body of water. (p.21)

municipal government (mū ni′ ci pəl guv′ ərn mənt) A local or city government. (p.291)

Pronunciation Key				
a at	ē me	ō old	ū use	ng song
ā ape	i it	ô fork	ü rule	th thin
ä far	ī ice	oi oil	u̇ pull	th this
âr care	îr pierce	ou out	ûr turn	zh measure
e end	o hot	u up	hw white	ə about, taken, pencil, lemon, circus

natural resource (nach′ ər əl rē′ sôrs) Something found in the environment that people can use. (p.15)

neutral (nü′ trəl) Not taking sides in a war or conflict. (p.256)

New Deal (nü dēl) Government programs started by President Franklin D. Roosevelt in the 1930s to aid people during the Great Depression. (p.257)

nonrenewable resource (non ri nü′ ə bəl rə′ sôrs) A natural resource that cannot be replaced. (p.35)

Northwest Passage (nôrth west′ pas′ ij) A water route through North America from Europe to Asia. (p.83)

opinion (ə pin′ yən) A statement of belief or feeling which cannot be proven true or false. (p.162)

option (op′ shən) A choice. (p.86)

outline (out′ līn) A written plan for organizing information about a subject. (p.268)

packet boat (pak′ it bôt) A boat that carries passengers, freight, and mail at set times over a set route. (p.106)

parallel (par′ ə lel) A line of latitude. (p.18)

Patriot (pā′ trē ət) A colonist who was opposed to British rule. (p.140)

patroon (pə trün′) A land owner in New Netherland who had to bring 50 settlers to the colony to help settle his land. (p.90)

pioneer (pī′ ə nēr) A person who is among the first of non-native people to settle a region. (p.173)

plateau (pla′ tō) A large area of flat land, higher than the surrounding country. (p.13)

political cartoon (pə lit′ i kəl kär tün′) A drawing that tells readers about events or people in the news. (p.186)

pollution (pə lü′ shən) Anything that dirties the air, soil, or water. (p.265)

population density (pop yə lā′ shən den′ si tē) A measurement of how many people live within a certain area. (p.178)

precipitation (pri si′ p i tā′ shən) Moisture that falls as rain, snow, sleet or hail. (p.26)

prehistory (pri his′ tə rē) The time before written records. (p.47)

primary source (prī′ mer ē sors) An artifact, photograph, or spoken or written eyewitness account of an event in the past. (p.40)

profit (prof′ it) The money a business earns after it pays for tools, salaries, and other costs. (p.90)

Prohibition (prō ə bish′ ən) The 18th amendment to the Constitution that made the sale of alcohol illegal. It was repealed in 1933. (p.256)

proprietor (prə prī′ i tər) Owner of a colony. (p.97)

public transportation (pub′ lik trans pər tā′ shən) Transportation systems, such as buses, subways, and trains, usually found in larger cities. (p.329)

ratify (ra′ tə fī) To formally approve. (p.161)

ration (rash′ ən) To use less of something. (p.261)

raw material (rô mə tir′ ē əl) An ore or other resource which must be changed for use in an economy. (p.37)

recreation (rek rē â′ shən) Things people do for relaxation and enjoyment. (p.322)

reform (ri fôrm′) A change to make things better. (p.247)

region (rē′ jən) An area with common features that set it apart from other areas. (p.15)

renewable resource (ri nü′ ə bəl rə′ sôrs) A natural resource that can be replaced. (p.35)

repeal (ri pəl′) To withdraw or cancel a law. (p.256)

representative (re pri zen′ tə tiv) A person chosen to speak or vote for others. (p.159)

reservation (res ûr vâ′ shən) An area protected or set aside for the use of Native Americans. (p.56)

retreat (ri trət′) To turn back. (p.145)

revolution (rev ə lü′ shən) The overthrow of a government; the colonists′ fight for freedom. (p.141)

road map (rôd map) A map that shows roads in one area. (p.324)

route (rüt) The course you take to get somewhere. (p.324)

Glossary

royal colony (roi′ əl kol′ ə nē) A colony that belongs to a king or queen. (p.109)

rural (rur′ əl) Of the countryside; including farms, small villages, or unsettled land. (p.246)

sachem (sā′ chəm) A member of the Grand Council of the Iroquois League. (p.63)

sea level (sē lev′ əl) The height of land where it meets the sea. (p.25)

secede (sə sēd′) To withdraw or break away from an organization such as a government. (p.218)

secondary source (se ′kən dār e sôrs) An account of an event from a person who did not see or experience it. (p.40)

Senate (sen′ it) The house of Congress in which each state has two members, regardless of its population. (p.308)

settlement house (set′ əl mənt hous) A place that offers education, hot meals, and other services to the poor. (p.238)

sheriff (she′ rif) The person who makes sure the laws are obeyed in a county. (p.109)

skyscraper (skī′ skrā pər) A tall building supported by a steel frame. (p.243)

slavery (slā′ və rē) The practice of making a person work for no money and without the freedom to leave. (p.90)

small-scale map (smôl skāl map) A map that shows few details of a large area. (p.148)

social worker (sô′ shəl wûr′ kər) A person who provides services to those in need. (p.238)

solution (sə lü′ shən) An answer to a problem. (p.28)

source (sôrs) The place where a river begins. (p.21)

Stamp Act (stamp akt) An act passed by Great Britain in 1765 that placed taxes on newspapers and paper sold in the 13 Colonies. (p.140)

stock (stok) A share of ownership in a company. (p.167)

stock exchange (stok eks chânj′) An organized market for buying and selling stocks. (p.167)

strike (strīk) A refusal of all the workers in a business to work until the owners meet their demands. (p.233)

suburb (sub′ ûrb) A smaller community near a larger city. (p.262)

Supreme Court (sə prēm′ krôt) The highest court in the United States. (p.308)

surplus (sûr′ plus) An amount greater than what is used or needed. (p.105)

surrender (sə ren′ dər) To give up. (p.145)

suspension bridge (sə spen′ shən brij) A bridge that hangs, or is suspended, from cables. (p.242)

sweatshop (swet′ shop) A factory where workers are paid low wages and work in unhealthy conditions. (p.248)

tanning (tan′ ing) A method of scraping and soaking animal skins to make leather. (p.189)

tax (taks) Money people pay to the government so that it can perform public services. (p.110)

temperature (tem′ pər ə chər) A measurement of how hot or cold something is, often the air. (p.25)

tenant farmer (ten′ ənt fär′ mər) A farmer who works land owned by someone else and pays rent in either cash or shares of the crops. (p.90)

tenement (ten′ ə mənt) A crowded, poorly maintained apartment building. (p.237)

terrorism (ter′ ə riz əm) Using violence or fear to achieve a political goal. (p.271)

time line (tīm līn) A diagram that shows a series of events in the order in which they happened. (p.38)

tolerance (tol′ ər əns) Accepting of differences. (p.90)

Pronunciation Key

a	at	ē	me	ō	old	ū	use	ng	song
ā	ape	i	it	ô	fork	ü	rule	th	thin
ä	far	ī	ice	oi	oil	ù	pull	th	this
âr	care	îr	pierce	ou	out	ûr	turn	zh	measure
e	end	o	hot	u	up	hw	white	ə	about, taken, pencil, lemon, circus

toll (tôl) A small fee people pay to use a canal, road or bridge. (p.183)

tow path (tô path) A path that ran along the side of a canal. (p.183)

trading post (trā′ ding pōst) A place to trade products with others. (p.84)

traitor (trā′ tər) Someone who acts against his or her own country. (p.151)

treaty (trē′ tē) A formal agreement between nations. (p.153)

Triangle Trade (trī′ ang′ gəl trād) Name for the trade routes that ran from Africa to the islands of the Caribbean and then to the American colonies. (p.116)

tributary (trib′ yə ter ē) A small river that flows into a larger river. (p.21)

Underground Railroad (un′ dər ground râl′ rôd) The system of secret routes used by people escaping slavery. (p.217)

Union (ūn′ yən) The states that make up the United States. Used during the Civil War to refer to the government of the Northern States. (p.223)

United Nations (ū nī′ tid nā′ shənz) An international peacekeeping organization that includes most of the countries of the world. (p.263)

urban (ûr′ bən) Of a city. (p.246)

urbanization (ûr′ bən iz tion) The process of cities replacing rural areas. (p.318)

URL (u r l) The web address of a site on the Internet. (p.294)

valley (va′ lē) The low land between hills or mountains, often with a river. (p.13)

veto (vē′ tô) To power of the executive branch to reject a bill passed by the legislative branch. (p.298)

wampum (wom′ pəm) Polished beads used in ceremonies by Iroquois and other Native Americans to represent certain ideas; also used in gift-giving and trading. (p.63)

weather (weth′ ər) The condition of the air that a certain time in a certain place, including temperature, precipitation, and wind. (p.24)

Web site (web sît) A location on the Internet. (p.294)

wigwam (wig′ wom) A round Native American home in which just one family lived made from arched poles covered with bark. (p.54)

World Wide Web (wûrld wîd web) A collection of information, programs, videos, songs and games on the Internet. (p.294)

Index

*This index lists many topics that appear in the book, along with the pages on which they are found. Page numbers after a *c* refer you to a chart or diagram, after a *g*, to a graph, after an *m*, to a map, after a *p*, to a photograph or picture, and after a *q*, to a quotation.

Index

Credits

Cover Photos: front cover: (t) Richard Berenholtz/CORBIS; (b) Derek Croucher/CORBIS. Back cover: (c) Alan Schein Photography/CORBIS.

Maps: XNR and Mapping Solutions

Illustration Credits: Bandelin Dacey Studios: pp. 284-285; Steve Barbaria: pp. 208-209 Kenneth Batelman: p. 303; Barbara-Higgins Bond: pp. 4-5, 164-165; Chuck Carter: p. 243; Steve Chorney: pp. 10, 111, 252, 282, 314; Stephen Conlin: p. 298; Robert Crawford: pp. 185, 328; Bill Farnsworth: pp. 147, 156, 212; Barbara Gibson: p. 217; Robert Gunn: pp. 80, 102, 170, 301; Stephen Harrington: p. 288; Jim Hays: pp. 234, 333; Christian Hook: p. 136; Richard Hook: p. 65; Robert Hunt: pp. 176-177; Inklink: pp. 54-55, 117, 182; Jui Ishida: pp. 6-7; Yuan Lee: pp. 58, 59, 76, 77, 214-215; Dennis Lyall: pp. 88-89; Angus McBride: pp. 60-61, 63; Greg Newbold: pp. 132-133; Frank Ordaz: pp. 44, 74-75, 130-131, 230; Frank Riccio: p. 159; Robert Van Nutt: pp. 113, 152

Photography Credits: All Photographs are by Macmillan/McGraw Hill (MMH) except as noted below.

2-3: Free Agents ltd./CORBIS. 8-9: Jim Schwabel/Index Stock. 10: Mike Briner. 11: (bl)Andre Jenny/Alamy; (bc) AP Wide World Photos; (br) Paul Katz/Index Stock. 12: Reuters/CORBIS. 13: Tom Van Sant/CORBIS. 14: Discovery Comm/Panoramic Images. 17: Siede Preis/Getty Images. 20: Patrick Watson/The Image Works. 22: (tl) AP Wide World Photos; (bl) Mitch Wojnarowicz/The Image Works; 22-23: Paul Rezendes Photography. 24-25: Eastcott/Momatiuk/The Image Works. 26-27: Peter Arnold, Inc. /Alamy. 27: CORBIS SYGMA. 28: (inset) Laura Lopez; (bkgd) Andy Olenick/Fotowerks. 34: (inset) Ariel Skelley/CORBIS. 34-35: (bkgd) Carl Heilman II/Panoramic Images. 35: Reuters/CORBIS. 37: (tc) Collection of The Corning Museum of Glass, Corning, NY; (tr) AP Wide World Photos. 38: (bc) Burke/Triolo Productions/Getty Images; (br) CORBIS. 39: (l) PhotoDisc; (r) Baldwin H. Ward & Kathryn C. Ward/CORBIS. 40: (bl) Werner Forman/CORBIS; (br) Courtesy, National Museum of the American Indian, Smithsonian Institution. Photo by NMAI Photo Services Staff. 41: (bl) Museum of American Indian/Smithsonian; (tr) The British Museum/HIP/The Image Works. 46-47: Michael Chu. 48: Printed with permission of the New York State Museum, Albany, New York 12230. 49: C Squared Studios/Getty Images. 50-51: J. A. Kraulis/Masterfile. 52-53: Nathan Benn/CORBIS. 55: (l) National Museum of American Indian; (c) National Museum of American Indian; (r) Marilyn Angel Wynn/Nativestock.com. 56: Mike Greenlar/The Image Works; 57: AP-Wide World Photos; 58: (tr) National Museum of American Indian; (br) Smithsonian American Art Museum, Washington, DC/Art Resource, NY. 59: (tl) National Museum of American Indian; National Museum of American Indian. 62: The Granger Collection, New York. 63: (b) Lawrence Migdale; Mike Greenlar/The Image Works. 64: City of Rochester/David Lassman/The Image Works. 72-73: Henry Westheim/Alamy. 75: The Granger Collection, New York. 78: Robert Brenner/Photo Edit. 82: The Granger Collection, New York. 83: New-York Historical Society, New York, USA. 85: The Granger Collection, New York; 1996 Image Farm Inc. (bkgd) ADAM JONES/DanitaDelimont.com. 86: (inset) Robert Lubeck/Earth Scenes. 88: New-York Historical Society, New York, USA. 90-91: The Granger Collection, New York; 1996 Image Farm Inc. 91: Kike Calvo/V&W/The Image Works. 92: Scala/Art Resource, NY. 94: Christie's Images/CORBIS. 97: The Granger Collection, New York; (bkgd) 1996 Image Farm Inc. 104: Bettmann/CORBIS. 105: Lee Snider/The Image Works. 106: The Image Bank/Getty Images; The Newark Museum/Art Resource, NY. 108: Mary Evans Picture Library. 110: Collection of the New-York Historical Society. 112: (bkgd) Lee Snider/Photo Images/CORBIS; (bl) Historic Hudson Valley. 112-113: (tcl) Lee Snider/Photo Images/CORBIS; Historic Hudson Valley. 114: Annie Griffiths Belt /CORBIS. 115: Ingram Publishing Royalty Free Photograph/Fotosearch; Mark Summerfield/Alamy. 118: (t) Hardie Truesdale/The Image Works; Darlene bordwell/www.darbaby.net; (t) Food Collection/Index Stock; (b) John Bollentin. 120: Courtesy New York State Museum, Albany New York. 123: Library of Congress prints and Photographs Division. 128-129: Mark E. Gibson/CORBIS. 134-135: North Wind Picture Archives/Alamy. 138: Edward Lamson Henry (1841-1919) 1903 Oil on canvas; 21 1/4 x 37 inches Albany Institute of History and Art Purchase 1993. 44. 140: (t) The Granger Collection, New York; (b) The Granger Collection, New York. 141: Bettmann/CORBIS; (bkgd) 1996 Image Farm Inc. 142: Royalty-Free/CORBIS. 140: Jim Zipp / ardea.com. 144-145: The Granger Collection, New York. 145: Courtesy National Park Service, Museum Management Program and Guilford Courthouse. 148-149: New-York Historical Society, New York, USA/The Bridgeman Art Library International. 151: Eastern National, Saratoga National Historical Park. 152: Photo by MPI/Getty Images. 153: Courtesy National Park Service, Museum Management Program and Guilford Courthouse. 158: Lee Snider/The Image Works. 160: The Granger Collection, New York. 162-163: The Granger Collection, New York. 164-165: (t Collection of The New-York Historical Society 1956.141h; (b) Collection of The New-York Historical Society 1944.224; 166: (tl) The Granger Collection, New York; (bl) Stan Ries /Panoramic Images. 167: Francis G. Mayer/CORBIS. 172: Scott Berner/Index Stock. 173: Paul J. Nelson. 174: Collection of The New-York Historical Society. 174:Yale Center for British Art, Paul Mellon Collection/Bridgeman Art Library International. 176-177: (bkgd) Rudi Von Briel/Index Stock Imagery; (tl) David Frazier/The Image Works; (tr) Sam Abell/National Geographic Image Collection; (tc) Annie Griffiths Belt/CORBIS; (c) Joseph Sohm; ChromoSohm Inc. /CORBIS. 178-179: (t) The Granger Collection, New York; (b) The Granger Collection, New York. 180-181: Bettmann/CORBIS. 184: The Granger Collection, New York. 188: Fulton County Museum; 189: SSPL/The Image Works; 190-191: The Granger Collection, New York; Bettmann/CORBIS. 192-193: Lee Snider/Photo Images/CORBIS; 194-195: The Granger Collection, New York; 197: (t) The Granger Collection, New York; The Granger Collection, New York; (b) The Granger Collection, New York. 204-205: C. Schmidt/zefa/CORBIS. 206-207: (l) The Granger Collection, New York; (c) The Granger Collection, New York; (r) The Granger Collection, New York; (l) George Eastman House/Contributor/Getty Images; (c) Mitsu Yasukawa; (r) Todd Plitt/Getty Images. 210: George Eastman House/Getty Images. 211: (t) The Granger Collection, New York; (b) COURTESY GEORGE EASTMAN HOUSE. 216-217: The Granger Collection, New York. 218: The Granger Collection, New York; The Granger Collection, New York. 219: Bettmann/CORBIS. 222-223: (bkgd) AP Wide World Photos; (inset) The Granger Collection, New York. 224: Brooks Kraft/CORBIS. 225: Bettmann/CORBIS. 226-227: The Granger Collection, New York; The Granger Collection, New York. 229: The Granger Collection, New York. 232-233: The Granger Collection, New York. 233: The Granger Collection, New York. 234-235: Pictorial Parade/Getty Images. 235: The Queens Borough Public Library, Long Island Division, Latimer Family Papers. 236-237: (inset) The Granger Collection, New York. 237: The Granger Collection, New York. 238: Scott B. Rosen/www.scottbrosen.com. 239: The Granger Collection, New York. 240: Bill Ross/CORBIS; CORBIS. 242: The Granger Collection, New York; 244-245: CORBIS; 245:(l)The Granger Collection, New York; (r) The Granger Collection, New York. 246: The Granger Collection, New York. 247: The Granger Collection, New York. 248: (t) The Granger Collection, New York; (b) PHILIPPE PSAILA/PHOTO RESEARCHERS, INC. 249: AP Wide World Photos; 254-255: Bettmann/CORBIS; Bettmann/CORBIS. 256-257: Bettmann/CORBIS; (bl) H. Armstrong Roberts/Retrofile; (br) The Granger Collection, New York; (tc) The Granger Collection, New York. 258: The Granger Collection, New York. 259: Photographs and Prints Division, Schomburg Center for Research in Black Culture, The New York Public Library, Astor, Leno and Tilden Foundations. 260-261: The Granger Collection, New York; Library of Congress Prints and Photographs Division #LC-USF34-009702-D. 262-263: (t)R. KRUBNER/Retrofile; (inset) Archive Holdings Inc/Getty Images. 264-265: (t) Bettmann/CORBIS; (b) Doug Armand/Getty Images; Bettmann/CORBIS; Joseph Sohm; ChromoSohm Inc. /CORBIS; Charles Gatewood / The Image Works; (t) Frank Johnston/Black Star Publishing/ Picture Quest. 266-267: (bkgd) Mary Iverson/CORBIS; (cl) J R EYERMAN/Getty Images; (tl) Hans Neleman/Getty Images; (cr) H. Armstrong Roberts/Retrostock; (l) CORBIS; William Gottlieb/CORBIS. 268-269: The Granger Collection, New York; 268-269: Bettmann/CORBIS; 270-271: Thomas E. Franklin/The Bergen Record/Contributor; Spencer Platt/Getty Images. 272: Gabe Palmer/zefa/CORBIS. 280-281: Andre Jenny/Alamy. 282-283: (r) ELLIS RICHARD/CORBIS SYGMA; (l) Brooks Kraft/CORBIS; (c) AP-Wide World Photos; (c) Michael Provost; (r) Harry Scull Jr./Stringer/Getty Images. 286-287: Andre Jenny/Alamy. 288-289: (bl) New York State of Appeals; (bc) SETH WENIG/Reuters/CORBIS; (br) Reuters/CORBIS. 290-291: Syracuse Newspapers/Gary Walts/The Image Works. 292: City of Rochester, New York. 294: Bettmann/CORBIS. 295: James Schwabel/Panoramic Images. 296-297: AP Wide World Photos. 299: Bruce McDonough. 302-303: (bkgd) Andre Jenny/Alamy; (t) AP Wide World Photos; (l) Andre Jenny/Alamy; (br) Andre Jenny/Alamy; (bc) Philip Scalia/Alamy; 304-305: (t) CORBIS. 306: Roy Ooms/Masterfile. 308: AP Wide World Photos. 310-311: (bkgd) J Sohm/VOA LLC /Panoramic Images. 314-315: (bl) Robert Brenner/PhotoEdit, Inc. ; (bc) Carolyn Schaefer/Panoramic Images. 315: James Schwabel/Panoramic Images; 316-317: (bkgd) James Schwabel/Panoramic Images; (inset) Darlene Bordwell/www.darbaby.net; 318: Ellen Senisi/The Image Works. 319: SZENES JASON/CORBIS SYGMA; (b) AP Wide World Photos. 320: Library of Congress, Prints & Photographs Division, [reproduction number, e.g., LC-B817-107672]; (bkgd) Syracuse Newspapers/John Berry/The Image Works, New York. 321: (t) Mary Evans Picture Library/The Image Works; (b) Phil Degginger/Alamy. 323: (t) Michael Provost; (b) Julie Lemberger/CORBIS. 324-325: James Schwabel /Panoramic Images. 326-327: (bkgd) Rudi Von Briel/PhotoEdit, Inc. ; (t) Syracuse Newspapers/Randi Anglin/The Image Works.

ACKNOWLEDGMENTS

continued from page ii

The Big One, by Linda L. Kiederer. From Yorktown Historical Society, January/February 1999 Feature. Copyright © 1998-2003 by Yorktown Historical Society. From <http://www.yorktownhistory.org/> All Rights Reserved. Used by Permission

Haudenosaunee and the American Revolution, Presentation to the United Nations July 18, 1995, by Carol Jacobs, Cayuga Bear Clan Mother. Published in Akwesasne Notes New Series, Fall, 1995, Volume 1. All Rights Reserved. Used by Permission.

Indian Storytelling Isn't Just Entertainment, by Seth Zuckerman. Published in Tidepool, March 29, 2001. All Rights Reserved. Used by Permission.

"Seneca." Britannica Concise Encyclopedia, 2005. From Encyclopedia Britannica. <http://concise.britannica.com/ebc/article?tocid=9378230> All Rights Reserved. Used by Permission.

The Iroquois Constitution, prepared by Gerald Murphy (The Cleveland Free-Net-aa300). Distributed by the Cybercasting Services Division of the National Public Telecomputing Network (NPTN). All Rights Reserved. Used by Permission. All Rights Reserved.

Cover Permission for **The Discovery of the Americas**, by Betsy and Giulio Maestro. Text Copyright © 1991 by Betsy C. Maestro. Illustrations Copyright © 1991 by Giulio Maestro. Published by William Morrow & Company, Inc. All rights reserved.

Cover Permission for **Hudson: The Story of a River**, by Robert Baron and Thomas Locker. Copyright © 2004 by Robert Baron and Thomas Locker. Published by Fulcrum Publishing. All Rights Reserved.

Cover Permission for **The Iroquois Indians**, by Bill Lund. Copyright © 1997 by Capstone Press. All Rights Reserved.

Rip Van Winkle, by Washington Irving; retold by Catherine Storr. Text Copyright © 1984 by Catherine Storr. Illustrations Copyright © 1984 by Peter Wingham. Published by Belitha Press, Ltd. All Rights Reserved. Used by Permission.

The Voyage of Giovanni de Verrazano: 1524-1528, edited by Lawrence C. Wroth. Copyright © 1970 by Yale University Press. All Rights Reserved. Used by Permission.

The History of New York State, edited by Dr. James Sullivan. Copyright © 1927 by Lewis Historical Publishing Company, Inc. All Rights Reserved. Used by Permission.

Cover Permission for **Life In New Amsterdam**, by Laura Fischer. Copyright © 2003 by Heinemann Library. All Rights Reserved.

Cover Permission for **Colonial Times: 1600 – 1700**, by Joy Masoff. Copyright © 2000 by Joy Masoff. Published by Scholastic, Inc. All Rights Reserved.

Cover Permission for **The New York Colony**, by Dennis B. Fradin. Copyright © 1988 by Regensteiner Publishing Enterprises, Inc. Published by Children's Press. All Rights Reserved.

The Arrow Over the Door, by Joseph Bruchac. Text Copyright © 1998 by Joseph Bruchac. Pictures Copyright © 1998 by James Watling. Published by Penguin Putnam Inc. All Rights Reserved. Used by Permission.

New York: The Empire State, by Jackie Ball and Kristen Behrens. Copyright © 2002 by World Almanac Library. All Rights Reserved. Used by Permission.

Georgiana Cole Halloran: An Autobiographical Account, from The Glovers of Fulton County. <http://www.albany.edu/history/glovers/index.html> All Rights Reserved. Used by Permission.

Cover Permission for **Redcoats and Petticoats**, by Katherine Kirkpatrick. Text Copyright © 1999 by Katherine Anne Kirkpatrick. Illustrations Copyright © 1999 by Ron Himler, Inc. Published by Holiday House. All Rights Reserved.

Cover Permission for **Shh! We're Writing the Constitution**, by Jean Fritz. Text Copyright © 1987 by Jean Fritz. Illustrations Copyright © 1987 by Tomie dePaola. Published by G.P. Putnam's Sons. All Rights Reserved.

Cover Permission for **The Amazing Impossible Erie Canal**, by Cheryl Harness. Copyright © 1995 by Cheryl Harness. Published by Simon & Schuster. All Rights Reserved.

Dreams, from The Collected Poems of Langston Hughes, edited by Arnold Rampersad. Copyright © 1994 by the Estate of Langston Hughes. Published by Alfred A. Knopf, Inc. All Rights Reserved. Used by Permission.

Lift Every Voice and Sing, by James Weldon Johnson. From Saint Peter Relates an Incident by James Weldon Johnson. Copyright © 1917, 1921, 1935 James Weldon Johnson, renewed 1963 by Grace Nail Johnson. Used by Permission of Viking Penguin, a division of Penguin Books USA Inc. Reprinted by Walker Publishing Company. All Rights Reserved. Used by Permission.

If You Should Go, from Hold Fast to Dreams: Poems Old & New Selected by Arna Bontemps. Originally from On These I Stand, by Countee Cullen. Copyright © 1925 by Harper & Brothers. All Rights Reserved. Used by Permission.

People, from The Collected Poems of Jean Toomer, edited by Robert B. Jones and Margery Toomer Latimer. Copyright © 1988 by The University of North Carolina Press. All Rights Reserved. Used by Permission.

Civil War: An Illustrated History, Narrative by Geoffrey C. Ward. Copyright © 1990 by American Documentaries, Inc. Published by Random House, Inc. All Rights Reserved. Used by Permission.

Windows on Henry Street, by Lillian Wald. Copyright © 1934 by Little, Brown and Company. All Rights Reserved. Used by Permission.

The American Spirit, Selected and Edited with Introduction and Commentary by Thomas A. Bailey and David M. Kennedy. Copyright © 1998 by The Board of Trustees of Leland Stanford, Jr. University and Trinity Partners. Published by Houghton Mifflin Company. All Rights Reserved. Used by Permission.

The Negro Artist and the Racial Mountain, by Langston Hughes. From The Nation, June, 1926. Copyright © 1926 by The Nation Company, L.P. All Rights Reserved. Used by Permission.

'Women's Liberation' Aims to Free Men, Too, by Gloria Steinem. From The Washington Post, Sunday, June 7, 1970. Copyright © 1970 by The Washington Post. All Rights Reserved. Used by Permission.

WTC Memorial Jury Statement for Winning Design, by Paula Grant Berry, Susan K. Freedman, Vartan Gregorian, Patricia Harris, Maya Lin, Michael McKeon, Julie Menin, Enrique Norten, Martin Puryear, Nancy Rosen, Lowery Stokes Sims, Michael Van Valkenburgh, and James E. Young. From World Trade Center Site Memorial Competition website: <http://www.wtcsitememorial.org> Used by Permission.

Maya Lin, from National Women's History Project. <http://www.nwhp.org/tlp/biographies/lin/lin_bio.html> All Rights Reserved. Used by Permission.

Cover Permission for **Her Story, Her Words**, by Frances E. Ruffin. Copyright © 2004 by The Rosen Publishing Group, Inc. All Rights Reserved.

Cover Permission for **The Story of the Statue of Liberty**, by Betsy and Giulio Maestro. Text Copyright © 1986 by Betsy C. Maestro. Illustrations Copyright © 1986 by Giulio Maestro. Published by HarperCollins. All Rights Reserved.

Cover Permission for **Dreaming of America: An Ellis Island Story**, by Eve Bunting. Text Copyright © 2000 by Edward D. Bunting and Anne Bunting. Trustees of the Edward D. Bunting and Anne E. Bunting Family Trust. Illustrations Copyright © 2000 by Ben F. Stahl. Published by BridgeWater Books. All Rights Reserved.

New York: An Illustrated History, by Ric Burns, James Sanders, and Lisa Ades. Copyright © 2003 by Alfred A. Knopf. Published by Random House, Inc. All Rights Reserved. Used by Permission.

I Want to Be a Fisherman, by Sandra Weiner. Copyright © 1977 by Sandra Weiner. Published by Macmillan Publishing Co., Inc. All Rights Reserved. Used by Permission.

Tell Us What You Like About UpState New York! by R.A. Wood Associates. Copyright 1996-2004 by R.A. Wood Associates. From website: <http://www.rawood.com/upstateny/UpStateNYWhatilikeolder4.html> Used by Permission.

I Love New York, by Paul Gerald. From Memphis Flyer, July 31, 2000. Published by Contemporary Media, Inc. All Rights Reserved. Used by Permission.

Go Pro Baseball Wise: Hall of Fame Visit, by PJ Dragseth. Copyright © 1995-2005 by PJ Dragseth Books. All Rights Reserved. Used by Permission. From <http://www.baseballwise.com/club/visithof.html>

Tania León, "Conversations with Three Symphonic Conductors: Dennis De Coteau, Tania León, John Robinson," by Anne Lundy. From The Black Perspective in Music, v. 16, no. 2, Fall, 1988. Published by Foundation for Research in the Afro-American Creative Arts. All Rights Reserved. Used by Permission.

World-Class Students, "International Flavor Makes H.W. Smith Elementary School Go `Round," by Lisa Slavin. From the Syracuse New Times. Copyright 2001 by Rway Communications, a division of RAS, Inc. All Rights Reserved. Used by Permission.

I Love New York, Words and Music by Steve Karmen. Copyright © 1977 by Elsmere Music, Inc. All Rights Reserved. Used by Permission.

Cover Permission for **Vote!**, by Eileen Christelow. Copyright © 2003 by Eileen Christelow. Published by Houghton Mifflin. All Rights Reserved.

Cover Permission for **A Very Important Day**, by Maggie Rugg Herold. Illustrated by Catherine Stock. Text Copyright © 1995 by Maggie Rugg Herold. Illustrations Copyright © 1995 by Catherine Stock. Published by William Morrow and Company, Inc. All Rights Reserved.

Cover Permission for **The Voice of the People: American Democracy in Action**, by Betsy Maestro and Giulio Maestro. Text Copyright © 1996 by Betsy C. Maestro. Illustrations Copyright © 1996 by Giulio Maestro. Published by William Morrow and Company, Inc. All Rights Reserved.